RELIGION, RACE, RIGHTS

The book highlights the interconnections between three framing concepts in the development of modern western law: religion, race, and rights. The author challenges the assumption that law is an objective, rational and secular enterprise by showing that the rule of law is historically grounded and linked to the particularities of Christian morality, the forces of capitalism dependent upon exploitation of minorities, and specific conceptions of individualism that surfaced with the Reformation in the sixteenth century and rapidly developed during the Enlightenment in the seventeenth and eighteenth centuries. Drawing upon landmark legal decisions and historical events, the book emphasises that justice is not blind, because our concept of justice changes over time and is linked to economic power, social values and moral sensibilities that are neither universal nor apolitical. Highlighting the historical interconnections between religion, race and rights aids our understanding of contemporary socio-legal issues. In the twenty-first century, the economic might of the USA and the west often leads to a myopic vision of law and a belief in its universal application. This ignores the cultural specificity of western legal concepts, and prevents us from appreciating that, analogous to previous colonial periods, in a global political economy Anglo-American law is not always transportable, transferable or translatable across political landscapes and religious communities.

Religion, Race, Rights

Landmarks in the History of Modern Anglo-American Law

Eve Darian-Smith

·HART·
PUBLISHING

OXFORD AND PORTLAND, OREGON
2010

Published in the United Kingdom by Hart Publishing Ltd
16C Worcester Place, Oxford, OX1 2JW
Telephone: +44 (0)1865 517530
Fax: +44 (0)1865 510710
E-mail: mail@hartpub.co.uk
Website: http://www.hartpub.co.uk

Published in North America (US and Canada) by
Hart Publishing
c/o International Specialized Book Services
920 NE 58th Avenue, Suite 300
Portland, OR 97213–3786
USA
Tel: +1 503 287 3093 or toll-free: (1) 800 944 6190
Fax: +1 503 280 8832
E-mail: orders@isbs.com
Website: http://www.isbs.com

British Library Cataloguing in Publication Data

Data Available

ISBN: 978-1-84113-729-2

Edited by www.textcollective.co.uk

Typeset by Columns Design Limited, Reading
Printed and bound in Great Britain by
TJ International Ltd, Padstow, Cornwall

To mum and dad

Contents

List of Figures

Figure 25. Supreme Court of the United States, Washington, DC.

Figure 26. Political cartoon depicting fear of immigrant workers, c 1881.

Figure 27. Photograph of child workers, 1909.

Figure 28. Anarchists. *Frank Leslie's Illustrated Newspaper,* 1886.

Figure 29. Indians in a Piegan Lodge, c 1911, Edward S Curtis.

Figure 30. Poster advertising the sale of Native American lands, 1911.

Figure 31. *A Family of New South Wales,* 1792, William Blake.

Figure 32. Photograph of girls praying beside their beds, Phoenix Indian School, Arizona, 1900.

Figure 33. View of Nuremberg in Ruins, 1945.

Figure 34. Robert H Jackson delivering his opening speech at Nuremberg, 1945.

Figure 35. *The New Christianity. 100% Aryan,* 1941, Philip Zec.

Figure 36. Billy Graham speaking in Trafalgar Square, London, 1945.

Figure 37. Chart used to explain the Nuremberg Laws, 1935.

Figure 38. Dorothy Counts' first day at a desegregated school, 1957.

Figure 39. Wal-Mart protest in Utah, 14 July 2005.

Figure 40. Spoof poster of the War on Terror. *Join Our Crusade.*

Figure 41. Two women in burqas, Afghanistan, 2009.

Acknowledgements

I would like to thank many people who have helped in the writing of this book. I am especially grateful to my professors at the University of Melbourne, Donna Merwick and Greg Dening, for helping me to think about history in new ways, and to Sally Falk Moore, John Comaroff and Peter Fitzpatrick for helping me appreciate some of the complexities of law. Special thanks to my dad, Ian Darian-Smith, for his encouragement, comments and input. Thanks also to Tom Hilbink, Austin Sarat, Kim Mills, Shelly Lowenkopf, Brian Clearwater and Kathie Moore, who have all contributed in various ways, and to Lisa Hajjar and graduate students on the Law and Society Program, UCSB, for providing comments on draft chapters. I am most grateful for the advice and support of Richard Hart throughout the writing process. Finally, warmest thanks to my husband, Philip McCarty, and my seven-year-old twins Ellie and Sam, for their constant love and kisses and helping to put things in perspective. Research for the book was supported by grants from the Institute for Social, Behavioral and Economic Research, the Interdisciplinary Humanities Center, and the Academic Senate at the University of California, Santa Barbara.

Preface

This book was written to highlight the importance of history in contemporary socio-legal scholarship. My hope is that by interesting the reader in past events, and illustrating how these events remain significant to our understanding of law in the present, I might convince the reader that history matters to our future. History may not help us predict the future, but it can show us that the challenges we face are not necessarily new, and that proposed solutions may not necessarily be the best solutions. History, as the historian Margaret MacMillan notes in her book *Dangerous Games: The Uses and Abuses of History*, is important for teaching us the limits of our understanding, and for nurturing humility, skepticism and an awareness of ourselves.

More specifically, I hope to show that the historical narratives that have developed over 400 years with respect to the development of modern western law—that law is objective, rational, universal and unbiased—are fundamentally flawed. By highlighting selected historical moments which I call 'legal landmarks', and focusing on the ways in which the concepts of religion, race and rights influenced the unfolding events, I suggest that Anglo-American law is deeply imbued with the ideologies, values and concepts that these discourses promoted. This point is of grave importance given the increasing cultural, religious and legal pluralism apparent in many countries in the early years of the twenty-first century.

I explore the development of Anglo-American law against the backdrop of great social, cultural, religious and economic revolutions. At times law facilitated these upheavals; at other times law was forced to respond, accommodate and adapt to new circumstances and conditions created by them. In short, Anglo-American law is both an architect and an artifact of social change. Most importantly, it is never value-free, floating abstractly above the melee of power and politics that informs everyday interactions.

The underlying question that frames the book, and the issue I leave the reader to ponder, is: Why is the narrative of law's neutrality still so compelling, perhaps even necessary, for contemporary western nations? Or, to put it another way, why do societies that employ Anglo-American law need to *believe*, perhaps now more than ever before, in the impartiality of the rule of law, despite many people's daily experiences to the contrary?

Introduction: Connecting Religion, Race and Rights

O
N 18 MARCH 2008, the US presidential candidate, Senator Barack Obama, gave an unprecedented speech on race and religion and their connection to inequality. The speech was a response to the fiery words of Obama's pastor, who—on media beamed around the world—had damned white Americans for their oppression of blacks. The public outrage over the pastor's address in turn forced Obama to face head-on the sticky topic of religion, race and rights. In a deeply moving speech reminiscent of a sermon, which reduced some to tears, Obama did what most politicians have failed to do—acknowledge and confront the complex intersections of religion, race and inequality in American society. By highlighting the histories of slavery, oppression and lack of opportunity that inform the bitter divide between black and white communities, Obama declared, 'I have never been so naive as to believe that we can get beyond our racial divisions in a single election cycle, or with a single candidacy—particularly a candidacy as imperfect as my own … This union may never be perfect, but generation after generation has shown that it can always be perfected.'[1]

The long-standing silence of politicians and commentators on the connections between religion, race and rights begs the question: Why? This book is about the relationship between religious faith, racist practices and the growth of legal rights in the history and development of modern European-Anglo-American law, or what I refer to as Anglo-American law or western law more generally. I argue that we cannot understand the enduring political, economic and social inequalities that plague our so-called democratic systems if we do not confront the question of how legal rights relate to religious and racist discourses at any one moment in time. While there have been wonderful books written about law and racism in the United States, including Patricia Williams' *Alchemy of Race and Rights* and Ian Lopez's *White By Law*, few scholars have engaged the historical relationship of law and religion. Among legal historians, most accounts of Anglo-American law

---

[1] Obama's speech was reminiscent of other famous speeches on race—most delivered by blacks. See Abraham Lincoln's speech at the Cooper Union in New York, 27 February 1860; Booker T Washington, 18 October 1895; President Lyndon B Johnson, 4 June 1965; and Jesse Jackson, 18 July 1984 (Wills 2008).

fail to speak about either race or religion at all. There are notable exceptions (Berman 1993, 2003; Witte 2002, 2006; Witte and Alexander 2008), but on the whole legal historians have tended to focus on changes in specific laws as a way to speak to wider societal transformations. Such accounts tend to prioritize the economic impulses of capitalism in the development of contract law, torts law, property law, family law, and so on. In short, issues of religion, race and rights are not always seen as connected in accounting for change in western legal cultures.

This book critically engages with the basic assumption that modern western law is an objective, unbiased and rational enterprise, and by implication the product of secular societies. Drawing upon what I call legal landmarks that involve conflict over religion, race and rights, I underscore the sacred, irrational and ideological elements embodied within modern law. I show that today's western understanding of the rule of law is historically grounded and linked to the particularities of Christian morality, the institutionalized exploitation of minorities, and specific conceptions of state and individual rights. These rights first surfaced during the Reformation in the sixteenth century, rapidly developed through the Enlightenment in the seventeenth and eighteenth centuries, and now form the basis of contemporary law, which pivots on the concept of an individual's legal entitlement to ownership of one's own life and property.

It is important to acknowledge the irrational and ideological elements in the development of western law in order to see that justice is not blind, because our concept of justice changes over time and is linked to economic power, social values and moral sensibilities that are not universal, apolitical or static. This point is of great significance in the early years of the twenty-first century, as the economic might of the United States and other industrialized nations often leads people to take a myopic vision of law, and adopt a readily asserted belief in its universal application. This perspective ignores the cultural specificity and ideological content of western legal concepts, and prevents us from appreciating that, analogous to past colonial periods, in today's global political economy Anglo-American law is not always transportable, transferable or translatable across political landscapes, cultural customs or religious communities. In other words, this perspective fails to recognize the tension inherent in western law between its claims to universalism on the one hand, and its particular historical development in unique social and cultural contexts on the other.

This book is organized around events, trials and people that were significant in the development of Anglo-American law. These landmarks occurred from the sixteenth century through to the present day, and have been selected because they are emblematic of greater social, cultural, economic and political forces that together have shaped (and are shaping) the profile of the modernist era. Some readers may feel that I have missed or ignored equally if not more important legal events, and it is true that other landmarks might serve just as well to illustrate my argument. However, I believe that the topics selected are significant as symptomatic of the jostling among communities and political groups representing various religious, economic, nationalist, ethnic and humanist interests in any one historical era. Other readers may argue that the discussion presented is too superficial—after all, each landmark could be the subject of a book or several books in its own right. I agree. That being said, though, I hope that the breadth of the historical narrative conveys an expansive outlook, one that prompts the reader to see links and connections across time.

The legal landmarks selected, and the tensions between the various group interests that they underscore, raise core questions that I explore throughout the book. How and in what ways did these groups access the legal system? Did the legal system support one faction over another, and if so, why? In what ways did conflict and opposition (and at other times unity and cooperation) between interest groups create opportunities for the growth of new legal concepts, legal reform and/or legal repression? How were discourses about religion, racism and rights constructed, mobilized or manipulated to serve the particular demands and needs of any one community or association? How did changes in legal practice affect wider social values, assumptions and common-sense understandings of national and/or cultural identity and related practices of racial differentiation? Did changes in public attitudes to religion and spiritual affiliation help to shape justifiable legal discrimination against minorities and racialized others? And as dominant attitudes shifted with respect to the relative importance of religion and race, how were these shifts connected to colonialism and capitalism? In other words, in what ways did colonialism, capitalism and their combined drive for cheap labor affect (both positively and negatively) the emerging concept of a rights-bearing citizen?

These sorts of questions indicate that this book does not present a conventional legal history. Rather, I am attempting a cultural study of law that explores the 'conceptual conditions that make possible that practice we understand as the rule of law' (Kahn 1999: 36–37). I use specific legal events as a lens through which large-scale paradigmatic shifts in legal thinking may be viewed. These in turn reflect people's commonplace assumptions and imaginings about law in their everyday activities. A cultural interpretation of specific legal events opens up for discussion the wider and often contested societal contexts involving religion and race that influence legal change. In this respect I take seriously Paul Kahn's argument that 'the rule of law is a social practice: it is a way of being in the world. To live under the rule of law is to maintain a set of beliefs about the self and community, time and space, authority and representation' (Kahn 1999: 36). My focus is on the shifting contours of those sets of beliefs over the centuries—particularly as they relate to ideas of religion and race—such that law appears at any one moment in time 'as the legitimate and even "natural" arrangement of our collective lives' (Kahn 1999: 36).

In thinking about the connections between discourses of religion, race and rights I refer to the concept of 'intersectionality'—a term associated with feminist theorists Kimberlé Crenshaw and Patricia Hill Collins—to emphasize that discourses of religion, race and rights are interrelated, dynamic and co-constitutive of each other (see Crenshaw 1989, 1991; Collins 1998; Grabham et al 2008). In short, I argue that these three categories are analytically distinct, but dialectically interconnected in practice and meaning. Wars of religion are always about something other than religion, and discriminatory practices are always about something other than simply marking racial difference. Similarly, the conceptual emergence of a citizen's legal rights cannot be discussed without also referring to who qualifies as 'human', as well as to issues of nationalism, internationalism and forces of capitalism that have informed the relationship between a nation and its citizenry.

In exploring the intersections of religion, race and rights I do not wish to suggest that these are the only forces at work in shaping legal concepts and norms. Class, gender and sexuality are obvious variables that also play a critical role. I do not exclude these elements, nor foreground them as the central pillars of my argument. Moreover, in exploring the connections between religion, race and rights I do not mean to suggest that at any given moment each prompted equal public attention or held equal political weight. Sometimes public debates over race were heard over those relating to religion. At other moments, concern with political and civil rights took center stage. For instance, in the early modern period leading up to the mid-eighteenth century, religious belief played a more explicit role in governing people's everyday thoughts, practices and political loyalties. Religion was central to explaining why the world was as harsh and brutal as it was. Albrecht Durer's famous woodcut, *The Four Horsemen of the Apocalypse* (1497), dramatically illustrates the sense of imminent death, famine, war and plague facing medieval societies as prophesized in the Book of Revelation 6: 1–8 (Figure 1). However, the centrality of religion in people's lives gradually declined with increasing industrialization and technology, and the growth of cosmopolitan city centers throughout the nineteenth century (McLeod 2000). Racist practices, too, fluctuated in their influence and political prominence over the centuries, coming to the fore in debates such as those over slavery, but deliberately glossed over during McCarthyism and the Cold War era. And while conceptualizing human rights is often associated with eighteenth-century Enlightenment philosophers, it was not until the post-World War II period that human rights assumed political prominence and became a force in international and intra-state negotiations. My general point is that, whether in public conversations or behind closed doors, debates about questions of religion, race and rights have always been in constant play in defining the western legal norms that inform today's national, international and transnational legal landscapes.

Finally, in exploring the intersections of religion, race and rights I do not want to suggest a causal or determinative relationship. Hence I am not arguing for a linear account, implying that shifts in religious faith caused shifts in constructing categories of race, which in turn created new social attitudes that are reflected in laws about property rights, citizenship qualifications, or the ability to vote. Rather, my contention is that the ebb and flow of religious practices, fluctuating racial tolerances, and the emerging idea of a rights-bearing individual are overlapping constitutive forces that together shape and have been shaped by legal

Figure 1. *The Four Horsemen of the Apocalypse*, 1497, Albrecht Durer. Staatliche Kunsthalle Karlsruhe.

The horseman holding a bow represents disease, the rider with a raised sword represents war, the rider with empty scales represents famine, and the rider holding a trident represents death.

processes. In my argument, law functions as the central axis around which discourses of religion, race and rights circulate, crystallize as ideological concepts, and become institutionalized through the administrative, bureaucratic and military agencies of the state. Law operates as a central site of organizing power, imbuing these debates with rationality, neutrality and legitimacy backed up by the ever-present threat of state-sanctioned violence.

DEFINING THE TERMS

Religion, race and rights are complex and difficult terms to define, and their meaning and application have been the focus of much scholarly and philosophical debate across historical epochs. I use the terms loosely to designate sets of belief that at particular historical moments have been mobilized to inform political ideologies, which in turn have shaped the development of Anglo-American law. For each landmark discussed in the book, I show that as proponents of particular beliefs with respect to religion, race and/or rights sought legal legitimacy for their perspectives, the rule of law and the status of the sovereign state shifted to accommodate, resist or empower believers according to wider historical contexts and social and economic forces.

Very briefly, *religion* is a belief in the existence of a supernatural force and the set of practices that substantiate that belief. Philosophers and scholars have sought to define the concept of religion for hundreds of years. Early descriptions of religion from sociological and anthropological perspectives were analyzed by Karl Marx, Max Weber, Emile Durkheim, Herbert Spencer, Edward Tylor and James Frazer in the latter half of the nineteenth and early twentieth centuries (see Fenn 2003; Clarke 2009). Some of these scholars, such as Durkheim, focused on the divide between the profane and the sacred as the defining feature of a religion and pointed to the collective dimensions of religious practice to create community solidarity. More recently, scholars such as Clifford Geertz and Thomas Luckmann have emphasized the deeper symbolism behind religious practices 'by which everyday life is brought into relation with a transcendent reality' (Hamilton 1995: 184). Arguably no single definition has adequately encapsulated the diversity and range of faith-based practices over the past 400 years. This becomes even more apparent given the range of religious practices in the early years of the twenty-first century. 'New Age, flying saucer cults, radical environmentalists, eco-feminism, human potential groups, holistic therapies—all have been identified as instances of a growing religious diversity quite different in character from the organized and exclusive practices of the church, denomination and sect' (Hamilton 1995: 15). Clearly, it is no longer possible to limit the identification of religion along the lines of recognizable and formal ritualized practices of mainstream religions. However, since this book is concerned with the moments when religious discourse is mobilized for the purposes of justifying and granting ethical legitimacy to a particular ideological position, it engages primarily with mainstream, institutionalized religious practices.

The concept of *race* is a social construct that shifts over time, as do the meanings that people attach to the concept. The idea that there are distinct human races existed in the Ancient and Greco-Roman worlds. However, with the emerging Enlightenment in the seventeenth century race began to be thought of in scientific terms. Gradually, early scientific theories hardened into social evolutionary racial hierarchies whereby white-skinned people were deemed 'naturally' superior to darker-skinned people. In other words, old ideas about racial difference were given a new meaning. As Ivan Hannaford notes in his illuminating book *Race: The History of an Idea in the West*, 'it was not until after the French and American Revolutions and the social upheavals that followed that the idea of race was fully conceptualized and became deeply embedded in our understandings and explanations of the world. In other words, the dispositions and presuppositions of race and ethnicity were introduced—some would say "invented" or "fabricated"—in modern times' (Hannaford 1996: 6; Gossett 1997: 3–16). Pseudo-scientific theories of race provided the logic to invent markers of racial difference, such as intelligence levels, physical ability, or personal dispositions such as laziness or dirtiness. These racial markers played enormously significant political and social roles in the eighteenth, nineteenth and twentieth centuries, and informed, amongst other things, laws determining who could claim civil and political rights and citizenship.

All humans belong to the species *homo sapiens* and there is no discernable genetic difference between people from different parts of the world, despite common physical traits between geographical regions, such as hair color or skin color. However, acknowledging that the concept of race has no scientific basis, and is in fact socially constructed, does not prevent the idea of distinct human 'races' operating within and across societies and shaping most people's everyday assumptions about cultural difference. False understandings of race continue to shape contemporary mainstream attitudes and social behaviors. 'It is in this context that race is both a falsehood and a fact, being false in its biological, scientific sense and factual in its very real effects on lived experience' (Sturm 2002: 15). An extremely disturbing aspect of all societies is how often popular misunderstandings about race pop up in political ideologies and surface in legislation and government policies such as those relating to immigration, access to social services, criminalization of particular ethnic groups, dismantling of affirmative action policies, and school voucher programs. In short, ideas of race, no matter how incorrect or misleading, cannot be disentangled from society's willingness to acknowledge an individual's right to equal opportunities and legal representation.

The concept of *rights* is also complicated and can be broken down into various categories, such as civil, political, economic, social and cultural rights. These different kinds of rights include, to varying degrees, the belief that all people are created equal in nature. Some of these rights, such as the right to vote and the right to be politically represented, are based on a person's status as a citizen of a state. In contrast, human rights, at least in theory, are not necessarily linked to a person's status with respect to state institutions but are supposedly determined on the basis of their intrinsic human dignity.

Modern ideas about rights developed relatively recently and are usually associated with the massive political and cultural shifts that occurred in European societies as a result of the Protestant Reformation of the sixteenth century. In this period, as historian John Witte Jr notes:

> Protestant doctrines of the person and society were recast into democratic social forms. Since all persons stand equal before God, they must stand equal before God's political agents in the state. Since God has vested all persons with natural liberties of life and belief, the state must ensure them of similar civil liberties. (Witte 2006: 40)

The Reformation's reliance on biblical texts to justify individuals' state-sanctioned right to freedom was gradually replaced in the seventeenth and eighteenth centuries by 'a new foundation of rights and political order' grounded in 'human nature and the social contract' (Witte 2006: 41; Ishay 2008). Philosophers and political commentators such as Thomas Hobbes, John Locke, Jean Jacques Rousseau, Thomas Paine and Thomas Jefferson argued that every person has the capacity to choose for him or herself the best way to achieve personal goals in what is known as the 'state of nature'. Unfortunately, in the state of nature people could be violent and selfish in their pursuit of self-interest. This required the intervention of the nation-state to bring order and control. And so, the argument went, a social contract was formed whereby people gave up some of their rights to the state, and in return the state was obliged to protect and defend them.

In Europe and the United States, against the turbulent background of the American War of Independence (1776) and the French Revolution (1789), the notion of human rights emerged based on a person's inalienable rights to life, freedom and liberty (Hunt 2008). Encapsulated in the French Declaration of the Rights of Man and of the Citizen (1789) and the American Bill of Rights (1791) was the idea that all individuals have, by virtue of their humanity, certain inalienable rights that the state is obligated to defend. In practical terms, this meant that a person's human rights were limited to the extent that the state would defend them. A person's status as citizen was seen as key in determining the degree to which a liberal democratic state would involve itself, or not, in defending any notion of rights and freedoms.

Unfortunately, the history of human rights is also a history of violence, oppression and exploitation. Colonialism, and the conquest and occupation of European nations over large areas of Africa, the Americas and Asia-Pacific regions from the sixteenth to the twentieth centuries, helped to establish schema whereby people were determined to be Christian or non-Christian, civilized or savage, citizens or non-citizens. These schema or hierarchies of mankind were based on social-evolutionary anthropological understandings of race which presumed that different human characteristics, such as intelligence, correlated to a person's ethnic identity and racial classification. In the nineteenth and early twentieth centuries, these pseudo-scientific arguments developed into popular theories associated with eugenics, which sought to classify mankind on the basis of genes and improve mankind through selective breeding, sterilization, and other horrifying social policies. As a result, 'While the colonizing West brought the constitutive aspects of the human rights tradition—sovereignty, constitutionalism, and ideas of freedom and equality—their beliefs about anthropology effectively excluded non-European peoples from human rights benefits' (Stacey 2009: 12).

With decolonization in the mid- to late twentieth century came a change in policies excluding non-European peoples from human rights benefits. The decolonization era saw the withdrawal of many European powers from their former colonies. International attention focused on the implementation of human rights in new self-governing systems. With the establishment of the United Nations in 1945 in the wake of World War II, and the issuing of the Universal Declaration of Human Rights in 1948, the subject of human rights was radically transformed. A number of formerly colonized countries joined the international forum of the United Nations and helped to draft the Universal Declaration. The Declaration's primary purpose was to protect individuals' human rights from violation by state governments, as had occurred under the Nazi regime which resulted in the mass extermination of millions of people. In an attempt to prevent such atrocities of war (and colonialism) from ever reoccurring, the Universal Declaration did not link human rights to citizenship but argued that people, as bearers of human rights, were self-determining, sovereign actors, whether or not a given state recognized them as such. In other words, the Universal Declaration attempted to move human rights discourse away from its former dependence on nation-states as the grantor and enforcer of a person's rights. While recent progress has been made in this regard, such as the establishment of the International Criminal Court in 2002, the conceptual innovations based on principles of self-determination introduced by the Universal Declaration of Human Rights have not yet been fully realized in national and international law (Stacey 2009).

Complicating the effectiveness of national and international human rights law is the premise that it is universal in its application. This premise is questioned by third world and postcolonial scholars, among others, who are skeptical that modern western law can operate as a rational and objective enterprise, devoid of cultural assumptions, values and biases (Preis 1996; Baxi 2006; Chimni 2006; Anghie et al 2003). This skepticism has an historical basis. In the past, the Enlightenment's triumphant narratives of reason and objectivity were employed by European leaders to argue that western law was universal and therefore applicable to colonized communities. Over the last 300 years, law has been a most effective weapon in institutionalizing colonial oppression and the imperial exploitation of non-European peoples. Against postcolonial scholars' critique of western law's universal claim, Anglo-American scholars have pointed to the secularization thesis, arguing that with the decline of religion in western societies through the nineteenth and twentieth centuries there has been a correlative rise in scientific logic and rationality. From a western perspective, law is interpreted as being a product of secularization, devoid of cultural particularities, and capable of being transferred and applied around the world. Modern Anglo-American law is a hallmark of modernity, and modernity, so the argument goes, is synonymous with secularization.

THE SECULARIZATION THESIS

Philosophers of the English and French Enlightenment such as Francis Bacon (1561–1626) and Voltaire (1694–1778) prophesied that with the rise of scientific experimentation and rational logic there would be a correlative decline in the importance of religion. These men argued that people would no longer depend so heavily on their spiritual beliefs to explain the world and their place in it. The natural and material worlds could be explained in empirical terms according to the laws of science. This prophecy turned out to be true, at least in part. During the eighteenth and nineteenth centuries European societies witnessed a steady decline in institutional religious practices, and public demonstrations of faith became less overt. This decline in public religiosity did not occur at the same rate or in the same manner in all countries and communities. However, it was sufficiently widespread across Europe and North America for Max Weber to argue in *The Protestant Ethic and the Spirit of Capitalism* that the rise of rationalization, particularly in the United States, had stripped the 'pursuit of wealth' of its religious and ethical meaning (Weber 1904: 182). Weber, along with other social commentators such as Karl Marx, subscribed to the secularization thesis, which assumes the inevitable decline of religion as a political and economic force in society and in the minds of individuals. Secularization, and the understanding that men and women are personally responsible for their actions and not subject to the whim of God, imbues ideas of 'progress' and 'improvement', which are emblematic of modern capitalist societies.

In recent years the secularization thesis has been hotly debated by sociologists of religion and church historians, divided on the issue of whether western society has become more, rather than less, religious since the Middle Ages. The issue in question is the degree to which the lessening power of religious institutions at the macro level correlates to a lessening of subjective religious belief at the individual level (Martin 2005; Gorski 2000; Demerath 2001; Norris and Inglehart 2004: 3–32). Peter Berger, a leading sociologist, summarizes the central problem:

> To be sure, modernization has had some secularizing effects, more in some places than in others. But it has also provoked powerful movements of counter-secularization. Also secularization on the societal level is not necessarily linked to secularization on the level of individual consciousness. Certain religious institutions have lost power and influence in many societies, but both old and new religious beliefs and practices have nevertheless continued in the lives of individuals, sometimes taking new institutional forms and sometimes leading to great explosions of religious fervor. Conversely, religiously identified institutions can play social or political roles even when very few people believe or practice the religion that the institutions represent. To say the least, the relation between religion and modernity is rather complicated. (Berger 1999: 2–3; Sheehan 2003)

Berger, along with other scholars, argues that it is increasingly clear that the secularization thesis is too simplistic and modernity is not synonymous with secularization. Yet if we accept this, can we reconcile the enduring presence of religion in western societies with the dominant assumption that law is a logical, rational and objective enterprise, free of any connection to subjective spiritual belief? As the legal historian AG Roeber has remarked, 'The reemergence of competing and possibly irreconcilable religious and legal systems in a postmodern twenty-first century unsettles much of the accumulated wisdom on the modernizing dimensions of early modern states and communities' (Roeber 2006: 201; see also Bhandar 2009). This questioning of the long-accepted secularization thesis has, in turn, prompted a reassessment of the development of modern nation-states and the role of secularization in their formation. There is an emerging appreciation that secular and religious practices are not unconnected or mutually exclusive. Hence, writes Nomi Stolzenberg:

> Contrary to the expectations of the likes of Marx and Proudhon, modern life has not been characterized by the 'withering away' of religion. Instead, we have witnessed the increasing polarization of religious and secular points of view. This polarization feeds on itself. It is all too easy to dismiss religious critiques of the law and the secular state as the products of fanaticism, religious fundamentalism, and political extremism, with which there is no possibility of constructive engagement. Conversely, it is all too easy for defenders of religious tradition to demonize the secular world. Both sides demonize the other; both sides talk past each other, without realizing that they share a common root. In fact, religious fundamentalism and modern secularism derive from—and yet are cut off from—a common political and religious heritage, an intellectual tradition borne of the struggle to reconcile the idea of divinity with the practical needs and limitations of the mortal world. (Stolzenberg 2007: 31–32)

Recognizing the limitations of the secularization thesis in explaining the development of modern liberal democracies has inspired a new body of thinking on the relationship between law and religion (see Cane 2008). There is a need to question the assumed separation of religion and state in modern liberal democracies, as well as a need to recognize that religious associations and apocalyptic visions continue to play a role in shaping political policies and public attitudes, particularly in the United States (Taylor 2007; Hall 2009; Micklethwait and Wooldridge 2009). As Mark Lilla, a scholar of modern theology and politics, has noted:

> The twilight of the idols [Bacon] has been postponed … Today we have progressed to the point where we are again fighting the battles of the sixteenth century—over revelation and reason, dogmatic purity and toleration, inspiration and consent, divine duty and common decency. We are disturbed and confused. We find it incomprehensible that theological ideas still inflame the minds of men, stirring up messianic passions that leave societies in ruins. We assumed that this was no longer possible, that human beings had learned to separate religious questions from political ones, that fanaticism was dead. We were wrong. (Lilla 2007: 3)

Religion and religious fervor appear to be alive and well, even among the most advanced industrialized societies typically characterized as secular. The presence of religious belief in political institutions is quickly revealed on an examination of the relationship between church and state. In Britain, the Bill of Rights (1688), Act of Settlement (1701) and Act of Union (1707) continue to exclude Roman Catholics from the throne. People who have fallen foul of this prohibition include Prince Michael of Kent and the Earl of St Andrews, who married Catholics in 1978 and 1988 respectively. Many British people believe that these laws are archaic, and legal challenges have been mounted on the basis that they conflict with the country's Human Rights Act (1998). According to a leading constitutional lawyer, Geoffrey Robertson QC, 'The Act of Settlement determined that the crown shall descend only on Protestant heads and that anyone "who holds communion with the church of Rome or marries a papist"—not to mention a Muslim, Hindu, Jew or Rastafarian—is excluded by force of law. This arcane and archaic legislation enshrined religious intolerance in the bedrock of the British constitution' (*Guardian Weekly*, 3 October 2008: 16).

In the United States, the distance between church and state is in many ways even less clear-cut than in Britain. According to Diana B Henriques, a *New York Times* reporter who has written extensively on the Bush administration's favoring certain religious organizations with tax exemptions, the church-state separation is a 'portable wall' (*New York Times*, 13 May 2007). Some legal scholars have shown not only that the concept of separation is open to interpretation, but that the concept has not always existed in US history, as is widely assumed. Philip Hamburger's *Separation of Church and State* (2002) is perhaps the most eloquent in debunking the myth that the founding fathers wanted to employ the doctrine of separation to guarantee religious freedom. On the contrary, he argues, the doctrine of separation was initially met with derision and criticism. However, in the late eighteenth century and into the nineteenth, the concept of separation was reinvigorated due to the rise of anti-Catholic organizations and others anxious to quell religious minorities. As a result, the concept of separation was installed as a central tenet in democratic governance. Hence the doctrine, now symbolic of democracy's tolerance of religious freedom, is arguably an historical product of religious discrimination and prejudice. Arguing against this view are distinguished scholars such as Isaac Kramnick and R Lawrence Moore, who in *The Godless Constitution: A Moral Defense of the Secular State* (2005) write about the foundational separation of church and state in American government.

Whatever side one takes in the complex debate about the separation of church and state in US constitutional history, it now seems clear that the widespread popular assumption that the rule of law epitomizes the secularism of modern society does not stand up. Despite a long-accepted narrative in liberal western societies, Anglo-American law cannot be simplistically characterized as a legal system premised on the separation of church and state. Nor can it be argued that the rule of law is entirely rationale, logical or pragmatic; law is not devoid of religious impulses either in the formation of its foundational concepts and myths of legitimacy, or in the religious battles and conflicts that have shaped its development over the centuries. 'Law, thought to be one of the exemplary domains of secularism, instead emerges as a signal location in which the sacred has resided and continues to reside alongside and as a fundamental part of the secular' (Umphrey et al 2007: 20; Schlag 1997; Novak 2000).

In this book I seek to recover some of the sacred dimensions of Anglo-American law that—for much of the modernist era—have been effectively silenced. This is an important platform from which to acknowledge that western law and its spiritual underpinnings may not be entirely appropriate or applicable to non-Christian cultures and their own religiously inspired systems of governance.

LAW AND RELIGION

The rise of science in the seventeenth and eighteenth centuries dovetailed with Enlightenment liberal ideology and together engendered skepticism that a Christian God is the inspirational source of all knowledge. Such skepticism had profound political consequences. In England it led to a public denunciation by parliament of the king's claim to 'divine authority', as dramatically displayed in the beheading of Charles I in 1649. Over the politically turbulent decades that followed, which included reinstating Charles II as king, a belief in God as the highest authority in the land was gradually replaced by a progressive system of constitutional democracy where men (not women) assumed responsibility for making legal rules through the application of what they thought of as logic, balance and reason. In the United States, the distancing between God and government played out in the signing of the Constitution (1787) and the Bill of Rights (1791). Together these documents created colonies free to govern themselves according to principles of equality and liberty, where one's personal religious affiliation was supposedly irrelevant (so long as one did not claim to be godless!). In the same period, the French Revolution of 1789 witnessed the rise of the Third Estate (primarily middle-class merchants) against the clergy and nobility. This revolt against traditional elites ultimately led to the decline of the *ancien régime* and the guillotining of King Louis XVI and his queen, Marie Antoinette. Importantly, in each of these three major revolutions in Britain, America and France, the separation of religion and state (and private and public spheres) was seen as exemplifying a transition from feudal society to modern self-governing societies free from supernatural intervention.

In contrast to the well-received revolutionary narratives of increasing secularization in Europe and America, this book presents three main arguments with respect to law and religion. First, I argue, in the spirit of legal theorist Austin Sarat, that 'modern law's relation to the sacred remains deeply ambivalent' (Sarat 2007: 188). While a hallmark of western law is that it is made by and for the people it serves, its ultimate validity seems to rest on some reference to a higher order of natural law and divine authority. Thus at the times when new regimes of western law were constructed, lawmakers typically invoked some concept of the sacred as a source of legitimacy for their actions (Asad 2003; Sarat et al 2007;

Fitzpatrick 1992: 51–63; Fitzpatrick 2004). As Martha Umphrey notes with respect to the American founders who evoked 'divine warrant' in the writing of the Declaration of Independence and the Constitution:

> God functions as an absolute that undergirds the legitimacy of the new order by virtue of its greater harmony with divinely ordained natural law. … Moreover, this turn to God comes at an extremely inharmonious moment: one of rupture and one that anticipates the impending revolutionary violence that inaugurates a new law, which will in turn legitimate the preceding violence. (Umphrey et al 2007: 11)

Secondly, I take seriously the idea that western legal concepts such as 'state', 'representative government', 'sovereignty', 'rights' and 'the individual' have their roots in Christianity (Mensch 2001; Roeber 2006: 200; Witte and Alexander 2008). Perhaps one of the more controversial proponents of this view is Carl Schmitt, who in his *Political Theology*, written amidst the turmoil of the German Weimer Republic in 1922, argued that 'all significant concepts of the modern theory of the state are secularized theological concepts' (Schmitt 1934: 36). In other words, according to Schmitt, a Catholic worldview permeates our understanding of the state apparatus. Notwithstanding whether one finds Schmitt's arguments compelling or repugnant given his subsequent association with the Nazi dictatorship, the point I would stress is that there is an intrinsic cultural affiliation between legal and Christian practices. This does not mean that the development of modern western law and the liberal nation-state can or should be understood solely from the perspective of Christian faith. However, as Elizabeth Mensch argues, 'much liberalism appropriated the forms and values of Christianity' (Mensch 2001: 61). She goes on to say:

> The medieval church employed the methodology of law to construct itself as a vast, legally constituted political entity. Moreover, by epistemologically combining the mystical and the legal, it invented a number of concepts still central to liberal legalism. For example, with the church as the first case in point, medieval canonists described a corporate body sufficiently of the present age to own property and enter contracts, yet sufficiently like the body of Christ to survive the death of any particular church official. From thence emerged the modern corporation, which has an existence apart from the mortality of any individual CEO or group of shareholders. Similarly, canonists produced something like a theory of representation: the pope was head of the church, with authority over members because he 'embodied' the whole church, which was in him. … The concept of embodiment was a first step toward a theory of representation: because the many were mysteriously present in the one, the one could legitimately make decisions on behalf of many. (Mensch 2001: 61)

Moreover, Mensch continues, the modern state is premised on its 'inquisitorial' character, which means that the state—like the Catholic Church in earlier centuries—assumes the ultimate power to authorize investigations into nonconformist behavior and implement sanctioned violence (Mensch 2001: 71–2; Derrida 1990; Kirsch 2009). The state's ability to use violence legitimately was most famously discussed by Max Weber in *Politics as a Vocation* (1919), where he defined the state as an entity having a monopoly on the legitimate use of physical force within a given territory. Hence law, as a mechanism of the state, embodies the potential to implement authorized violence, a point graphically made by Michel Foucault in his analysis of the transition from public executions to panopticon prison systems in *Discipline and Punish* (1995). Today the state's legitimate exercise of violence can be seen in everyday forms of policing as well as in its marshalling of military force in times of perceived crisis and potential conflict.

Thirdly, I argue that, analogous to the ways in which western law developed over time through negotiation of categories of race, class and gender which determined who qualified as 'citizen' at any given moment in time, law also developed over time as a result of negotiations about categories of religious affiliation. This point is important but rarely discussed. Often glossed over in explorations of the development of Anglo-American law are its histories of conflict and legal discrimination between Christians and non-Christians (ie colonists against native peoples), as well as between members of different Christian faiths (ie Protestants against Catholics). These conflicts determined a person's standing and status before the law. Just as the color of a person's skin was and is used as a way of demarcating 'us' and 'them', a person's spiritual affiliation also historically functioned and continues to function as a marker of cultural identity and differentiation that can justify both explicit and implicit legalized intolerance. Significantly, racial and religious intolerance are not mutually exclusive practices; in many cases prejudices dovetail and overlap. In countries such as Australia, Britain and the United States this was most recently demonstrated by legislative endorsement of racial profiling against dark-skinned people of Islamic faith in the wake of the 9/11 terrorist attacks. Today it may be possible to say that, similar to previous historical eras, religion has again emerged as being more significant than race as a primary indicator of ethnicity and difference.

LAW AND RACE

A fact often forgotten or ignored in the public domain is that Anglo-American law is an effective mechanism for institutionalizing racial discrimination. Despite the existence of an extensive body of scholarship on law and its role in implementing or resisting racial discrimination, little recognition is given to the ways in which law underpins racial discrimination in the public consciousness. One reason for this amnesia is that, following the civil rights era in the 1960s, it is now illegal in most liberal democracies to differentiate between people on the basis of skin color, cultural affiliation and/or gender. In the twenty-first century all citizens governed through democratic legal systems ostensibly have equal rights to vote, go to court, buy a house, seek employment, and so on. In a superficial sense, the battle for racial equality has been won. However, racism is still pervasive and Du Bois' 'color line' has not been eradicated but rather made more difficult to articulate and define (Du Bois 1903: 10). By this I mean that contemporary discriminatory practices are more insidious and tricky to attack precisely because they can and do operate outside formal legal rules, and because racial formations are dynamic and constantly changing (Calavita 2007: 19; Omni and Winant 1986;Winant 2004).

In any discussion of law and racism, it is important to foreground capitalism and its drive for material resources, cheap labor, and the constant need to open up new consumer markets. Of course capitalism did not produce racism, and racist practices existed long before the modern capitalist system was first institutionalized in England under a Protestant regime in the sixteenth and seventeenth centuries. That being said, full-scale capitalist enterprise has been very much a central concern in the creation of labor hierarchies. And labor hierarchies have pivoted primarily on racial differences that determine an individual's capacity to garner higher or lower wages.

We can see these forces today in the growing gap between rich and poor. As has been remarked upon by many scholars and economists, the exploitation of the many by the few is today's economic reality (Carbado 2002). What we are currently experiencing is a post-Fordist process whereby economic and political power settles in a core group of entrepreneurs who outsource work to a floating periphery of temporary workers both locally and overseas. Often glossed over in mainstream media, racial and gender minorities are disproportionately represented in western countries' most disadvantaged classes (see eg Winant 2004). Moreover, outsourcing is most profitable when the overseas labor pools are poor and desperate workers willing to accept terrible working conditions, job insecurity and minimal wages. As a result, the gap between the wealthy north and impoverished south has not been closed—nor has it come even close to it—since the decolonization movements in the middle of the last century. Significantly, there remains a racialized differentiation between developed and developing geopolitical regions that has its roots in and perpetuates the racial distinctions of former colonial eras (Winant 2004). What we are witnessing today, then, is a global political economy that still depends on maintaining racial hierarchies and marginalized communities both within and between western and non-western states. Anglo-American law and international legal agencies, albeit perhaps unintentionally, play a significant role in denying adequate legal access to marginalized communities and in turn sustaining and enforcing racial biases in favor of the capitalist enterprise.

LAW AND RIGHTS

In discussing individual rights, one is forced to engage with issues of power. Throughout the modern era, liberal democratic states have been the grantor and enforcer of people's rights, be these with respect to voting, access to social services, or claims to educational opportunities. Against societal demands to protect the

16

rights and freedoms of individuals, as well as to extend these rights progressively to marginalized groups such as women and ethnic minorities, national governments have to contend with the self-serving economic and political interests of those in power. It should come as no surprise that historically, Anglo-American law has typically worked to the benefit of the rich and powerful.[2]

In the twenty-first century, the phenomenon of law servicing the interests of powerful elites is evident on a global scale. Susan Silbey's work on globalization, or what she calls 'postmodern colonialism', highlights the role that legal institutions play in facilitating new forms of economic domination across borders and transnational spaces. 'Significantly', she argues, 'this is not something happening outside the law or without the active collaboration of law and legal scholars' (Silbey 1997: 220). For the past 300 years modern western law has 'provided the "infrastructure" for capitalist investment and development' (Silbey 1997: 221; Tigar 2000). Today law continues to facilitate, on a global scale, a largely deregulated free market system loosened from centralized state accountability and control. The acknowledgement and enforcement of ordinary people's legal rights has been sacrificed in this process.

Of course Anglo-American law (and its western and non-western practitioners) does not represent a system of total power and domination.[3] There are moments of resistance against the forces of capitalism, as seen in the periods of colonialism in the eighteenth, nineteenth and twentieth centuries as well as in the current postcolonial era (Merry 2004). There are also numerous instances of law being mobilized to empower marginalized people through a recognition of their political, economic and civil rights, and provide leverage for the demands made by actors within social movements (eg Rodriguez-Garavito and Arenas 2005). But, as Silbey concedes, the worry is that despite these moments of local resistance and victory, the dominant narratives of globalization, which draw on Enlightenment ideologies of reason and progress, mask the realities of how power actually operates

---

[2] This is not a new insight. Socio-legal scholars associated with the Critical Legal Studies (CLS) movement, which began in the 1970s in the United States and Britain, argued that all legal decision-making is in fact political despite claims that it is neutral and objective. CLS scholars drew on the insights of the earlier legal realist movement, whose proponents argued that all law is political, and that 'Every decision [judges] made was a moral and political choice' (Mensch 1990: 22; Unger 1986; Kelman 1990; Altman 1993; Douzinas et al 1994).

[3] '[I]n a world of transnational movement and cross-border transactions it is still an open question whether international law will simply be the law of the powerful or whether, indeed, local practices working around the edges of the formal law will be of far greater import. Many business agreements now incorporate by reference the law of England or an American state as governing in the event of a dispute. But that may only mean that trade agreements, based on nonlegal ties, will become all the more important, or that allowing a Western nation's law to apply in the business realm will actually give greater scope to the use of local laws for matters of criminal law or family law jurisdiction. Whatever the results, studies of history and culture suggest two factors that are likely to remain extremely important in the face of seeming globalization: the local always has a way of reasserting itself as people keep responding to the cultural imperative of category experimentation, and the changes will be reciprocal despite the seemingly incommensurate array of powers' (Rosen 2006: 167–68).

17

(Silbey 1997). And by masking how power operates, economic exploitation and political manipulation are presented as somehow 'natural', inevitable, and no one's fault (see Foucault 1995). Thus the notion of any form of social responsibility, held by either a government or a specific leader on behalf of society, is erased from the public consciousness. As a consequence the structures of inequality are made invisible as popular dissent is silenced. As Silbey notes, 'the dominant narratives of globalization deny the existence of a recognizable and powerful other from whom one can demand justice' (Silbey 1997: 228).

The great ideological promise of the Enlightenment, with its belief in modern law as the source of equal protection and enforceable rights for all, has clearly not been fulfilled. Certainly democratic states have vastly improved living and labor conditions for many people, particularly with the increasing international recognition of human rights in the wake of World War II. Nonetheless, violence and atrocities still occur, and civil wars and genocides taint the history of the twentieth and twenty-first centuries. With vast movements of people across borders and regions, many are increasingly caught literally in-between states without full or partial citizenship status and so without the capacity to appeal to state enforcement agencies. Refugees, undocumented immigrants, and those displaced by natural disasters such as the victims of Hurricane Katrina occupy extremely ambiguous legal spaces where rights and liberties are severely compromised, if recognized at all. An increasing recognition of human rights and the proliferation of international legal instruments seeking to protect those rights are clearly insufficient to counter the massive institutional structures that sustain global inequities and violence. Despite industrialized nations' overwhelming wealth and range of advantages over the global south, western law's narratives of freedom, reason, progress and justice fall short of what many ordinary people experience in their everyday lives, whether they live in Britain, the United States, Japan, India or Russia.

The book is divided into three parts that follow an approximate historical chronology. The first part explores the ways in which the development of Anglo-American law is the product of the Reformation and the Enlightenment. The second part shows how the law has been shaped by its role in slavery, labor and colonialism. The third part focuses on events since World War II that reveal the ways in which law has been changed by international and world affairs and the forces of a global political economy. The general thrust of this historical narrative is to demonstrate how law is made and shaped through its encounters with political, economic and cultural forces, and how ideologies of religion, racism and rights played out in these encounters.

I

Moving toward Separation of Church and State

1

Martin Luther and the Challenge to the Catholic Church (1517)

FOR MANY PEOPLE, particularly those living in the United States, the name Martin Luther does not conjure up the sixteenth-century German monk and the Reformation, but rather Martin Luther King Jr and the civil rights era of the 1960s. Over 400 years separates the two men, and on the surface there appears to be, apart from sharing the same name, very little in common between the Catholic monk and the twentieth-century African-American activist and Baptist minister.

Despite the many centuries that separate the two men, and their vastly different worldviews, especially with respect to the role of religion, it could be argued that there are similarities and continuities between them. Both men drew upon their deep religious faith as an aid to incite and navigate political revolution. Both men were dedicated to the ideal of equality and self-determination. Both men objected to 'top-down' religious hierarchies that dictated to the congregation. And neither man—each from relatively humble and modest backgrounds—could have foreseen their personal role in opening up the political space for profound social and legal change.

In a sense, Martin Luther the monk ushered in the modernist age by highlighting the abuses of a clerical hierarchy, citing what he viewed as extreme corruption within the Catholic Church. Such abuses and corruption, he argued, denied ordinary people access to salvation and divine justice. Some 400 years later, Martin Luther King Jr continued this trajectory by highlighting the institutional discrimination in the US legal system, demanding that all individuals, of whatever religion or race, should have access to secular justice. Indeed, in his 'Letter from a Birmingham Jail', Martin Luther King makes express reference to the monk and his so-called 'extremist' non-violent position which King saw himself as following. Perhaps what both men shared more than anything else was the belief that law—be it divine or secular in origin—was vital in guaranteeing individuals some measure of equality and independence from abuses of power by religious and political leaders.

RELIGION: PROTEST AND REFORM

In this chapter I examine the role played by Martin Luther in bringing about the Reformation in the first half of the sixteenth century. First and foremost, it is important to keep in mind that in 1500 in western Europe, the Protestant Church and its many descendent denominations and branches such as Lutheranism, Calvinism, Anabaptism, Anglicanism, Presbyterianism, Baptism, Methodism, Pentecostalism, Adventism, and so on simply did not exist. In the early sixteenth century the only sanctioned Christian religion in existence was Catholicism. It had undergone internal challenges and earlier, in the eleventh century, had split into two branches. This split or schism resulted in the western Catholic Church, centered in Rome, and the eastern Orthodox Church, with its center in Constantinople (current day Istanbul). Technically, this divide still exists today between these two branches of the original Catholic Church.

Martin Luther is primarily remembered for challenging the Catholic Church and breaking its dominant and enormously powerful political, economic and social hold over western Europe. He achieved this massive destabilization by establishing a radical theological basis for a new Christian Protestant faith, which in time developed into an alternative set of religious, legal and political institutions and a profound restructuring of the way people thought and behaved in society (Witte 2006: 38–41, 49–62). For the first time in hundreds of years, Luther pressed people—both those who were attracted to his ideas and those who were not—to be self-conscious about their faith and to reflect upon religion as something conceptually distinct from their everyday activities, behaviors and thoughts. For the first time in hundreds of years, the 'religious culture' of the medieval worldview was challenged. It could no longer be taken for granted that Catholic values permeated all thought or that the Catholic Church dictated all human endeavor (Berman 2003; MacCulloch 2003).

Despite Luther's fierce attack on the Catholic Church, he was not an activist or agitator in the sense that he deliberately set out to disrupt society. On the contrary, Luther was a deeply spiritual man who was horrified by the abuses of power of the Vatican in Rome and the corrupting influences of the Catholic Church across the vast Holy Roman Empire. Like his contemporary Erasmus, arguably the most eminent humanist scholar and Catholic theologian of the period, Luther called for a return to the early church and a simplified gospel devoid of ritual and excess. Luther, at least in the early years of his writing, did not advocate a new conception of faith but rather pushed for *reform* of the church from within (hence Reformation). However, in his *protestations* against the church (hence Protestantism) Luther inadvertently acted as a catalyst for massive religious, social, economic, political and cultural upheavals. These upheavals forever changed the historical trajectory of western Europe and the New World.

In a sense, Luther's theological position created a conceptual bridge between a declining European medieval world controlled by the overarching authority of the Catholic Church, and an emerging modern era characterized by humanist thinking and new forms of nationalism, capitalism, and ideas about the appropriate relationship between church and government. In the immediate decades prior to Luther's attack, political and economic discontent had been brewing among northern Europeans, fueled by popular anxiety about the turn of the century and the coming apocalypse (Figure 1). In this period of general discontent, Luther's public sermons provided the theological impetus for change. Luther's personal charisma, the effectiveness of the printing press in spreading his teachings across Europe, and the failure by Pope Leo X in Rome (and Charles V, Emperor of the Holy Roman Empire) to take immediate action and silence him for heresy, provided a unique moment for widespread revolution. Luther approved of some aspects of this revolution and denounced others such as the calls for change expressed in the Peasants' War of 1524–25 and the Anabaptist revolts in Germany, Switzerland and Austria.

Luther's thoughts and writings, and their widespread impact across western Europe, were indicative of a general shift in thinking among ordinary people that characterized the early modern era. An important element in this shift was a new emphasis given to secular law and forms of governance over the previously accepted authority of an overarching ecclesiastical power. This rising legal consciousness and turn to secular law did not mean that men such as Luther no longer believed in the omnipresence of a god. Rather, Luther articulated the division between earthly and spiritual kingdoms and called for each to have its own independent laws and authority. For the first time in European society there was open discussion and debate about the relationship between individuals and God, which in time led to what we today recognize as the separation of church and state.[1]

The degree to which changes in people's personal religious beliefs in the Reformation period directly caused changes in law, legal philosophy and legal practice remains open to academic debate (see Roeber 2006). What is indisputable is that Luther, albeit largely unwittingly, created the opportunity and momentum for a radical revolution in western legal philosophy and practice by highlighting the religious abuses of the Church and the canon law that supported it (Berman 2003, 1993; Gorski 2003; Witte 2002). In demonstrating a connection between theological and legal reform, this chapter contextualizes Luther's challenge to religious practices against a wider backdrop of political, social and economic upheavals that were taking place at the beginning of the early modern period. This wider context helps to underscore why Luther was viewed by the Church as a heretic and excommunicated, living a good part of his life in exile

---

[1] 'The move toward separation [of church and state] is commonly attributed to the Reformation, but the real separation that occurred during the Reformation occurred at a deeper level and did not lead directly to church-state separation at all. Rather, it entailed a separation of individual faith from the sacralized, integrative ordering of the High Middle Ages and a return to the Augustinian insistence on a radical disjuncture between God and human beings' (Mensch 2001: 63).

and in constant threat of danger, and more importantly, why Luther's challenge to the Catholic faith had such an enormous impact on German and west European legal, political and social institutions. This broader historical context is essential to understanding why this book on the development of modern Anglo-American law begins with Martin Luther, and why a reader in the twenty-first century should care about a monk who lived nearly 500 years ago.

There is another important reason why this book begins with Martin Luther as the first legal landmark in the development of modern western law. By taking Luther and the Reformation period as the starting point, the reader may see that the origins of what we think of as Anglo-American law are grounded in numerous European and non-European legal cultures and traditions. In the early 1500s, when Luther began to challenge the practices of the Church, the legal system in place in much of Europe was extraordinarily complicated and drew its authority and meaning from ancient cultures and various religious traditions not exclusively Christian in origin. As the legal historian Raol Van Caenegem has noted, 'medieval and modern Europe has not only borrowed many of its constituent elements from elsewhere, but has borrowed (from various cultural traditions) elements that were not only different, but contradictory and at first sight mutually exclusive' (Van Caenegem 1991: 117).[2] Appreciating the complex foundations of European law is vital in order to break down a prevailing and commonplace view—that has existed since the early modern period began in the 1500s—that western law is intrinsically unique, superior, and has very different historical foundations from the laws that existed in Islamic, Asian and other non-European societies.

Who was Martin Luther?

Luther was born in 1483 in Eisleben, Germany, to Hans and Margarethe Luther. In 1501, at the age of 17, Martin attended the University of Erfurt, where he excelled in philosophy and law. In 1505 he gave up his legal career, much to the disappointment of his father, and entered the monastery of the Augustinian Eremites. Ordained in 1507, he received his doctorate at the new university of Wittenberg and was subsequently appointed professor of theology (Figure 2). Elector Frederick of Saxony, the founder and patron of the new university, was delighted by Luther's steadily growing reputation as a significant scholar and theologian (Maland 1982: 84).

---

[2] '… to many historians it is a constant source of surprise to find the European achievement fed by such diverse streams as the Greek World (with its polytheism, Aristotelian naturalism, free scientific enquiry and cyclical view of history), Judaism (with its monotheism, other-worldliness and rectilinear "providential" history), Christianity (which sprang from Judaism and yet was rejected by it and developed in bitter opposition to it), the Romans (with their unspeculative, legal and administrative mind and their centralizing and imperialistic bent) and the Germanic nations (which, though attracted by the Mediterranean world, were so utterly different from most of its ways and values), not to mention the Arabic, Celtic and Slav influences' (Van Caenegem 1991: 117).

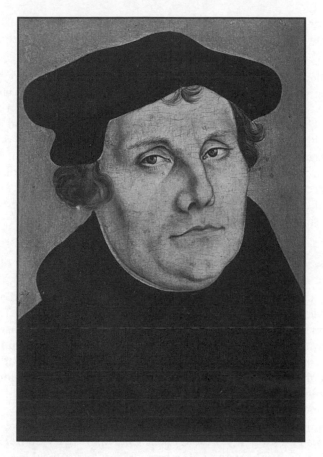

Figure 2. *Luther at Age 46, 1529, Lucas Cranach the Elder. Hessisches Landesmuseum Darmstadt.*

Cranach (1472–1553) became a court painter to Frederick the Wise of Saxony in 1504. Over the years he produced portraits of many of the Saxon Electors, members of the court, and leaders of the Reformation. Cranach was a close friend of Martin Luther; he engraved a picture of him in 1520 and later painted him in 1529. Cranach was present at Luther's marriage to Katharina von Bora and was godfather to his first child.

Martin Luther was an intensely spiritual man, but was weighted down with feelings of anguish and despair. According to David Maland, an historian of the sixteenth and seventeenth centuries:

Luther's dilemma can be simply stated. He believed that God required him to keep His law in all points; he also believed that this was beyond his ability and that therefore he was damned. Nothing in the ordered life could give him comfort. Neither the discipline of the monastery nor the rigorous mortification of the flesh could assuage the over-powering sense of guilt which beset him. 'I was a good monk' he wrote in later life 'and I kept the rule of my Order so strictly that I may say that if ever a monk got to

25

Heaven by his monkery, it was I … if I had kept on any longer I should have killed myself with vigils, prayers, reading, and other works'. (Maland 1982: 84–85)

For years Luther suffered in the belief that he would never receive God's grace and salvation. However, around 1514, upon re-reading the Greek text of the Epistles, he started to reinterpret the term 'righteousness' and the text 'the just shall live by faith alone'. Luther began to see in this reinterpretation promise of hope and liberation. He wrote, 'I grasped that the justice of God justifies us through faith. Whereupon I felt myself to be reborn and to have gone through open doors into paradise' (Maland 1982: 86). This new interpretation of scripture lifted a heavy weight from Luther's heart and allowed him to rejoice in God's righteousness rather than be oppressed and frightened by it. For Luther, faith alone justified humanity. Thus no amount of penitence could absolve one of one's sins, since what was required from an individual was true and pure belief.

Luther's 95 Theses

According to historical tradition, on 31 October 1517, Luther posted on the door of the castle church in Wittenberg a document known as the 95 Theses. This posting was deliberately done on the eve of All Saints Day when many pilgrims were in town for a celebration, and Luther was assured that his document would receive maximum exposure and publicity. While it may seem odd to post a document on the door of a local castle or church, this was quite common in the sixteenth century if a person wanted to raise a subject for general consideration in the town or village.

Luther's document listed 95 concerns that he had with what he saw as the corruption and dishonesty of the Catholic Church. As noted above, Luther was not the first to highlight these problems. In fact other theologians, scholars, artists and social commentators had leveled similar criticisms at the Church from the latter part of the fifteenth century onwards. However, unlike these other critics, Luther managed to ignite a social movement of widespread and enormous impact. His major complaint against the Church was its practice of selling letters of indulgence or paper decrees that could be bought from a papal commissioner. Theoretically, the buying of indulgences ensured absolution by releasing a sinner from having to perform some form of earthly penitence. The Church endorsed the idea that indulgences could in effect buy God's pardon, absolve one from sin, and secure the purchaser's salvation. In short, papal letters were seen as an aid to securing one's place in heaven. 'They were hawked about as letters of credit on God Himself, and their spheres of influence was even extended to souls in purgatory so that their time of ordeal might be reduced' (Maland 1982: 79). According to a saying of the time, 'As soon as the coin in the coffer rings, the soul from purgatory springs' (Bainton 1995: 6; Maland 1982: 79).

Luther was disgusted with this practice, arguing that only God could pardon one's earthly sins. Thus there was no need to spend money on a piece of paper since the sale of indulgences was, in essence, a hoax foisted on naive parishioners by shrewd and ruthless clergymen. In Luther's opinion, all individuals were free to make their own determination with God. Hence there was no need for salvation to be in any way mediated by and through members of the church hierarchy. In Luther's words:

> there is no true, basic difference between laymen and priests, princes, and bishops, between religious and secular, except for the sake of office and work, but not for the sake of status. ... Therefore ... those who are now called 'spiritual', that is priests, bishops, or popes, are neither different from other Christians nor superior to them. (Luther cited in Porter 1974: 41)

In Luther's call for a return to the religion's early teachings and a simpler relationship with God based on love and faith, his ideas explicitly undermined the rituals of the Church and its symbolic power. Given the complex interconnections of religion, politics and economics in the sixteenth century, it was impossible to confine Luther's criticisms of the Church to a debate about theological interpretation of scripture. The sale of indulgences was a highly lucrative commercial business. The profits from indulgences paid churchmen's salaries and debts, and were politically important in supporting the standing of the clergy within the church hierarchy. Luther's criticism of the sale of indulgences not only brought into question prevailing church practices with respect to an individual's salvation, it also attacked a revenue stream that sustained the opulent lifestyle of the pope and the upkeep of the Vatican in Rome, as well as the building and preservation of monasteries across the Holy Roman Empire (Maland 1982: 87).[3]

Luther's 95 Theses was quickly picked up by a local Wittenberg printer and disseminated across Europe. By 1519 students from England, France and Italy were flocking to hear his lectures and sermons. The pope, who had been sent a copy of the 95 Theses by the cardinal responsible for the town of Wittenberg, Albert of Hohenzollern, grew increasingly alarmed by Luther's success. Pope Leo X issued a papal bull warning Luther to retract 41 'mistakes', some of which had appeared in the 95 Theses. Luther refused to retract the sentences, and burnt his copy of the papal bull alongside volumes of canon law (Catholic court law) on 20 December 1520. The pope had little choice but to officially excommunicate Luther from the Church, which he did on 3 January 1521.

The Diet of Worms

The pope's excommunication of Luther forced Charles V, Emperor of the Holy Roman Empire, to take action. Charles V, as the temporal governing authority, was responsible for his subjects' safety and well-being and for dealing with

---

[3] Debate within the Catholic Church over the appropriateness of indulgences resurfaced in 2009. The sale of indulgences was banned in 1567, but today they can be earned through charitable contributions, prayer, and other pious acts. See *New York Times*, 10 February 2009, 1.

heretics and disrupters of the peace. He summoned Luther to the Diet of Worms, a general assembly (*Diet*) of secular leaders which met in the small German town of Worms. Prince Frederick III, Elector of Saxony, was sympathetic to Luther and obtained an assurance from Charles V that Luther would be guaranteed safe passage to and from the Diet. At the assembly on 22 January 1521, Luther was shown a table on which were heaped copies of his works and books. He was asked if he still believed in what he had written and taught what they contained. Luther, after consulting with his friends and spiritual aids, declared to the Diet the following day, 'I neither can nor will make any retraction, since it is neither safe nor honourable to act against conscience. God help me. Amen.'

Luther quickly left Worms with a 20-day safe conduct pass, but upon its lapse was declared an outlaw. His literature was banned, and an arrest warrant was issued by Charles V under the Edict of Worms on 25 May 1521. According to the Edict:

> He [Luther] destroys all civil police and hierarchical and ecclesiastical order, so that people are led to rebel against their superiors, spiritual and temporal ... Furthermore, he institutes a way of life by which people do whatever they please, like beasts. They behave like men without any law, condemning and despising all civil and canon laws ... Daily, several books full of evil doctrine and bad examples are being written and published. There are also many pictures and illustrations circulated so that the enemy of human nature, through various tricks, might capture the souls of Christians. Because of these books and unreasonable pictures, Christians fall into transgression and start doubting their own faith and customs, thus causing scandals and hatreds. From day to day, and more and more, rebellions, divisions, and dissensions are taking place in this kingdom and in all the provinces and cities of Christendom. This is much to be feared.
>
> ... [W]e forbid anyone from this time forward to date, either by words or deeds, to receive, defend, sustain, or favor the said Martin Luther. On the contrary, we want him to be apprehended and punished as a notorious heretic, as he deserves ... (Jensen 1975: 87, 101, 107)

Frederick III, fearing for Luther's life, kept him in hiding in Wartburg Castle, where he remained on and off for some years. During this period he continued to be prolific; amongst other writings he translated the Greek bible into German. In 1523 he married a nun, Katharina von Bora, who subsequently bore him six children.

The Importance of the Printing Press

It has been suggested that initially the pope did not take Luther's protestations seriously and dismissed him as a 'drunken German' who 'when sober will change his mind' (Polack 1931: 45). Such a dismissal, if it occurred, reflected widespread attitudes held by Italians about northern German peoples. In this period, Italians liked to think of themselves as representing the learning, innovation and humanist aesthetic of the Renaissance and Classical Rome, and often talked about

Germans as culturally inferior. The Italian-based Catholic Church's disparagement of Germany may in part explain why Pope Leo X did not take Luther seriously, charge him immediately with heresy, and stem the dissemination of his radical ideas.

While the Catholic Church hesitated over how best to deal with Luther, the monk made effective use of the printing press. It allowed for the mass production of Luther's writings and enabled him to communicate to a wider audience, which in turn led to his ultimate success in establishing a religious movement that 'presented the new belief as a popular movement with a mass base' (Scribner 1981: 1). It is hard today, given computer technology and the lightning speed with which some of us communicate with others around the world, to appreciate the innovation and importance of mass-produced printed text. But up until the 1440s, there had been no such thing as a printing press. Texts had to be copied by hand, which was an extremely expensive and time-consuming process. This type of work was usually left to monastic scribes, who dedicated themselves to the painstaking copying of ecclesiastical manuscripts.[4] Copying page after page of dense Latin text onto parchment by quill, scribes often embellished their work with beautiful designs of letters, flowers, animals and domestic scenes in gold gilt and other rich colors.[5] These illuminated manuscripts were extremely rare and valuable, and the people who had access to them were typically educated male nobility and churchmen. Women generally did not handle such documents, although nuns living in monasteries were sometimes allowed access to them (see Lindgren 2009).

Johannes Gutenberg dramatically changed the social, political and literary landscape of late medieval Europe when he invented the first moveable metal typeset in the mid-fifteenth century, approximately 70 years before Luther posted his 95 Theses on the church door at Wittenberg. The invention of the metal typeset enabled mass reproduction of a page of text, and even more importantly meant that new words could be assembled quickly, producing new pages of text (Figure 3). It 'laid the foundations of modern publicity' and foreshadowed the periodical press, or newspaper (Steinberg 1996: 6–7).

---

[4] In contrast to church documents, the demand for legal texts was more urgent. As law schools began to flourish in the 12th and 13th centuries, legal texts were often produced by 'independent semi-educated individuals' working out of their own home or a workshop (L'Engle 2001: 43).

[5] In the early medieval period, parchment was the usual medium for illuminated manuscripts. Parchment was made by taking the leathery skin of animals and then cleaning and treating it to create a strong and smooth writing surface that typically could be written on on both sides. Vellum was the skin taken from new or stillborn calves and was even softer and more flexible. Before the use of leather, papyrus, which grew on the banks of the Nile in Egypt, had been used in the production of manuscripts. However, Ptolemy V of Egypt (2nd century BC) had stopped its export and parchment was developed as an alternative. By the 14th century, paper was often used in preference to parchment or vellum. Paper was an invention of the Chinese, introduced into Europe by the Arabs in Spain. Paper manuscripts were then distributed throughout Germany and Italy along trade routes, and it did not take long for paper production to become established. According to historical evidence, the first paper-mill was set up in Nuremberg, Germany, in 1386 (Geck 1968: 12).

Figure 3. The Print Shop of Johannes Gutenberg, 1580, Theodor Galle after Johannes Stradanus (Jan van der Straet). Plate 4 of the *Nova Reperta* (New Discoveries). Engraving. Metropolitan Museum of Art, New York.

The discovery of printing was considered a wonder of the new age. Note the men on the left putting the movable typeset in place, the pressman on the right pulling down the bar, and the wet sheets drying above.

Unfortunately for Gutenberg, he did not make an enormous fortune from his invention. Plagued by financial woes, he managed to borrow some money and set up a print shop in the German city of Mainz in the 1440s (Geck 1968: 19–28). He began by publishing small items such as indulgences. Production of indulgences was a mainstay for the new printing firms that quickly established themselves across Europe. For instance, by 1498, Johann Luschner was printing 18,000 letters of indulgence for the abbey of Monserrat in Barcelona (Steinberg 1996: 63). Not only does this attest to the rapid success of the printing press, it also underscores the scale of the sale of indulgences by the Catholic Church and why Luther was so concerned with them in his 95 Theses.

Gutenberg is remembered primarily for printing the first full-length book. Between the years 1452 and 1455 he printed approximately 200 copies of what is known as the Gutenberg bible. A few of these were printed on parchment but the majority were printed on paper. The Gutenberg bible was published in Latin— not the German vernacular—and so the local market for the book was limited given that it could only be read by highly educated men. Gutenberg astutely sold the bibles to international book dealers in Frankfurt, who distributed them across Europe to their clientele, which consisted mostly of learned professors and churchmen (Geck 1968: 54).[6]

As word of the marvelous bible spread across Europe, so did the new printing technology. '[W]ithin fifteen years after Gutenberg's death in 1468 printing-presses had been set up in every country of western Christendom from Sweden to Sicily and from Spain to Poland and Hungary' (Steinberg 1996: 9). Although printing developed at a different pace and in different ways across Europe, the main centers of European commerce such as London, Paris, Rome, Cologne, Basel, Valencia, Seville, Naples and Venice quickly became hubs of print media (Hirsch 1967: 104). As 'thriving centres of trading, banking and shipping, and seats of secular and ecclesiastical courts' these cities provided the greatest clientele (Steinberg 1996: 18). Although the actual figures are difficult to estimate—given the lack of reliable records and destruction of books over time—it is projected that by 1500 approximately 45,000 books had been printed and printing presses had been set up in 206 cities. In the following decades there was a proliferation of both religious and secular books. These became increasingly affordable and accessible to a range of people across all socioeconomic classes, and for the first time women had reasonable access to literary works. Apart from the bible, popular books were *Aesop's Fables* (1484), Geoffrey Chaucer's *The Canterbury Tales* (1483), Erasmus' *Ship of Fools* (1494), Thomas More's *Utopia* (1517), and Niccolo Machiavelli's *The Prince* (1532).

Politics, Propaganda, and Publishing in the Vernacular

One of Luther's primary concerns was that the laity should be able to mediate their own relationship with God without intervention from the church. He believed that people should be able to read the bible and other texts in their own language, and not be dependent upon the clergy for interpreting God's words for them. Around 1500, only 40 titles had been published in German, but by 1523 there were 498, one-third of which had been written by Luther (Scribner 1981: 2). These figures point to both Luther's writing productivity and his commitment to publishing in the vernacular. Publishing in German was quite revolutionary given that almost all books at that time, especially those associated with religious matters, appeared in Latin.

In the three years following Luther's posting of the 95 Theses, 30 editions of this document were printed—those authorized by Luther as well as other

---

[6] Typically the bibles were sold unbound to allow individual collectors to bind according to personal taste. Today, only 48 copies of the Gutenberg bible are known to exist. The British Museum, London, owns both a paper and a vellum copy and has a wonderful website that enables a direct comparison of the two to be made: see www.bl.uk/treasures/gutenberg/homepage.html.

editions that were illegally copied.[7] In 1520 Luther published three important treatises which set out his views on necessary church reforms. These tracts were *To the Christian Nobility of the German Nation*, *Prelude on the Babylonian Captivity of the Church*, and *On the Freedom of a Christian*. The *Prelude* was a theological tract and hence was published initially in Latin, though it was soon translated into German. The other two tracts were published in both German and Latin, but the German version sold twice as fast. Just to give a sense of the number of sales, according to historical records, *To the Christian Nobility of the German Nation* sold over 4,000 copies in just five days (Steinberg 1996: 64–65). Together these three treatises reflected Luther's increasing conviction that a break with the Catholic Church was necessary. In the second of these tracts, Luther's tone is aggressive. He explicitly calls the pope the Antichrist. Erasmus, after reading these treatises, withdrew his open support of Luther, and the two men became increasingly divergent in their opinions about the Catholic Church (see MacCulloch 2003: 97–105).

Luther's bible, which he translated from Greek into German and published in 1522, achieved the most spectacular sales. This was not the first bible to be printed in the German vernacular, but it was certainly the most popular. Luther's first edition was illustrated with woodcuts by the well-known artist Lucas Cranach, and despite it being quite expensive, the first 5,000 copies sold out in a few weeks. Over the course of Luther's life, approximately 400 editions of the German bible were printed (Steinberg 1996: 65). This great interest in vernacular bibles was not confined to Germany. After 1522, most European countries began printing the bible in their mother tongue. The Netherlands produced a vernacular bible in 1523, England in 1524, Denmark in 1524, Sweden in 1526, Iceland in 1540, Hungary in 1541, Spain and Croatia in 1543, Poland in 1552, and Lithuania in 1579 (Steinberg 1996: 57).

The Reformation and its lines of attack did not occur purely in the pulpit nor involve only theological issues of absolution and salvation. It was as much a political/cultural revolution as a religious one, since challenges to the dominance of the Church necessarily implied vast social transformations that shook the very foundations of ordinary people's understanding of their place, class, function and obligations in the world. As Scribner has noted, Protestant ideas involved the breaking down of old values and ways of thinking and creating new structures of allegiance or a new 'symbolic universe' (Scribner 1981: 9).

There were many people—besides Luther and other radical churchmen—who had a stake in dismantling the old system. Members of the growing middle classes such as printers, artisans, burghers and entrepreneurs felt that the Catholic Church's grip on German society was too tight and oppressive. Many Germans

---

[7] For a fascinating discussion of the problem of unauthorized reprints, and specifically Luther's bad experience with illegal editions of his bible and writings, see Flood 1998: 51–54. In an attempt to curb the production of unauthorized versions, Luther introduced special markings in his official editions, which amounted in practice to an early form of copyright.

felt allegiance and loyalty to local princes and dukes, not the clerical hierarchy of the faraway Roman Church. And the German princes and aristocracy involved in the 'expansion and elaboration of secular rule' were increasingly rubbing up against the presence of Catholic institutions (Vale 1988: 297). Many of these supporters of reform made effective use of the printing press, and print media played a vital role in disseminating a general feeling of discontent across northern Europe.

An important aspect of the printing revolution, and one that is often over-looked, was the power of oral communication and visual imagery in spreading the Protestant message. Thus the introduction of the printing press did not mean a sudden and exclusive use of literary text, nor did it mean that one had to be formally literate to be influenced or affected by newly printed ideas.[8] The reality was a much more complex relationship between oral, visual and textual commu-nication in the sixteenth century, and how these media functioned in spreading new ideas about the Reformation (Scribner 1981: 3). Printed texts were often read aloud and cited in public debates and sermons. Luther was well known for his public readings and students gathered from across Europe to hear him speak. He was also very aware of the power of visual imagery to communicate to a range of people. As argued by Elizabeth Eisenstein, the increasing presence of printed text did not wipe out the use of visual media, particularly among peasants, artisans, and others not involved in the elite practice of reading books. On the contrary, 'after the advent of printing, visual aids multiplied, signs and symbols were codified; different kinds of iconographic and nonphonetic communication were rapidly developed' (Eistenstein 1983: 37).

One of the most effective forms of visual communication was the use of the woodcut in the production of broadsheets, which typically appeared in the form of a simple folded pamphlet or single page. When woodcut imagery was printed in conjunction with accompanying text, this hybridized publication served as a

> meeting place point between the illiterate, the semi-literate, and the literate. For those unable to read, the message of a popular broadsheet could be read from the visual images alone. More effectively, its printed text could be read out by someone who could read, creating a situation of oral interchange which was probably the most powerful means of spreading the Reformation. (Scribner 1981: 6)

Broadsheets (with or without text) communicated to the general public, often through propagandist means. This in turn made possible the articulation of

---

[8] Clearly, the invention of the printing press and the use of print media played a vital role in disseminating the general feeling of discontent and ideas of religious, political and social reform across the German region. Still, it is important not to jump to the conclusion that this in turn was evidence of increasing rates of literacy. As some scholars have noted, it is very difficult actually to measure levels of literacy (Eisenstein 1983: 29–34; Scribner 1981: 1–2). That being said, the dramatic jump in the number of books published in German in the early years of the 16th century is staggering, and does suggest an overall increase in literacy rates, especially by the second half of the century (see Gilmont 1998: 13–14).

complex ideas in simple, popular, visual and strategic terms. Printed materials opened up a space for public debate in ways that had not existed before. Because the printing press enabled new ideas to be widely circulated in a standardized and replicable format, people in Germany were reading, seeing and hearing very similar—if not identical—printed materials to those read, looked at and heard in Austria or France. So, despite the increase in vernacular publications, which emphasized national and cultural differences across western Europe, there was also a standardization of literature and visual imagery that facilitated communication among citizens of different territories, as well as within local areas between members of different classes and arenas of social life (see Eistenstein 1983; Gilmont 1998; Scribner 1981). In short, religious *and* political issues had never been so openly discussed by so many people.

Luther was fully aware of the power of propaganda and visual imagery to unite people from various regions and socioeconomic classes.[9] In 1545 he published a small polemical picturebook entitled *Depiction of the Papacy,* which featured nine illustrations and a brief accompanying text. Some of these images depicted vulgar and mocking representations of monks and clergymen (see for example Rublack 2005: 63; Scribner 1981). Others showed the demonic and evil origins of the pope as Antichrist and were quickly copied and reproduced in broadsheets and disseminated widely (Figure 4). Luther and other Protestant propagandists made extensive use of the monster motif both in depictions of the pope and in caricatures of monks and nuns, who were all considered to be working in collusion with Satan (see Hsia 2004).

In Luther's *Table Talk,* he is quoted as having said, 'Antichrist is the pope and the Turk together; a beast full of life must have a body and soul; the spirit or soul of antichrist is the pope, his flesh or body the Turk' (Hazlitt 1856: 193). Luther's equating the pope with the figure of the Antichrist—the very antithesis of Christ—triggered an extremely powerful and provocative medieval iconography and visual code.[10]

---

[9] For an interesting analysis of Luther's shifting thoughts on visual imagery, and the extent to which he thought visual imagery should be abolished or judiciously used in combination with text to further the cause of religious reform, see Dillenberger 1999: 89–95, 173–88; also Michalski 1993: 1–42. Note that iconoclasm, or the destruction of visual imagery in decoration or art, was very much promoted by other radical evangelicals such as Luther's colleague Karlstadt at the University of Wittenberg, as well as Zwingli, Calvin and the Anabaptists. These reformers believed that it was wrong to worship images, especially religious images, which they claimed were devilish idols. A notable exception to this belief was the use of illustrations in bibles, primarily on the ground that such illustrations were important in the education of the illiterate.

[10] According to legend, the Antichrist was born to the 'whore of Babylon' (Babylon is about 50 miles south of Baghdad) and was very much associated with non-Christian Islamic culture and faith. His life was lived as an inverted parallel to that of Christ. The Antichrist, for instance, died when he faked his death and resurrection and tried to ape Christ's ascension from Mount Olivet (Scribner 1981: 148). The figure of the Antichrist drew its symbolism from the classic apocalyptic texts of the Book of Daniel and Thessalonians.

Figure 4. *The Devil with a Bagpipe* (c. 1535). By Erhard Schoen.

This broadsheet shows the devil playing a tune through the ears and mouth of a monk, suggesting that the monk has become a two-headed monster. The lower right hand corner is where messages of dissent were printed (see Scribner 1981:134). British Museum, London.

> The code was one of the most effective and lasting creations of evangelical propaganda. … It involved the evangelical believer in a cosmic struggle against absolute evil. The sense of an imminent crisis was present before the Reformation. The evangelical movement drew upon popular belief to involve the believer in a struggle intimately involved with that crisis, the final confrontation with the papal Antichrist and the world turned upside-down. (Scribner 1981: 183, 187–8)

The visual code stressed that the Antichrist was evil personified, and signaled both an inversion of the order of things and the coming of the end of the world. The Antichrist figure was also linked with disbelievers, heretics and foreigners, who were often depicted in racial terms, such as visual and written descriptions of the Antichrist's servant, the dark-skinned Turk.[11]

---

[11] Whether the Turk was the Antichrist or only the servant of the Antichrist was considered a serious question and was debated by evangelical theologians, including Luther (Scribner 1981: 181).

RACE: THE INFIDEL TURK

It is hard to understand today the sense of impending crisis presented by the threat of the appearance of the Antichrist. But in sixteenth-century western Europe, Christian religion played a central role in almost everyone's lives. Thus Luther's bringing into question the authority and legitimacy of the pope had profound implications on all fronts for an individual's spiritual and personal existence. No one could afford simply to ignore claims that the Antichrist was working within the Catholic Church. One's very soul was at stake.

Still, Luther was not the first to call the pope the Antichrist and openly criticize the excesses of the church system. What made Luther's attack so compelling and appealing to a mass audience, and successful in terms of bringing about radical change, was his ability to mobilize multi-layered associations that linked people's spiritual, material and political interests and in turn created an exceedingly receptive audience. For instance, Luther argued that the Catholic Church was leading ordinary people not toward salvation, but hell, in his tract *On the Babylonian Captivity of the Catholic Church* (1521). Explicitly linking the corruption of the church with satanic Babylon and the so-called Turkish infidel evoked long-standing fears that resonated with many west Europeans who lived in dread of an invading Ottoman Empire (see below). In short, one of the reasons for the dramatic success of evangelical literature and imagery was that it connected collective anxiety over spiritual salvation with real fears about invading armies and racist prejudices against foreign Islamic peoples. For many west Europeans the threat of the world being turned 'upside-down' was not some vague danger but a real and hovering menace.

Crusades and Infidels

West European fear and hatred of Arabs and Turks had existed for many centuries. Crusades or 'holy wars' were launched against the Islamic world as early as 1095, when Pope Urban II led the attack against the so-called infidel. The ostensible aim of the crusades was to secure the Christian kingdom against Muslim territories and recover control of Palestine and specifically Jerusalem, which was revered by Christians as a site of pilgrimage and devotion. Leading the crusades were Christian knights, who were heralded as the defenders of Christendom and the true faith. Conveniently, the knights' status was enhanced by a romanticized cult of chivalry that helped to gloss over the less than Christian aspects of the holy wars.[12]

---

[12] Because of the association of crusading Christian knights with romanticism and chivalry, it is often forgotten that the crusading battles were fought primarily by ordinary foot soldiers whose experience of war was typically very different from that of their leaders. Thousands of men from across England, France, Italy and northern Europe joined the Christian forces, often under duress by the clergy or their feudal lords. Many died from disease or starvation. For many poor peasants and laborers, the only redeeming feature was that popes typically promised full remission of sins and a place in heaven to anyone who participated in the holy mission.

In reality, the geopolitics of the crusades involved securing land, money, trading networks and power for the papacy as well as for the knights, lords and mercenaries who led the armies and the merchants who quickly followed the victorious forces (see Runciman 1987; Tyerman 2006). After Jerusalem was taken in 1099 and the Seljuk Turks pushed out of western Asia Minor, the Muslim territories of Jerusalem Tripoli, Antioch and Edessa along the coast of Palestine were established as Christian states. In addition to expanding the authority of the Christian empire, these states became significant trading centers throughout the eastern Mediterranean region and the occupiers gained considerable wealth and power. Crusaders discovered sophisticated civilizations in the east that had advanced medical learning, accounting practices, mathematical systems, and commercial legal codes (Lewis 2009).

The presence of Christian forces in former Muslim territories could not be indefinitely maintained. As noted by the historian Christopher Tyerman, secular authorities back in Europe began to demand attention from the Church. As a consequence, bloody wars in far off lands, even those fought in defense of Christianity, began to lose some of their appeal and rationale through the twelfth and thirteenth centuries (Tyerman 2006). Eventually Muslim forces mobilized and pushed back to regain control of Jerusalem in 1187. However some of the Christian states that had been established in the Middle East stood fast, and the strongholds of Tripoli and Acre were not regained by the Muslims until 1291. As the number of crusades began to taper off in their intensity and broad appeal through the thirteenth century, relations between Christian and non-Christian regions were left bitter and divisive. From the perspective of Christian Europe, the Holy Land was once again abandoned to barbaric and heathen Islam. From the perspective of the Middle East, Europeans had aggressively invaded Arab and Turkish territories over a number of centuries and displayed excessive violence and racism against Muslim and Jewish peoples (see Maalouf 1989).

The uneasy relationship between east and west again exploded in 1453 when the Ottoman Empire captured the city of Constantinople (current day Istanbul), ousted the Byzantine emperor Constantine XI, and dismantled the Eastern Roman Empire.[13] This occupation consolidated the Ottoman Empire's status as the most powerful force in the eastern Mediterranean region and southeastern Europe. The power of the Ottoman Empire was dramatically demonstrated by the conversion of the oldest and most famous Christian building in the city, Hagia Sofia, into a mosque (Figure 5). Under Sultan Selim (1512–20) and his successor Süleyman the Magnificent (1520–66), the Empire extended its reach into Egypt and developed a substantial naval force that dominated the Red Sea and much of the Mediterranean. Süleyman took occupation of Belgrade and the territories of current-day Hungary and other central European regions in 1526.

---

[13] Constantinople remained the capital of the Ottoman Empire until the empire's dissolution in 1922, and was renamed Istanbul in 1930 by the Turkish Republic.

Figure 5. Hagia Sofia, Istanbul. Photograph by Andreas Wahra.

When the Turks took Constantinople in 1453, the oldest and most famous Christian building in the city, the Church of Holy Wisdom, or Hagia Sofia, was converted into a mosque and Arabic calligraphy replaced the Christian mosaics. Hagia Sofia became a museum in 1935. Today, both Christian iconography and Islamic calligraphy can be seen side by side as a reminder of the building's turbulent religious and political history.

Three years later, in 1529, Süleyman laid siege to Vienna, but due to harsh winter conditions his troops were forced to retreat. This threat to a prominent Christian city created enormous alarm throughout Austria and Germany, and underscored the proximity and threat of Turkish occupation in other parts of western Europe. At the time of Luther's writings and sermons, the Turkish threat was very real and imminent (Bohnstedt 1968: 7).

Racializing Religious Difference

Talad Asad, in a book on secularism and its connections to both Christianity and Islam, argues that today, as much as in the past, west Europeans are profoundly disturbed by the presence of Muslim communities within the borders of Europe (Asad 2003: 159). He notes that a central reason for this anxiety comes from the fact that many west Europeans draw their cultural identity in opposition to Islamic peoples, and that Islam functions as Europe's 'primary alter' (Asad 2003: 169). This oppositional cultural distinction exists despite the common roots of European and Islamic peoples in the traditions and heritage of ancient Hellenic Greece (Asad 2003: 168; see also Lewis 2009).

Throughout the period of the medieval crusades and into the early years of the sixteenth century, Islam did not threaten Europe so much as Christendom, 'since Europe was not then distinct from Christendom' (Asad 2003: 162). As the historian Denys Hay has pointed out, 'If the Turk was not different under natural law he was certainly different under divine law: the Turk was not far short of a "natural enemy" of Christians' (Hay 1957: 113–14). The Catholic Church fully exploited this sense of difference, and in rallying the troops and resources for the crusades deployed considerable propaganda against the so-called infidel, including attacking the authenticity of the Qur'an and the Prophet Muhammad. The papacy promoted religious and political intolerance toward Muslims (as well as Jews, Asians and Others) based upon a simple dichotomy: people were either Christian or non-Christian. As Diarmaid MacCulloch has argued:

> western Christianity before 1500 must rank as one of the most intolerant religions in the world: its record in comparison to medieval Islamic civilization is embarrassingly poor. It put up with Jews (more or less) only because they played a part in the Church's view of its own future, it hated and feared Islam and did its best to destroy it whenever possible. Its attitude to Greek Christianity was at best condescending, and at worst contemptuous, resulting in consistent failure for medieval negotiations on Christian reunion. (MacCulloch 2003: 676)

Across western Europe, stories about Muslims being satanic, evil, pagan, beastly and barbaric were commonplace. 'There was much discussion of the Turkish menace to Christendom, not only in Germany and Italy but even in countries that were in no sense exposed to Moslem attacks, as for example in France, England, and the Netherlands' (Bohnstedt 1968: 9). Stereotypes of Muslims titillated the European imagination, on the one hand creating an image of monstrosity, violence and evil, and on the other hand enabling Christian Europeans to define themselves in opposition as virtuous, civil and good (Blanks 1999: 3). Such stereotypes helped to establish a common moral code and symbolic iconography that was mobilized throughout the crusades, the later medieval period and on through the sixteenth and seventeenth centuries (Vitkus 1999; Blanks and Frassetto 1999; Daniel 1993). Unfortunately, these derogatory images continue to exist in the twenty-first century in enduring Orientalist discourses and political rhetoric about Islam as 'evil' and 'barbaric' in the War on Terror.

On War Against the Turks

Luther promoted textual and visual stereotypes of the pope as Antichrist and clergy as collaborators with the infidel. By drawing on established iconographic cues and commonplace assumptions about Muslim peoples as barbaric and evil, and linking these images with his criticism of the papacy, Luther helped to assemble a powerful propaganda machine made effective by mass printing.

In Luther's tract *On War Against the Turks* (1529) he set out a complex argument about why people should fight the Turks in the wake of the Ottoman Empire's near occupation of Vienna a few months earlier. First, unlike the earlier crusades which Luther had denounced,[14] he firmly believed that the emperor must wage war since this time the Turks were now the aggressors:

> The Turk certainly has no right or command to begin war and to attack lands that are not his ... The Turk does not fight from necessity or to protect his land in peace, as the right kind of a ruler does; but, like a pirate or a highwayman, he seeks to rob and ravage other lands which do and have done nothing to him. He is God's rod and the devil's servant, there is no doubt about that. (Luther cited in Porter 1974: 125)

Second, Luther argued that despite there being a real and immediate threat of a Turkish incursion into western Europe, people should not blindly follow the directions of the papacy, which has no business exerting physical force on others. Rather, they should obey the temporal leadership of the emperor Charles V, whose job it was to keep his subjects safe within the borders of the Holy Roman Empire. Luther urged men to obey the temporal authority of the emperor over the spiritual authority of the pope when dealing with the Turkish invasion.

> If there is to be a war against the Turk, it should be fought at the emperor's command, under his banner, and in his name. Then everyone can be sure in his conscience that he is obeying the ordinance of God, since we know that the emperor is our true overlord and head and that whoever obeys him in such a case obeys God also ... (Luther cited in Porter 1974: 129)

---

[14] Luther openly criticized the misuse of papal power in the medieval crusades in his tract *On War Against the Turks* (1529). 'The popes had never seriously intended to wage war against the Turk; instead they used the Turkish war as a cover for their game and robbed Germany of money by means of indulgences whenever they took the notion. The whole world knew it but now it is forgotten. ... They undertook to fight against the Turk in the name of Christ, and taught and incited men to do this, as though our people were an army of Christians against the Turks, who were the enemies of Christ. This is absolutely contrary to Christ's doctrine and name. It is against his doctrine because he says Christians shall not resist evil, fight, or quarrel, nor take revenge or insist on rights [Matt.5: 39]' (Luther cited in Porter 1974: 123).

Furthermore, when fighting under the direction of the emperor, Luther implored men to fight simply and in fulfillment of their oath of obedience to a temporal government. Luther cautioned against soldiers relying upon the reasons promoted by the pope:

> such as the winning of great honor, glory, and wealth, the extension of the territory, or wrath and revenge and other such reasons. By waging war for these reasons men seek only their own self-interest, not what is right ... (Luther cited in Porter 1974: 130)

Finally, Luther emphasized that war against Turks should be fought as a 'just war' and not a holy war against unbelievers and in defense of the Christian faith. Foreshadowing some of the arguments Hugo Grotius would make 100 years later in his three-volume treatise *On the Laws of War and Peace* (1625), where he laid out his 'just war' doctrine, Luther believed in the right of the secular leader to wage war under certain conditions (see Bull et al 1990; Stumpf 2006). Fighting the Turks should be thought of as a purely secular war to defend property, lives, land and territories. Luther argued that this distinction was important.

> If the emperor were supposed to destroy the unbelievers and non-Christians, he would have to begin with the pope, bishops, and clergy, and perhaps not spare us or himself; for there is enough horrible idolatry in his own empire to make it unnecessary for him to fight the Turks for this reason. There are entirely too many Turks, Jews, heathen, and non-Christians among us with open false doctrine and with offensive, shameful lives. Let the Turk believe and live as he will, just as one lets the papacy and other false Christians live. The emperor's sword has nothing to do with the faith; it belongs to physical, worldly things ... (Luther cited in Porter 1974: 130)

Luther's tract *On War Against the Turks* is perhaps most significant because it drives a wedge into the taken-for-granted western narrative of one overarching Christian kingdom governed by one supreme God. Moreover, Luther disrupted the assumption that western Europe was equivalent to Christendom. As argued by Luther in the above quotation, his contention was that it was no longer a simple battle between European Christians and Muslim non-Christians. By pointing to the Antichrist and evoking the collaboration between pope and Turk, Luther claimed that the dichotomy between 'us' and 'them' had become blurry and there was now evil within Europe disguised in the form of the Catholic Church. In short, Luther mobilized existing racist stereotypes to complicate the simplistic 'us v them' dichotomy and focus attention on the non-Christian element within western Europe itself. By associating Catholicism with Islamic forces and arguing that the enemy could now exist in the form of one's local priest or nun, Luther escalated widespread alarm of an imminent external *and* internal threat.[15]

---

[15] In Luther's later writings, this vehement attack was explicitly widened to include Jews. See Luther *On the Jews and Their Lies* (1543) and for a commentary see Witte 2002: 297–98; Oberman 2003: 81–85.

RIGHTS: DEMANDING SECULAR LAW

The Medieval Legal System

At the time that Luther posted his 95 Theses, the legal landscape in western Europe was extremely complicated. By 1500, Europeans had to navigate three different systems of law: customary Germanic law, civil (Roman) law, and canon (Catholic) law. As noted by Van Caenegem,

> we cannot speak of one medieval law, or the Law of the Middle Ages; rather there was a multitude of legal systems, sometimes co-existing. … So numerous were the legal problems and solutions, and so passionate the arguments that medieval man devoted to them, that the period must be considered one of the richest treasure houses of human experience in the field of law. (Van Caenegem 1991: 115)

Custom-based Germanic law was dominant through most of the medieval period, particularly in northern Europe where Roman law had almost been eradicated. Germanic customary law was the articulation of laws that were declared to have existed since ancient times, and derived in part from the earlier invasions of Germanic peoples into west Europe that included central Asian Huns as well as Goths and Slavs, and later Danes, Swedes and Norwegians in the fourth, fifth and sixth centuries. Germanic customary law had its foundations in a variety of ancient cultural traditions and jurisprudential sources (see Kelley 2000: 99–108).

Germanic customary law was a largely unwritten but widely accepted code of legal behaviors and norms.[16] It was very important in governing localized feudal societies and the complicated relations between agricultural serfs and their lords. Feudal relationships were by their nature parochial, dependent upon a sense of mutual obligation, loyalty and trust between tenant farmers and the local lord. The serf tilled the fields, grew the food, and soldiered for the lord if necessary. In turn, the master provided protection and charity for the serf and his family in times of war or famine. Germanic customary law was complicated in that it reinforced a top-down social hierarchy and yet at the same time bolstered the notion of reciprocity by providing (at least in theory) the legal avenues for a lowly serf to make an appeal if a lord failed to meet his societal obligations.

Germanic customary law upheld the supremacy of law over kings—meaning that even kings were not above the law. This doctrine was embodied in the 'right of resistance' and was reinforced in Magna Carta of 1215, a legal document forced upon King John of England by his barons and important for its upholding the right of nobles to use law to control the arbitrary power of kings. This

---

[16] For a marvelous essay on the role of nonverbal communication in preliterate and marginally literate medieval societies, see Hibbitts 1992.

concept of a right of resistance would be revived and have immense significance in the English, American and French Revolutions in subsequent centuries. The concept underscored that:

> The king and his people both stood under a mutual obligation to preserve the law from infringement or corruption and in some cases when the king clearly failed to do his duty we find his subjects taking matters into their own hands and deposing him. (Morrall cited in Tamanaha 2004: 24)

Civil Law and its 'Rediscovery' in Western Europe

In contrast to the communal and reciprocal underpinnings in Germanic customary law, civil (Roman) law helped to articulate and reinforce a hierarchical set of social relations that was removed from localized norms and very much favored a power elite. The story of the rise and fall and rise again of Roman law is fascinating. Roman law was rationalized and then codified by the Byzantine emperor Justinian I between 529 and 534 in the document known as the *Corpus Juris Civilis* (body of civil law) (Kelley 1990: 53–66). Then, so the story goes, for many centuries the *Corpus Juris Civilis* lay hidden in some forgotten library or monastery and was in effect lost to western Europe until its rediscovery in the twelfth century. Perhaps surprisingly from a contemporary perspective, Roman law was not considered archaic and irrelevant despite not having been used for some 700 years. On the contrary, 'like the Bible, [it] was not seen as a product of a particular and transient historic phase, but as an eternal paradigm, a treasure-house of timeless wisdom and a revelation for all time' (Van Caenegem 1991: 129).

However, as noted by Michael Tigar in his history of capitalism, the story of the rediscovery of Roman law by Europeans is not entirely correct. He cautions that 'it would be conveniently ethnocentric to take this view, for it makes commercial civilization from 1000 onward a Western invention' (Tigar 2000: 76). It also suggests that Roman law was and remained a purely European creation, rediscovered in the twelfth century, and then over the subsequent centuries of colonial rule transported and transferred around the world. Against this European interpretation, the crusades in fact provided the opportunity for 'extensive borrowings from the legal learning and mercantile practice of Arab and Byzantium civilizations' (Tigar 2000: 78).

One of the attractions of Roman law was that it enabled a certain degree of standardization in legal procedures, and hence was widely used in commercial trading networks across the Mediterranean and into Palestine and Syria. Thus one of the most enduring consequences of the medieval crusades in the eleventh and twelfth centuries was European traders returning home from the east and bringing with them elements of Roman and Arab law conducive to commercial contracts and negotiations. As a result Justinian's *Corpus Juris Civilis* formed the basis of legal textbooks that then became the focus of study in the new universities established in the twelfth and thirteenth centuries in Bologna, Paris, Pisa, Salamanca, Prague, Oxford and Cambridge. Roman law—in contrast to the customary intricacies of German feudal law—was centralized, written and codified primarily in Latin, and removed from having to heed local norms and behaviors. As a result, Roman law provided the basis for establishing a technically trained professional class of legal experts who could negotiate on behalf of their employers across borders and geo-political regions. It contributed greatly to the 'creation of modern organization and administration' and helped to build a new social class of 'qualified officials, judges and administrators' (Van Caenegem 1991: 135).

The Significance of Canon (Catholic) Law

Canon law developed alongside civil Roman law and derived many of its rules and practices from it. Canon law began to be compiled from the twelfth century onward in texts that were known as the *Concordia Discordantium Canonum* or more commonly the *Decretum* (see Helmholz 2008).[17] Canon law embraced internationalism. It 'ranged over large international, intercultural, and even universal boundaries' and 'took as its field of competence the entire "modern law of nations"' (Kelley 2000: 157). Canon law became widely accepted by the rising legal profession as a set of rules or norms of general application that transcended—or at least had the potential to transcend—national borders and territorial regions (Bellomo 1995). Canon lawyers took their orders from the Church and drew their political and economic status from its hierarchical and immensely powerful bureaucratic structure. As the Catholic Church became increasingly corrupt and its members overtly greedy, church lawyers clung more and more to the authority of the pope as being above the law of the land and the supreme arbiter of all things. By declaring the pope supreme, church lawyers could ignore local civil laws and appeal directly to Rome for adjudication (Clarke 2001: 27). Canon law, in short, provided a line of divinely authorized defense against prosecution of individual clergy members, as well as against general German disgruntlement over the excessive practices of the Catholic Church.

Canon law was also significant in terms of focusing on the individual's relationship with God; it helped to articulate public and private spheres as well as laying the foundations for the concept of individual rights that would become so important in the seventeenth and eighteenth centuries. Canonists 'emphasized the liberty—the "free will"—of the individual soul, and thereby his (and increasingly her) responsibility before the law' (Kelley 2000: 153). Aligned to the canonists' focus on the individual's free will and capacity to own personal

---

[17] The *Decretum* is *part* of a larger collection of legal texts known as the *Corpus Iuris Canonici*. The *Corpus* maintained its legal authority in the Catholic Church up until Pentecost Sunday, 27 May 1917, when Pope Benedict XV issued a revised Code of Canon Law.

property, draw up private wills, or testify before an ecclesiastical court, laws developed that determined what kind of individual qualified as having standing before the law. As a result, the legal revival in the medieval period also witnessed increasing efforts to define individuals' legal worth, based on their faith and culture. With respect to European Jews, their legal status differed over time and 'depended heavily upon local religion and politics' (Bell 2008: 206). While there are certainly examples of tolerance and accommodation of Jewish people, overall 'the early modern period remained fundamentally anti-Jewish' (Bell 2008: 212). Under canon law, the testimony of Jews in courts typically counted for far less than that of a Christian, and the testimony of a Muslim counted not at all. Anti-Judaism was also endorsed in civil law and in some cities Jews could not become magistrates or physicians (MacCulloch 2003: 126). These procedural rules of law and legalized limits on secular behavior formalized discriminatory practices and buttressed racial prejudice within western European societies towards non-Christian others.

Civil Law versus Canon Law

In the thirteenth and fourteenth centuries commentaries on and analyses of legal thought proliferated, as did the production and demand for specialized university legal textbooks. Overall, the field of jurisprudence assumed great significance in the medieval and early modern periods, and certainly among Europe's educated and powerful there was a considerable rise in legal consciousness (see Clarke 2001; Van Caenegem 1991: 119–122; Musson 2001). One of the primary reasons for this heightened engagement with law was that as a system of rules it established legal precedents, reinforcing shared expectations and a sense of predictability in such things as the laws of inheritance, property rights, contracts and taxation that very much helped the burgeoning mercantile classes. This sense of order should not be underestimated given that people's lives were typically harsh, violent, disorderly and short.

Despite major differences, together the civil and canon law texts created a common body of legal knowledge known as the *ius commune*, which was studied across Europe in law school curriculums (Kelley 2000: 148). However, while in practice there was much shared knowledge and overlap among jurists who specialized in civil law or canon law, these two groups of legal experts tended to represent different interest groups.[18] Hence the civil and ecclesiastical court systems were endorsed by competing sections of society jostling for power and sovereign authority over such things as property rights and the control of taxes.

---

[18] Because civil and canon law were treated as separate fields of jurisprudence, they were visually distinct in manuscripts. A jurist could glance at a manuscript and tell immediately if it concerned civil or canon law. Typically in a civil law manuscript the first initial in the text paragraphs was decorated in blue, while in a canon law manuscript the first initial alternated between blue and red (L'Engle 2001: 64–66).

These competing groups were represented on the one hand by princes, electors, lesser nobility and merchant burghers who favored civil law because it helped to consolidate private ownership in the hands of a few and lent itself to the capitalist enterprise, and on the other hand by the ecclesiastical clerics who were anxious to defend the imperial interests of the Catholic Church and provide legal immunity to their own increasingly reprehensible clergy members.

In Germany and through most of western Europe, Catholic canon law steadily gained dominance over civil law during the 1500s and 1600s. This created great aggravation in Germany, where a growing nationalist movement of elites, merchants and ordinary working people were becoming increasingly incensed by the injustices experienced at the hands of the Italian clergy. Anger and conflict came to a head at the Diet of Worms in 1521, where, as mentioned above, Martin Luther was brought before the emperor, Charles V, to answer charges of heresy. At this hearing the emperor asked the German Estates (made up of princes and electors) to list their concerns with papal activities and the 'burdens placed on the German nation', and so the *Statement of Grievances Presented to the Diet of Worms in 1521*, listing over 100 specific grievances, was produced. In addition to being the first official catalog of the Estate's grievances against Catholic institutions, the document underscores the degree to which ecclesiastical courts were a dominant presence that influenced and controlled all aspects of public and private activity.

Luther held specific views on law and in 1520 denounced all jurists—both church and civil. According to Luther, 'Jurists are bad Christians' and 'Every jurist is an enemy of Christ' (cited in Witte 2002: 119–76). From Luther's perspective at the time, it was difficult to differentiate between church law and clerical authority on the one hand, and civil law and secular authority on the other (Witte 2002: 2). The historian Harold Berman has called this the 'apocalyptic phase of the Revolution', a period in which Luther 'coupled his theological doctrine of heavenly kingdom, in which law is replaced by grace, with a broadside attack on the prevailing legal order in the German principalities and in the empire, as well as on jurists generally' (Berman 2003: 63).

In this 'apocalyptic phase' Luther did not anticipate the societal crisis his attack on the Catholic Church would generate. While he brought optimism to many people with his calls for spiritual renewal, this optimism depended on a concurrent undermining of the power of the ecclesiastical courts, which had formerly lent a degree of predictability to life and social and economic relations. Luther's demands for spiritual reform destabilized the authority of canon law and made it ineffective in those cities and towns where Lutheranism was embraced (Witte 2002). As the ecclesiastical courts began to be dismantled, people across all classes of society were left confused and afraid, not knowing where to turn for legal adjudication on even basic matters of property dispute or divorce. As a result,

> Prostitution, concubinage, gambling, drunkenness, and usury reached new heights. Crime, delinquency, truancy, vagabondage, and mendicancy soared. Schools, charities,

hospices, and other welfare institutions fell into massive disarray. Requirements for marriage, annulment, divorce, and inheritance became hopeless confused. A generation of orphans, bastards, students, spinsters, and others found themselves without the support and sanctuary traditionally afforded to monasteries, cloisters, and ecclesiastical guilds. All these subjects, and many more, the Catholic canon law had governed in detail for many centuries in Germany. The new Protestant civil law, where it existed at all, was too primitive to address these subjects properly. (Witte 2002: 3)

Throughout the 1520s Luther was forced to confront the panic and crisis created by the dismantling of ecclesiastical courts in the cities that supported him. Moreover, he began to realize that he must engage with sympathetic jurists who approved of spiritual reformation, and decide how best to help them in the building of new bureaucracies and legal authorities appropriate to the Protestant faith. As Luther developed his ideas in response to unfolding political events such as the Peasants' War (1524–25) and the Ottoman Empire's occupation of Belgrade (1526), he began to envisage a clear division of duties between a spiritual jurisdiction governed by divine authority and a temporal jurisdiction governed by the emperor's secular authority.

The Two Kingdoms of Church and State

Luther's tract *On War Against the Turks* (1529) undermined the legitimacy of the Catholic Church and challenged the medieval assumption that the pope was the overarching spiritual *and* temporal authority on all things. In Luther's opinion, while God was the supreme spiritual head, when it came to earthly governance and secular matters the emperor was in charge as the 'true overlord'. Scholars debate how to define secularism and secular legal authority in the context of the Reformation. Harold Berman has argued that the term 'secular' has changed radically since the sixteenth century, and a current conception of secularism that equates it with rational pragmatism and modernity does not take into account Luther's understanding of secularism as one 'in which God is present' (Berman 2003: 194, 179). According to Berman, Luther drew upon the bible as the source of law and the result was 'a process of spiritualization of secular responsibilities and activities' (Berman 2003: 369). If we ignore this spiritualization process, Berman argues, 'we have broken with Lutheran thought by denying to the law of the state the function of expressly fostering "spiritual gifts" through adoption of theologically determined and theologically formulated church laws, marriage laws, school laws, laws of moral discipline, and poor laws ...' (Berman 2003: 193).

It should come as no surprise that Luther attributed spiritual guidance and discipline in the work of a secular authority and its legal system. Luther was a deeply religious man who never faltered in his belief of a divine omnipresence. Despite this belief, or perhaps because of it, Luther claimed that splitting godly from temporal authority was absolutely necessary. His argument drew on an earlier tract that local German princes had urged him to write, entitled *Temporal*

Authority: To What Extent it Should be Obeyed (1523). In this earlier document Luther first articulated his concept of the 'two kingdoms' and the necessity of dividing power and authority between spiritual and earthly governments. According to Luther:

> ... the world and the masses are and always will be un-Christian, even if they are all baptized and Christian in name. Christians are few and far between (as the saying is). Therefore, it is out of the question that there should be a common Christian government over the whole world, or indeed over a single country or any considerable body of people, for the wicked always outnumber the good ... For this reason God has ordained two governments: the spiritual, by which the Holy Spirit produces Christians and righteous people under Christ; and the temporal, which restrains the un-Christian and the wicked so that ... they will be obliged to keep still and maintain an outward peace. (Luther in Porter 1974: 56, 55)

Furthermore, Luther argued, these two kingdoms or governments should be autonomous in their exercise of power and each should have its own laws because:

> without law no kingdom or government can survive, as everyday experience amply shows. The temporal government has laws which extend no further to life and property and external affairs on earth, for God cannot and will not permit anyone but himself to rule over the soul. (Luther in Porter 1974: 61)

In enunciating the distinct duties and obligations of the emperor as distinct from divine spiritual authority, Luther forced ordinary people to rethink their relationship to religious and political institutions and appreciate that they were not necessarily one and same entity. For the first time since the Classical Roman empire, blind loyalty to the institutions and laws of the Catholic Church were not assumed as a given and the role of the secular state had to be directly confronted.[19] Luther, by claiming that the war against the Turks was a problem for the emperor—not the pope—helped to open up a space for public discussion about temporal governance. And as public conversation spread, heightened by racist fears of the foreign infidel and local peasant insurgents, debate over what would be the most appropriate form of law and government to keep the peace in what Luther called the 'distressed and wretched nation' became intense (Luther in Porter 1974: 38). If the emperor was in charge, what exactly was the relationship between the emperor and local secular authorities? Did canon [Catholic] law still hold precedence over German rules and statutes? What should replace canon

---

[19] However, as Diarmaid MacCulloch reminds us, the idea of the 'state' in the context of the Reformation is not equivalent to modern nation-states that developed in Europe in the 18th and 19th centuries and involved, amongst other things, 'a common consciousness created within a consolidated territory ... producing a public rhetoric of a single national will' (MacCulloch 2003: 43). In the late 15th and early 16th centuries the notion of a secular state existed in an immature form and people's loyalty to a geographical location, local culture, or ruling dynastic family was mediated through a sense of a 'God-given created order' rather than a sense of deliberately orchestrated human endeavor (MacCulloch 2003: 44).

law, and how would that law be determined? What role would the rising middle class of burghers and merchants play in German city administration? And what, if any, were the rights of the working-class plebeians and peasants against abusive clergy, princes, lords and guild masters?

CONCLUSION

Reflections on how law and governance related to the distribution of power within society's class structure, and how best to secure law and order in a period of massive discontent, were new in the early years of sixteenth-century Europe. Such thinking represented a profound shift in public attitudes across all strata of society. It marked a transition away from a medieval mindset which believed that everything was governed and caused by a supreme Christian god toward a mindset characteristic of the early modern period which was increasingly centered on the authority of secular government and the individual's rights and relationship to it. I do not want to suggest that these changes happened overnight or even in the course of Luther's lifetime. The transition in Germany from a religious culture (where all actions and thoughts are in some way related to religious practices) to a secular culture (where conscious effort is needed to connect religion to human action) was slow, gradual, and faltering. However, Luther did sow the seeds of revolution that forever changed the political, spiritual, legal and cultural landscape of western Europe.

This shift in popular attitude was triggered in part by widespread discontentment with the abuses of the Catholic Church and the injustices of ecclesiastical courts. But the shift was also due to a growth in German nationalist identity, which in turn was nurtured by a rising mercantile class concerned with individual and corporate rights vis-a-vis the state, as well as its heavy investment in securing legal predictability and enforceability beneficial to the capitalist enterprise. Intellectuals and bureaucrats also increasingly favored the concept of a centralized secular government with sovereign authority independent of a greedy Catholic Church and the ineffectual and cumbersome administration of the Holy Roman Empire.

A great deal more could be said about Luther and his life, Luther's contentious relationship with insurgent peasants, Luther's impact on the reformation as a whole, the differing views of radical reformers such as John Calvin and Ulrich Zwingli, and the subsequent Counter-Reformation movement including the Spanish Inquisition. However, I am leaving this chapter here in the hope that the above narrative has helped the reader to appreciate the importance of Martin Luther in destabilizing the medieval way of understanding the world and opening up religious, intellectual, political and social space to envisage or imagine a new way of being (Matheson 2000: 7). This new way of being cannot be disentangled from a xenophobic conception of the racially superior European in contrast to inferior Muslims, Jews, and other foreign 'barbarians'. Nor can it be disentangled from an emerging legal consciousness that involved various demands for new forms of secular governance, as well as a growth in German nationalist identity at both community and individual levels.

The next chapter turns to England, which was the first state to institutionalize the Protestant faith, only 17 years after Luther posted his 95 Theses. The backdrop to the chapter is the growing secularization of English society. The central concern is the emergent separation of religious authority and secular government, and specifically the rising tension between centralized state absolutism on the one hand and the developing concept of representative parliamentary democracy on the other. This tension came to a head at the trial of King Charles I and his beheading in 1649 by order of parliament. The outcome of the case ultimately rested on the old customary notion of a 'right to resistance' against tyranny and the belief that no one—not even the king—is above the law. In the early years of the twenty-first century, which witnessed the Bush administration claim that it was at times above the law, it would seem that Charles I's unsuccessful defense that it is a king's prerogative to enjoy state immunity is neither irrelevant nor yet resolved.

Recommended Reading

Asad, Talad (2003) *Formations of the Secular: Christianity, Islam, Modernity.* Stanford, CA: Stanford University Press.

Berman, Harold J (1993, 2000 edn) *Faith and Order: The Reconciliation of Law and Religion.* Grand Rapids, MI and Cambridge, UK: William B Eerdmans Publishing Co.

Berman, Harold J (2003) *Law and Revolution, II: The Impact of the Protestant Reformations on the Western Legal Tradition.* Cambridge, MA: The Belknap Press of Harvard University Press.

Eisenstein, EL (1993) *The Printing Revolution in Early Modern Europe.* Cambridge: Cambridge University Press.

Kelley, Donald R (2000) *The Human Measure: Social Thought in the Western Legal Tradition.* Cambridge, MA: Harvard University Press.

Lewis, David Levering (2009) *God's Crucible: Islam and the Making of Modern Europe, 570–1215.* New York: WW Norton & Co.

MacCulloch, Diarmaid (2003) *The Reformation: Europe's House Divided 1490–1700.* New York: Penguin.

Strauss, Gerald (ed and trans) (1971) *Manifestations of Discontent in Germany on the Eve of the Reformation.* Bloomington: Indiana University Press.

Tyerman, Christopher (2006) *God's War: A New History of the Crusades.* Cambridge, MA: The Belknap Press of Harvard University Press.

Van Caenegem, RC (1991) *Legal History: A European Perspective.* London and Rio Grande: The Hambledon Press.

Witte, John Jr (2002) *Law and Protestantism: The Legal Teachings of the Lutheran Reformation.* Cambridge: Cambridge University Press.

Witte, John Jr (2006) *God's Joust, God's Justice: Law and Religion in the Western Tradition*. Grand Rapids, MI and Cambridge, UK: William B Eerdmans Publishing Co.

Witte, John Jr (2007) *The Reformation of Rights: Law, Religion, and Human Rights in Early Modern Calvinism*. Cambridge: Cambridge University Press.

2

Executing the King: The Trial of Charles I (1649)

GERMANY'S PROTESTANT Reformation had a considerable impact in England, and by extension Scotland and Ireland, in the first half of the seventeenth century. During these years, society experienced massive shifts in political and theological ideas; these shifts challenged the very foundations of religious authority, and by implication altered the status of secular state authority. By the mid-1600s—just over a century after Martin Luther had posted his 95 Theses on the castle church in Wittenberg—the long-held medieval assumption that the head of the church was also the indisputable head of state was profoundly contested. How did these changes come about, and why did they happen in England? What were the implications of this political challenge for God's authority with respect to the development of modern English law? More generally, to what extent did England's overseas colonies and its engagement with other European states affect popular attitudes towards the legal system and generate demands for legal reform?

The trial and execution of Charles I of England is a highly symbolic milestone in the historical development of modern western law. For the first time the common law, which ostensibly represented society's concepts of rights and justice, was seen as overcoming medieval assumptions about God's ultimate authority over the material world. Specifically, the execution underscored that no one, not even the king, could oppress and wage war on his own people. The concept of a monarch's immunity from any form of state scrutiny and accountability was shattered. Divine law could not trump secular law, at least during this period in England.[1]

It is important to note that Charles I was not poisoned, assassinated, disappeared or dealt with behind the closed doors of a court martial. He was tried in Westminster Hall, the 'center of English justice', before 70 judges and thousands

---

[1] This was not the case in France, where under Louis XIV and his successors the doctrine of the divine right of kings and absolute monarchy flourished. The doctrine drew heavily on the later writings of Jacques-Benigne Bossuet, who in his 1709 treatise *Politics Drawn from the Very Words of Scripture* wrote that absolute rule did not mean arbitrary rule, since God institutes the monarch for the welfare of the people; therefore, he/she must act in the best interests of his/her people.

of subjects. Those members of parliament who participated in the trial—a substantial number did not participate or vote (Robertson 2005)—regarded it as crucial to the legitimacy of the trial and execution that proceedings be carefully recorded, that evidence be gathered systematically, and that due process be, and be seen to be, fully complied with. This concern for legal justice underscores that throughout the conflicts and battles between king, state and people during the first half of the seventeenth century there was a growing awareness of the need to defend the legitimacy of the English common law. This legitimacy was forged on the basis of its apparent objectivity and a sense that it should prevail over time, outliving the dictates of specific monarchs and operating beyond political influence and pressure.[2]

In order to understand why the trial and execution of Charles I occurred in 1649, we look to 1605 and the Gunpowder Plot, which resulted in another dramatic trial and public execution. On the surface these events may appear to have little connection, separated as they are by 44 years, different monarchies, civil wars, and the establishment of England's first North American colonies. However, I suggest that in order to put Charles I's execution in religious, social and political context, it is necessary to step back some years and follow the sequence of events that led up to it.

The Gunpowder Plot was a bold and daring attempt by Catholic radicals to blow up the king and most of the Protestant aristocracy attending a state opening of the Houses of Parliament. In response to the Gunpowder Plot, laws discriminating against Catholics were more strictly enforced in the first half of the seventeenth century, the religious intolerance of Puritanism began to take a firm hold, and James I of England (formerly James VI of Scotland) increasingly came to support the doctrine of the 'divine right of kings' as a way to justify his supreme sovereign control. This doctrine was easily adapted to justify absolutism, and caused extreme anxiety among parliamentarians who feared that the king would simply dissolve parliament. And under James I's son, Charles I, this is exactly what happened. Charles I ruled as a dictator in the years 1629–40, refusing to consult the elected representatives of his country. Charles' explicit disrespect for the rights of his elected members set the stage for an ultimate clash between divine and secular authority, resulting in two bloody civil wars and his trial and death by order of parliament.

In England, the bitter conflict in the first half of the seventeenth century over whether the king (as God's earthly representative) or parliament held sovereign

---

[2] The Church of England provided the primary source of education for the masses, with local parsons and rectors doing the majority of the teaching. Other schoolteachers had to be approved and licensed by the Church. The clergy also controlled higher institutions of learning, such as the Universities of Oxford and Cambridge, and students had to take an oath professing loyalty to the Church of England. However, a notable exception was the teaching of common law to lawyers at the Inns of Court, which helped to reinforce the sense that the common law belonged to the English people and as a mechanism of power was beyond the direct control of king and church (see Hill 1975: 149–56).

control marks, in a sense, the beginning of the modern era. The beheading of Charles I established, once and for all, the capacity of the English aristocracy, gentry and merchants jointly to stake a claim in the governance of the nation and establish their right as Anglo-Saxon, male and propertied individuals to participate in the practice of law-making. Certainly these battles over power were not resolved in any definitive way by the execution of Charles I. Charles II (Charles I's son) was restored as monarch in 1660 after an interim republic led by Oliver Cromwell, and sought to institutionalize his divine right as king. However, Charles I's beheading was an extreme instance of usurpation of power by the English parliament, and essential for highlighting the vulnerability and limited power of the sovereign. In England, the notion that the king held absolute authority—a theory debated by jurists and political philosophers such as Jean Bodin in his *Six livres de la République* (1576) and ultimately supported in France and Spain (Franklin 2009)—was dramatically and irreversibly undermined. Intellectually and politically, the way was paved for subsequent popular revolutions in America and France over 100 years later that were to champion a more democratic sharing of executive power. For this reason Charles I's public execution is a highly symbolic and substantively significant legal landmark in the history of modern law.

RELIGION: PROTESTANT AND CATHOLIC VIOLENCE

In the early hours of the morning of 24 March 1603, Elizabeth I, virgin queen of England, died amidst great mourning and alarm. It was still not clear, at least to the general populace, who would succeed her since the queen had no direct heirs and had forbidden all public discussion of a successor under penalty of imprisonment. Among Elizabeth's most intimate advisors, the plan was hatched that James VI of Scotland, the queen's cousin and godson, would take the throne. As Elizabeth lay dying, Robert Carey was dispatched to ride to bring James news of his status, and deliver him safely to London for crowning.

As news that James VI of Scotland was to become James I of England spread, English Catholics sighed with relief and viewed the turn of events with optimism. Under Elizabeth's reign, Catholics had been persecuted and penalized and Jesuits banned from the country. Elizabeth was excommunicated by Pope Pius V in 1570 for her open hostility toward the Catholic Church. Elizabeth in turn brought to trial and executed Mary Queen of Scots, James VI's mother, for treason because of her Catholic faith in 1587. Laws against Catholics constantly threatened the lives and property of those practicing mass and confession, no matter how private the rituals of faith.[3] Moreover, Catholic men could not attend university

---

[3] Under the Act of Uniformity and Act of Supremacy (1559) legal restrictions were placed on Catholics which forced many to practice their faith underground. Attendance at Protestant church services was compulsory and enforced by threat of fines. The laws were not entirely successful, forcing

or enter government service since both required the taking of the Oath of Supremacy and a declaration of loyalty to the Church of England (see Tutino 2007). Under Elizabeth, Catholicism had been driven underground and was largely harbored in the private estates of wealthy nobility (particularly women) who could afford to hire priests as tutors and build secret temples within the inner walls of their vast manors. Because women at the time did not have any form of legal rights and so were deemed not legally responsible for their actions, they played a pivotal role in nurturing and maintaining Catholicism within the domestic realm. Often their husbands conformed to the practices of the Church of England, while the wives practiced Catholicism behind closed doors (see Sharpe 2005: 24–25; Fraser 1996: 19–36; Questier 2006).

English Catholics expected things to change with the death of Elizabeth and the installation of the new king. James VI, despite having been brought up in Scotland as a member of the Calvinist church, was known to be sympathetic toward Catholics and had tolerated 'honest papists'. Not only had his mother been Catholic, but his wife, Anne of Denmark, secretly converted from Lutheranism to Catholicism in 1600 and was known to be writing letters to the pope. James did little to quell his wife's activities or rumors of his own potential conversion to Catholicism, playing his diplomatic hand well by hinting that all options were open. So while English Catholics greeted the new monarch with high expectations, in courtly circles there was a general feeling of unease that the new king of England might once again throw the country into a state of instability by allowing—perhaps inadvertently—Catholic forces to marshal their resources and possibly overthrow the Protestant state.[4]

The English Reformation and Establishing the Church of England

The English people's fears of bloody conflict between Protestants and Catholics were real and justified. As early as 1531, just 14 years after Martin Luther had publicly begun his attack on the Catholic Church, King Henry VIII denounced the pope's authority over the English people and established a rival state religion,

---

parliament to enact harsher laws against Catholics in 1571 which increased monetary fines for non-attendance at Protestant services, imposed life imprisonment for refusals to take the Oath of Supremacy, and applied the death penalty to all missionaries and Catholic priests. In the latter part of Elizabeth's reign, over 100 Jesuits and Catholics were executed. Under the earlier reign of the Catholic Mary Tudor (1553–58), it was said that Protestants numbering 237 men and 55 women were burnt at the stake between 1555 and 1558.

[4] In the years immediately prior to Elizabeth's death, James was living in Scotland and wrote private letters to Robert Cecil in London regarding his imminent accession to the throne. In one of these letters James expressly indicated his leniency toward Catholics so long as they did not become politically threatening and jeopardize his position as king: 'I will never allow in my conscience that the blood of any man should be shed for diversity of opinions in religion, but I should be sorry that Catholics should so multiply as they might be able to practice their old principles upon us [and] at last become master' (Fraser 1996: 38). While there remains some debate as to the actual increase in the number of Catholics in the early years of James' rule, alarm about the increase was real (Fraser 1996: 81).

the Church of England.[5] The ensuing conflicts between English Catholics and Protestants marred the subsequent decades, with imprisonments, executions, massacres, and a long costly war with Spain in which Englishmen were tortured under the Inquisition (see Tutino 2007; Questier 2006; Kirsch 2009; see Figure 6). Beyond England, in 1572 thousands of French Protestants, the Huguenots, were slaughtered in the streets of Paris in what came to be known as the St Bartholomew's Day Massacre. Such events served as constant reminders of what many English people regarded as the tyranny of the Catholic Church.

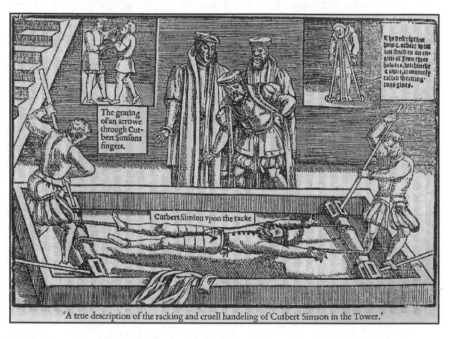

'A true description of the racking and cruell handeling of Cutbert Simson in the Tower.'

Figure 6. Scenes of torture and persecution of English Protestants by English Catholics in John Foxe's very popular book of propaganda *Book of Martyrs* or *Actes and Monuments of these Latter and Perilous Days, touching Matters of the Church* (1563). Folger Shakespeare Library, Washington D.C.

Henry VIII's distancing of England from Rome was fueled by both political and religious interests. In England nationalism was on the rise and the country was emerging as a significant seafaring power that was increasingly resentful of Rome's hold over it. Moreover, Henry VIII was in desperate need of a male heir to the throne and was anxious to declare his marriage to Catherine of Aragon

[5] Originally, Henry VIII had attacked Martin Luther in a 1521 publication entitled *The Defence of the Seven* Sacraments, which was a hugely popular book and went through approximately 20 editions in England and Europe. Pope Leo X awarded Henry VIII the title 'Defender of the Faith' for his championing of the Catholic Church.

'blighted in the eyes of God' and so be free to marry his new love Ann Boleyn. Unfortunately, Pope Clement VII refused to annul Henry's marriage to Catherine, which the pope argued was valid according to canon (church) law. England's subsequent break with Rome meant that Henry VIII did not need the pope's dispensation for his marriage annulment and he could move ahead with divorcing Catherine and marrying the second of his six wives.[6]

Supporting England's political and economic break with Rome were new theological ideas introduced by the German reformer Martin Luther and his followers, who opposed the corrupt practices of the Catholic Church. The reformers' radical ideas about the need to change the practice of Christianity swept across northern Europe in the latter part of the fifteenth and early sixteenth centuries, ushering in Protestantism as a new and competing Christian faith. This historical period embodied a new era of thinking—for some individuals—about one's personal relationship to God. This shift in spiritual perspective also created a new consciousness about one's role in society, both as an individual and as part of a collective nation. Hence emerging alongside new ways of knowing oneself in relation to God ('justification by faith alone') was a new understanding of individuals' rights in relation to the king. Nurturing such ideas was a growing interest in the concept of empirical science, the introduction of technologies such as the printing press, the development of a bureaucratic nation-state, the creation of a mercantile middle class, the economic impetus for colonization of overseas territories, and the sustained contact of Englishmen with darker-skinned non-Christian others. These factors created an environment that more readily accommodated the pursuit of individual and national aspirations of wealth and power, and the justification of those aspirations in terms of religious and racial superiority.

The Gunpowder Plot

On the eve of 5 November 1605, in the cellars beneath London's Houses of Parliament, a large number of barrels containing gunpowder were discovered. Guards had uncovered a Catholic plot to blow up James I, his wife, and the country's Protestant aristocracy of parliamentarians that made up the House of Lords and House of Commons. According to the English Jesuit Father Oswald Tesimond in a near contemporary account:

---

[6] Anne Boleyn was closely linked to an increasingly powerful Episcopal faction led by the radical Thomas Cromwell, who bitterly resented the Catholic clergy and their hold on the laity through political influence and the exertion of canon law. Cromwell led his armed forces in the charge to break up Catholic monasteries and abbeys throughout the 1530s. This dissolution of the monasteries provided Henry VIII with immense state revenues, but it also threw the country into violent turmoil, and reckless vandalism ensued as the pastoral system of charity provided by the Catholic Church was slowly dismantled. Cromwell was executed in 1540 for his participation in the dissolution process, as Henry VIII tried to quell the public outcry and re-establish a more conservative reform agenda through the Act of Six Articles (1539) and other demonstrations of leniency toward Catholic clergy.

Parliament was due to begin on Tuesday, 5 November. On the Monday night preceding, Sir Thomas Knyvett, a gentleman of the King's household, was sent to search the lower rooms and cellars beneath the actual chamber where Parliament met. He was to make his search as if he were concerned with other matters. But notice that at the entrance of the outer chambers he meets a man fully dressed, booted and spurred! Since it was already past midnight, this seemed to him rather strange. ... They had the man search[ed] whom they had just seized. Three fuses, or matches, were found on him ... These would serve to ignite the powder on the following morning. (cited in Sharpe 2005: 5)

The leader of the Gunpowder Plot was Robert Catesby. But the man charged with executing the deed was Guy Fawkes, a devout Catholic who had served with Spain in the Netherlands against the Protestant Dutch and was skilled in the use of explosives and gunpowder.[7] There were 13 conspirators in all, most connected by family or marriage, growing up together in a tight-knit Catholic community held together by faith and secrecy (Fraser 1996: 99).[8]

The date was set for the planned explosion in late 1604, but the opening of parliament was delayed and the date had to be pushed back again and again. As time wore on, more and more men were added to the conspiratorial team and despite being sworn to utmost secrecy there increasingly arose opportunities for betrayal and disclosure. The plotters began to grow nervous, with some very distressed at the thought of innocents, some of them Catholic, being caught up in the explosion (Fraser 1996: 106–07). So it was not particularly surprising that someone eventually squealed. On the night of 26 October 1605, a letter was delivered by a mysterious stranger to the house of Lord Monteagle, a well-known sympathizer of the Catholic cause and connected by marriage to Elizabeth Tresham, a member of a leading Catholic family (cited in Fraser 1996: 150).

Perceiving the seriousness of the warning, Monteagle took the letter to the Secretary of State, Robert Cecil, Earl of Salisbury. Cecil, for reasons still unclear, did not immediately inform the king of the treasonable plan; he waited until the king returned from a hunting trip some days later. Upon hearing the news, the king was alarmed and demanded that search parties be sent to inspect the precinct around parliament. Suspicions were raised over a large pile of firewood found in an underground cellar, and a second search was conducted around midnight.

The man discovered in the cellar was Guy Fawkes. For the first day of his imprisonment he pretended that his name was 'John Johnson' in an effort not to implicate his fellow conspirators. Unfortunately, Fawkes' efforts to remain silent

---

[7] 'The Plotters may have been original in the daring and scope of their concept, but they were certainly not original in choosing gunpowder to carry out the "blow". In 1585 five hundred of the besiegers of Antwerp had been killed by the use of an explosive-packed machine, invented by one Giambelli' (Fraser 1996: 122).

[8] Some historians have argued that the men involved in the plot had been scheming for many years prior to Elizabeth's death to bring about a Spanish succession, and that the disappointments of James' early years as king of England were largely irrelevant (see Wormald 1985).

did not prevail when the rack was applied on 7 November by order of the king.[9] As Fawkes endured intense torture over the following days (as attested by his increasingly faltering signature following torture sessions), information leaked out and his fellow plotters were rounded up from their estates and hiding places. Some took their own lives; some were killed during attempts to imprison them. The seven who were captured alive were put on trial with Guy Fawkes and hung, drawn and quartered on 30 and 31 January 1606.

Some historians have argued that the Gunpowder Plot was a Protestant conspiracy perpetrated by the king and his courtiers in order to bolster the monarchy and justify the severity of laws against English Catholics. One of the difficulties in determining the actual facts is that contemporary accounts are clearly biased, expressing either Catholic or Protestant views. Complicating the matter further, the confessions of the actual plotters were extracted under torture and in all probability represent a distortion of the facts (Sharpe 2005: 46). While the significance of Guy Fawkes and the Gunpowder Plot has changed somewhat over time (see Sharpe 2005), it nonetheless still represents one of the most bold and treacherous offenses against king and government in European history. It is annually commemorated on 5 November each year, on what is known as Guy Fawkes Night, when firecrackers, bonfires and effigies of Guy are lit to remind local communities of the treachery of the plotters.

What is not commemorated in the annual Guy Fawkes celebrations is that the failed Plot provided the English monarchy with an excuse to roll back advances made in institutionalizing electoral representation in parliament and granting certain political rights to propertied males. It also empowered James I, and his son Charles I, to act without accountability and justify their actions under the doctrine of divine right. This allowed them to claim that God was the highest authority and source of law, and that government derived its powers from this divine authority and not from the consent of the governed. Somewhat surprisingly, this appeal to God as the source of governance endures into the twenty-first century. One of the most egregious examples of this in recent times was former US President George W Bush's evocation of his 'divine mission' in his attacks on Afghanistan and Iraq. Bush's position was supported by legal luminaries such as US Supreme Court Justice Scalia, who has noted that the trouble with democracy is that it has a tendency 'to obscure the divine authority behind government' (Scalia 2002). The reaction of the English monarchy to the Gunpowder Plot in

---

[9] In England during this period, torture was used only in extreme cases. It was generally only justified when a prisoner was suspected of treason, not because of that person's religious faith. This contrasted with the use of torture by the Catholic Church in its various inquisitions. In England there was only one rack, housed at the Tower of London. 'The rack was a large open frame of oak, raised from the ground. The prisoner was laid on it with his back to the floor, his wrists and ankles attached by cords to rollers at either end. Levers were operated which stretched the prisoner quite slowly, while he was urged to confess. The rack, inevitably, caused permanent damage and dislocation to the prisoner. So feared was the instrument, indeed, that sometimes the mere sight of it was enough to cow the prisoner into giving information' (Fraser 1996: 179).

the seventeenth century foreshadowed this kind of contemporary thinking, and paved the way for the use of torture to provide evidence deemed legitimate and acceptable in an English court of law—a contentious issue that over 400 years later continues to be hotly debated in legal and political circles.

The Doctrine of the Divine Right of Kings

The Gunpowder Plot punctuated the religious extremism that permeated seventeenth century England. On a personal front, James was fearful for his own safety and the safety of his wife and children. In his address to parliament on 9 November, five days after the discovery of the Plot, James referred to the concept of divine right by arguing that his escape from certain death was nothing short of a divine miracle, which was appropriate given that kings were divinely appointed by God.

The doctrine of the divine right of kings was not a new concept developed by James as a result of his Gunpowder Plot scare. Rather, the Plot made his earlier thoughts on the divine authority of the monarch more pertinent and applicable to the challenges he faced with the growing presence of English Catholics and Jesuits, some of whom were fanatics, as well as the growing demands of Puritans for greater church reform. By evoking his divine right to act, James could on the one hand occupy a position of spiritual authority equivalent to the pope, and on the other hand assume a supreme legitimacy that was not granted under Calvinism. This ambiguity in turn gave him religious and ideological flexibility in his dealings with the complex religious factions and conflicts of the period.

The doctrine of divine right was a traditional medieval concept upheld by Elizabeth I and other English monarchs before James, but, whereas Elizabeth had merely hinted at the doctrine's existence, James felt the need to explicitly spell out the idea of divine right in official terms. Before his accession to the throne of England in 1603, James had written texts supporting the notion of the divine right of kings, and continued to do so over the course of his reign. The principal books were *The Trew Law of Free Monarchies* (1598), *Basilikon Doron* (1599), *An Apologie for the Oath of Allegiance* (1607), and *A Defense of the Right of Kings against Cardinal Perron* (1615). The *Basilikon Doron* was a manual written by James to educate his four-year old son in the duties of kingship (see Wormald 1991). In this manual, James wrote that a good king:

> Acknowledgeth himself ordained for his people, having received from God a burden of government, whereof he must be countable. The idea of a divine right to rule has appeared in many cultures Eastern and Western spanning all the way back to the first God king Gilgamesh ... A good King will frame his actions to be according to the law, yet he is not bound thereto but of his good will.

Despite James' spoken and written words on the supreme authority of kings, he did not in fact practice absolutism. In an important speech to parliament on

21 March 1610, James reminded his courtiers and parliament that he held powers comparable to those of God, and that kings could 'make or unmake their subjects; they have the power of raising and casting down; of life, and of death, judges over all their subjects, and in all causes, and yet accountable to none but God only' (cited in Houston 1973: 116). And yet in this same speech James made it clear that a king must rule according to the law of the land. A king, James said:

> binds himself by a double oath to the observation of the fundamental laws of the Kingdom: tacitly, as by being a king, and so bound to protect as well the people as the laws of his kingdom: and expressly, by his oath at his coronation. So, as every just king in a settled kingdom is bound to observe that paction [agreement] made to his people by his laws, in framing his government agreeable thereto ... I will not content that my power be disputed upon, but I shall ever be willing to make the reason appear of all my doings, and rule my actions according to my laws. (cited in Houston 1973: 117)

It seems that James was genuinely keen to present himself as a moderate monarch who consulted his courtiers, judges and parliamentarians, and who acted only within his constitutional prerogative. That being said, James was quick to invoke the doctrine of divine right as a convenient way of stemming the increasing encroachment of the House of Commons over his kingly authority to raise taxes and revenues. In short, the doctrine of the divine right of kings provided a mechanism whereby James could be elevated above the melee of murky politics, granting him supreme spiritual authority to govern without constantly having to seek the approval of his parliamentarians. So, as parliament increasingly tried to reframe its relationship to the king and garner more power and control over the jurisdictional rights of the monarch, James explicitly turned to the doctrine of divine right to argue his position. He went so far as to test the doctrine's legitimacy in the courts. This constant invocation of the doctrine infuriated members of the Commons, who were thwarted in their attempts to restrain James and distrustful of his 'foreign' ways and his open disrespect for their privileges and position as a representative assembly.[10] A constant fear that ran through all the political quarrels between James and members of the Commons was that the king, in asserting his prerogative to act, was creating the conditions by which he—or his successor—could ultimately dispense with parliament altogether.

---

[10] The Commons' distrust of James was not unjustified. For instance, after the disastrous 1614 parliament which James dissolved after eight weeks when the Commons refused to grant him additional funds, James said to the Spanish Ambassador: 'the House of Commons is a body without a head. The members give their opinions in a disorderly manner. At their meetings nothing is heard but cries, shouts, and confusions. I am surprised that my ancestors should ever have allowed such as institution to come into existence' (cited in Houston 1973: 38).

The Importance of English Common Law

Distrust and at times open conflict between King James and members of the House of Commons undermined James' reign until his death in 1625. Throughout this period, the growing status of England's common law—as opposed to civil law—was seen as a significant mechanism to contain the absolutist tendencies built into James' reliance on the divine right. The English common law also helped to crystallize and consolidate a sense of English nationalism, both in relation to Catholics in Ireland, France and Spain, and against the foreign peoples of England's overseas dominions and trading ports in the New and Old Worlds (see Cormack 2007).

In the early years of seventeenth century England, the common law was not the only legal system in use, though it was the dominant one. Civil law had replaced canon or papal law, and it existed alongside the common law but was exercised only in the ecclesiastical courts and the Court of Admiralty. As a result, civil law lawyers were considerably outnumbered by common law lawyers—approximately 200 to 2,000. Moreover, unlike civil law, which operated at a greater level of abstractionism, common law was self-referential and the legal profession argued that it could adequately deal with all legal issues within its domestic jurisdiction (Burgess 1993: 119). Under the common law there was no need to refer to some higher notion of natural law or some independently formulated code of reason. Rather, the English common law drew its authority from the concept of an ancient constitution and its specific application to the needs of a localized English citizenry (Burgess 1993: 1–78; see also Barnes 2008).

A central feature of the common law lay in its relationship to nationalist ideals and the concept of English identity and race. This relationship was brought to the fore when James, as king of both Scotland and England after 1603, argued for the political union of the two kingdoms in the third session of the 1606–07 parliament (Wormald 1983). James' reasoning reflected a medieval mindset appropriate to dynastic leadership since he believed that an individual's allegiance was owed to a king because of that person's subjection to that king, not because of a personal or contractual relationship to the state through the institution of monarchy.[11] On the basis of this reasoning James proposed that the two countries should share one religion, one law, and one government system. This scheme would open up commerce between the two regions and dismantle

---

[11] However, there is evidence that even James subscribed to some notion of contract between the king and the people. In *The Trew Law of Free Monarchies* (1598) he wrote: 'I confess that a king at his coronation, or at the entry to his kingdom, willingly promises to his people to discharge honorably and truly the office given him by God over them. But, presuming that thereafter he breaks his promise unto them never so inexcusably, the question is, who should be the judge of the break ...' The answer for James was that only God could determine whether a king had broken his contractual obligations (Wootton 1986: 103).

their legally defined borders. Most importantly, James argued for mutual naturalization whereby any person born after 1603 would automatically be considered a subject of both England and Scotland.

The plan for Scottish and English union was met with much hostility from the English and the Scots, though for different reasons. The Scots were wary of the English, who treated the northern kingdom as an inferior province to be colonized and assimilated. The English found the idea of union intolerable because it would dilute the greatness of the English constitution and its people (Wormald 1992). '[A]ll sections of articulate English society, politicians, courtiers, merchants, lawyers, threatened in their national pride and in their pockets, argued passionately against the Scots' (Wormald 1983: 206). It was not until 1707, a full century later, that union was officially recognized and the name 'Britain' begrudgingly accepted (Levack 1987). The English bitterly resented the notion of a common citizenship, arguing that law represented the soul of the country and legal citizenship should be granted only to those of English ancestry. Citizenship was not something that could be parleyed according to the whims of a monarch. Moreover, in England there was a strong sentiment that citizens held some sort of contractual relationship or reciprocal right in relation to the state. While it would be some decades before this contractual relationship was explicitly discussed in the political writings of Thomas Hobbes, John Locke and others, it nonetheless informed a visceral resistance to James' proposition for union. In short, the Commons maintained that Scots could not become English simply on the basis of their allegiance to James as king. 'To many English gentlemen, who instinctively identified allegiance with law, and therefore limits, this notion of a purely personal subjection was offensive' (Russell 2006: 2; see also Hulsebosch 2006: 190).

Central to English sensibilities was the notion that allegiance should be made to the English common law, and that this allegiance would endure over time despite the changing personage of the king himself. This sensibility dovetailed with English pride in being a sovereign nation, independent and unique, which in turn fueled a growing sense of nationalist identity. Importantly, both sovereignty and nationalism were embodied within and articulated through the English common law, which 'was the only fully national system of law in Europe at that time' (Russell 2006: 9; Levack 1987: 18).

Against this background, it is easier to understand why the hostility that met James' push for union between Scotland and England focused on a sense that English common law would become diluted and degenerated by an amalgamation with Scotland's inferior law. There were also fears that 'honest Englishmen might find themselves tried before a Scottish court' (Wormald 1983: 206).[12] Since

---

[12] In addition, protestors were anxious that union would result in an influx of poor Scotsmen, who would interbreed and diminish the significance of the English race and identity (Hulsebosch 2006: 191). Interestingly, this notion of an invading wave of economically and racially inferior people has informed much of England's resistance to the concept of a united Britain, which under the Acts of

Scotland would not give up its legal system and become subordinate to English common law, this meant that the king would be left to rule, in effect, through two legal systems. This was quite simply unacceptable to many Englishmen, who conceptually framed their national identity in terms of obedience to England's state institutions and its common law. In *Calvin's Case* (1608), an important decision spelling out the legal relationship between England and its external territories, Judge Foster declared: 'England and Scotland are two nations. As two nations, so two peoples, so two lawes.' Justice Walmsely in the same case supported this view when he said:

> The kingdomes meete in the king but are not therfore united or confounded ... The kingdomes remaine the same still. 2 crownes, 2 scepters, 2 lawes, 2 distinct Parliaments, composed of people, nobilitie and royaltie, which are not mixt nor confounded. (cited in Russell 2006: 9)

England's forging of a nationalist identity that rested heavily on the notion of a unique common law system must be understood in the context of its expansionist policies of empire building overseas. In 1607, the Colony of Ulster in Northern Ireland and the Colony of Virginia in North America were established. This overseas expansion in both the New and Old Worlds was essential in fueling a growing national consciousness back home that relied heavily on the significance of English common law. As noted by the legal historian Daniel Hulsebosch:

> At the same time that the English began expanding beyond the realm to create what became know as an empire, they also innovated upon old scripts of fundamental law to define their national constitution—to define the English nation. Constitutional ideas and imperial expansion developed simultaneously and reciprocally ... English legal nationalism was in part a response to imperial expansion ... (Hulsebosch 2006: 188, 201)

The existence of colonies forced legal theorists such as Sir Edward Coke in *Calvin's Case* to rethink elements of English common law, and to determine the extent to which it could be exported overseas (MacMillan 2006: 31–41).[13] Coke was a leading legal figure, serving as Attorney General under Elizabeth I, then appointed Lord Chief Justice of England in 1613 by James I, only to be removed

Union in 1707 joined England and Scotland and dissolved the Scottish parliament. Over the ensuing centuries, antagonism and conflict periodically flared up between Scotland and England. In recent decades, with the rise of the European Union, Scotland and Wales have called for greater independence from England. This has resulted in a number of measures that bolster regional nationalism, such as the coining of Welsh money, and Scotland reopening its parliament after 300 years in 1999 (see Darian-Smith 1999; Russell 2006).

[13] *Calvin's Case* (1608) was a leading decision of the period, and is most often associated with the writings and judgment of Sir Edward Coke and his advocacy of constitutionalism and a national legal order that could resist and limit the royal prerogative of the king. The interpretation of Coke's writings by American revolutionaries in the 18th century and by subsequent American lawyers and historians is not entirely correct. Coke's interpretation of the English common law and its ability to be exported to the New World colonies was more modest than many Americans would have it (Hulsebosch 2006).

from office three years later. He firmly believed in the supremacy of the common law over divine authority. He also believed that the common law, as a system of rules, could only operate within the territorial boundaries of England, and be applied and remedied through its lawyers, courts, prisons and enforcement agencies. At the same time, Coke was mindful of the need for Englishmen living overseas to access certain laws, particularly those pertaining to rights over property. A compromise was established whereby English male citizens—of a certain socioeconomic background and class—could bring an action in an English court so long as that English court had jurisdiction over the matter. Since legal cases in the dominions were beyond the jurisdictional reach of England, concessions for self-government by colonists was to a large degree conceded. This early trajectory of self-rule created the conditions for increasing conflict between colonial dominions and mother England, setting the scene for the eventual break by America's 13 colonies following the American War of Independence (1775–83).[14]

RACE: RELIGIOUS INTOLERANCE AND LEGALIZING RACISM

In Europe, the intersections between religion, race and nationalist identity became very much more complicated in the later sixteenth and early seventeenth centuries. Prior to the German Reformation, the great divide between 'us' and 'them' pivoted to a great extent on whether one was Christian or not. Crusades and conquests between Christians, Muslims and Jews provided the central narrative of conflict and difference throughout the medieval period (Vitkus 1999). Modern nation-states were in the early stages of development, and more often than not people identified with a region or local city or village. And so it was one's religious identity that was first and foremost used as a signifier of difference, denoting European from non-European in the pre-modern era.

Following the Reformation and the splitting of Christianity along lines of Catholicism and reformed Protestant churches, religious pluralism proliferated and conflict became much more divisive both within Europe and at European nations' colonial peripheries. In Europe, most of the north was associated with Lutheranism, Calvinism and other Episcopal churches, while much of southern Europe (as well as Ireland and France) was associated with Catholicism and the overarching jurisdiction of the pope. Hence Catholics living in England, connected as they were to papal Rome, were considered by many as being foreign and un-English.

---

[14] 'Far from England, thinly populated, rich in natural resources, and occupied by men and women who knew their own minds and grasped a bargain when they saw it, the colonies edged toward self-government. When English authorities tried to make the imperial system more effective and responsive to the wishes of the crown, colonial elites cited their old liberties and dug in their feet. The pattern appeared early in Virginia's history and persisted until the final crisis, in 1776' (Hoffer 1998: 15).

Beyond the reaches of Europe, religious differences also played a significant role in the acquisition of overseas territories and the various practices of conquest, occupation and alliance by European countries such as England, Portugal, Spain and the Netherlands (see Benton 2002). It is important to note that throughout this period of early colonialism religious differences increasingly took on a state-militarized dimension. Both within Europe and between European powers seeking overseas territories, there was an increasing coalescence of religious affiliation and nationalist identity that carried with it various rights to property and legal redress associated with belonging to a legally defined, jurisdictionally bound community.

Claims that one faith was superior to another were reinforced by and dovetailed with ideas of racial differentiation. In England, the topic of religious conflict featured explicitly in political debates and governmental proclamations aimed at dealing with religious pluralism, which involved competition between Catholics, Protestants, Anglicans, Puritans, and many independent nonconformist and sectarian splinter faiths. In contrast, public discussion about race was far less obvious and often veiled. However, this is not to say that people were not aware of, or did not participate in, racial discourse. Ideas about race circulated throughout society and informed taken-for-granted assumptions about what it meant to be English, and how this connected to England's role in the world. The idea of a superior, civilized, law-abiding Anglo-Saxon race, which had long been nurtured in the English collective memory through highly cherished origin myths (MacDougall 1982), was given new vigor and meaning in its articulation through the lens of a Protestant state-based religion.

Theories of Race in Early Modern Europe

In Europe prior to the Reformation, discourses of difference between European and non-European people largely pivoted on the spiritual, cultural and physical divides that existed between Christians, Jews, Muslims, and other religious/ethnic communities. In this early pre-modern period, notions of race and racial difference did not evoke the pseudo-scientific justifications that are associated with the Enlightenment and nineteenth-century social-evolutionary theories of racism. Rather, pre-modern notions of difference are often assumed to have been more fluid and porous because difference was articulated not on the basis of a biological schema but rather depended to a great degree on cultural differences between peoples expressed through dress, religion, diet, language, marriage customs, and so on.[15] As a consequence, scholars who study the history of racial

---

[15] Nineteenth-century categories of racism are assumed to be relatively rigid in their comparative and hierarchical focus on skin color, blood lines, genealogical descent, and cranial and brain size. These physical features, it was argued at the time, in turn correlated to particular moral and social values and rational capacities, such that a person of brown skin could be declared to be violent in nature and intellectually incapable of reading.

discrimination often overlook the Renaissance and early modern period and tend to focus almost exclusively on the better developed social evolutionary models of racial hierarchy associated with the Enlightenment and post-Enlightenment eras.

Against this dominant trend, Ania Loomba and Jonathan Burton argue eloquently in *Race in Early Modern England* that in order to understand the shifting conceptualizations of race over time we should pay closer attention to 'both the unique characteristics of early modern ideas about race and cultural difference, and their connections with later ideologies and practices' (Loomba and Burton 2007: 2; see also Erickson and Hulse 2000). This argument highlights that racism cannot be thought of as only a consequence of colonialism; rather, early discourses of race shaped the 'particular forms taken by modern European colonialism and slavery'. Drawing on a range of documents and literature, Loomba and Burton show that sixteenth and early seventeenth century ideas about human difference were hotly debated and discussed at length in the writings of English explorers, missionaries, merchants, scientists and philosophers. This fascination with otherness can also be seen in more popular literature, poetry, travelogues and performances. For instance, sophisticated racial codes and symbolism permeate Shakespeare's plays *Othello, Antony and Cleopatra* and *The Merchant of Venice,* which were performed before and appreciated by much of English society during this period (Floyd-Wilson 2006; Bovilsky 2008). There was no single explanation for social and physical difference. Rather, a range of theories—often contradictory—were postulated that overlapped and reinforced a sense of difference on a number of fronts, be it class, religion, morals, skin color, or capacity to labor.

With respect to the connections between race, rights and power, England's theories of racism pivoted on a person's religion or perceived lack of religion. Central to this was whether a person was Christian (ie Protestant) or was capable of being converted to Christianity; if the answer was no, they were usually deemed racially inferior, subhuman, and in turn rightly destroyed or enslaved.[16] The Catholic Spanish and Portuguese who conquered much of Latin America were as cruel and exploitative of the native peoples as the English; however, in contrast, the rationale for their oppression depended not so much on religiously justified racism as on a system of explicit economic profiteering (see Anghie 2005: 13–31; Williams 1990; Hannaford 1996: 150; Smedley 1999: 41). In this regard the works of the Spanish theologians Bartolomé de Las Casas (1474–1566) and Franciso de Vitoria (1480–1536) were important because they argued against the prevailing view that non-Christians were non-human. Rather, each scholar argued that native peoples were relatively sophisticated and could reason, hold rights and own property. According to Vitoria, Indians have 'polities which are

---

[16] Queen Elizabeth herself in the latter part of her reign proclaimed that because of England's war with Spain, the numbers of 'Negroes and blackamoors' (Muslims and dark skinned non-Muslims) had grown and they should be expelled from England. Her justification was that 'most of them are infidels having no understanding of Christ or his Gospel' (cited in Loomba and Burton 2007: 159).

orderly arranged and they have definite marriage and magistrates, overlords, laws and workshops, and a system of exchange, all of which call for the use of reason' (Anghie 2005: 20; Pagden 1993: 69–87). As a result of the writings of both Las Casas and Vitoria, laws were implemented that attempted to modify the brutal exploitation of Indians by the Spanish conquistadors and settlers in 1542.

While it is important to appreciate the different weighting given to racist discourse by the English in North America and the Spanish and Portuguese in Central and South America, it is also important to note the similarities that existed within all European colonizing nations at this time and their mutual desire to control people and resources in the burgeoning pursuit of capitalist profits. According to Loomba and Burton:

> England has a very specific history of racial thought, shaped by its rivalries with other European nations, by its own emergent nationalism and relation with its margins, and by its own sense of its past. An eclectic range of racial markers therefore appear in texts seeking to distinguish the English from the Irish they colonized, the Spanish they battled, the Africans they enslaved, the Turks with whom they traded, and the allegedly barbaric ancient Britons from whom they were descended. … At the same time, even when self-consciously different, the English discourses of race need to be seen as part of a larger transnational history. (Loomba and Burton 2007: 5)

The New World and Encountering Native Peoples

Throughout the 1500s as European explorers and traders ventured overseas, stories and gossip circulated about encounters with strange foreigners in Ireland, Africa, India and Asia. This fascination with others took on a new dimension with the opening up of the New World. Among all ranks and classes of English society there was a growing fascination with otherness and both its positive and negative qualities. Descriptions of the behaviors and ways of native peoples were made immediate and tangible to an increasingly broad spectrum of English society through the printing press. Some English people read, but many more listened to, travel diaries and accounts of contact. A few works did have some factual basis, such as Peter Martyr's collection of explorers' accounts including that of Columbus, which was published as *De Orbe Novo* in 1530 and translated into English by 1577. However, many of these accounts were based on very little—if any—evidence, and repeated long-standing narratives telling of fantastical creatures, cannibalism and untold riches that had been circulating across Europe in a variety of forms since the fifteenth century (see Lestringant 1997; Figure 7).

As plans for English colonization in North America began to take shape from the 1570s onwards, considerable efforts were made to counter the often lurid depictions of native peoples that were circulating in English society. Entrepreneurs were anxious to present a positive image of the New World. Promotional literature encouraged the wealthy to become stockholders and invest in overseas ventures. Ordinary people were urged to pack up their lives and belongings and

Figure 7. *America*, 1575–80, Johannes Stradanus (Jan Van Der Straet).

This allegorical engraving shows the Italian explorer and cartographer Amerigo Vespucci in the New World, confronting the figure of America in her hammock. In the background we see cannibals round a fire, and in the foreground a strange beast licks the ground. The continent of America is thought to have derived its name from the feminized Latin version of Vespucci's first name. Image courtesy of New York Public Library.

set out for the unknown. Metaphors of Virginia being a bountiful garden of Eden, as well as an ideal site from which to convert the infidel and spread Protestant Christianity, were repeated again and again in descriptions of the new settlement in North America (Adams 2001: 110–55). Selected images of the North Carolina coast and the Algonquian peoples by the English artist John White, brought back to London in the 1580s, provided an effective visual supplement to the positive propaganda machine (Sloan 2007).[17]

---

[17] Richard Hakluyt the elder, a prominent lawyer, wrote a list of 'Inducements' in 1585 stating the many advantages of setting up a colony in Virginia. First he summed up why people should voyage to Northern America in the first place, listing the establishment of Christianity as the primary motivation. He then went on to caution against open warfare with the natives, which would not, in his opinion, be conducive to profiteering. In his own words: 'The ends of this voyage are these: 1. To plant Christian religion. 2. To trafficke [trade]. 3. To conquer. Or, to do all three. To plant Christian religion without conquest, will bee hard. Trafficke easily followeth conquest: conquest is not easie. Trafficke without conquest seemeth possible, and not uneasie. What is to be done, is the question ...' (Hakluyt cited in Mancall 1995: 39–41).

A group of wealthy English merchants and gentry received James I's approval to set up the London based Virginia Company and in 1606 financed an expedition to the New World. One hundred and four men and boys set sail. A year later, Jamestown, named after King James, was established as the first permanent settlement in North America. While the promoters of Jamestown were keen to highlight its religious mission, all were well aware that the general intent was to make money by producing crops to send back to England. From the start, this goal of seeking profit underscored the arrogance with which the English treated the native peoples, whom they saw as uncivilized and inferior in their perceived inability (and unwillingness) to extract maximum resources from the land.

The colony did not fare well from the start, with many Englishmen dying from typhoid, malaria or dysentery. George Percy's 'A Discourse of the Plantation of the Southern Colonie in Virginia 1606–1607' (cited in Mancall 1995: doc 6) presents a clear record of disease, malnutrition and depression among the few surviving settlers, as well as early signs of tension and conflict with the local native chief, Powhatan. Powhatan governed 30 regional tribes in Virginia and he could marshal thousands of men, in contrast to the 100 or so who lived in Jamestown in the early years between 1607 and 1610. Powhatan maintained a strategic relationship with the English, carefully controlling their access to food and undermining their feeble attempts to grow crops. The Indians 'alternated hostilities and aid, as Powhatan tried to benefit from trade with the English and use them to consolidate his power in the region while discouraging them from settling in large numbers and taking land' (Adams 2001: 112).

Both sides conducted guerrilla raids, and the English used bullying tactics and threats to secure corn from the Indians during the desperately cold winter months (Horn 2006: Woolley 2008). However, the attacks by the English on Indian villages, which included massacres of native women and children and wanton destruction of Indian cornfields, stain the settlement's record and its attempts to present itself as having a benevolent relationship with the natives (Morgan 1975: 71–91). Tensions abated for a short period after Powhatan's daughter, Pocahontas, was captured by English traders and eventually married the colonist John Rolfe. According to contemporary accounts, the marriage helped to create peaceful conditions between colonists and natives (Hamor 1615: 809). However, after Chief Powhatan's death in 1618, his younger brother Opechancanough took control and decided upon a much more aggressive trajectory, which resulted in hundreds of settlers (347 men, women and children) being killed in a surprise attack in 1622.

Justifying Indian Annihilation

With the dramatic massacre in 1622 of almost a third of the existing Jamestown colony, any remaining pretense of peaceful co-existence or belief in the eventual assimilation of natives into English culture and 'civilization' was irreparably shattered. The gloves came off, so to speak. And so began a steady erosion of the English narrative of co-existence between Europeans and non-Europeans with the conversion of Indians to Christianity. Another narrative gained dominance over the first, and this second story maintained that Indians were incapable of conversion and civility and so were endowed with brutish and beastly qualities. In short, English settlers promoted the message that Indians were nothing more than marauders and murderers. In a history of the settlement at Plymouth Plantation, William Bradford summed up this new sensibility when he said that surrounding the settlers was an uncivilized 'hideous and desolate wilderness, full of wild beasts and wild men' (cited in Tomlins 2001: 19).

Approximately 50 years later, the narrative of Indians as subhuman beasts was reaffirmed in the political philosophy of John Locke. In his *Second Treatis*, Locke argued that American land was for the 'use of the Industrious and Rational' and anyone who interfered with Europeans' appropriation of that land might 'be destroyed as a *Lyon* or a *Tyger*, one of those wild Savage Beasts, with whom men can have no Society nor Security' (cited in Tomlins 2001: 46). Such language justified the necessary elimination of native peoples on the basis of their bestiality and (by definition) racial inferiority. According to Stephen Adams, 'The English tried to hold onto their most self-flattering and benevolent scripts as long as possible and then took to seeing themselves as the new Israelites commissioned by God to rid the Promised Land of intractable heathens' (Adams 2001: 126).

By reducing Indians to inhuman beasts, any notion that they inhabited and owned the land prior to contact could be dismissed. As beasts, they were non-legal entities, incapable of land possession and production, and so deserved to forfeit all rights to ownership. Hence the wild lands could be thought of as 'terra nullius'[18] or empty in the sense that they did not belong to anyone and were conceptually waiting to be ordered through the imposition of legal jurisdiction and the allocation of possessory rights to those capable (and morally worthy) of holding them (Tomlins 2001: 19–22). In 1622, the same year as the massacre of over 300 English settlers, John Donne, in a sermon preached before members of the Virginia Company, claimed that 'a land never inhabited by, or utterly derelict and immemorially abandoned by the former inhabitants, becomes theirs that will possess it' (cited in Tomlins 2001: 21). And once possessed, land could be made to be productive—tilled, planted and reaped.

---

[18]   The legal argument that the land was 'terra nullius' or empty land was used in later colonial ventures as well, such as Captain Cook's taking possession of Australia in 1787. In Cook's reports back to England, he described the land as being one of a 'pure state of nature', populated by aboriginal peoples who however 'did not cultivate the land or erect permanent habitations upon it' (Cook cited in Day 1997: 26). More often than not, the very existence of native peoples was denied or overlooked by the colonialists, allowing the myth of an empty land to endure over time and justify possession of the continent by Europeans (Reynolds 1989; Banner 2005a). It was not until 1992 that the Australian High Court finally denied that the legal doctrine of terra nullius could be used to justify aboriginal dispossession or limit claims for compensation by holders of rights to indigenous land.

Figure 8. Harvesting Tobacco at Jamestown, c 1650, painting by Sidney E King. From John L Cotter and J Paul Hudson, *Project Gutenberg ebook of New Discoveries at Jamestown* (2005).

In the ensuing years, the growing of tobacco provided the means to make Jamestown a viable commercial colony by the mid-1620s (Figure 8). But it was not just the financial rewards that tobacco provided. Through its cultivation, tobacco imposed an aesthetic order on the landscape and substantiated the need for towns, markets, laws, courthouses, judges, juries, tax collection and land registration, as well as a bureaucratic system of regulatory agencies.[19] As Peter Hoffer notes:

> English newcomers thus did not claim land by reading aloud a legal proclamation to the Indians, like the Spanish, or by organizing a procession and giving presents, like the French, or by drawing a map and establishing a trading post, like the Dutch, or even by taking readings of the position of the stars, like the Portuguese. The English constructed houses, laid out gardens, and put up fences—all kinds of fences. Indeed the stouter the fence (or stone wall), the happier the English were. Bounding the land, whether by survey, grant, or actual occupation, fulfilled the letter and spirit of England's land law in her colonies as in the home counties. (Hoffer 1998: 25)

During the early years of English colonialism in North America, an unwavering faith in the power of law to bring order to a chaotic and dangerous world sustained a sense of community. Law provided a mechanism for determining insider from outsider, man from beast. 'The colonists believed in the possibilities of a lawful world, and their demands for legal redress grew from and sustained this faith' (Hoffer 1998: xii). Such faith in the law dovetailed, particularly in the New England colonies, with a strict Calvinist faith or Puritanism that firmly

---

[19] For a wonderful discussion of the 'geography of sovereignty' see Tomlins 2001: 34.

upheld law and God's rule as the guiding principles for survival (Hoffer 1998: 1–26). Harold Berman has called this combination of faith and law the 'spiritualization of the secular' (Berman 2003). Together God and government provided a platform on which developed a complex layering of capitalist ideology, material commercial needs, land rights claims, racist categories of inclusion and exclusion, and the imposition and gradual adaptation of English law to a new world geography. The compilation of laws for Plymouth Plantation in 1636 has been described as the first comprehensive body of law enacted in North America. English law and custom provided the basis for some of its clauses, but other clauses were unknown in England, such as the 'provision for civil marriage, equality of descent, liberal provisions for women and widows, and the institution of a recording system'. Among other things, these clauses reflected the changing role and status of women and were 'partly an attempt to fill the needs of a frontier society and partly the Puritan predilection to enact laws based upon scriptural authority' (Cushing 1977: xiv).

The Beginnings of the Trans-Atlantic Slave Trade

In 1619, merchants in Jamestown bought approximately 20 Africans who had arrived on the shores of the Chesapeake, brought to the New World by a Dutch trader. This was the first recorded shipment of Africans to North America. The men were brought to the new plantation colony as a cheap source of labor and were initially classified as indentured servants. There was a growing need for such servants as tobacco plantations began to turn a profit and the demand for cheap labor steadily increased. So-called white indentured servants, or 'white slaves', mostly street children, beggars, gypsies, convicts and dissidents sent to the New World from England, Ireland and Scotland, simply could not provide sufficient labor pools (Jordan and Walsh 2008), hence the turn to Africa. And so the number of Africans brought to the New World slowly increased (Davis 2006). The transition from the use of white indentured servants to black slaves in the labor forces of the American colonies did not happen overnight, and did not happen at the same pace in all the colonies. But in the settlements that depended upon relatively large-scale agricultural farming, the need for unskilled labor increasingly made the relative costs of black slave labor more attractive and economically more profitable than the labor of indentured white servants, who in theory could one day win their freedom (Galenson 1981).

Conveniently, the manipulation of English legal practice and procedure to justify the exploitation—and in many instances genocide—of native peoples set the precedent for legal innovations to legitimize the enslavement of 'heathen' Africans (Wawrzyczek 2001). Law provided the symbolic authority and practical mechanics by which Christians and non-Christians were differentiated, in turn gradually denying Africans the right to sue their masters and rendering those originally classified as indentured servants unable to own property that was technically within their means. In the 50 years following the first appearance of Africans on North American shores, slavery as a legal institution was formally recognized. Massachusetts was the first to legalize slavery in 1642, closely followed by Connecticut in 1650, Virginia in 1661, Maryland in 1663, and New York and New Jersey in 1664. By the later years of the seventeenth century, the transatlantic slave trade had picked up momentum, peaking over 100 years later toward the end of the eighteenth century. The institution of slavery itself would not be made illegal across the United States until 1865, following the American Civil War and the ratification of the Thirteenth Amendment.

RIGHTS: DEFINING THE RIGHTS OF KING, PARLIAMENT AND SUBJECT

As the early English colonists in the New World grappled with erecting their own legal system, back in London James I's son, Charles I, took over the throne in 1625 and proceeded to run the country in a manner so divisive that civil wars ensued and his public execution in 1649 was the ultimate outcome. Given the spiritual underpinnings and relative stability of the English crown under James, it seems extraordinary that less than 50 years after his succession, his son would be tried for treason and executed by order of parliament. For the first time in modern European history the sacred authority of the sovereign was deemed an inadequate justification for the king to ignore the demands and rights of his people. Certainly not all of English society believed that it was necessary or appropriate to take the king's life. However, there was a general consensus that divine law was not above secular law and the king was obliged to govern according to the laws of the land set by government. Divine majesty, in short, did not grant the king legal immunity, and secular law prevailed as the ultimate authority and basis of justice.

Events Leading to the Trial of Charles I

James I, Charles I's father, had promoted the ideology of the divine right of kings. However, whereas James had used this ideology in an understated way, Charles used it in a heavy-handed fashion and quickly became oppressive. According to many accounts, Charles I was a rather unpleasant man—sickly as a child, he grew up obstinate, insecure and inflexible. 'Charles was an excellent connoisseur of the visual arts, but as a reigning monarch he was woefully inadequate' (Reeve 1989: 3, 172–225). These personal characteristics helped to promote his sense of supreme Godly entitlement, which he explicitly referred to in public and which ultimately curtailed his ability to navigate the religious and political factions of government and court life. Charles' inflexible personality and claims to Godly entitlement caused great alarmed among members of the House of Commons, who increasingly feared that Charles might dissolve parliament in a fit of temper and impose absolute monarchy, under which all power would be vested in the king alone.

Conflict between the House of Commons and Charles I reached boiling point in 1627, only two years after his succession to the throne. Charles, with England at war with France and Spain, had raised taxes to pay for the war effort without the approval of parliament. He had also overstepped his authority by forcing wealthy nobles to grant him loans, failing to enforce habeas corpus and due process under martial law, and generally interfering with the property rights of the wealthy in an attempt to appropriate funds for the crown. Members of the Commons were outraged at this flagrant disregard for their basic rights as Englishmen. In 1628 they presented the *Petition of Right* to the king, setting out his abuse of power and requesting redress on a number of issues. Charles' response was to dissolve parliament and rule without the Commons' consent or advice for the following 11 years, which came to be known as the Eleven Years' Tyranny.

During this turbulent period, for first time the terminology of political 'rights'—as opposed to previous uses of 'liberties' and 'privileges'—entered the pages of constitutional history (Baker 2004). However:

> these ancient rights of which parliamentarians spoke were not universal 'human' rights or rights derived from some abstract regime superior to municipal law. They were the rights and liberties of Englishmen, inherited by birth like other forms of franchise or property, guaranteed over the centuries by charters of liberties and statutes of due process, and believed to be superior to such rights as might belong to the peoples of benighted nations. There was little practical reason to reflect upon universal rights of man in an island which believed its own rights superior to those of mankind in general. (Baker 2004: para 3)

Charles I openly courted England's long-despised Catholic faction, aggravating the Commons' suspicion and fears of absolutism. In 1625 he married Henrietta Maria, sister of Louis XIII of France, despite great opposition from members of parliament, who were fearful that this new Catholic queen would encourage leniency toward English Catholics (Figure 9). Charles promised that he would not ease restrictions on Catholics, but such promises contradicted the secret marriage treaty he had made with France. He then set about 'reforming' the Church of England and Church of Scotland over the following decade. This essentially amounted to imposing a new Book of Common Prayer and introducing high Anglican ceremonies into church rituals, which many viewed as resembling Catholic practices.

The Scottish parliament revolted against the church reforms and in 1639 declared Charles I's claim to absolute power null and void (see Macinnes 2009; Braddick 2008: 3–39; Adamson 2009). Charles proceeded to wage war on Scotland, forcing him to recall parliament in order to raise more funds. Parliament again refused to grant him the right to raise taxes for war, whereupon Charles quickly dissolved the House of Commons in what became known as the Short Parliament. At war with Scotland and desperate for money, Charles was soon forced to call parliament again in November 1640, in what is now called the

Figure 9.   Charles 1 and Henrietta Maria with her two eldest children, 1633.
By Anthony van Dyck.

Anthony van Dyck was a Flemish artist who was invited to England by Charles 1 in 1632 to become the court painter. By this stage he was well known throughout Europe for his vivid courtly style, luxuriously painted dresses and clothing, and warm intimate portraits of families with children and dogs. Van Dyck is said to have painted approximately forty portraits of the king, and many of the king's wife and children. In this painting, the king and queen are depicted with their sons Charles, Prince of Wales (Charles II) next to his father and James, Duke of York (James II) who sits on his mother's lap. Van Dyck died in 1641 but his influence on British portraiture lasted for over three hundred years.

Long Parliament (Holmes 2006: 1–34). The Commons yet again refused to grant further funds for war against Scotland, whereupon Charles negotiated with Catholics in Ireland to raise an army to invade Scotland.

A dim view of Charles' overt flirtation with Catholicism was taken among his dominant Presbyterian and Calvinist subjects in both England and Scotland. However, when the king negotiated with the Irish Catholics to invade Scotland in 1640 on his behalf, in return granting them political concessions, many Englishmen saw his actions as traitorous and outside the acceptable boundaries of warfare (Braddick 2008: 156–81). This sense of outrage and betrayal escalated through late 1640 and into 1641 and mobilized the rise of mass political factions among the working and middle classes, particularly in London (Lindley 1997: 4–35). It led to the imprisonment and execution of Thomas Wentworth, 1st Earl of Strafford, who had become, alongside Archbishop William Laud, Charles' principal advisor. Strafford was seen by many as having violated constitutional principles and the rights of all Englishmen in his zealous work for the king. He came to symbolize the king's demand for absolute rule and his affection for Catholics. As large mobs assembled in the streets of London calling for Strafford's imprisonment, the House of Commons deemed it necessary to remove him from office and passed a bill of attainder on 13 April 1641 which declared Strafford guilty. On 8 May, under considerable pressure from thousands of street demonstrators and mounting fear of a popish plot, the Lords passed the attainder as well. The final assent of Charles sealed Strafford's fate and without proper trial he was executed on 12 May before jubilant crowds numbering 100,000 (Lindley 1997: 19–26; Braddick 2008: 134–39; Adamson 2009).

Political and social tensions did not abate with Strafford's death, but through the second half of 1641 'there was a drift of opinion towards the King' (Braddick 2008: 161). However, this leaning toward compromise was dramatically undermined when news broke of a massacre of English and Scottish subjects in Ireland. Gossip circulated that Charles had been complicit in the Irish rebellion, and rumors abounded of the atrocities perpetrated by the Catholic Irish on English colonial settlers, including burning women and children alive and perpetrating sadistic tortures (Braddick 2008: 167–68). As noted by Robertson:

> The native Irish had combined with 'Old English' Catholics to wreak revenge upon the newly settled Protestants from England and Scotland with a genocidal ferocity. The impact of atrocity pictures—woodcuts of 'wild Irish' skewering pregnant women on their pikes and barbequing babies—was heightened by rumours that the King was seeking support from Strafford's Catholic army, which was implicated in the massacres. … The impact of the news in London was dramatic: it swung many moderates … against the King. (Robertson 2005: 61)

'[L]ittle more than two months after news of the Irish rising reached London any pretense of normal parliamentary government had collapsed' (Braddick 2008: 168). At this point the Commons granted itself certain powers, including the right to call itself even if the king refused. As parliament railed against the king's royal prerogative in the 'Grand Remonstrance', a document of grievances that was presented to the king on 1 December 1641, discontent continued to brew and parliamentarians found themselves divided according to whether they supported or opposed the king. Fears of popish conspiracies were fueled by an outpouring of propaganda pamphlets and political publicity. Various political factions formed coalitions—those who feared a popish plot and those who feared a rise in Puritan populism—and plans were made to impeach Charles' Catholic queen. Upon hearing this news, Charles stormed parliament on 4 January 1642, hoping to round up and imprison his most staunch opponents, but they had been warned and had already fled (Braddick 2008: 172–80).

Charles now faced angry resistance on many fronts from an increasingly powerful puritan faction and he raced away from London to Nottingham. What then ensued was a bitter attempt to mobilize support amongst the provinces and districts beyond the immediate influence of London. Broadsheets and pamphlets circulated, both denouncing and praising the king. In parliament executive orders were written, committees formed, and petitions submitted (Braddick 2008: 184). Charles' refusal to cooperate with or accommodate the wishes of his parliamentarians and subjects ultimately forced him to declare civil war on 22 August 1642. Years of death and destruction ensued and over 100,000 lives were lost. Charles finally surrendered to Scottish Presbyterian forces in 1646 and returned to London in 1647 (C Holmes 2006: 71–92). Charles managed to instigate a second civil war, which broke out during 1648. However, his royalist forces were ill prepared; they scattered and were quickly overcome by the New Model Army, led by Sir Thomas Fairfax with Oliver Cromwell second-in-command (Gentles 2009). Charles was imprisoned and put on trial in January 1649.

Reverberations from the Colonies

The Irish Rebellion of 1641 confirmed for many Englishmen the depravity of the Irish. English Protestant settlers in Ireland had long disparaged the people they had conquered (Garner 2003). Similar to the racial stereotypes of native peoples that were emerging in the Americas, the Irish were considered by many Englishmen to be 'wild' and inhuman. Contributing to this opinion was the fact that many Irish were pastoralists and nomadic and did not hold the same views as the English about property and contract, and had a very different sense of legal rights (Smedley 1999: 49, 53–59). The English saw the Irish 'wasting' good agricultural land and took this to be indicative of their sub-normal intelligence and barbaric ways. Ultimately, the Irish were considered uncivilized and incapable of being saved, in part because of their Catholic faith and in part because of their barbarism. On the basis of being considered irredeemable, the Irish were treated with great hostility by the English settlers, who ran them off their lands, killed their animals, and enslaved those that did not escape to work the largely unsuccessful agricultural plantations.

As England's first colony, Ireland provided a model of colonial conquest that would be adopted and adapted for the North American plantations. Moreover, the English imagery and ideology of Irish inferiority was picked up and circulated among the colonists in Virginia and New England. Irish 'savages' helped to make the New World 'savages' more familiar. In turn, pictorial representations of indigenous peoples (discussed above) were transported back to England and similarities were drawn between what were perceived to be the animal-like qualities of Native Americans, Africans, Jews and Irish peasants (Loomba and Burton 2007). For instance, the engraver Theodorus de Bry published an illustration of a Pict woman (a member of an ancient Celtic tribe) in a book by Thomas Hariot on the native peoples of North America entitled *A Brief and True Report of the New Found Land of Virginia* (1590) (Figure 10). The book was extremely popular, and included among the illustrations of native peoples five images of Picts to show that the ancient people of Britain were just as 'savage' as those of the New World (Hariot 1972; van Groesen 2008: 190, 247). This complex layering of racial imagery derived from both the New and Old Worlds helped to unite and consolidate the oppositional frames used to distinguish the civilized from the barbaric, the Christian from the heathen, the lawful from the lawless and—in the case of increasing political and social opposition mobilizing against Charles I—authentic Englishmen from untrustworthy, Catholic-loving imposters.

Images of natives were not the only thing that found their way back to England to fuel a range of new ideas about English society. The manipulation of the common law by trading company charters to suit the needs of the new North American plantation colonies did not go unnoticed by government officials, parliamentarians and merchants back in London. In particular, the new legal system established in Plymouth underscored the adaptability of English common law in building a new form of representative government devoid of hereditary monarchs. The Pilgrims in North America also stirred up debate about the rights of individuals and their relationship to king and government. They argued that while they might disagree with the dictates of the king and his reform of the Church of England, they were still to be considered loyal English subjects. This kind of thinking helped to foster radical ideas back in London, and through the 1630s and 40s it became more acceptable to voice disapproval of and yet maintain one's loyalty to the English nation. Through the use of cheap pamphlets and theatrical performances that deliberately appealed to the masses, the political landscape was opened up to a range of new political philosophies and debates (Lake 2002; Braddick 2008: 439). This fermentation of ideas generated widespread public sympathy for those who disagreed with the king and questioned his claim to divine authority and tendency toward absolute monarchy (see Spurr 1998, 2006).

Figure 10.   *The True Picture of a Woman Picte*, 1588, engraving by Theodor de Bry. Courtesy of North Carolina Collection/ University of North Carolina Libraries.

The Picts were an ancient Celtic tribe, and the woman in this image is shown in a 'savage' state with tattoos adorning her skin and holding spears. The image was first published in a book on the paintings of colonist John White by Thomas Hariot, *A Brief and True Report of the New Found Land of Virginia*. In this book Native Americans and Picts were illustrated together, underscoring English attitudes that Native and Irish peoples were similarly 'primitive'. The English stereotype of the Irish being barbaric and intellectually inferior was sustained for centuries, and became a popular theme in nineteenth century England and the United States.

On mainland Europe during this period, Germany, Spain, Austria, Sweden, the Netherlands and France were reeling from bitter clashes between Catholics and Protestants that had raged throughout the Thirty Years' War (1618–48). The Peace of Westphalia was finally concluded in 1648, bringing the war to an end by forcing the Holy Roman Empire to recognize the sovereignty of the German Princes over their own domestic dominions. While no parties were entirely happy with the Peace, and the pope condemned it because it considerably weakened the hold of the Catholic Church over northern Europe, the Peace did highlight the widespread need for political and legal reform. Back in England, as the country dealt with its own internal civil wars throughout the 1640s, the impact of the Peace negotiations was relatively muted. That being said, the negotiations did highlight the limited authority of a divine authority (ie the pope) over secular state affairs. Ideas filtering into London from mainland Europe and from England's colonial periphery together fed into the country's volatile and in many ways desperate intellectual climate, which was becoming increasingly receptive to new ideas and strategies. Across England, Scotland and Ireland the stage was being set for a final clash between Charles I and his subjects, culminating in the king's trial and beheading.

The Trial of Charles I

Under an Act of Parliament, the House of Commons established a special court to adjudicate the trial of Charles 1 (see Robertson 2005; C Holmes 2006; Braddick 2008: 551–81). The first session of the trial began on 20 January 1649 in Westminster Hall, the 'center of English justice'. Heavy on legal and regal symbolism, the Hall was richly decorated in scarlet cloth and defended by 200 guards stationed around the building, carrying 'rich javelins with velvet and fringe' (see Kelsey 2001: 81). Ironically, 43 years earlier, the Hall had been the site of the Gunpowder Plot prosecution, as a result of which eight Catholic men were condemned to death for their treasonable attempt to blow up king and parliament. At that point, only extreme Catholics would have argued for the necessity of taking the king's life. Now, over four decades later, a good percentage of the English population was calling Charles a traitor for waging war against his own people, an action punishable by death.

The Puritan-dominated parliament charged the king with exercising tyranny against his subjects. The preamble to the charge indicates that England was conceived as a corporate state to which Charles had been trusted to rule with limited powers granted to him. In a sense, the jurists envisaged the king's role as being similar to that of a chief magistrate (Orr 2001: 121, 127). If a chief magistrate fails to abide by the limited powers bestowed upon him, he can be removed by the state; so too the king for waging war upon his people. The preamble reads:

> That the said Charles Stuart, being admitted King of England, and therein trusted with a limited power to govern by and according to the laws of the land, and not otherwise; and by his trust, oath, and office, being obliged to use the power committed to him for the good and benefit of the people, and for the preservation of their rights and liberties; yet, nevertheless, out of a wicked design to erect and uphold in himself an unlimited and tyrannical power to rule according to his will, and to overthrow the rights and liberties of the people ... (cited in Orr 2001: 127)

Before 59 judges (though accounts differ on this number) and thousands of subjects, the king was described as a 'tyrant, traitor, murderer' (Wedgewood

1967: 147). The king was then asked how he would plead to the charge. Charles demanded to know by what lawful authority he had been brought before the court. His refusal to answer on the basis of the court having no lawful jurisdiction was repeated again and again, and the same refrain used in the second and third sessions the following two days. Given these refusals, the court was left with no alternative but to convict Charles under the *pro confessor* rule, which stated that a refusal to plead amounted to a tacit confession.

From the court's point of view this was unfortunate, since if there was no contest there was no need to publicly present evidence against the king. A compromise was reached whereby evidence was presented to the judges in private session to help them decide on an appropriate course of action (Robertson 2005: 151–76). The evidence showed that Charles was guilty of murder, destruction of property, approving the torture of prisoners, and waging war against parliament. 'Even more damaging were his secret letters, full of double dealings and attempts to procure military assistance from Catholic powers and from Ireland and Scotland' (Robertson 2005: 175).

At the fourth session Charles was nervous and grim; he pleaded that a special session of parliament be held at which he would address the Lords and Commons as their king. His request—not surprisingly—was denied. After an adjournment by the judges and further confusion and hesitation, Bradshawe, the delivering judge, spoke for a good half hour about the failure of the king to abide by parliament and the elected representatives of the people (Robertson 2005: 185). According to Bradshawe, the king had set himself above the highest court of justice in England, the House of Commons in parliament. By so doing, he had set himself above 'that which was itself "superior to the law" as "parent and the author of the Law ... the People of England"' (cited in Orr 2001: 130).

Judge Bradshawe went on to discuss the longstanding contractual relationship that existed between the monarch and his or her subjects, which he argued Charles had violated:

> For there is a contract and bargain made between the king and his people, and the oath is taken for the performance, and certainly, Sir, the bond is reciprocal, for as you are their liege Lord, so they are your liege subjects ... the one tie, the one bond, is the bond of protection that is due from the sovereign, the other is the bond of subjection that is due from the subject. Sir, if this bond be once broken, farewell sovereignty! (cited in Robertson 2005: 185)

'Farewell sovereignty'—such a concept was entirely new in the history of English law. This is not to say that the judges departed from prevailing thinking about king, government and society and invented a new rationale to fit their inclination to dispatch the king. The contractual relationship between king and subject was a longstanding legal concept harking back to feudal times. In short, the judges 'depended on a pre-existing public law vocabulary' to make their case (Orr 2001: 133). However, in talking about the 'state' and conceiving it as an abstract corporation above the power of the king, as mentioned above, they described his position as that of a chief magistrate who holds an office bestowed upon him. The net result was that the judges anxiously, and rather ironically, called to mind a 'monarchical past they were in the process of rejecting' (Orr 2001: 133).

Describing the king as an officer of the state provided the basis on which the judges could argue that Charles had overstepped his powers by waging war on the English people. According to historian Geoffrey Robertson, in his account of John Cooke, the barrister who prepared the brief against Charles, the justification for Charles' death was based on the invention of an entirely new crime—tyranny. According to Roberston, Cooke devised a means to circumvent the claim of sovereign immunity by

> formulating the crime of tyranny to punish a leader who destroys law and liberty, or who bears command responsibility for the killing of his own people, or who orders the plunder of innocent civilians and the torture of prisoners of war ... the King's trial may now be seen as the earliest precedent for trials of modern heads of state—political and military leaders like Pinochet and Milosevic, who attempt (just like Charles I) to plead sovereign immunity when arraigned for killing their own people ... The cause has now taken shape in the International Criminal Court, and it is (so to speak) a crowning irony that the Bush administration, for all its proclaimed Puritan religiousity, is seeking so obsessively to destroy the one institution that can deliver on Cooke's proposition that rulers who oppress their people must be brought to justice. (Robertson 2005: 3, 6, 7)

Charles I, as an officer of the state who had overstepped his duties and obligations by waging tyrannical war including torture on his people, was publicly executed on 30 January 1649. According to accounts of Charles' execution, it was a day of sobriety and jubilation. 'The bitter January frost was still unbroken and the King, anxious that he might feel the cold, put on two shirts so that he would not shiver when he came to prepare for the block and so give the impression of fear' (Wedgewood 1967: 204). So began Charles I's procession toward a scaffold specially erected adjacent to the Banqueting House in White-hall, London. The platform was decked in black cloth, and crowded with the executioner and other officials. Charles gave a short speech, during which he talked about his duties as a Christian, his understanding of the injustice of events that had led him to the platform, and his declaration that he died a member of the Church of England.

> The King stood for a moment raising his hands and eyes to Heaven and praying in silence, then slipped off his cloak and lay down with his neck on the block. ... A fearful silence had now fallen on the little knot of people on the scaffold, on the surrounding troops, and on the crowd. Within a few seconds the King stretched out his hands and the executioner on the instant at one blow severed his head from his body. (Wedgewood 1967: 219)

CONCLUSION

The execution of Charles I in 1649 did not resolve the contested issue of religion in England's increasingly secular society (Sommerville 1992; Spurr 1998, 2006). Following Charles' execution there was a short lived republican commonwealth governed by Oliver Cromwell (1649–58)—a period known as the Interregnum. Cromwell, a devout Puritan, ruled as a dictator and amongst other things ruthlessly pursued the genocide of Irish Catholics (Hill 1970; see also Little 2009). In 1660 Charles I's son, Charles II, was reinstated and made king in the period known as the Restoration (Harris 2006). Despite Charles II's personal desire for religious tolerance, he was forced by parliament to enact harsh anti-Puritan laws in an attempt to bolster the Anglican faction and the re-establishment of the Church of England. Charles II's reign was full of conflict with parliament, as well as religious plots and intrigue. Upon his deathbed he reportedly converted to Catholicism.

Bitter conflict over religion continued in the subsequent reign of James II (1685–88), a devout Catholic. Upon becoming king, James II quickly purged the church and army of leading Protestants, replacing them with men of the Catholic faith. Conspiracies against him evolved within various religious and political factions and it was planned that William Henry of Orange and his wife Mary, the Protestant daughter of James II, should oust the king and assume the throne. In what is often referred to as the 'Glorious Revolution' of 1688 because it supposedly occurred without bloodshed or violence, Dutch armies led by William arrived on the shores of England, quickly overthrew James and installed William and Mary. The following year, the Bill of Rights was passed by parliament, limiting forever the absolute power of the monarch and guaranteeing, amongst other things, parliamentary democracy and the right of subjects to petition the king (Harris 2008). To this day the Bill of Rights remains one of the cornerstones of modern English common law. In terms of religion, following the Glorious Revolution Catholics were persecuted, harassed, and denied the right to vote or become members of parliament for over a century.

Charles I's execution did not stop violent religious conflict, or prevent future kings from claiming immunity from prosecution by evoking their divine authority in the face of conflict with parliament or their subjects. Nor did it prevent Charles II (the son of Charles I), when restored to the throne in 1660, from rounding up the 59 petitioners who had signed his father's death warrant and exacting bloody revenge. The 1660 regicide trial, as it was known, was a shameful and 'discreditable affair'. According to Robertson, 'The defendants had been locked up for months in plague-infested prisons, and were brought to the Old Bailey in shackles and leg-irons to be viciously mocked and abused by partisan judges of Charles II, who instructed vetted jurors to convict without bothering to leave the jury-box' (Robertson 2005: 3).

What Charles I's execution did achieve was to set a legal precedent: parliament exercised a supreme form of independence free from royal prerogative. This assertion of parliamentary sovereignty and call for observance of civil liberties on behalf of the people—at least on behalf of the ruling elite in England—in turn set the stage for the American and French Revolutions over 100 years later. It represented a new perspective on the relationship between a king and his subjects, and in a sense heralded the modern era. 'It is from the claim that all subjects have the right to overthrow a tyrannical government and have a say in its replacement that modern democratic theory takes its origins' (Wootton 1986: 40). In a profound sense Charles' execution was a necessary precursor to the eventual declaration of the rights of citizens and constitutional democratic principles of government that are the hallmarks of modern Anglo-American law. Echoes of the prosecution's arguments against Charles made in defense of citizens' rights and civil liberties can be found in political theories of the later seventeenth and eighteenth centuries. More recently, echoes of these legal arguments can be heard in the Nuremberg trials in the late 1940s (see chapter seven), the Universal Declaration of Human Rights of 1948, and the debates in the past two decades about the need for humanitarian intervention in cases of tyrannical genocide which provided the impetus for the establishment of the International Criminal Court in 2002.

In thinking about the intersections and connections between religion, race and rights in the lead up to and execution of Charles I, it is easy to focus on religion as being at the forefront of English society's concerns in the seventeenth century. From the Gunpowder Plot and civil wars through to the king's execution, bitter conflict and violence raged between English Catholics, Protestants and Puritans (to name the obvious religious camps). However, historians have suggested that disagreement over religious ideology and ritual did not have much of an impact on the majority of ordinary English people. Rather, religious conflict was primarily a preoccupation among the few in power, or those jostling to claim power. This does not mean that people did not think of themselves as religious, rather that 'the vast majority of the population were churchgoers and their religion was of a rather tepid kind, well integrated with their own needs and interests, but undemanding' (Spurr 2006: 298). If this thesis is correct and the 'Protestantizing of England owed ... comparatively little to religious fervor' (Carswell 1934: 4), then it is necessary to look beyond religious conflict to focus on other social, political and economic forces that characterized the period. Despite the dominance of religion in England's political discourse, a lot more was going on that often could only be thought about or spoken of in religious terms (Wootton 1986: 27). As John Spurr reminds us, in post-reformation seventeenth century, it was still impossible to separate religion from politics (Spurr 2006: 4) In short, the language of religion provided the framework and foil for debate and public conversation about a range of other matters.

Such matters included growing public interest in racial differentiation between Europeans and non-Europeans encountered in the New World—an interest that cannot be uncoupled from an emerging English nationalism and identity. Specifically, the early plantations set up in Virginia by English colonists in the early seventeenth century, and the tensions between Englishmen and the native peoples they encountered, gave impetus to an ideology of English superiority and sustained the idea of an Anglo-Saxon race. In response to escalating violence between European and non-Europeans, the common law was used adaptively to endorse racist practices that helped to justify and consolidate English landhold-ings against native claims. Significantly, these racist practices also established the legal conditions conducive to promoting the transatlantic slave trade that took off during this period.

Underlying the sensibility of English nationalism was a collective cultural and economic investment in a common law system that protected the property rights of certain male individuals, particularly the growing merchant and gentry classes determined to play a role in government both at home and overseas. Together the language of race and the language of rights were factors in the growth of law's secularization. As Harold Berman notes, this process of secularization involved not only the transfer of ecclesiastical authority to lay courts and institutions, but also a process of 'spiritualization of secular responsibilities and activities' (Ber-man 2003: 369–70). This overlay of faith and law provided an extremely conveni-ent mechanism for building and justifying imperial goals. Berman writes, 'At the heart of the transformation of English law in the seventeenth century was the Anglo-Calvinist belief that God had made a covenant with the English people, that England was an elect nation, chosen, as the children of Israel had once been chosen, to be "a light to all the nations"' (Berman 2003: 376). This belief sustained the early puritan colonists who first migrated to the New World to 'build a city upon a hill' (Witte 2006: 143–68, 2007: 277–320), as well as the idea of manifest destiny and subsequent US imperial ventures in the nineteenth, twentieth and twenty-first centuries (Stephanson 1995).

As will be discussed in the next chapter, colonialism, capitalism and secularism together nurtured new political theories espoused by thinkers such as Hobbes, Voltaire and Rousseau. The writings of these Enlightenment theorists were in turn essential to political radicals such as Thomas Paine, whose thinking about human rights played a central role in the development of modern law in the eighteenth century, shaped as it was by the cumulative impact of the American War of Independence (1776) and the French Revolution (1789).

Recommended Reading

Adamson, John (2009) *The Noble Revolt: The Overthrow of Charles 1*. London: Weidenfeld & Nicolson.

Benton, Lauren (2002) *Law and Colonial Cultures: Legal Regimes in World History.* Cambridge: Cambridge University Press.

Berman, Harold J (2003) *Law and Revolution, II: The Impact of the Protestant Reformations on the Western Legal Tradition*. Cambridge, MA: The Belknap Press of Harvard Univer-sity Press.

Braddick, Michael (2008) *God's Fury, England's Fire: A New History of the English Civil Wars*. London: Allen Lane.

Harris, Tim (2006) *Restoration: Charles II and His Kingdoms, 1660–1685*. New York: Penguin Global.

Harris, Tim (2008) *Revolution: The Great Crisis of the British Monarchy, 1685–1720*. New York: Penguin Global.

Holmes, Clive (2006) *Why Was Charles I Executed?* London: Hambledon Continuum.

Lake, Peter with Michael Questier (2002) *The Anti-Christ's Lewd Hat: Protestants, Papists and Players in Post-Reformation England*. New Haven, CT: Yale University Press.

MacMillan, Ken (2006) *Sovereignty and Possession in the English New World: The Legal Foundations of Empire 1576–1640*. Cambridge: Cambridge University Press.

Pagden, Anthony (1993) *European Encounters with the New World*. New Haven, CT: Yale University Press.

Robertson, Geoffrey (2005) *The Tyrannicide Brief: The Story of the Man who sent Charles I to the Scaffold*. London: Chatto & Windus.

Sommerville, C John (1992) *The Secularization of Early Modern England*. New York: Oxford University Press.

Spurr, John (2006) *The Post-Reformation 1603–1714*. Harlow: Pearson Education.

3

Revolution and Thomas Paine's Rights of Man *(1791)*

THIS CHAPTER TAKES as its legal landmark the publication of Thomas Paine's essay *Rights of Man*. Written in 1791, in the midst of the French Revolution, *Rights of Man* drew on Paine's earlier publications and in particular an essay entitled *Common Sense*, which he wrote over 20 years earlier on the eve of the American War of Independence in 1776. Both essays were considered radical at the time, and both were essential in bringing about dramatic legal and political change. In short, these works changed the course of popular thinking in North America and Britain by openly calling for the rejection of monarchy and divine authority and advocating the right of ordinary people to be actively involved in government. *Rights of Man* called for representative democracy based on the recognition of an individual's 'natural' or inalienable rights to life, justice and well-being. In a profound sense, Paine was instrumental in paving the way for the growth and development of a universal human rights discourse which today plays a large part in national, international and transnational law and legal negotiations.

Paine was not the first person to think in terms of democratic principles based on an individual's rights. He was heavily influenced by men such as Locke, Voltaire, Rousseau and Montesquieu. His ideas represent the culmination of a long trajectory of political and legal philosophy concerned with the relationship of the individual to the state. This trajectory arguably began in the wake of the English Civil War and King Charles I's public execution over 100 years earlier in 1649. However, while Paine was not the first to think about and use the terminology of political rights, he was original in his belief that these rights pertain to all humans regardless of their specific religious or spiritual belief system. Up to this point, most Europeans believed that a Christian God ruled supreme and political and legal rights were granted to individuals—if at all— only if one was of a certain Christian faith, racial background and socioeconomic class, and male in gender. African slaves and native peoples encountered in the New World were not Christians and so were denied any entitlement. Paine challenged this premise head-on, arguing that all peoples by virtue of their humanity should be shown respect and justice, and be treated equally. He was, in short, one of the first, if not *the* first, to talk in terms of rights being universal.

Paine's *Common Sense* and *Rights of Man* were instrumental in forging a new legal, political and social environment that today characterizes what we know and understand as the modern age. It is difficult to talk about contemporary democracy and legal rights—be these political, civil or human rights—without appreciating the context in which the concept of rights first materialized and how and why it has changed over time. Given our assumptions about all of us holding certain rights, such as the right to due process by petition of habeas corpus, it is important (and humbling) to know that these assumptions have only been around for about 200 years and for most of that period legal rights were only held by white males who enjoyed a certain status and property.

Paine's pamphlet *The Age of Reason* was written in 1793, two years after completing the *Rights of Man*. In *The Age of Reason* Paine presented his views on religion, which were very much informed by his belief in rationalism and scientific empiricism. While Theodore Roosevelt later described Paine as a 'filthy little atheist' (Spater 1987: 144), Paine in fact always professed to be a spiritual man who believed in a universal deity but openly spurned state sponsored churches and religion. Moreover, in direct conflict with the British system, Paine argued strongly for the disassociation of church and state because of the inherent problems he saw in any government dictating an individual's personal belief system. In *The Age of Reason*, Paine specifically argued against atheism, and promoted the enlightenment philosophy of deism, which had been so influential on American revolutionaries including Thomas Jefferson, Benjamin Franklin and George Washington.

Why begin with Paine's views on religion when he is primarily known for his innovative articulation of equality and universal rights? As discussed in the Introduction, I argue that the intersections and interactions between discourses of religion, race and rights cannot be disentangled from each other. With respect to Paine, according to one of his recent biographers, it is impossible to discuss *Rights of Man* without also talking about *The Age of Reason* because the latter is 'in a sense its counterpart and completion' (Hitchens 2006: 123). Hence I begin with Paine's views on religion, and in particular his interest in the ways science raised questions with respect to religion, as a window onto his writings on political and civil rights.

While Paine's interest in science was a driving force in his ability to think innovatively with respect to political rights, it also allowed him to think radically with respect to peoples of different ethnic and cultural backgrounds. In his essay *African Slavery in America* (1775) he railed against slavery, challenging the dominant pseudo-scientific discourse which provided the rationale for blacks' racial inferiority. Paine was well aware that such explanations conveniently justified black enslavement and indigenous genocide. Drawing on his immediate experience of slavery, which at the time was practiced widely across American society and by some of his closest colleagues and friends, Paine wrote against prevailing societal norms and publicly criticized racist practices. He was extremely radical in his bitter attacks on slavery and the exploitation of the working class (including women), and in his criticism of colonialism and the suppression and genocide of Native Americans. Paine's writings on the natural and universal rights of all men were deeply influenced by his immediate experience and repugnance of racially justified oppression of men and women.

In the final part of this chapter I address Paine's *Rights of Man*, and discuss his contribution to the development of American law and government in the period of the early Republic. In exploring Paine's influence on men such as Thomas Jefferson I examine the doctrine of the separation of church and state, which is often held up as emblematic of modern western democracy. I argue that, contrary to many modern Americans' view of their institutions of government, the principle of separation of church and state was not established by the First Amendment to the United States Constitution. Nor was the concept of separation of church and state widely accepted in France in the wake of the French Revolution. Much to the disappointment of Paine, the doctrine of separation was not endorsed or implemented in the United States or anywhere in Europe until many decades later.

My general argument—and one made by Paine himself throughout his various writings—is that a person's perspective on religion, race, and law and governance are inextricably linked. If one believes in religious tolerance it is then possible to embrace an ideology of cultural diversity and be at least willing to think about equal legal rights for all people. In the United States in both the pre- and post-revolutionary eras, religious tolerance was greater than it had ever been in Europe. That being said, tolerance was largely restricted to the Christian faith. Atheism and paganism were socially and politically unacceptable, and Buddhist, Muslim and Jewish faiths barely tolerated. Hence the radical American and French Revolutions of 1776 and 1789, which ushered in the concepts of modern representative government and inalienable legal rights as articulated in Paine's *Rights of Man*, were indeed revolutionary but were in fact limited in their immediate impact. This was largely because prevailing ideologies about racial inferiority dovetailed with mainstream ideologies about religious hierarchies to sustain socioeconomic disparities between classes, genders and ethnic communities.

Thomas Paine was born in 1737 in England and raised in a Quaker household. His father made corsets for a living. He did not have a remarkable youth or career, moving between jobs as an excise officer, schoolteacher and preacher. He had a longstanding interest in scientific inquiry, dabbling in inventions to build a single-span iron bridge, smokeless candles, and early models of steam engines. Paine became involved in political affairs in his 30s, and helped to lobby the British parliament for better pay and conditions for his fellow excise officers. On this subject he wrote a pamphlet and distributed 4,000 copies to members of parliament in 1774, which resulted in him losing his job and being forced to sell his household possessions to pay off debtors. Politically and socially isolated and without financial means, Paine met Benjamin Franklin through a mutual acquaintance and the two quickly became firm friends (Nelson 2006: 48–49). Franklin suggested to Paine that he emigrate to the British colonies and join him in Philadelphia, supplying him with letters of introduction. In November 1774

Paine arrived—though desperately ill from typhoid contracted on the long transatlantic voyage—in the New World. From these unlikely beginnings, Paine went on to become a powerful intellectual and political force in pre-revolutionary America (Figure 11). As argued by recent biographers, his radical and progressive ways of thinking made him in many ways a man ahead of his time (Hitchens 2006; Kaye 2005; Nelson 2006).

Figure 11. *Thomas Paine*, 1794, engraving by William Sharp from a George Romney Portrait. From the Library of Congress, Prints and Photographs Division.

Paine died in obscurity and poverty in upstate New York in 1809, attended by a funeral procession of six people, two of whom were reported to be black.[1] He was

---

[1] New York State awarded Paine 277 acres in New Rochelle in 1784 for the role he played in the American War of Independence. However, according to David W Chen in an article in the *New York Times*, 'Residents in what was a Tory stronghold disdained him. He was prevented from voting and branded an atheist. Finally, he retreated to Manhattan, where he died in 1809, childless, scorned, and impoverished. Ten years later, his body was exhumed from his farm and shipped to England by a zealous supporter who hoped that Paine would be accorded more respect. Instead, legend has it that

quickly forgotten or denounced for his radicalism and revolutionary ideals and remained largely unappreciated for nearly 200 years, until a recent spate of biographies appeared in the first decade of the twenty-first century (Keane 2003; Kaye 2005; Hitchens 2006; Nelson 2006). This recent interest in Paine, I believe, reflects the escalating crisis in the United States and other western nations subsequent to 9/11 with the War on Terror and the denial by the former Bush administration of basic civil liberties for which Paine fought so valiantly. It is not insignificant that President Obama, in his inaugural address of 20 January 2009, used the word 'crisis' four times, referred to 'the rights of man', and ended with a quote from Paine's earlier writings. Interestingly, George Washington had ordered this same quote to be read to his troops in their fight for independence against the British. Despite Paine's relative obscurity in many of the most prominent history books on western law and jurisprudence, in this chapter I hope to leave the reader with a sense of his immense significance and influence in terms of how we think today as modern legal subjects and citizens (Figure 12).

Figure 12. Anti-war rally and protest, 24 September 2005, Washington, DC.
© Bert Schlauch, Minneapolis, MN.

some of his bones were recycled into buttons, and others were either tossed into the garbage or lost to history. On the other hand, specific pieces said to be parts of his body include a skull owned by a family in Australia. … According to historians, Paine's body was exhumed in 1819 by William Cobbett, a one time Paine foe who later became an admirer. Cobbett felt that Paine was not being given his posthumous due, so he decided that England, where Paine spent the first thirty-seven years of his life, was a more appropriate burial site. The trouble was, hardly anyone else cared. So Paine's remains were kept in a trunk in Cobbett's attic. When Cobbett died in 1835, his son was apparently unsuccessful in auctioning off the bones, and may have buried them in the family plot, said Mr McCartin. Or maybe he didn't: in the 1850s, a Unitarian minister in England said that he had Paine's skull and right hand, and in the 1930s, a woman in Brighton insisted that she had Paine's jawbone' (Chen 2001).

RELIGION: *THE AGE OF REASON* AND THE CHALLENGE OF SCIENCE

The Enlightenment—a term usually used to denote Europe in the eighteenth century—was a complex historical movement that has come to epitomize the dawning of the west's modern age. While the Enlightenment period is not easily defined, philosophers, scientists and scholars during the seventeenth century in England, and the eighteenth century in Europe and America, began to challenge conventional ways of thinking and started to ask new questions about the nature of people in the world. These questions profoundly challenged the prevailing medieval mindset, which had largely accepted that one's position in life was determined by fate and pre-ordained by a divine God. In contrast, throughout the Enlightenment more and more ordinary people were beginning to ask questions that challenged God's all encompassing power, such as: How do people know what they know? Is there another authority for knowledge other than God? For what purpose are we here on earth? How can cultural and religious diversity among people be explained? Why are some people born to rule and others to be enslaved? To what degree can people resist the status quo and advocate improvement and change?

These questions—and the schools of thought they inspired—came to be referred to as the 'new learning'. Today we associate this term with the rise of scientific enquiry, empirical reasoning, and a general demand for intellectual reform based not on belief or faith but on experiential inductive reasoning. In England, four men were particularly important in nurturing the rise of scientific reasoning: Francis Bacon (1561–1626),[2] Thomas Hobbes (1588–1679),[3] John

---

[2] Francis Bacon was a diplomat, lawyer, and member of parliament for 37 years. Under James I he was made Lord Chancellor of England in 1618 before being thrown into the Tower of London for accepting bribes three years later. However, for all his influence in affairs of state and religion, he is most widely known for his contribution to forging the new field of applied modern scientific inquiry. Disillusioned with an Aristotelian model of reasoning that deduced 'logical implications from abstract first principles', Bacon advocated the use of human sensory experience and experimentation. According to Bacon, it was only through a systematic approach to material reality that one could determine a universal structure of human understanding. However, this first required that one's mind be clear of prior beliefs that might cloud one's ability to interpret objectively. On this front, Bacon argued for the purging of the 'four idols' in the first part of the *Novum Organum* (1620). In what is a truly innovative contribution, Bacon was one of the first philosophers to recognize that all people are influenced by their own personal psychologies (idols of the cave), ethnic prejudices (idols of the tribe), linguistic and social frames (idols of the marketplace) and ideological beliefs (idols of the theater). Having cleared one's mind, Bacon thought that it was possible to follow the pursuit of objective reasoning through careful empirical experimentation, from which could be inferred rational law-like principles. Nature, he argued, was to provide the only sure basis for a claim of truth. Importantly, the goal of this new scientific methodology was to tame and control nature.

[3] Thomas Hobbes, who had been Bacon's secretary in his early career and had assisted him in writing his *Essays* (1601), was highly influenced by Bacon's rejection of traditional philosophical knowledge passed down by Plato, Aristotle, and others. However, Hobbes argued that Bacon's experimental approach was also flawed in its inability to provide indisputable universal structures of understanding. For Hobbes, what was required was a mechanistic and materialist approach that took mathematical theory as its explanatory force, and reduced complex phenomena to their simplest elements. Hobbes' deductive approach to reason, which derived general principles from stated original

Locke (1632–1704)[4] and Isaac Newton (1642–1727).[5] Voltaire wrote in his *Letters Concerning the English Nation*, published in 1733, that Bacon and Newton (as well as his fellow Frenchman Descartes) were central in ushering in new forms of knowledge and thinking (cited in Kramnick 1995: 52; see Porter 2000). The Royal Society, established in London in 1660, epitomized the new wave of interest in

premises—as opposed to Bacon's inductive approach, which derived general principles from specific instances of fact—led him to question the authority of sacred texts. While Hobbes was not an atheist, he was often labeled as such because he argued that the bible could not be proven to be the word of God, and therefore life after death was not a demonstrable fact. Hobbes, like Bacon, by introducing an evidentiary burden, profoundly challenged *a priori* assumptions about the indisputable existence of God.

[4] The notion of a rational deity was essential in the thinking of John Locke as well. In his *Essay Concerning Human Understanding* (1690) Locke argued that a rational God had granted man the power to reason through his own sensory experience. Hence divinely revealed knowledge (faith) should be subject to experience and reason, and rejected if found irrational or subjective. To do otherwise and blindly believe in divine revelation only led to bitter wars and misery. Locke argued that 'religion, which should most distinguish us from beasts, and ought most peculiarly to elevate us as rational creatures above brutes, is that wherein men often appear most irrational, and more senseless than beasts themselves' (Locke 1690: 358). Locke's concern to distinguish between faith and reason, and his desire to establish a new relationship between government and religion, was to a large degree fostered by his anxiety over the threat of Catholicism again taking hold in England. The Civil Wars (1642–48), the beheading of Charles I (1649), the republican dictatorship of Oliver Cromwell (1653–58), the Restoration of Charles II (1660–85) and the Glorious Revolution (1688) were all very recent events that had consumed Britain in violent sectarian factionalism. Against this historical backdrop, Locke wrote *A Letter Concerning Toleration* in 1689 where he argued for a broader acceptance of various Christian denominations. Locke put forward the argument that the state should look after the external interests of civil society such as welfare and defense, and that the church should look after one's internal soul and salvation. According to Locke, these should be thought of as two distinct jurisdictions with separate powers and functions, a position that echoed Martin Luther's argument over a century earlier for the two kingdoms of church and state (see chapter one). In *A Letter Concerning Toleration,* Locke wrote that 'absolute liberty, just and true liberty, equal and impartial liberty, is the thing we stand in need of'. While Locke espoused toleration, he was Protestant in his religious faith and did not go so far as to argue for the toleration of atheists or Catholics. However, inadvertently or otherwise, his writings on religious toleration and in particular his very popular and widely read *Essay Concerning Human Understanding* did help to move public debate toward conceptualizing a more universally conceived Christian God without getting bogged down in detailed arguments about the scriptural practices and rituals of specific religious groups. Moreover, Locke's ideas on tolerance and his open distaste for state intervention in people's private spirituality helped to articulate and consolidate many of the fundamental principles for which the American revolutionaries fought so hard in establishing their independence and liberty from Britain 100 years later.

[5] In a similar fashion to Bacon and Hobbes, Isaac Newton did not intentionally set out to dispute the existence of divine intervention in his exploration of science and in particular the laws of physics (see Gay 1969: 140–41). Like Hobbes, however, he was sure that mathematics provided the key to uniform and universal knowledge. According to Newton, a Supreme Being created the world but the universal laws of nature (such as gravity) governed all human experience, which in turn could be understood through reasoned empirical experimentation. Newton's enormous contribution to physics, astronomy, chemistry and in particular his demonstration of the universal laws of gravity, which also helped to explain the circulation of the planets around the sun, profoundly changed scientific thinking. These discoveries were enormously influential in promoting the emergence of scientific 'clubs' (such as the Lunar Society) that consisted of men getting together to ponder and play with light, chemicals and mechanical instruments (Holmes 2009; Uglow 2003; Golinski 1992). This new fascination with the laws of nature can be seen in Newton's *Philosophiae Naturalis Princeipia Mathematica* (1687). By presenting uniform laws and principles capable of explaining physical reality, Newton verified 'the soundness of Bacon's empiricist method' which in turn 'pointed to the existence of a *rational deity*' (Walters 1993: 8–9, my emphasis).

scientific learning based on experimentation and factual determination (see Holmes 2009; Uglow 2003; Golinski 1992).

Inadvertently, the quest for scientific understanding helped to nurture a sense of skepticism in institutionalized religion and the explanation that God was solely responsible for both spiritual and earthly worlds. Skepticism among scientists and intellectuals fostered a growing sense that man was an active participant in his daily life and well-being and encountered God not through formal religious institutions or rituals, but through personal experience and reason. This does not mean that religious faith was less important to intellectuals, or that a rise in scientific interest necessarily correlated to a growing secularism in society (Thomson 2008: 13–17). Rather, alternative ideas about religion that emerged during this period, particularly among men of science, can be interpreted 'not as refutation of religion but an attempt to rescue it from clericalism … superstition, and fanaticism' (Thomson 2008: 15). Quite a number of scientists embraced deism, which was a philosophical movement that was very important among American and French revolutionaries and in particular the 'founding fathers' of the United States. Deists believed in a God, but typically rejected formal religion as being corrupt. Deists held that a universal God created the material world, but it was the laws of nature and human reason that governed man's experience of the world (see below). As historians have noted, the influence of men such as Bacon, Locke and Newton 'on eighteenth century thought (and, by association, deism) can hardly be exaggerated' (Walters 1993: 7).

English Deism and American Radicalism

The English Enlightenment fostered new ideas about religion and religious tolerance. One offshoot of this more inclusive perspective on religion was the growth of deism, which was a position on religion that many found very attractive in the pre-revolutionary period in America. Very simply, deists believed in a universal God existing outside the institutions of formal religion. Deists did not uphold God as the only source of knowledge and authority, nor did they maintain that Christianity was the supreme or only legitimate religion. In short, deism as a philosophical movement challenged conventional understandings of divinity and took issue with the bible and other holy books as the definitive word and authority of God.

Deism and the deist movement in England were not particularly widespread or influential. However the deists' thinking and presence in theological and political debates were indicative of the general mood of the later seventeenth and early eighteenth centuries whereby scientific exploration and explanation began to challenge conventional attitudes to scriptural authority. As Peter Gay has noted:

> Deism reflected and articulated a critical transition in religious consciousness, but by reflecting and articulating it so plainly, so coarsely, it hastened the transition. The impact of the deist polemic was felt whenever men reasoned about religion. The secular Enlightenment, which was by no means dominated by deists, is the deists' rightful heir.

... Deism, we might say, is the product of the confluence of three strong emotions: hate, love, and hope. The deists hated priests and priestcraft, mystery-mongering, and assaults on common sense. They loved the ethical teachings of the classical philosophers, the grand unalterable regularity of nature, the sense of freedom granted the man liberated from superstition. They hoped that the problems of life—of private conduct and public policy—could be solved by the application of unaided human reason, and that the mysteries of the universe could be, if not solved, at least defined and circumscribed by man's scientific inquiry ... They were powerful agents of modernity. (Gay 1968: 13)

While deism attracted attention and controversy in England in the early years of the eighteenth century, by the 1730s it was in serious decline.[6] As a theological position it had been attacked by astute intellectuals such as David Hume[7] and prominent churchmen such as Bishop Joseph Butler (Gay 1968: 140–42). However, 'English deism, it seems, traveled well. ... As deism waned in England, it waxed in France and the German states' (Gay 1968: 143). Voltaire, building on the work of his predecessor Montesquieu and on his own exposure to deism during his two years in London between 1726 and 1728, wrote essays and pamphlets advocating the deist principles of toleration and justice. These writings were often burnt for being seditious and Voltaire was forced on occasion to hide in the homes of friends to avoid persecution and imprisonment. In his later years, Voltaire openly declared himself a deist and his pamphlets and essays became increasingly propagandist in tone. For instance, in his *Sermon of the Fifty* (1755) Voltaire eloquently called for a universal God or 'Supreme Being', and rejected the notion of separate churches which embroiled nation-states in wars and violence:

---

[6] Some scholars claim that John Locke was influential in the deist movement, despite the fact that he critically addressed the deists in his *Essay Concerning Human Understanding*. Certainly there are both similarities and differences between Locke's thinking and that of the English Deists (see Hefelbower 1918). Both Locke and the deists argued that the laws of nature could be comprehended by reason. And both Locke and the deists were critical of absolute monarchy for the way it imposed religious belief on people and for being, as Locke noted, 'inconsistent with civil society' in that it denied the right of individuals to come together voluntarily and give up some of their natural rights for the security and well-being of the collective 'commonwealth' (cited in Kramnick 1995: 401). However, Locke ultimately maintained that natural religion was insufficient to curb the 'limitless expression of subjective will' existing in a state of nature (Syse 2007: 233). Hence he argued that natural religion must be supplemented by traditional religion in the form of supernatural revelation, miracles and the bible's scriptural authority. In this way Locke was religiously conservative, arguing against established state religion, but not willing to give up the legitimacy of formal church institutions and rituals. The deists, on the other hand, were more radical (and perhaps more optimistic) in their dismissal of revelation and holy books as authoritative sources of God's power and instead argued for a return to a natural theology in which God was responsible for the universal laws of nature.

[7] In calling for a pure, unadulterated religion, some deists saw connections with the religious practices of 'savage' native peoples and equated true original Christianity with an original natural religion (ie Matthew Tindal, *Christianity as Old as the Creation* (XIV) (1730)). In *Natural History of Religion* (1757) David Hume aggressively attacked such claims, arguing that polytheism and not monotheism was the first religion of early peoples. Moreover, Hume argued that religious belief was the result of fear of the unknown, not of reason, and so denounced the primary claim of the deists that religious belief must be experienced through rationalism.

My brethren, religion is the secret voice of God which speaks to all men; it should unite, and not divide, them all: hence any religion that belongs to only one people is false. Ours is in its basic principle the religion of the entire universe; for we worship a Supreme Being as all nations worship him, we practice the justice that all nations teach, and we reject all those lies with which all nations reproach one another: thus, in agreement with them in the principle that reconciles them, we differ from them in the matters over which they fight. (cited in Gay 1968: 146)

In America, deism became increasingly popular from the 1730s onwards, and by the middle of the eighteenth century orthodox clergy were warning their congregations against the deist movement (Holmes 2006: 49). Deism held a strong position in many of the 13 colonies' colleges such as Harvard and Yale, and it is was in these centers of learning that young people embraced the radical deist ideals of universal education, religious tolerance, freedom of the press, and the separation of church and state. It is important to underscore that Puritans, Catholics, Anglicans, Lutherans and Calvinists all believed in the union of church and state, and bitterly opposed the notion of separation. Deism, which argued for separation, was particularly attractive in the colonies' pre-revolutionary atmosphere of the 1770s. Deism provided a spiritual rationale for a general political and intellectual movement seeking to challenge an oppressive British government based on divine authority and determined to rule without input from the colonists.

Paine's *Common Sense* (1776) and *The Crisis* (1776)

Thomas Paine's arrival in the New World coincided with a tumultuous period of increasing colonial resistance to an overbearing Britain. Having regained his health following the terrible transatlantic crossing, he quickly became involved in local politics in Philadelphia and set about editing the *Pennsylvania Magazine* and writing pamphlets and broadsheets advocating the colonies' independence from Britain. One of the unique aspects of Paine's writings was his use of common language. Drawing on his own modest background, Paine was able to speak to ordinary working people of the lower and middle classes and as a result his writings had a profound ability to stir up public debate and galvanize public opinion. Aiding this process was the fact that pamphlets could be quickly printed, were cheap to buy, and were easily listened to or read.

Paine's pamphlet *Common Sense* (1776) sold 150,000 copies within three months in the colonies (Kaye 2005: 43). As Harvey Kaye remarks, 'The equivalent sales today would be 15 million, making it, proportionally, the nation's greatest best-seller ever. By one estimation, half a million copies were sold in the course of the Revolution. Plus, copies were shared, and those who could not read it heard it read aloud in homes, taverns, workshops, and fields' (Kaye 2005: 43). *Common Sense* also had a marked impact on Europeans, many of whom were thinking along similar revolutionary lines in the build up to the French Revolution.

Common Sense combined elements of lay preaching with rationalist logic, and 'it can be said, without any risk of cliché, that it was a catalyst that altered the course of history' (Hitchens 2006: 30, 37). Within months of publishing *Common Sense*, Paine published a series of pamphlets called *The Crisis* (1776), and General George Washington ordered these pamphlets to be read aloud to his troops to inspire them in their battles with the British. Together *Common Sense* and *The Crisis* were exceedingly important in helping to marshal colonial resistance, galvanize a new form of nationalism based on American exceptionalism, and give voice to the despair suffered during the long war for independence. It was Paine who first proposed the name *United States of America*. And it was Paine who in his first *Crisis* pamphlet wrote the famous words, 'These are the times that try men's souls'.

Paine's deist sentiments were well known and admired by many American revolutionary leaders, who to varying degrees shared his Newtonian belief in the laws of nature, a natural theology that upheld the vision of a universal creator, and a belief in the right of all to be treated equally. Paine's ideas drew heavily on the earlier writings of John Locke, Montesquieu and Rousseau, and the senti-ments of equality and universal spiritualism can be clearly seen in Thomas Jefferson's opening paragraph of the 1776 Declaration of Independence, which reads:

> When in the Course of human events it becomes necessary for one people to dissolve the political bands which have connected them with another and to assume among the powers of the earth, the separate and equal station to which the Laws of Nature and of Nature's God entitle them, a decent respect to the opinions of mankind requires that they should declare the causes which impel them to the separation. We hold these truths to be self-evident, that all men are created equal, and that they are endowed by their Creator with certain unalienable Rights, that among these are Life, Liberty, and the pursuit of Happiness …

However, while Paine was a darling of the revolutionary period, in the post-revolutionary period his radical ideas increasingly irritated the growing number of conservative American republicans through the 1780s. By 1787 Paine had had enough of their antagonism, and took off to Europe in search of a sponsor willing to finance his invention of a single-span iron bridge. In Paris he was surrounded by men such as Thomas Jefferson, in residence as the American Minster to France, as well as Lafayette and a dissident set of French intellectuals who openly admired the American Declaration of Independence and hoped for a similar overturning of the absolutist regime in France. In 1791 Paine published the first part of his *Rights of Man*, which immediately sold 50,000 copies. Below I discuss the content and impact of the *Rights of Man* and its political implications in terms of its call for representative democracy, universal suffrage, and the rejection of all forms of inherited power. At this point it is important to appreciate that while Paine was considered seditious for publishing *Rights of Man* and outlawed in Britain, his popularity in France was immense.

In 1792 Paine was appointed to the French National Assembly despite being unable to speak French. However, things quickly turned sour as the French Revolution spun out of control and the Reign of Terror set in. Political and military factions competed for control of Paris and up to 40,000 people were imprisoned and guillotined. General disillusionment and horror at the unfolding events of the French Revolution were felt across Britain, France and the United States. Paine was similarly distressed by the revolutionaries' extremism, and in particular Robespierre's 'Committee of Public Safety' and 'Revolutionary Tribunal' which were responsible for rounding up people on the slightest suspicion and creating an environment of mass hysteria. Paine had difficulty holding his tongue, and became unpopular with the more radical Jacobins for arguing against capital punishment and the execution of Louis XVI and his queen, Marie Antoinette. In late 1793 a new rule was made which prohibited foreigners from participating in the French National Assembly, resulting in Paine's arrest and imprisonment, where by a lucky escape he avoided execution. He was released in 1794, largely with the aid of the new American Minster to France—and later president of the United States—James Monroe.

Paine's *The Age of Reason* (1793)

Paine wrote the first part of *The Age of Reason* in the period immediately preceding his imprisonment. Recalling his association with the American Revolution by dedicating his work to his 'Fellow Citizens of the United States', Paine railed against the French revolutionaries' persecution of Catholic priests and the bloody revenge unleashed on individuals associated with the church. Paine agreed with the dismantling of state sponsored Catholicism in France and what he considered to be its illegitimate institutions of power. However, he disagreed with the violent rampage that bloodied the streets of Paris. He wrote:

> It has been my intention, for several years, to publish my thoughts upon religion. ... The circumstance that has now taken place in France, of the total abolition of the national order of priesthood, and of everything pertaining to compulsive systems of religion, and compulsive articles of faith, has not only precipitated my intention, but rendered a work of this kind exceedingly necessary, lest, in the general wreck of superstition, of false systems of government, and false theology, we lose sight of morality, of humanity, and of theology that is true. (Paine 2007: 356)

Paine went on to profess his faith. Note that in his declaration of what he does not believe in, he rejects all formal religious institutions and argues that faith should be experienced through an individual's reason when he states: 'My own mind is my own church'. Note also that Paine lumped together Christianity with Judaic and Muslim belief, which, given the racist thinking of most British, French and American people at this time, was considered profoundly offensive and blasphemous:

> I believe in one God, and no more; and I hope for happiness beyond this life.
>
> I believe in the equality of man, and I believe that religious duties consist in doing justice, loving mercy, and endeavoring to make our fellow-creatures happy.
>
> I do not believe in the creed professed by the Jewish church, by the Roman church, by the Greek church, by the Turkish church, by the Protestant church, nor by any church that I know of. My own mind is my own church.
>
> All national institutions of churches, whether Jewish, Christian, or Turkish, appear to me no other than human inventions set up to terrify and enslave mankind, and monopolize power and profit. (Paine 2007: 356)

Paine denounced state sponsored religions, arguing that they suppress free thought through violence. He argued that what was needed was a separation of church and state. And he envisaged that with a change in government would come a change in religious attitudes and the ability to think in terms of a universal single God:

> Soon after I had published the pamphlet *Common Sense*, in America, I saw the exceeding probability that a revolution in the system of government would be followed by a revolution in the system of religion. The adulterous connection of church and state, wherever it has taken place, whether Jewish, Christian, or Turkish, has so effectually prohibited, by pains and penalties, every discussion upon established creeds, and upon first principles of religion, that until the system of government should be changed, those subjects could not be brought fairly and openly before the world: but that whenever this should be done, a revolution in the system of religion would follow. Human interventions and priest-craft would be detected; and man would return to the pure, unmixed, and unadulterated belief of one God, and no more. (Paine 2007: 357)

Following a detailed discussion of the Old and New Testaments, Paine engaged with 'The Effects of Christianism on Education' in Chapter XII of Part One of *The Age of Reason*. Here Paine discussed how ancient civilizations drew on scientific knowledge and mathematics to study astronomy, astrology and the natural world in general. However, such scientific knowledge was restricted with the rise of Catholicism, precisely because it brought into question 'the truth of their system of faith'. In short, Paine saw a basic conflict between scientific approaches to understanding the world and the maintenance of the hierarchical power structure of the Catholic Church through 'mystery, miracle, and prophecy'. Interestingly, he also articulated what he saw as a 'natural association' between the sciences and liberalism. According to Paine, 'The event that served more than any other to break the first link in this long chain of despotic ignorance, is that known by the name of the Reformation by Luther. From that time ... the Sciences began to revive, and Liberality, their natural associate, began to appear' (Paine 2007: 387–88).

In Part III of *The Age of Reason* Paine discussed the immorality of Christianity, arguing that church-goers go through the motions of church attendance and ritual but do not really express true faith. Paine believed in the equality of all men, and it is here that his disgust with what man is capable of doing to others is apparent. He wrote:

The prejudice of unfounded belief, often degenerates into the prejudice of custom, and becomes at last rank hypocrisy. When men, from custom or fashion or any worldly motive, profess or pretend to believe what they do not believe, nor can give any reason for believing, they unship the helm of their morality, and being no longer honest to their own minds they feel no moral difficulty in being unjust to others. ... Morality has no hold on their minds, no restraint on their actions. (Paine 2007: 477)

The impact of *The Age of Reason* was varied. It explicitly and aggressively promoted deism at the expense of the bible and orthodox Christianity. Paine's 'vulgar' and unpolished language, which made the pamphlet accessible to the middle and lower classes, also meant that he was able to communicate with a large audience; therefore his irreverent attack on church institutions was potentially very dangerous. In Britain, publishers and booksellers caught peddling *The Age of Reason* pamphlet were prosecuted and imprisoned. In France, *The Age of Reason* had limited impact, mostly because its main ideas were already very familiar. In the United States, the pamphlet initially created a resurgence of interest in deism and thousands of copies were sold. But this enthusiasm was short lived. Over the next few years, especially upon Paine's return to the United States in 1802 at the invitation of Jefferson, he was called all manner of names by conservative Federalists and churchmen, such as 'infamous scavenger', 'lying, drunken, brutal infidel', and 'loathsome ... a drunken atheist, and the scavenger of faction' (cited in Kaye 2005: 91).

RACE: QUESTIONING SLAVERY AND DISCRIMINATION

Paine's thinking about religion, race and rights dramatically illustrates the complex interweaving of these three issues in his grappling with the concepts of justice and humanity. His argument for representative democracy based on the concept of human rights and the separation of church and state cannot be disassociated from his tolerance of religious pluralism and his own deist faith with its universal, non-interventionist God. Similarly, his radical political and religious views cannot be disassociated from his sincere belief in egalitarianism and his concern over the unequal treatment of minorities, which in the context of the early American republic primarily constituted African slaves, indigenous peoples, and of course women (Figure 13).

Paine was not the first to speak openly against slavery in America.[8] Still, it was Paine who made the criticism of slavery a public issue, and his accessible writings were without doubt the most influential. In 1775 he published an essay entitled *African Slavery in America*, which appeared in the *Pennsylvania Journal and Weekly Advertiser*. In this essay Paine called slaves 'an unnatural commodity' and

---

[8] For instance the Quaker John Woolman openly attacked slavery in his tract *Consideration on the Keeping of Negros* (1762). Woolman insightfully commented on the difficulty of overcoming prejudice given 'the idea of slavery being connected with the black color, and liberty with the white' (cited in Kramnick 1995: 634).

Figure 13. Slave quarters on a South Carolina plantation, 1860.

argued that the practice of slavery went against all Christian principles. The essay was relatively well received in the pre-revolutionary period, capturing the mood of egalitarianism and freedom from oppression that colonists were demanding from Britain. Within weeks of its publication the first anti-slavery society, the Society for the Relief of Free Negroes Unlawfully Held In Bondage, was established in the United States, and Paine was one of its founding members.

In his essay Paine underscored that slavery went against Christian values. He also stressed that all people have a natural right to their freedom, independent of their religion, culture and the color of their skin:

> Christians are taught to count all men their neighbors; and love their neighbors as themselves; and do to all men as they would be done by; to do good to all men; and Man-stealing is ranked with enormous crimes. Is the barbarous enslaving of our inoffensive neighbors, and treating them like wild beasts subdued by force, reconcilable with Divine precepts! Is this doing to them as we would desire they should do to us? If they carry off and enslave some thousands of us, would we think it just? ... as the true owner has a right to reclaim his goods that were stolen, and sold; so the slave, who is

proper owner of his freedom, has a right to reclaim it, however often sold. … As these people are not convicted of forfeiting freedom, they still have a natural, perfect right to it; and the governments whenever they come should, in justice set them free, and punish those who hold them in slavery.

Paine's views directly challenged mainstream attitudes and prejudices, given that many colonists owned slaves or benefited indirectly from their cheap labor. That being said, Paine's writings and their anti-slavery rhetoric were tolerated in the pre and post-revolutionary euphoria that gripped the 13 colonies. And from 1775 on, particularly in the northeastern states, an increasing number of lay societies advocating the abolition of slavery appeared. The primary reason given for abolition was that it went against Christian values. Very few abolitionists, however, endorsed Paine's more radical argument that Africans were equal to Americans and possessed freedom as a natural inalienable right based on their common humanity. Most abolitionists continued to believe in the pseudo-scientific rationales prevailing at the time which justified the notion that white European males were racially superior. This distinction between showing charity toward others versus legally recognizing a person's inalienable right to freedom is important, as will be discussed further in chapter four.

Among influential politicians and leaders, many of whom owned slaves, such as George Washington and Thomas Jefferson, there was cautious support for Paine's egalitarian views. For instance, Jefferson, who was deeply influenced by Paine, originally drafted a paragraph calling for the abolition of the slave trade in the Declaration of Independence, but Congress removed this before voting on its approval and publication (Hitchens 2006: 38; Lewis 1947). The anti-slavery movement progressed relatively slowly in the north, with some states such as Pennsylvania introducing gradual emancipation in 1780 such that all children born to slaves would become free upon turning 28 years of age. In the south, the anti-slavery movement was almost non-existent. At the federal level, in 1787 Congress passed the Northwest Ordinance barring slavery from the Northwest Territory, though this took years actually to enforce.[9] That same year, Congress outlawed the import of slaves after 1808, though because the slave population was self-reproducing this law did not have much of an impact on the practice of slavery within the United States itself.

Paine attacked not just slavery and the slave trade. He was also deeply distressed by the treatment of native peoples by colonists and early republicans, and he spoke openly about this abuse. In some of his earliest writing in 1775 as editor of the *Pennsylvania Magazine* Paine wrote that if independence was won

---

[9] The Northwest Ordinance also mentioned Native Americans, saying that their lands and rights should be respected and observed. Unfortunately, this was largely ignored by Americans pushing westward, who often coerced natives to sign treaties and when met with resistance by Indian tribes resorted to brutality and violence in an effort to clear them off the lands. The Northwest Ordinance reads: 'The utmost faith shall always be observed towards the Indians; their land and property shall never be taken without their consent; and, in their property, rights and liberty, they shall never be invaded or disturbed.'

from Britain, 'then may our first gratitude be shown by an act of continental legislation, which shall put a stop to the importation of Negroes for sale, soften the hard fate of those already here [ie Indians], and in time procure their freedom' (cited in Kaye 2005: 37). This rhetoric of egalitarianism and liberty was also expressed with respect to women. While uncertainty remains as to its authorship, Paine is commonly attributed as the author of a piece in the *Pennsylvania Magazine* which surveys the treatment of women across the ages and finds that 'women, almost—without exception—at all times and in all places, [have been] adored and oppressed' (cited in Kramnick 1995: 586). This acknowledgement of both women's plight and their right to be recognized as equal to men in a universal collective helped to nurture feminist sentiment. For instance, Abigail Adams, wife of John Adams, a prominent political figure who went on to become the second president of the United States (1797–1801), was influenced by Paine's ideas and in writing to her husband pointedly stated:

> In the new Code of Laws which I suppose it will be necessary for you to make, I desire that you would remember the ladies. … Do not put such unlimited power into the hands of the Husbands. Remember all Men would be tyrants if they could. If particular care and attention is not paid to the Ladies we are determined to ferment a Rebellion, and will not hold ourselves bound by any Laws in which we have no voice, or Representation. (cited in Kaye 2005: 52)

Perhaps the most innovative, and in many ways most interesting, of Paine's writings is *Agrarian Justice*, in which he argued against the structural inequalities that create poverty and discrimination. Written in 1797 when Paine was still in France, *Agrarian Justice* was a response to Bishop Watson's *An Apology for the Bible*, which denounced Paine's *The Age of Reason*. What really disturbed Paine was Watson's claim that God had, in his wisdom and goodness, created both rich and poor, and so inequality among people was scripturally justified. Paine fiercely rejected this claim and argued:

> It is wrong to say God made rich and poor; He made only male and female, and He gave them the earth for their inheritance. … The most affluent and the most miserable of the human race are to be found in the countries that are called civilized … To understand what the state of society ought to be, it is necessary to have some idea of the natural and primitive state of man; such as it is at this day among the Indians of North America. There is not, in that state, any of those spectacles of human misery which poverty and want present to our eyes in all the towns and streets of Europe. … Poverty, therefore, is a thing created by that which is called civilized life. … Civilization, therefore, or that which is so-called, has operated in two ways: to make one part of society more affluent, and the other more wretched, than would have been the lot of either in a natural state. (Paine 2007: 523)

Agrarian Justice takes as its premise that the earth prior to cultivation and civilization was the common property of all. 'There could be no such thing as landed property originally', argued Paine. However, certain men through cultivation of the land came to take possession, and this possession was defended through the development of property law. Paine noted that such cultivation was a good thing and he defended property rights. But he also argued that those who own property have a duty toward those they dispossessed of their 'natural inheritance'. This duty is to 'create a national fund' from which all people—both men and women, rich and poor—should be paid 'fifteen pounds sterling' upon reaching 21 years of age for compensation in part, for the loss of his or her natural inheritance (Paine 2007: 525).[10]

Paine's idea of a national fund as part of a welfare system, organized through the state, was incredibly radical for the times. Based on the concept of society's collective benefits in helping the poor, Paine repeatedly declared in *Agrarian Justice* that:

> It is not a charity but a right, not bounty but justice, that I am pleading for. ... The plan here proposed will reach the whole. It will immediately relieve and take out of view three classes of wretchedness—the blind, the lame, and the aged poor; and it will do this without deranging or interfering with any national measures. (Paine 2007: 528–29)

Perhaps most perceptively of all, Paine noted that if society did not compensate those people dispossessed of their original rights to land in some way, poverty among certain peoples would become entrenched. 'The great mass of the poor in countries are becoming a hereditary race, and it is next to impossible [for] them to get out of that state themselves. It also must be observed that this mass increases in all countries that are called civilized' (Paine 2007: 528–30). Coupled with the rising divide between rich and poor—which brings to mind the gross and entrenched socioeconomic inequalities of the twenty-first century within developed nations and between developed and developing nations—Paine noted that this divide had come about through exploitation of labor in the first place. In a truly original insight that foreshadows Marx and other nineteenth century political theorists and activists concerned with issues of labor, Paine stated:

> ... for if we examine the case minutely it will be found that the accumulation of personal property is, in many instances, the effect of paying too little for the labor that produced it; the consequence of which is that the working hand perishes in old age, and the employer abounds in affluence. (Paine 2007: 531)

Agrarian Justice was not well received, and it was quickly denounced by politicians and entrepreneurs. If ever there were a reason for the Federalists, industrialists and burgeoning capitalist classes in the United States, Britain and France to denounce Paine as a radical revolutionary and deliberately ignore or

---

[10] Paine wrote, 'Separate an individual from society, and give him an island or a continent to possess, and he cannot acquire personal property. He cannot be rich. So inseparably are the means connected with the end, in all cases, that where the former do no exist the latter cannot be obtained. All accumulation, therefore, of personal property, beyond what a man's own hands produce, is derived to him by living in society; and he owes on every principle of justice, of gratitude, and of civilization, a part of that accumulation back again to society from whence the whole came' (Paine 2007: 530).

deny his political significance, it could be found in the profoundly threatening language of egalitarianism and welfarism expressed in *Agrarian Justice*. Despite its limited reception, however, many of Paine's views in *Agrarian Justice* were to have a significant impact—though often unacknowledged—on future generations advocating labor reform and a minimum wage. In many ways Paine's explicit opposition to racial, class and gender discrimination foreshadowed the political debates and legal landmarks that marked much of the colonial and industrial nineteenth century, such as the practice and abolition of slavery (chapter four), workers' demands for the eight-hour workday (chapter five), and the US government's treatment of native peoples (chapter six).

RIGHTS: LAW'S COMING OF AGE IN *RIGHTS OF MAN*

Paine's *Rights of Man*, written in the midst of the French Revolution and drawing heavily on the 1789 French Declaration of the Rights of Man and of the Citizen, outlined a new political philosophy that spoke to ordinary people and provided them with hope and optimism. It stated in unequivocal terms that power lay in the hands of individuals working together. Not surprisingly, it was eagerly read by the literate working classes, whose exploitation and poverty at this time was extreme. Even in England, where Paine was outlawed for writing *Rights of Man* and people were imprisoned if found with a copy in their possession, many intellectuals and working-class people embraced its central tenets.

In a profound sense, *Rights of Man* represents a turning point in the development of modern Anglo-American law by opening up the minds of ordinary people to thinking about new possibilities and opportunities with respect to representational government and suffrage. In 1822, according to the English radical reformer William Cobbett, Paine '"had awakened ... the spirit of enquiry" in the common man' (cited in Dyck 1987: 135). For the first time there was an accessible and internationally received political manifesto available that advocated tolerance, civil liberties and political equality, and which spoke—at least theoretically—to women,[11] slaves, indentured servants, religious and ethnic minorities, and the great mass of impoverished working classes. Paine's *Rights of Man* translated and incorporated the spirit of the French Revolution and a civil law tradition into a document that spoke to a working class English-speaking audience whose legal system was based in the common law. In short, Paine played a central role in helping to launch a new modernist era where the definition and enforcement of legal rights became a constant core issue in legal reform.

---

[11] Still Paine came under attack for not expressly referring to women in his *Rights of Man*. In America and France a few outspoken women, such as Olympe de Gouges, were beginning to take a stand and call for women's rights to be recognized. In 1792, the Englishwoman Mary Wollstonecraft wrote *Vindication of the Rights of Women*, which today is considered one of the founding documents of the feminist movement.

Paine wrote *Rights of Man* in 1791 in angry response to Edmund Burke's *Reflections on the Revolution in France* of that same year. In *Reflections*, Burke denounced the French revolutionary movement and advocated the return of an absolutist monarchy. Burke, much to the surprise of many people, including Paine who was a long-time friend, proved in the end to be a hardcore royalist and determinedly antagonistic towards France. Paine was convinced that Burke had sold his soul in defense of England's historic 1688 'Glorious Revolution', which resulted in the reinstatement of the authority of the hereditary monarch.[12] In contrast, Paine denounced all forms of hereditary government both in the form of inherited monarchy and in the maintenance of an elite birth-right aristocracy which in England formed the House of Lords. Hereditary government, Paine argued, should be replaced with representative democracy in which all citizens should have a voice, irrespective of one's parentage.

In stark opposition to Burke's royalist defense of kingship, Paine's *Rights of Man* presented a new articulation of republicanism adopted by Jefferson and other US presidents such as Madison and Monroe. Admittedly, some of the ideas set out in *Rights of Man*, such as the concept of inalienable rights, appeared in Paine's earlier writings and in particular *Common Sense*. But unlike his earlier works, *Rights of Man* presented a more thorough and thoughtful account of how a republic and constitution would actually work in practice. It covered a range of topics, including a commentary on the origin of old governments, a comparison of old and new systems of government, a discussion of the value of constitutions, and advice as to how Britain could best reform politically. Dedicated to George Washington and the Marquis de Lafayette, *Rights of Man* acknowledged the roles played by both the American and the French Revolutions in helping to shape Paine's final treatise.

The basic premise in *Rights of Man* is that all people since the beginning of time have been created equal. This equality, manifested in an individual's rights, derives from the laws of nature and as such cannot be taken away or denied either by another person or by government. Paine adroitly referred to both a spiritual and a temporal interpretation of creation, thereby accommodating formal and informal religious perspectives such as deism (Paine 2007: 200). He then differentiated between an individual's natural rights and civil rights, and argued that certain natural rights are exchanged for civil rights, such as those that relate to security and protection of the individual by the state:

---

[12] Paine wrote, 'When the French Revolution broke out, it certainly afforded to Mr Burke an opportunity of doing some good, had he been disposed to it; instead of which, no sooner did he see the old prejudices wearing away, than he immediately began sowing the seeds of a new inveteracy, as if he were afraid that England and France would cease to be enemies. [England and France entered war in 1793.] That there are men in all countries who get their living by war, and by keeping up the quarrels of Nations, is as shocking as it is true; but when those who are concerned in the government of a country, make it their study to sow discord and cultivate prejudices between Nations, it becomes the more unpardonable' (from Paine's Preface to the English edition of *Rights of Man*; Paine 2007: 180).

Natural rights are those which pertain to man in right of his existence. Of this kind are all the intellectual rights, or rights of the mind, and also all those rights of acting as an individual for his own comfort and happiness, which are not injurious to the natural rights of others … consequently religion is one of those rights. … Civil rights are those which appertain to man in right of his being a member of society. Every civil right has for its foundation some natural right pre-existing in the individual … (Paine 2007: 201–02)

In Paine's commentary on types of government, he made the distinction between archaic systems based on 'superstition', systems based on divine right and 'power', and new systems that are to be based on 'reason' and 'the common rights of man'. Since Paine believed that common rights exist prior to the establishment of any form of government, he rejected the idea of a social contract, a key theme in the earlier writings of political philosophers such as Hobbes, Locke and Rousseau. According to Paine:

It has been thought a considerable advance towards establishing the principles of Freedom to say that Government is a compact between those who govern and those who are governed; but this cannot be true, because it is putting the effect before the cause; for as man must have existed before governments existed, there necessarily was a time when governments did not exist, and consequently there could originally exist no governors to form such a compact with. The fact therefore must be that the individuals themselves, each in his own personal and sovereign right, entered into a compact with each other to produce a government: and this is the only mode in which governments have a right to arise, and the only principle on which they have a right to exist. (Paine 2007: 203)

Finally, Paine referred in his *Rights of Man* to the French National Assembly and its passing in 1789 of the Declaration of the Rights of Man and of the Citizen, which set out a list of 17 rights to be enjoyed by all men. Paine noted with approval that in the presence of a 'Supreme Being', the Assembly recognized the 'sacred rights of men and of citizens' and so referenced a natural theology grounded in the laws of nature (Figure 14). Today, this list of rights has become emblematic of the modern age and a new approach to law and government which incorporates recognition of individual rights. For the sake of brevity, I cite only the most significant of these rights below:

1. Men are born and remain free and equal in rights; social distinctions may be based only upon general usefulness.
2. The aim of every political association is the preservation of the natural and inalienable rights of man; these rights are liberty, property, security, and resistance to oppression.
3. The source of all sovereignty resides essentially in the nation; no group, no individual, may exercise authority not emanating expressly therefrom. …
6. Law is the expression of the general will; all citizens have the right to concur personally, or through their representatives, in its formation; it must be the same for all, whether it protects or punishes. All citizens, being equal before

Figure 14. *Declaration of the Rights of Man and of the Citizen,* 1793, artist unknown. This image includes a fascinating mix of symbols. By arranging the articles on tablets, the artist clearly meant to associate this document with the Ten Commandments. Such a link could establish the revolutionaries' handiwork as equivalent to that of God. Reinforcing this is the all-seeing eye located at the top. However, this is not the God of biblical revelation but of the Masonic order, which espoused a deistic vision of a benevolent creator and founder of general laws. The all-seeing eye also appears on the reverse of the Great Seal of the United States (1782) and has been printed on the back of the American one-dollar bill since 1935 (see Stolleis 2008). Courtesy of Centre historique des Archives Nationales, Paris.

it, are equally admissible to all public offices, positions, and employments, according to their capacity, and without other distinction than that of virtues and talents.

7. No man may be accused, arrested, or detained except in the cases determined by law …

10. No one is to be disquieted because of his opinions, even religious, provided their manifestation does not disturb the public order established by law.

11. Free communication of ideas and opinions is one of the most precious of the rights of man. Consequently, every citizen may speak, write, and print freely, subject to responsibility for the abuse of such liberty in the cases determined by law. …

16. Every society in which the guarantee of rights is not assured or the separation of powers not determined has no constitution at all. (cited in Kramnick 1995: 466–68)

Separation of Church and State?

In eighteenth-century North America, the landscape of religious practice was extremely complex. A vast number of sects and denominations, some of which were concentrated geographically in particular states or regions, peppered the colonies. While only eight of the 13 colonies had an official or established state religion, all had some form of explicit or implicit system whereby distinctions were made on the basis of one's religious affiliation. Such discrimination in some cases prevented individuals from taking public office or voting if they did not practice the approved religion, and in other cases took the form of tax benefits and other financial incentives for those who did. While most Americans were 'largely free of direct penalties on religion' after the American War of Independence in 1776, there remained in most states legal evidence of privileges available to those who practiced state-supported religions (Hamburger 2002: 90; Witte 2005: 101) (Figure 15).

In this climate of explicit and implicit religious discrimination, those who dissented from their state-supported religion argued fiercely for religious liberty, which was the right to practice one's spiritual faith without reprisal or recrimination. They argued that the state, in short, should not favor one religion over another, nor should the state intervene in preventing the practice of any faith. However, this demand for religious liberty was not equivalent to demanding separation of church and state. On the contrary, most people readily accepted a moral or spiritual dimension to government and were anxious that religious liberty would allow all churches to flourish and have the opportunity to influence state affairs.[13] The general sentiment was that there could—and should—be alliances and collaboration between states and churches.

David Holmes, in *The Faiths of the Founding Fathers* (2006), has argued that the founding fathers represented a range of perspectives on and allegiances to religion and in so doing reflected the various sentiments of the early colonial period (see also Waldman 2009). Each figure was in some way associated with the established churches of his colony. Church attendance was a necessary part of colonial life, and certainly a precondition for anyone with political ambitions. That being said, there is no doubt that men such as Benjamin Franklin, George

---

[13]   The assumption is that churches in this context were Christian. Supporters of religious liberty did not extend the concept to incorporate Jews, Muslims, Hindus or atheists.

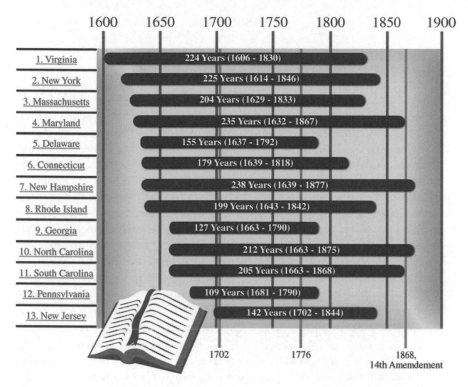

Figure 15. Time between original colonial charter and the end of state-supported religion. © ProCon.org, a 501c3 nonprofit charity online at www.procon.org (image accessed 15 August 2009).

Washington and Thomas Jefferson were deists. Deism enabled these men to find a spiritual justification for the break with mother England and its deeply entrenched class system, and allowed them to think creatively in political terms regarding the idea of a new American government based on the concepts of equality and religious tolerance. In short, deism was important in its confluence with the nurturing and emergence of new political ideas in the 13 colonies. According to Holmes, 'Deism influenced, in one way or another, most of the political leaders who designed the new American government' (Holmes 2006: 50–51).

The central concern, then, of deists and the vast numbers of other religious dissenters was to ensure religious liberty, not the separation of church and state. As Hamburger argues, the concept of a separation or wall between church and state simply did not make sense to the majority of Americans in the latter part of the eighteenth century. Moreover, he notes, support for the concept of separation was most often used as a slur and accusation against one's enemies (Hamburger 2002: 66).

CONCLUSION

In recent decades, driven by the politicizing of evangelicalism in the United States, there has been much debate about whether the country was founded as a 'Christian nation', or upon more secular ideologies (Walters 1992; Ellis 2005; DL Holmes 2006; Lambert 2006; Novack and Novack 2007; Waldman 2009). Today's evangelicals and conservatives are anxious to claim the founding fathers as their own, despite the fact that none of the founding fathers were in fact evangelical (Holmes 2006: 31, 165). This controversy over whether the United States was created as a 'Christian nation' has in turn raised a secondary question of whether the founding fathers were Christian in their personal beliefs. One of the problems in this secondary discussion is a rather simplistic and naive presentation of deists as non-Christian, as if the two positions were mutually exclusive. While it may be hard for us to understand today, many deists during the revolutionary and early republican period, despite criticizing formalized church religion, would nonetheless have considered themselves Christian, albeit in an unorthodox sense. For instance, Jefferson, openly condemned by the Federalists in the late 1790s for his deist position and tolerance of religious pluralism, wrote about his religious belief in a letter to Benjamin Rush, dated 1803:

> ... I then promised you, one day or other, I would give you my views of it [religion]. They are a result of a life of inquiry and reflection, and very different from the anti-Christian system imputed to me by those who know nothing of my opinions. To the corruptions of Christianity I am, indeed, opposed; but not to the genuine precepts of Jesus himself. I am a Christian, in the only sense he wished any one to be; sincerely attached to his doctrines, in preference to all others ... (cited in Kramnick 1995: 163)

Deists and other religious dissenters in late eighteenth-century North America all desired religious liberty, but not all of them supported the concept of separation of church and state. The conceptual distinction between religious liberty and separation of church and state is difficult for twenty-first-century readers, particularly those immersed in a mythic American history of separation written into the Constitution under the First Amendment. The idea of separation of church and state has assumed iconic stature, and many consider it to be emblematic of US democracy and freedom. However, if one examines the public debates and discussions in Congress at the time (Witte 2005: 71–106), listens to the words of James Madison in his presentation of the constitutional amendments to Congress (Hamburger 2002: 105), and reads the First Amendment carefully, separation does not appear to have been the original intention of the writers of the Bill of Rights when they wrote, 'Congress shall make no law respecting an establishment of religion, or prohibiting the free exercise thereof ...'. According to Hamburger:

> The religious dissenters who participated in the campaign against establishment and whose claims seem to have affected the wording of the constitutional guarantees against establishments made demands for religious liberty that limited civil government,

especially civil legislation, rather than for a religious liberty conceived as a separation of church and state. Moreover, in attempting to prohibit the civil legislation that would establish religion, they sought to preserve the power of government to legislate on religion in other ways. Accordingly, American constitutions, whether those of the states or that of the United States, said nothing about separation. Nor should this be a surprise. ... Instead, these dissenters typically sought constitutional limitations on the power of government, particularly on government's power to legislate an establishment (Hamburger 2002: 107).

Throughout his writings, Paine argued vehemently for the separation of church and state—to remedy what he, and others, called an 'adulterous connection' (Hamburger 2002: 27–28). Drawing upon his unwavering belief in religious tolerance, Paine argued that only with such a separation could all religions be practiced openly without state intervention or coercion. However, it is not clear that Paine condemned all connections between church and state. Like many religious dissenters in America, Paine attacked established churches backed by state governments. And what he was arguing for was religious liberty—the ability to practice one's spirituality without fear of fine or punishment, or denial of employment and other resources granted to citizens who did practice state religion. Paine may have gone further than most religious dissenters in either England or America in calling for separation of church and state institutions. However, his argument for separation was not widely supported and had dropped out of public conversation by the late 1790s.

In the context of the United States, the concept of separation of church and state was not widely endorsed until the nineteenth century, when it became— amongst other things—a symbol of secular industrial society and American Protestant identity in contrast to the influx of a large Catholic immigrant population. The transformation of the idea of religious liberty of the late eighteenth century into that of separation of church and state in the nineteenth bolstered the image of a just and egalitarian American society that did not discriminate on the basis of religion. This popular idea of American society as an inclusive 'melting pot' implied that the rule of law operated in a rarified atmosphere of objectivity and universality, beyond the reaches of religious intervention. That politics and lawmaking remained highly influenced by and influential in matters of religion—despite the concept of separation—is picked up in the next chapter on slavery, where in the United States and Britain racial injustice and the denial of legal rights to black Africans were to a large degree justified on the basis that they were non-Christian.

Recommended Reading

Gay, Peter (1968) *The Enlightenment: An Interpretation: The Science of Freedom*. New York: WW Norton.

Hamburger, Philip (2002) *Separation of Church and State*. Cambridge, MA: Harvard University Press.

Hitchens, Christopher (2006) *Thomas Paine's Rights of Man*. New York: Atlantic Monthly Press.

Holmes, David L (2006) *The Faiths of the Founding Fathers*. Oxford: Oxford University Press.

Holmes, Richard (2009) *The Age of Wonder: How the Romantic Generation Discovered the Beauty and Terror of Science*. New York: Pantheon.

Kaye, Harvey J (2005) *Thomas Paine and the Promise of America*. New York: Hill and Wang.

Kramnick, Isaac (ed) (1995) *The Portable Enlightenment Reader*. New York; Penguin.

Locke, John (1690) *An Essay Concerning Human Understanding*. Oxford: Clarendon Press (1924).

Nelson, Craig (2006) *Thomas Paine: Enlightenment, Revolution, and the Birth of Modern Nations*. New York: Penguin.

Paine, Thomas (2007) *The Thomas Paine Reader*. Radford, VA: Wilder Publications.

Porter, Roy (2000) *The Creation of the Modern World: The Untold Story of the British Enlightenment*. New York: WW Norton.

Waldman, Steven (2009) *Founding Faith: How Our Founding Fathers Forged a Radical New Approach to Religious Liberty*. New York: Random House.

Witte, John Jr (2005, 2nd edn) *Religion and the American Constitutional Experiment*. Boulder, CO: Westview.

II

Capitalism, Colonialism and Nationalism

4

Sugar, Slaves, Rebellion, Murder (1865)

WITH ITS TROPICAL climate, sparkling beaches and misty blue mountain peaks, Jamaica is considered a most desirable tourist destination. As the largest English-speaking island in the Caribbean, Jamaica annually attracts thousands of leisure-seekers to its sandy shores. Most tourists visiting the island are unaware of its bloody and violent history—of the Spanish decimation of its native Arawak population in the seventeenth century and the British importation and massacre of African slaves brought to the island to work the sugar plantations in the eighteenth and nineteenth centuries.

The legal landmark explored in this chapter revolves around the Morant Bay ex-slave riot of 1865, and the retaliatory British massacre on the island colony of Jamaica in the British West Indies. Hundreds of black Jamaicans were killed by soldiers as they rampaged through the countryside, and another 354 were tried under martial law and summarily executed. An additional 600 men and women were flogged and tortured, and over a thousand homes were burnt to the ground. The Jamaican Governor, Edward John Eyre, was brought back to England in August 1866 and put on trial for his excesses in dealing with the rebellion, and in particular for his involvement in the court martial and execution of a Jamaican mulatto called George William Gordon. The trial is considered a legal landmark because it forced British society to engage with how it should officially and legally treat ex-slaves.[1] Up to this point, British citizens had largely been insulated from the realities of colonial rule and oppression of native peoples. Even after events such as the Indian Mutiny of 1857, in which 100,000 Indians died, the English did not typically engage with why such atrocities occurred, or what they suggested about colonial control. Most people were satisfied to leave the actual mechanics of colonial rule to the Colonial Office and its overseas governors. However, the

---

[1] The case of *Phillips v Eyre* (1870) LR 6 QB 1 also set a legal precedent regarding the criteria that must be satisfied in order to sue a person in England for a tort committed outside the country in a British colony. Very simply, the act in question must be actionable both in England and in the place where it was committed. Before Eyre left Jamaica to return to England, he passed an Act that made his actions under martial law legal. As a result the court held that he could not be later charged in England.

Eyre controversy dramatically brought the harsh realities of colonialism into England's domestic arena. The controversy set family members against each other, and fostered conflict among eminent scientists, intellectuals, and England's two foremost judges.

While the Jamaican uprising and massacre was very much a British imperial affair, the ensuing controversy cannot be disentangled from concurrent events in the United States. The Morant Bay riot occurred only six months after the end of the American Civil War in April 1865. The bloody battles that had divided the American North from South over four long years, the assassination of President Lincoln, and the difficulties encountered in accommodating an emancipated slave population in the reconstruction era, featured in the minds of many British people. Unlike the United States, Britain did not experience a civil war over the issue of slavery. Nonetheless it was—in many ways similar to the United States—a country politically and socially divided along the lines of those who argued for racial equality and those who fundamentally believed in the inferiority of non-whites. As one historian has noted, the Eyre controversy in Britain represented an 'intellectual civil war' (Dutton 1982: 126).

The Morant Bay riot raises many historical questions: Why did Jamaica's black peasantry, who had been emancipated from slavery in 1838 under the Slavery Abolition Act (1833), suddenly rise up 30 years later and strike at the British colonial government? What were the economic and social reasons for their disgruntlement? And once martial law was declared, why did British military officers react so savagely toward the African population of ex-slaves? The details of the actual events have occupied historians over the years (see Semmel 1969; Dutton 1982; Heuman 1994; Hall 2002; Evans 2005). My focus here is on Edward John Eyre's return to England in 1866 following the riot, and the subsequent three years of controversy over his actions, which were hotly debated in the British Houses of Parliament, the law courts, and popular newspapers, pamphlets and political cartoons (Figure 16).

The Eyre controversy provides a context to discuss how ex-slaves were 'managed' and treated in Anglo-American law. More specifically, it enables us to examine how discourses involving issues of religion, race, and the emerging recognition of political and civil rights as they pertained to non-whites, developed and played out in the second half of the nineteenth century. On two occasions Edward John Eyre was brought before judges and tried for the murder of George William Gordon, and in each case he was acquitted. What is fascinating are the discussions about the legal rights of British citizens in relation to the legal rights of black colonial subjects in both public debates and court decision-making (see Wiener 2009). The trials fixed on the role of British law in maintaining order and civility in a far-away colonial outpost. Among politicians, lawyers and bureaucrats, the central question was whether Eyre's imposition of

Figure 16. *Edward John Eyre,* 1867, Julia Margaret Cameron. Courtesy of National Portrait Gallery, Canberra, Australia.
Presented by Sir Roy Strong and the late Dr Julia Trevelyan Oman in memory of their friendship with Gordon Darling and Marilyn Darling 2006

martial law, which was in force for a month, was a justifiable and lawful act.[2] Was Eyre simply performing his duty as governor and colonial representative of Britain in Jamaica, or did his excessive actions speak of incompetence, compulsiveness and inhumanity?

The Eyre controversy was about much more than the legality of events, as attested to by the intense responses raised by the trial among English citizens. Issues involving religion certainly played a part—Eyre was attacked as being ungodly and unchristian, especially by Baptists and other non-conformist religious members who were both outraged by the death of black Baptists and

---

[2] Martial law is the temporary military takeover of civilian law enforcement. It typically involves the suspension of a number of rights, including the right to habeas corpus, the right to legal counsel, and the right to a verdict by a jury of peers. Once martial law is lifted, it is presumed that a reinstated civilian court cannot try actions committed under martial law. However, as Rande Kostal argues with respect to martial law in the 1860s, amongst English lawyers the definition of martial law was not clear, hence much of the confusion over the term throughout the debates during the Eyre controversy (Kostal 2005: 9).

anxious to denounce Eyre's self-righteous Anglicanism. Race played an even bigger role than religion; despite race not being openly discussed in the parliamentary debates and law courts, racism was clearly at the heart of the matter. It must be remembered that at this time in Jamaica ex-slaves outnumbered whites by 30 to one. According to the 1861 census, there were 13,816 white, 81,065 brown, and 346,374 black people living in Jamaica (Evans 2005: 171 fn 2). The question, then, was this: to what extent could martial law be justified—and the death of innocent blacks deemed acceptable—when there was a very real threat to white people? More generally, what should be done with a population of ex-slaves who were demanding civil and political rights equal to British citizens, but who were still considered by mainstream English society to be socially and culturally inferior? And the intelligentsia of mid-Victorian England were troubled by a further question: how could one uphold British law as the embodiment of western democracy and freedom when the ultimate result of applying law was the enduring suppression, and in some cases unwarranted death, of non-white communities?

The Triangular Slave Trade

The slave and sugar cane trades were both well established in the Roman Empire; sugar plantations were distributed around the Mediterranean and slave trading was concentrated in Iberia and along the northwest coast of Africa. Until the early sixteenth century, both sugar and slave economies were limited by a lack of agricultural land and access to large labor pools. However, with the Portuguese and Spanish discovery and colonization of the New World, and the later entry of the British into the Caribbean, this all changed significantly. The transatlantic triangular trading route became firmly established in the late seventeenth century, and the number of exported slaves and the production of sugar cane increased substantially (Mintz 1986; Figure 17). According to scholar and former prime minister of Trinidad and Tobago, Eric Williams, in his famous 1944 book *Capitalism and Slavery*:

> In this triangular trade England—France and Colonial America equally—supplied the exports and the ships; Africa the human merchandise; the plantations the colonial raw materials. The slave ship sailed from the home country with a cargo of manufactured goods. These were exchanged at a profit on the coast of Africa for Negroes, who were traded on the plantations, at another profit, in exchange for a cargo of colonial produce to be taken back to the home country. ... The West Indian islands became the hub of the British Empire, of immense importance to the grandeur and prosperity of England. It was the Negro slaves who made these sugar colonies the most precious colonies ever recorded in the whole annals of imperialism. (Williams 1944: 51–52; 53–84, 98–107)

Throughout the eighteenth century, sugar production exploded in the French and British colonies in the West Indies, driven by the changing dietary habits of

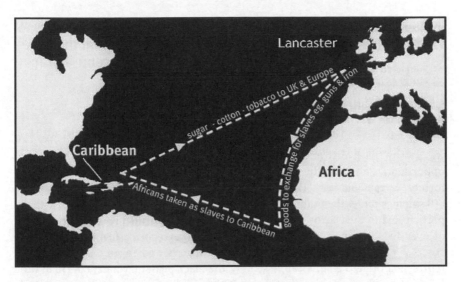

Figure 17. The triangle slave trade was a very effective system whereby Africans were enslaved and shipped from Africa to the Caribbean and the east coast of North America. There the ships were loaded with products produced by slave labor, such as cotton, tobacco, rum, sugar and coffee, and sailed to England and European ports. Having unloaded these goods, the ships were filled with European products such as guns, cloth, pots, pans, alcohol and other goods used to purchase enslaved Africans on the southern leg of the journey. Map produced by Mike Ely (kasamaproject.org).

many Europeans and the increasing consumption of sugar in tea and coffee, as well as a range of jams, jellies and chocolates. Average consumption in Britain 'rose from four pounds per head in 1700 to eighteen pounds in 1800' (Ponting 2000: 698; see Mintz 1986). The sugar production colonies required huge numbers of laborers to work the sugarcane fields, and millions of Africans were shipped to the British West Indian islands throughout the eighteenth century. It is estimated that four million slaves were sent to Jamaica alone (Williams 1994).

However, in the later years of the eighteenth century sugar exports to Britain dropped as cheaper sugar from India and Cuba cut into the Jamaican market. The Napoleonic Wars between 1803 and 1815 further disrupted foreign shipments. Jamaica's economy slumped and sugar began to stockpile at its ports. Williams notes: 'In 1806 the surplus of sugar in England amounted to six thousand tons. Production had to be curtailed. To restrict production, the slave trade must be abolished. ... The war and Bonaparte's continental blockade made abolition imperative if the older colonies were to survive' (Williams 1994: 149, 150). Somewhat ironically, abolition was widely supported by many West Indian planters and plantation owners, who saw it is a way out of their economic woes.

However, abolition did not bring the planters economic good fortune, nor did the emancipation of slaves have the desired effect of liberating blacks from oppression.

Jamaican Rebellion

In October 1865 a bloody uprising took place in Jamaica: the Morant Bay riot was led by black African peasants who, as ex-slaves, were tired of the limited opportunities afforded them by the ruling white and mulatto elite. Theoretically former slaves could vote. However, since voting required payment of a high fee (10 shillings under the Franchise Act of 1859), in reality very few freemen actually participated in the electoral process. In the elections of 1864, out of a population of over 400,000, only 2,000 people voted and, apart from a few mulattos, these voters were white. Starving, forced to pay harsh taxes, and angered by their lack of representation in the Jamaican Assembly, the black peasantry hatched a plan for a rebellion and began to mobilize forces. This mobilization was carried out largely through black Baptist connections and parish networks (see Heuman 1994; Gordon 1998; Evans 2005: 130–32).

The disgruntled peasants used a specific event to trigger the rebellion. Led by Paul Bogle, a Baptist Deacon (Figure 18), around 200 people marched on the town of Morant Bay. Ostensibly they were protesting against the earlier arrest of a black man who had been charged with trespassing on abandoned land. Bogle and 27 others rescued the man, who was being held by soldiers, and warrants were promptly issued for their arrest for assaulting police and rioting. Bogle and his followers then decided to march on Morant Bay, attack the police station and grab arms, and make their way to the courthouse where a meeting of officials was taking place.

> The crowd that day was unlike any other which has ever made its way to Morant Bay ... Only a small number had guns, but most of the others had either sharpened sticks or cutlasses. The crowd was also highly organized; the men marched four abreast, with the women on their flanks. As one observer noted, they 'came in rows ... they were well packed together close behind each other, but not at all straggling: they advanced slowly and deliberately'. Though dressed in ordinary laborers' clothes, they looked more like troops than like an irregular mob. ... Even more menacing was the statement of the leading members of the crowd. As they passed by the druggist's shop on the way into town, they knelt down and tasted some dirt and swore 'we will kill every white and Mulatto man in the Bay, and when we finish, we will return and go to the estates'. (cited in Heuman 1994: 3–40)

As Bogle and the crowd reached the Morant Bay courthouse, a local group of militia panicked and opened fire, killing seven blacks. The crowd retaliated, killing 18 whites, including the chief magistrate, and wounding another 30, most of whom were white. The rebels then took control of the town and were joined by

Figure 18. Paul Bogle, c 1865. Courtesy of the Jamaica Historical Society.

more peasants. Over the following days general chaos ensued; two white plantation owners were killed and properties were set alight.

In an effort to suppress the uprising, Governor Edward John Eyre, in consultation with the Jamaican Assembly, imposed martial rule. Lawlessness and terror reigned. Over the course of a month hundreds of blacks were killed and many more were tortured and flogged. George William Gordon, a mulatto member of the Jamaican House of Assembly and as an open supporter of emancipated blacks a long-time enemy of Eyre, was deliberately taken from Kingston to Morant Bay, where he would be subject to martial law. Two days after his court martial, he was executed.[3] This execution occurred despite there being no legal evidence of

---

[3] '... Gordon had been Eyre's longtime opponent in the public arena. In the Assembly, he dismissed Eyre as "groveling, pretentious, and prevaricating" and communicated his opinion of the governor to the Anti-Slavery Society in Britain. Although born a slave, Gordon was freed by his wealthy planter father, married an Irish woman and pursued a career in business and politics with

Gordon's involvement in the rebellion. As news of the uprising filtered back to England, there was widespread horror at what had apparently transpired on the ill-fated colonial island. According to the reports of Eyre's officers:

> I found a number of special constables, who had captured a number of prisoners from the rebel camp. Finding their guilt clear, and being unable to either take or leave them, I had them all shot. The constables then hung them up on trees—eleven in number. (Colonel Hobbs, cited in Semmel 1969: 14)

> Within a mile of us every black man who did not stand at our approach to give an account of himself was shot … I am of the opinion that upwards of sixty rebels were killed yesterday by the troops under my command. (Captain Hole, cited in Semmel 1969: 15)

> On returning to Golden Grove in the evening, sixty-seven prisoners had been sent in … I disposed of [shot] as many as possible, but was too tired to continue after dark … (Lieutenant Adcock, cited in Semmel 1969: 15)

> We made a raid of thirty men; flogging nine men and burning their negro houses. We held a court martial on the prisoners, who amounted to about fifty or sixty. Several were flogged without court martial, from a simple examination. (Captain Ford, cited in Semmel 1969: 15)

RELIGION: THE 'DIVINE INSTITUTION' OF SLAVERY

News of the atrocities and excessive use of violence on Jamaican blacks, many of them women and children, polarized English society. The two resultant camps produced coalitions representing a variety of religious, economic and political interests. However it was religious groups, many from non-conformist evangelical denominations such as Baptists, Quakers, Methodists and Unitarians, that first led the charge against Eyre, calling for his immediate removal from office. Not only were members of these non-conformist groups heavily involved in anti-slavery activism, the Baptist missionaries in particular were outraged that Eyre had acted with such violence against their new black Christian converts. As Catherine Hall points out, Baptists had a long-standing involvement in Jamaica and considered their missionary work there to be extremely important (Hall 2002; see also Gordon 1998).

Representing one side of the Eyre controversy was the Jamaica Committee, established in December 1865 shortly after news of the events in Jamaica was printed in the London newspapers. The Committee's specific agenda was to call for the resignation of Eyre and to have him put on trial for murder. The Committee included leading liberal intellectuals and political economists such as John Stuart Mill, scientists Charles Darwin and Thomas Huxley, politicians

mixed success. In the 1860s, as Eyre discovered, Gordon's politics became increasingly radical and his advocacy for the poverty-stricken was known throughout Jamaica. … He was re-elected to the Assembly in 1863 with the support of small settlers and Native Baptists' (Evans 2005: 134–35).

Thomas Hughes and Peter Taylor, as well as a variety of professors and members of the clergy (Figure 19). It mainly represented the interests of middle-class philanthropists, humanitarians and liberals. Many of its members belonged to the British and Foreign Anti-Slavery Society, which upon hearing of the atrocities perpetrated on black Jamaicans sent a delegation of 250 people to the Colonial Secretary demanding Eyre's immediate removal from office. A few days later a delegation from the London Missionary Society also called upon the Colonial Secretary demanding Eyre's suspension (Semmel 1969: 22). These liberal protestations were joined by mass demonstrations of working-class people, who empathized with the poor labor conditions of black Jamaicans.

Jamaica Committee	Eyre Defence Committee
John Stuart Mill	Thomas Carlyle
Charles Darwin	John Ruskin
Thomas Huxley	Charles Dickens
Herbert Spencer	Rev. Charles Kingsley
John Bright	Alfred Lord Tennyson
Thomas Hughes	

Figure 19. Leading Public Figures in the Jamaica Committee and Eyre Defence Committee

Representing the other side of the controversy was the Eyre Defence Committee, which supported Eyre and his use of martial law, arguing that it was necessary to bring about a swift restoration of order in Jamaica. The Defence Committee was led by Thomas Carlyle, who was joined by other leading writers of the time including John Ruskin, Charles Dickens and Alfred Lord Tennyson. Also on the Defence Committee were John Tyndall, a physicist and close friend of Huxley, and Lord Elcho, who opposed electoral reform. In very general terms, the Defence Committee represented the views of the established Anglican church (Governor Eyre was a devout Anglican) as well as the political position of Tory conservatives. It was associated with the opinions of the imperial elite, who above all else worshipped law and order, and were intent on maintaining the status quo. These members were fearful of mass demonstrations and the threat of mob violence, and anxiously repressed calls for legal reform, be they at home by working-class laborers or in overseas colonies by Irishmen, natives or emancipated slaves.[4]

---

[4] 'The Eyre Defence Fund eventually listed among its contributors seventy-one peers, six bishops, twenty MPs, forty generals, twenty-six admirals, four hundred clergymen, and thirty thousand other individuals'. In contrast, the Jamaica Committee, reflecting its working-class appeal, 'eventually mustered over 800 members, but it could whip up crowds of over 10,000' (Dutton 1982: 115).

The Eyre controversy split English society according to whether or not one supported the emancipation of slaves *and* the granting of civil and political rights to blacks.[5] Many members of the non-conformist religious groups who rushed to publicly condemn Eyre had been instrumental in the British and American anti-slavery movement throughout the later decades of the eighteenth century and into the first half of the nineteenth century. The relationship between evangelical thinking and anti-slavery activism is significant.

> Not that all anti-slavery people were evangelicals—they were not … But evangelicals' world-view and theology created an especially conducive mental context for anti-slavery action. Many abolitionists believed themselves to be the 'righteous remnant' of the evangelical tradition. The preacher's insistence on immediate repentance of sin became a model for abolitionists' demands for immediate repentance of slaveholding. The strenuous pursuit of a holy life became a metaphor, or perhaps more accurately, a prescription for reform activity. The patterns of thought, the norms of behavior, the earnestness of moral exertion, the legitimating experience of the indwelling of the Holy Spirit—all shaped the mental-moral context within which abolitionists sallied forth to battle with slavery. (Mathews 1980: 209)

As discussed in the previous chapter, Thomas Paine published the first American pamphlet condemning slavery in 1775 in Philadelphia and that same year joined the Society for the Relief of Free Negros Unlawfully Held In Bondage, an abolitionist group made up primarily of Quakers. The first British abolitionist group was formed a few years later in 1783 by a group of people, again mostly Quakers, who drew up a petition seeking to stop British involvement in the trafficking and sale of slaves in the British colonies, particularly in the West Indies (Hochschild 2005; Davis 2006: 231–49). These early abolitionists were influenced by a range of ideas circulating in England about non-European peoples, such as those published by Captain James Cook in his journals on his first Pacific voyage on the ship *The Endeavour* (1768–71). Cook, an exceptional navigator and famous for his advancement of knowledge of latitude and longitude (Richardson 2005), expressed genuine interest in and generosity toward the indigenous peoples of Tahiti and the eastern coast of Australia (see Aughton 2002; Collingridge 2003). British abolitionists were also influenced by French Enlightenment philosophers such as Diderot, who in his *Supplement to Bougainville's Voyage* (1772) angrily condemned colonialism and the enslavement of native peoples. Writing a fictional account of the French explorer Bougainville's arrival in Tahiti from the perspective of a native leader, Diderot wrote:

> The Tahitian you want to seize like a wild animal is your brother. … what right have you over him that he has not over you? When you came, did we rush upon you, did we pillage your ship? Did we seize you and expose you to the arrows of our enemies? Did

---

[5] A person can—at least in theory—support the end of slavery, but remain profoundly racist in his or her actual dealings with minority peoples. In short, there is a distinction between showing charity toward others on the one hand, and recognizing a person's inalienable legal rights to freedom, vote, own property, etc on the other.

we yoke you with the animals for toil in our fields? No. We respected our own likeness in you. Leave us to our ways; they are wiser and more honest than yours. We do not want to barter what you call ignorance [in us] for your useless civilization. (cited in Kramnick 1995: 641)

While many Quakers responded warmly to the ideas of Diderot and other French *philosophes*, they were prevented from exercising much influence in political circles. This was because in Britain during this period Quakers were considered religious dissenters and so were prohibited from participating in parliament, and barred from the professions and universities (Davis 2006: 233). Therefore it was men such as the Anglican evangelical William Wilberforce who led the parliamentary campaign against the transatlantic slave trade and was instrumental in establishing the Committee for the Abolition of the Slave Trade in 1787.

Gradually, as a result of the promotion of anti-slavery ideas through the distribution of pamphlets, holding of church meetings, signing of petitions, publication of tracts and related books such as the ex-slave Equiano's autobiography,[6] a network of abolitionist groups sprung up across the country (for an excellent account of this movement see Hochschild 2005). These groups reflected the rise of popular sentiment supporting the idea of a universal family of mankind, in which blacks and whites could be considered brothers and sisters. This sentiment was strongly felt among members of all social classes of British society, many of whom demonstrated their support for the abolition movement by refusing to buy sugar imported from West Indian slave colonies (Walvin 1980: 152). The humanizing of slaves was visually reinforced by the well-known potter and designer, Josiah Wedgwood, who produced a popular 'slave medallion' depicting a kneeling slave in chains surrounded by the motto 'Am I not a man and a Brother'. Throughout the 1790s these ceramic medallions were distributed in the thousands, and the image was further promoted as a fashionable decoration on hat pins, cameo brooches and snuff boxes. Wedgwood also sent crates of the cameos to Benjamin Franklin in Philadelphia to help him in his anti-slavery efforts in the United States.

The popularity of Wedgwood's cameos and hat pins underscores another important aspect of the anti-slavery movement. For the first time many women were actively engaged in political debate and activism, 'and found in the abolition movement a valid way to engage in the nation's public life' (Cooper 1996: 196). More specifically, since some women regarded the subjugation of women by men

---

[6] The widespread appeal of abolitionism was nurtured by, and reflected in, the enormous interest in the autobiography of the ex-slave Olaudah Equiano. Equiano published his book *The Interesting Narrative of the Life of Olaudah Equiano or Gustavus Vassa the African* in 1789, whereupon it was quickly reprinted. In the book, Equiano tells of his kidnapping from his Nigerian village and his subsequent subjection to multiple horrors as a slave on a Virginia plantation. The autobiography was extremely effective in underscoring the inhumanity of slavery and promoting the anti-slavery movement (Carretta 2005).

as analogous to the subjugation of slaves by masters, promoting ideas of equality and sisterhood spoke to the hope of reforming the subordinate position of women in English life (Midgley 1995).

A 'Divine Institution'

One of the core agendas of the anti-slavery movement was to fight the assumption that slavery was sanctioned in the bible. This assumption was particularly prevalent among North American pro-slavery advocates, who often referred to slavery as a 'divine institution' and the separation of the races as 'ordained by God'. Accordingly, these pro-slavery advocates held that the relationship between slave and master was morally acceptable and legal in the sense that it was divinely sanctioned. Moreover, it was argued, slaves should be grateful since their servitude provided a means by which they could be introduced to the gospel, become Christian, and ultimately have their 'heathen' souls saved (Buswell 1964: 5–18).

John Campbell, an historian and member of the Social Improvement Society of Philadelphia, wrote a treatise in 1851 called *Negro-Mania: Examination of the Falsely Assumed Equality of the Various Races of Men*. In this manifesto, Campbell outlined the reasons why it was ludicrous to think of all men as being equal. Whilst stating in his introduction that he was neither for nor against slavery, nonetheless all of Campbell's arguments supported the notion that whites were superior to blacks and the idea that whites were 'naturally' more intelligent than blacks, as evidenced by their never having been enslaved. In support of his argument about the obvious physical and intellectual advantages of whites, Campbell referred to the scriptures as evidence of God's will in making all men not equal.

> Why all this rant about Negro equality, seeing that neither nature or nature's God ever established such equality? ... The manifest moral intellectual and physical inferiority of the Negro issues from the decree of God which no efforts of many can either alter or abrogate. Even modification must be but partial at least. It is the destiny of the Negro if by himself to be a savage; if by the white to be a serf.

Campbell was not alone in his view that God made men unequal. A few years later, in 1853, Arthur de Gobineau wrote *An Essay on the Inequality of the Human Races* which supported Campbell's argument that God had made white men superior. Five years later, Thomas R Cobb wrote *An Inquiry Into the Law of Negro Slavery in the United States of America*, arguing that God had ordained black inferiority so that blacks could be most suited to the lowliest of work:

> The Great Architect had framed them [negroes] both physically and mentally to fill the sphere in which they were thrown, and His wisdom and mercy combined in constituting them thus suited to the degraded position they were destined to occupy. Hence their submissiveness, their obedience, their contentment.

To counter the use of the bible as a justification for slavery, anti-slavery activists also turned to scripture to point out God's love for all people and the dignity of humanity regardless of color or race. Referring to imagery such as God's family and a united brotherhood, anti-slavery advocates often drew on Luke and Isaiah. For instance, Robert Robinson, a radical English Baptist minister, preached a sermon entitled *Slavery Inconsistent with the Spirit of Christianity* in which he declared to his congregation in 1788 that religion should be used to subvert the system of slavery (Robinson 1788). This view was famously taken up and expressed in the United States by Frederick Douglas, who wrote that not only was slavery contrary to Christian teachings, the church had been actively involved in perpetrating 'this horrible blasphemy'. In 1852, as the northern abolitionists began to gain political momentum, Douglas damningly wrote in an essay entitled *The Meaning of July Fourth for the Negro*:

> But the church of this country is not only indifferent to the wrongs of the slave, it actually takes sides with the oppressors. It has made itself the bulwark of American slavery, and the shield of American slave-hunters. Many of its most eloquent Divines, who stand as the very lights of the church, have shamelessly given the sanction of religion and the Bible to the whole slave system. They have taught that man may, properly, be a slave; that the relation of master and slave is ordained by God; that to send back an escaped bondman to his master is clearly the duty of all the followers of the Lord Jesus Christ; and this horrible blasphemy is palmed off upon the world for Christianity.

In Britain, unlike the United States, there were few African slaves.[7] Moreover, slave labor was not essential to the nation's economy as it was in the American colonies, particularly in the southern plantation states. Certainly some British merchants profited greatly from the slave trade, but the country's wealth was not based on a slave economy and as a result there was more open debate about the plight of slaves. Aiding the British anti-slavery movement was the legal system. Unlike in the United States, in Britain in the latter part of the eighteenth century slaves were not considered legal chattels or property that could be bought and sold (Figure 20). This basic legal principle, established in the 1772 *Somerset* case—that under common law slaves were not regarded as property and therefore the practice of owning slaves was illegal—promoted an intellectual and emotional environment in Britain that could more readily respond to calls denouncing the slave trade.[8] In material terms this meant that the prohibition of the slave trade in Britain did not necessitate the disavowal of anyone's property rights or raise the problem of monetary compensation, as it would in the American colonies. It also meant that slaves bought in other jurisdictions were not recognized as slaves if they were subsequently transported to Britain, further undermining the economic incentives for owning slaves.

---

[7]   In the 1770s in London it is estimated that approximately 3% of the population were black, and most of them were slaves (Wise 2005: 8). For a visual account of blacks in English society, see Dabydeen 1987.

[8]   For a marvelous account of the Somerset case see Steven Wise's *Though the Heavens May Fall: The Landmark Trial that Led to the End of Human Slavery* (2005).

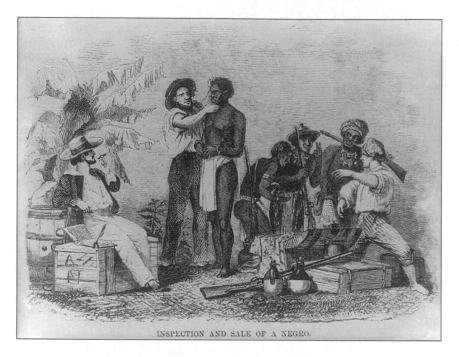

INSPECTION AND SALE OF A NEGRO.

Figure 20. *An African man being inspected for sale into slavery while a white man talks with African slave traders, 1854.* This engraving appeared in the detailed account of a former slave ship captain, Theodore Canot. The book was entitled *Captain Canot: Twenty Years of an African Slaver,* edited by Brantz Mayer, and was published in New York in 1854. © Library of Congress Prints and Photographs Division Washington, DC. Reproduction Number: LC-USZ62–15392.

Given no obvious legal impediment to the dismantling of the slave trade, coupled with the widespread religious and secular appeal of the anti-slavery movement, the British parliament passed the Slave Trade Act in 1807 which made it illegal to participate in the slave trade anywhere in the Empire. However, it was not until the 1820s with the establishment of the Anti-Slavery Society and the rekindling of public interest that the institution of slavery itself was to be condemned. In 1833 the Slavery Abolition Act was passed, which mandated that after a period of apprenticeship had been served, all slaves in Britain and the British colonies must be set free.

Emancipation in Jamaica

In Jamaica, the Slavery Abolition Act of 1833 did not come into full force until 1838 as a result of pressure from British anti-slavery groups on plantation owners to declare slave apprenticeships over and blacks officially free. With the help of resettlement loans to ex-slaves provided by the British and Foreign Anti-Slavery

Society, most blacks left the plantations of their former masters, who had paid them minimal wages for their labor. These ex-slaves took up small land-holdings in the Jamaican hills in an attempt to live off the land out of reach of colonial control.

To make up for the absence of labor, embittered plantation owners were forced to import 'coolies' from India, who were different from slaves in that they were supposedly indentured for a set period of time only. However, unlike Trinidad and Guiana, Jamaica did not import sufficient numbers of indentured laborers to make the plantations operable to the extent they had been prior to emancipation. As a result, sugar production dropped dramatically through the 1840s and 50s. Furthermore, the economic woes of Jamaica were compounded during this period when the preferential tariff protection on sugar produced in the British colonies was dropped. In accordance with laissez-faire free market economic theory, the Sugar Equalization Duties Act of 1851 was introduced. This Act determined that sugar could be imported to Britain from anywhere in the world at competitive prices. Therefore sugar produced in Brazil and Cuba—which continued to enjoy cheap slave labor—as well as a rise in the use of European beet-sugar, meant that the sugar monopoly formerly enjoyed by Jamaica and other British colonies was over.

Adding to the economic decline was Jamaica's political mismanagement. Unlike most of the British colonial islands, at the time of the Morant Bay riot Jamaica was not a Crown colony but operated under a charter of self-government. This meant that Governor Eyre had in effect very little political power; most power lay almost exclusively in the corrupt and disorderly Assembly made up of white and mulatto plantation owners and merchants. The Assembly had no coherent financial policy. In the face of such problems as drought, the rising cost of imports, declining production and sale of sugar, and the necessity of building new roads and infrastructure, the Assembly's response was simply to raise taxes. This infuriated the black peasantry, who were already hard pressed to make ends meet. To make matters worse, fulfillment of the promise of a black franchise and representation in the Assembly became increasingly remote. Assembly members were anxious to retain their economic and political control, and so it was conveniently determined that non-representation was the fault of the ex-slaves since 'the people at large are not sufficiently educated to have opinions on public affairs' (cited in Evans 2005: 119).

Debating the 'Negro Question' in Jamaica

The economic collapse of Jamaica and the freeing of its slaves were addressed by Thomas Carlyle, a Scottish historian and prominent intellectual in Victorian England. Carlyle published an essay in 1849 entitled 'Occasional Discourse on the

Negro Question' in which he evoked 'the immortal gods' and divinity as the source and authority for his writings. In this essay he damned the British and Foreign Anti-Slavery Society, sarcastically calling it the 'Sluggard and Scoundrel Protection Society'. Carlyle's acidic attack on the anti-slavery movement was motivated by his strong Calvinist work ethic, which valued the need to 'work' above all. Carlyle believed that the anti-slavery movement had helped to liberate slaves who then chose to sit in idleness and poverty, refusing to work. Accordingly, he argued that the only right a black man had was 'an indisputable and perpetual *right* to be compelled, by the real proprietors of said land, to do competent work for a living' (Carlyle 1850: 531). Not surprisingly, Carlyle claimed that under the laws of nature and the Maker who created them, 'it is the Saxon British' who are the real proprietors of Jamaica because of their hard work in making the island economically productive. Carlyle went on:

> ... till the European white man first saw them, some three short centuries ago, those islands had produced mere jungle, savagery, poison reptiles and swamp malaria until the white European first saw them, they were, as if not yet created: their noble elements of cinnamon—sugar, coffee, pepper, black and gray, lying all asleep, waiting the white Enchanter, who should say to them, awake! ... Not a square inch of soil in those fruitful isles, purchased by British blood, shall any black man hold to grow pumpkins for him, except on terms that are fair toward Britain. (Carlyle 1850: 533–35)

Carlyle argued that it was the 'unhappy wedlock' of philanthropic liberalism and laissez-faire political economic theory that had brought about the terrible demise of Jamaica. It should be noted that it was political economists such as John Stuart Mill who had strongly supported the dismantling of the colonial sugar monopolies. Mill, once friend but now public enemy of Carlyle, responded to Carlyle's attack in his essay 'The Negro Question' (1850).[9] Mill pointed out that the anti-slavery movement was not some sentimental philanthropic movement to be mocked and lampooned; rather it 'triumphed because it was the cause of justice; and in the estimation of the great majority of its supporters, of religion' (Mill 1850: 465). Mill went on to accuse Carlyle of doing the work of the devil, particularly because Carlyle provided pro-slavery advocates in North America with literary ammunition. Mill wrote, 'the owners of human flesh ... will welcome such as auxiliary' (Mill 1850: 469). Perhaps most importantly of all, Mill attacked the pseduo-scientific laws of nature that Carlyle invoked to endorse his racist attitudes. In the words of Carlyle, blacks will have to be servants 'to those that are born wiser than you, that are born lords of you'. In response, Mill wrote that Carlyle had made 'the vulgar error of imputing every difference which he finds among human beings to an original difference of nature' (Mill 1850: 468).

[9] The story goes that in 1835 Mill's maid accidentally burnt the first volume of Carlyle's three-volume *The French Revolution, A History*. Carlyle went on to write volumes two and three and then returned to re-write the first volume from memory (Cummings 2004: 181). One wonders to what extent this event tainted their friendship.

This critique of natural law is significant. Carlyle's essay 'Occasional Discourse on the Negro Question' makes one of the first references to scientific racism, reflecting a shift in public debate about the relationship between blacks and whites. As noted by the historian Catherine Hall, Carlyle's essay 'marked the moment when it became legitimate for public men to profess a belief in the essential inferiority of black people, and to claim that they were born to be mastered and could never attain the level of European civilization' (Hall 2002: 48).

As mentioned above, prior to emancipation, the concept of a universal family of mankind attracted widespread support from religious groups and philanthropic societies across British society. Brotherhood and sisterhood was the dominant rhetorical theme in the 1820s and 30s. However, with emancipation came new problems that had not been foreseen by most. In the British colonies, freed slaves were still oppressed and discriminated against and were increasingly aggressive in asserting their demands to be treated equally. 'Indeed, it was emancipation which provoked the rise of new ways of categorizing racial difference, for it raised the spectre of black peoples as free and equal' (Hall 2002: 48). As a result, from the 1840s there was 'an increasing turn to the language of race to explain and justify the inequalities and persistent differences between peoples' (Hall 2002: 339).[10]

With the early signs of a crumbling British Empire, as epitomized by the demise of the sugar colonies, old animosities and new fears surfaced to galvanize religious and political coalitions and factions across British society. On the side *against* Edward John Eyre was the evangelical, pro-abolition, liberal-minded Jamaica Committee (led by John Stuart Mill). Among these members there was concern at the failure of emancipation to establish rights for blacks. This concern was further heightened by a growing dismay at the increasing social acceptability of blatant racist talk that could be used to justify violence and discrimination. On the side *for* Eyre was the conservative and openly racist Eyre Defence Committee (led by Thomas Carlyle). Among these members there was a palpable fear of what Carlyle had called 'black anarchy'—the threat of a lawless mob that could rise up and take by force the political and civil rights that emancipation had in theory granted them (Carlyle 1850: 528).

RACE: SCIENTIFIC RACISM

In both the emancipated British colonies and during the reconstruction era in the United States, freedom did not bring ex-slaves social equality or equal legal treatment. One of the biggest hurdles in establishing equality was an increasingly

---

[10] '"[W]hen race first emerged, it was secondary to slavery, for which it furnished a justification". Following emancipation, however, the concept of race became activated as "racialization". Racialization served to *embody* discrimination, making the former legal division between Blacks and Whites [and other racialized groups] now both "absolute and natural"' (Wolfe cited in Evans 2005: 139).

entrenched ideology that non-white people were intellectually and socially infe-rior. This attitude had been voiced earlier by eighteenth century Enlightenment philosophers such as David Hume and Immanuel Kant, and repeated by men of learning such as the historian James Long, who wrote in his book *The History of Jamaica* (1774), 'We find them [negroes] marked with the same bestial manners, stupidity, and vices, which debase their brethren on the continent' (cited in Kramnick 1995: 644).

However, what made the mid-nineteenth century public discussion about race rather different from that expressed in the previous century was the use of a pseudo-scientific rationale (see Lorimer 1978). This new rhetoric, couched in the language of biology and experimentation, set out to 'prove' a hierarchy of man that positioned white Caucasian males at the top and typically indigenous Australians (who are very dark in skin tone) at the bottom. Sometimes referred to as scientific racism or social Darwinian theory, this model of mankind was very much associated with the new science of anthropology (see Gould 1996; Hobsbawm 2003: 311–14). According to most anthropologists at the time, the darker a person's skin the more removed that person was from civilized society. In this way individuals could be biologically determined as being superior or inferior, and granted the legal rights that 'naturally' correlated to their level of savagery.

Aiding this notion of a hierarchy of mankind was the theory of polygenism, which held that humans originated from different lineages.[11] Its most famous proponent was Louis Agassiz, a Swiss naturalist who emigrated to the United States and became a Harvard professor and director of the Museum of Comparative Zoology until 1873. Agassiz was very much a public intellectual, pious, and a 'devout creationist who lived long enough to become the only major scientific opponent of evolution' (Gould 1996).

In contrast to Agassiz's lack of data or scientific proof for his polygenist theory, Samuel George Morton, a Philadelphia doctor, set out (unsuccessfully) to dem-onstrate empirically that human races were in fact separate species. Morton amassed a huge collection of skulls in order to measure the difference in skull size between the races. Focusing primarily on Native American skulls, Morton's publications sought to show objectively the intellectual inferiority of other races in contrast to caucasians. Predictably, the 'Negro Group', which constituted Africans and Australian Aborigines, were shown to have the smallest cranial capacity (Gould 1996: 87). While Morton died in 1851, his polygenist thesis lived on in the words of other scientists and naturalists (Figure 21). Many of Morton's writings became the basis for the eugenics movement, which became prominent amongst American scholars in the later nineteenth and early twentieth centuries.

---

[11] '… it was one of the first theories of largely American origin that won the attention and respect of European scientists—so much so that Europeans referred to polygeny as the "American school" of anthropology. Polygeny had European antecedents … but Americans developed the data cited in its support and based a large body of research on its tenets' (Gould 1996: 74).

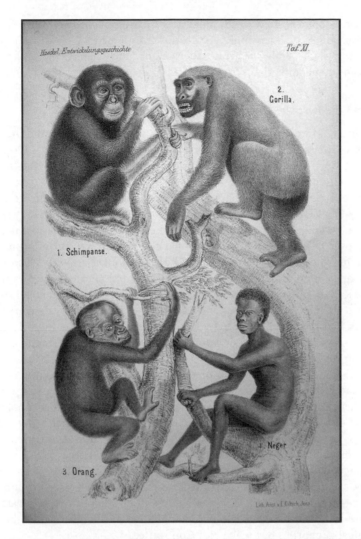

Figure 21. Ernst Haeckel's *The History of Creation*, 1868. Published in English in 1876. From 6th editon, New York, D Appleton and Co, 1914, 2 volumes.

Not surprisingly, the polygenist theory of a hierarchy of races also helped to reinforce a hierarchy of social classes. In this way science could be used to justify the enormous economic disparity between elite capitalist entrepreneurs and the masses of exploited industrial workers that swelled the ranks of the working classes in the second half of the nineteenth century. In short, race dovetailed with class to perpetuate gross social inequalities, both in colonial outposts and in urban metropolitan centers. Liberal reformers advocating equality found it hard to attack the popular and prominent polygenist racial argument, couched as it was in terms of objectively true 'science'. Hence the blatant legal discrimination

135

in this era—both in the United States and in Britain—against other racialized groups of people such as immigrant groups from Poland, Germany and Ireland demanding rights with respect to their labor (see chapter five), and Native Americans demanding rights to tribal land (see chapter six).

Race and the Eyre Controversy

The politics of race in Victorian England cannot be disentangled from the intense emotions expressed by those either for or against ex-governor Edward John Eyre. Members of the liberal-minded Jamaica Committee, such as the scientists Charles Darwin and his more vocal colleague Thomas Huxley, were staunch opponents of social evolutionary theory and angrily attacked the concept of polygeny (see Shipman 1994: 17–72). In *On the Origin of the Species*, written in 1859, Darwin argued for the monogenist thesis, which held that mankind had evolved over thousands of years in a single common descent from primates. He was careful to point out, particularly in his later book *Descent of Man* in 1871, that there were not different races of man that could be categorized as separate species. Rather, diversity and physiological differences between people could be explained as the effects of thousands of years of adaptation to environmental elements. The conclusions drawn by Darwin, Huxley and other biological evolutionary scientists were based on immensely detailed studies of animal species, ranging from barnacles to humans.

. Darwin and Huxley were very much aware that the thesis of evolution could be manipulated by those seeking to promote racism and the oppression of blacks and other minorities. Darwin's deep personal commitment to abolition is explored in the marvelous work of Adrian Desmond and James Moore entitled *Darwin's Sacred Cause: How a Hatred of Slavery Shaped Darwin's Views on Human Evolution*. Darwin and Huxley were involved in the Jamaica Committee and shared with many of its members a deep belief in abolition and human equality. While not openly religious men—Huxley referred to himself as agnostic—nonetheless these scientists' ideological perspectives correlated well with the more obviously religious ideologies of the Baptists and other nonconformist supporters of the Jamaica Committee.

In contrast, the Eyre Defence Committee, the opposing camp supporting Edward John Eyre, was dominated by men who espoused the racist idea that blacks were naturally inferior. This form of support sits uncomfortably with Eyre's personal history of sympathy and respect for Australian Aboriginal peoples. In his early career as explorer and leader of overland expeditions, Eyre had traveled with a young Aboriginal man called Wylie who proved to be a long-term faithful companion and showed Eyre how to survive in the harsh Australian wilderness. Eyre's published *Journals* detailing his journeys indicate a unique level of concern for indigenous peoples and Eyre strongly criticized the injustices they experienced at the hands of white Europeans. In short, in his early career Eyre had stood out amongst the colonialists for his relatively non-racist attitudes and his obvious respect for 'primitive' blacks. His ability to work well with Aborigines was confirmed when the Colonial Office appointed Eyre Resident Magistrate and Assistant-Protector of Aborigines at Moorunde in 1841. This appointment was made in a desperate bid to restore peace between native and colonial settlements on the Murray River (Evans 2005; Dutton 1982).[12]

Given Eyre's friendship with and appreciation of indigenous Australians, it seems a tragedy that 20 years later he was accused of racism toward black Africans when governor of Jamaica. Over the course of Eyre's career, English attitudes toward colonized peoples had changed dramatically with the rise of scientific racist discourse. 'Accordingly, humanitarian hopes and expectations that social inequality would be redressed by educating both former slaves and Indigenous peoples to become like Europeans were challenged by the conviction that social inferiority was determined biologically, and was, therefore, irremediable' (Evans 2005: 100). Moreover, Eyre, as an Australian explorer, had been beholden to no one, and his drive to conquer the land was largely about fulfilling his personal ambitions. However, as colonial governor in New Zealand and later the Caribbean in the 1850s and 60s, he was acting as a representative of the British Empire. This meant that Eyre's attitudes in this later period were in part shaped by his sense of duty to control the colony in ways that best suited the interests of British settlers.

Eyre became governor of Jamaica post-emancipation. At this time most of the black peasantry were impoverished and destitute, denied fair wages and openly discriminated against by plantation owners angry at being denied an exploitable labor force. Eyre, in trying to find solutions and explanations for the obvious problems besieging the sugar colony, increasingly came to speak in ways that put responsibility and blame on the shoulders of the black peasants. Accusing them of laziness and theft, Eyre stepped up laws governing criminal activity, and increased the length of jail sentences and use of the whip. Between 1861 and 1864 the number of peasants in jail doubled. For Eyre, this escalation was proof of their moral deficiencies, due, in turn, to their being biologically inferior. Indeed, noted Eyre, even among peasants who possess

> lands, carts, horses mules and other property, who profess to be members of religious bodies, and who, on Sundays and holidays, are always well dressed, at their own homes, and in their social habits and relations little better than absolute savages. (cited in Evans 2005: 123)

Eyre's use of racist discourse escalated as rumors of organized rebellion began to circulate and events intensified in Jamaica throughout 1865. This intensification was due in large part to Eyre's strategic mistake in publicly distributing copies of the 'Underhill Letter', which harshly criticized the British and Jamaican governments for failing to support black peasants. The general 'deterioration,

---

[12] Eyre is considered an Australian hero for his important pioneering ventures. Lake Eyre, Eyre Peninsula, Eyre Creek and Eyre Highway are all named in his honor.

decadence, and decay' in the colony was explained in terms of race that echoed and reinforced the polygenist theories of scientists back in Britain. In the words of Eyre:

> Persons of position, education and influence of the white race, are dying off or leaving the Country, and their places are not supplied by any fresh influx of European energy, intelligence, experience, enlightened views and moral principles, qualities which are so essential as examples to stimulate and influence races only just emerging from, and without such influences likely to fall rapidly back into, a state of barbarism. (cited in Evans 2005: 126)

This racialized account also justified the use of violence by the Colonial Office and its overseas representatives in suppressing potential rebellion and resistance by blacks. Racist sentiment, in short, correlated well with the aspirations and interests of the British Empire, which was anxious to keep its exploitative hold on the natives in its overseas colonies. Eyre confirmed many of the prevailing racist views circulating in London, and reproduced these in the colonial setting. So while Eyre 'appropriated certain elements of contemporary scientific thought' in his reference to a racial hierarchy, his manifestation of race and racial difference 'was also *produced through* specifically colonial interests' (Evans 2005: 128).

RIGHTS: EMPIRE'S RIGHT TO MASSACRE

The complex relationship between the London metropolis and the British Empire's peripheral colonies has been the subject of increasing attention for historians and cultural analysts over the past three decades, especially in the wake of the work of Edward Said and the emergence of post-colonial studies (Gilroy 1991; Stoler 1995; Cooper and Stoler 1997; Hall 2002). It is now widely accepted that in order to understand English society one must take into account how people's attitudes, ideologies and beliefs filtered through an orientalist imaginary and the material artifacts of colonialism as they impacted the 'mother country'. In this regard, the production and determination of law was no different from any other arena of British life (see Mawani 2009). Law, and the constant refinement of rules as applied in Britain's domestic jurisdictions of England, Wales, Scotland and Northern Ireland, was constantly filtered through the rules of law as they applied in its overseas colonies.

In the latter half of the nineteenth century colonized people were becoming more and more resistant to British imperialism. As a result, British citizens at all levels of society were increasingly forced to confront the tenuousness of their country's hold on its colonies. This sense of vulnerability was reinforced by tales of barbarous blacks circulating in the collective imaginary. Hovering behind British sensibilities with regard to blacks were memories of the 1791 revolt of

African slaves against the colonial French regime on the island of Saint-Dominque (Haiti), which ended in the establishment of the first free republic governed by blacks. The brutal violence of the Haitian Revolution led by Toussaint L'Ouverture—violence perpetrated by both Africans and Europeans—created a specter of horror that was never entirely forgotten (Nesbitt 2008; Davis 2006: 157–74; Bell 2007).

The British public's anxiety about the possibility of rebellion was further heightened by numerous colonial conflicts, such as the ongoing Maori Wars which occupied the country's colonial settlements in New Zealand between 1845 and 1872. Added to this was the constant friction between natives and British settlers in Australia, Canada and other colonial settlements. Historians, however, have argued that the most significant event in the nineteenth century in terms of galvanizing Victorian opinion against 'murderous' and 'barbarous' foreigners was the Indian Rebellion of 1857 (see Brantlinger 1990; Chakravarty 2004). It is estimated that 100,000 Indians were killed by a vicious British military determined to exact revenge for the deaths of their compatriots. Indians were killed by mass executions, strung up in front of cannons and their bodies blown apart, or bundled into sacks and burnt to death. The ferocity and scale of British violence against Indian men, women and children were by all accounts horrifying.

Yet what was perhaps even more horrible was the 'general taste for blood exhibited by the British public which rejoiced in the stories of the terrible vengeance' (Semmel 1969: 20). For instance, Charles Dickens (a member of the Eyre Defence Committee), whose novels such as *Hard Times* (1854) showed enormous empathy for Britain's industrial poor and who staunchly supported reforms to health and sanitation, nonetheless conformed to racist stereotypes when it came to attacks on the British Empire. In late 1857 Dickens published an essay about the Indian Mutiny in his journal *Household Words*. Dickens wrote 'I wish I were a commander in chief in India … I should do my utmost to exterminate the race upon whom the stain of the late cruelties rested' (cited in Brantlinger 1990). Dickens, along with many members of English society, considered the British retaliation against Indians appalling but in the circumstances justifiably appropriate.

One result of the escalation of resistance to Empire was that in the eyes of Britain's politicians, bureaucrats and general populace the rule of law was seen as a mechanism for maintaining order in faraway 'primitive' colonies. Above all else, the British firmly believed that law—both a symbol of civilization and a weapon of order—must hold strong against the thronging lawless masses. Emblematic of this popular sentiment was *Punch* magazine's strikingly violent image of the female figure of Justice beating down the barbarous Indian mutineers (Figure 22).

Figure 22.   *Justice* by John Tenniel, *Punch*, September 1857. This cartoon refers to the appropriate response to the Indian Mutiny of 1857.

Eyre's Justification

Against a backdrop of concern for the maintenance, security and economic vitality of the British colonies, news of the Morant Bay riot in Jamaica was received with some trepidation in England. British investors in West Indian sugar had already lost considerable sums as a result of abolition, rising labor costs, and increasingly dilapidated sugar plantations. Predictably, upon hearing the first official reports, the Colonial Office offered immediate praise for the way Governor Eyre had handled the situation. The rioters had been swiftly suppressed, the rebellion had not spread to other ports and regions of the island, there had been relatively few British casualties, and the financial investments of Englishmen had

140

not been seriously harmed. That Eyre had imposed martial law for a month, and that during this period hundreds of blacks were murdered and tortured, did not initially cause a hue and cry among most members of British government.

However, as news of Eyre's harsh retribution against riotous blacks filtered into the English newspapers, calls were made for a public inquiry. As discussed above, this movement against Eyre was expressed most vocally by members of anti-conformist religious groups and progressive liberals, many of whom had been abolitionist activists. The British government was forced to accommodate this shift in public opinion and appointed a Royal Commission, led by leading lawyer Sir Henry Storks, to go to Jamaica and assess the legality of Eyre's actions (Kostal 2005: 127–31). Following extensive hearings and witness interviews, the Commission announced in April 1866 that Eyre had acted with 'skill, promptitude, and vigor' in bringing the rebellion to a swift halt. In the circumstances it was held that the use of martial law was legitimate.

However, the Commission also found that Gordon had not been directly involved in the rebellion, and so Eyre's actions in trying Gordon before a court martial which resulted in his execution were questionable. Moreover, the Commission determined that Eyre's imposition of martial law for a month was unnecessary, the punishments excessive, the floggings 'reckless' and at times 'barbarous', and the burning of a thousand houses 'wanton and cruel' (Evans 2005: 137). Eyre was dismissed from office and his career in the Colonial Office finished, though he did eventually receive a government pension. He returned with his family to England in July 1866 to face trial over what was considered to be excessive retaliation against black Jamaicans.

For the next three years Eyre was the focus of public opinion, parliamentary debate and court proceedings. Throughout this period, he was adamant that his actions should be understood in the context of events leading up to the outbreak of rebellion, and not judged by British people sitting comfortably in their living rooms and in complete ignorance of the realities of Jamaican politics and society. Writing from Jamaica to Edward Cardwell, Secretary of State, in the weeks immediately following the rebellion, Eyre explained his actions by claiming:

> The whole Colony has been upon a mine, which required but a spark to ignite it. Disaffection and disloyalty exist in nearly all the [Baptist] Parishes of the Island, and had there been the least hesitation or delay in dealing with them in the parishes where they became developed in rebellion, I confidently believe that the insurrection would have been universal throughout the entire Island, and that either the Colony would have been lost to the Mother Country, or an almost interminable war and an unknown expense have had to be incurred in suppressing it. (cited in Evans 2005: 142)

Eyre wrote of the black peasantry:

> … nor do I doubt but that the object was to exterminate the white and colored [mulatto] classes, and obtain possession of the country for themselves. However wild and visionary such a scheme may appear to Englishmen, it must be borne in mind that the success which attended the efforts of the Haytians against the French, and more

recently of the St Domingans against the Spaniards, afforded examples and encouragement which from the vicinity of those republics to Jamaica, were constantly before the peasantry of this country. (cited in Evans 2005: 144)

Reinforcing a sense of crisis, Eyre resorted to the specter of race as a means to justify his actions. Again in his writings to Cardwell in London, Eyre pandered to the pseudo-scientific explanations which held that white Europeans were 'naturally' superior by affirming popular ideas about natives as ignorant and excitable children and biologically prone to unchristian and lawless acts. Eyre evoked the new language of scientific racism in his use of the word 'negro', arguing:

> It is scarcely necessary to point out that the Negro is a creature of impulse and imitation, easily misled, very excitable, and a perfect fiend when under the influence of an excitement which stirs up all the evil passions of a race little removed in many respects from absolute savages. (cited in Evans 2005: 143)

Back in London, parliament debated Eyre's actions. While racism underscored British society's thinking about the Jamaican controversy, it is interesting to note that race was not openly discussed as an explanation for Eyre's harsh retaliation. One person who attempted to do so was WE Forster, formerly Liberal Under-Secretary for the Colonies, who suggested that the real reason for Eyre's excessive actions was that the Jamaican rebels were black. Forster declared to the House of Commons:

> Now, how was it that Governor Eyre, whom he believed to be a humane and conscientious man, sanctioned proceedings of this kind, and how was it that British officers perpetrated atrocities from which they would have shrunk had the victims been white people? The reason was that they were not free, and he did not know that he himself or any Member of the House would have been free, from the race feeling— feeling of contempt for what was regarded as an inferior race. (cited in Dutton 1982: 120)

Forster's comment was met by silence and no later speaker took up this line of thinking. It seems that explicit discourse about race was to a large degree silenced in public debate. By 1865 most people in British society accepted the arguments that non-whites were biologically inferior to blacks (Pitts 2005: 150–62). Even many former abolitionists were reticent about claiming that whites and blacks were equal in all respects. As a result, racial politics informed the Eyre controversy, but to a large extent such politics were taken for granted and did not require much comment or debate.

Nation's Rights versus Subjects' Rights

Most of the contemporary debates on the Eyre controversy focused on the issue of martial law and whether Eyre was legally justified in using it. Against the findings of the Royal Commission, members of the Jamaica Committee argued that Eyre had wrongfully imposed martial law since Jamaica was not a crown colony at the time but operated under a charter of self-government. As such, common law prevailed in Jamaica, not military law as is typical in colonial settlements. The Lord Chief Justice of England, Sir Alexander Cockburn, agreed with the Jamaica Committee that Eyre had acted outside the parameters of his legal authority. Cockburn argued that since martial law was prohibited in England, it should not be considered legal in Jamaica either.

Not everyone, however, accepted this legal interpretation. In July 1867, a full year after Eyre's return to England, the House of Commons debated whether the government could use martial law in situations of necessity, even in Britain. Driven by growing fears of rioting lawless blacks abroad (and the working-class rabble at home), the majority of the House voted to keep martial law available to those representing the state in 'distant spheres' and who may need it in order to uphold 'the authority of the Crown and the rights of the country' (cited in Evans 2005: 147). Judging from the favorable newspaper reactions to the House's majority ruling, it seems that the wider public also agreed that martial law was necessary in order to defend the ultimate rights of the country in relation to its black subjects.

With the legitimacy of martial law determined by parliament, why then did the Eyre controversy continue to excite passionate debate through 1867 and into 1868? According to the historian Rande Kostal, politicians, judges and juries, faced with determining Eyre's actions in the three private prosecutions initiated against him by the Jamaica Committee, focused on a rather different issue. Kostal notes, 'the Jamaica affair mainly concerned the moral and legal framework governing white Englishmen at home, not black subjects abroad', hence 'the Jamaica suppression became controversial because it called into the question the moral—and hence legal—integrity of the English people' (Kostal 2005: 20). In other words, the reason why the Eyre controversy was so intense and prolonged was that it raised concern over the very nature of English law. Law was a symbol of democracy and civilization, emblematic of national identity and the greatness of the British nation. Moreover, law was central to Britain's imperial mission, functioning as a marker of Protestant Christianity and the country's enlightened superiority over others. Challenging the integrity of English law raised a variety of intense emotions. 'Law, not religion, secured personal security and property from the innate selfishness and savagery of all men. Law, not religion was the deeper reservoir of public conscience. No one knew law better, lived it better, than did the English' (Kostal 2005: 461).

The Eyre controversy brought to the fore a central question: to what extent could or should law in the colonies differ from law in England? The issue at stake was how to reconcile the Empire's excessive use of force in its colonies and the massacre of innocent blacks with the widely accepted concept of limited state power in its domestic arena. For no matter how dire the apparent threat to the British government, the state could not legitimately murder innocents on the streets of London by the second half of the nineteenth century (Semmel 1969:

142). Allowing law to be applied differently in the colonies was admitting to law's ambiguities, partialities, and inherent injustices. How, then, could one accept these contradictions without undermining the basic integrity of English law's assumption of universalism and its legitimacy as a mechanism of colonial control?[13]

As argued by Frederic Harrison, barrister for the Jamaica Committee and defender of the legal rights of trade unions:

> The precise issue we raise is this—that through our empire the British rule shall be the rule of law; that every British citizen, white, brown, or black in skin, shall be subject to definite, and not to indefinite powers ...

Moreover:

> English law is of that kind, if you play fast and loose with it, it vanishes ... what is done in the colony today may be done in Ireland tomorrow, and in England hereafter ... the sacred principles for which the English people once fought and struggled we now invoke for the loftier end of checking the English people themselves from imitating the tyranny they crushed. (cited in Semmel 1969: 137)

Harrison, along with the other members of the Jamaica Committee, simply could not understand how parliament could endorse the use of martial law, albeit in principle only in the colonies. For these men the debate over martial law and the state's right to unfettered executive power was seen as 'one of the most important constitutional battles in which Englishmen have for many years been engaged' (Huxley cited in Semmel 1969: 134; see also Pitts 2005: 150–62).

Working-class Discontent and the Second Reform Act

Despite the efforts of the Jamaica Committee to educate society through pamphlets, public lectures and newspaper articles, by the end of 1866 it was clear that popular support for the Committee's criticism of Eyre was drying up. Among the elite and middle classes there was now widespread support for Eyre. Why this apparent shift in attitude among the middle classes, and why would these classes act to limit their own power? According to Semmel, the middle classes, made up of small employers, property owners and tradesmen, 'were convinced that they *were* defending the British constitution—defending it against the threat of revolution by the "democratic rabble"' (Semmel 1969: 138). In other words, the middle classes were willing to concede to the British state rights over and above their own as subjects so long as the state kept the peace and controlled blacks overseas as well as the working classes within England.

---

[13] It was believed (and often still is) that while English law had emerged over the centuries from a unique Anglo-Saxon people, it was universal in its ability to transcend cultural difference and apply to the country's colonial periphery. The rule of law was the Empire's most effective weapon (see Fitzpatrick 1992).

In order to understand middle-class support for Eyre and for dismantling some of the limits on state executive power, one has to appreciate the complex interplay between the metropole and the colonies in the English imagination (Hall 2000; Mawani 2009: 4). As parliament and country were arguing about the use of law in Jamaica with respect to the rights of ex-slaves, parliament and country were also arguing about law with respect to the domestic rights of working-class men and women in England. At the time of the Eyre controversy the middle classes had cause to be alarmed by what many viewed as the extreme dangers presented by working-class demands for the vote and for labor reforms. Huge rallies in Hyde Park and Trafalgar Square in the later part of 1886, organized by John Bright and John Stuart Mill (both members of the Jamaica Committee), brought together thousands of disgruntled industrial laborers, disappointed with the limited improvements introduced by the First Reform Act (1832) and the dashed dreams for universal suffrage raised by the Chartist movement through the 1830s and 40s. Bread riots broke out in London in January in 1867 as rates of unemployment and levels of poverty skyrocketed. In Ireland there were also grave fears for public safety as Fenian[14] activists attacked the British military. In December 1867 a bomb was thrown at a London jail in a failed effort to free imprisoned Irishmen, resulting in the deaths of innocent bystanders.

Such working-class agitation for legal reform could not be ignored by either the Whig or Tory parties. As a result of mass pressure, the Second Reform Act was passed on 15 August 1867, widening the male franchise to include one in three men in the boroughs (though still excluding all women). The 1867 Reform Act opened up voting to more middle-class men, and in so doing recognized them as full members of society who could participate in the British polity. This recognition helped to shift middle-class interests to coincide more explicitly with that of the conservative elite. Hence the middle classes agreed with the elite that in the best interests of society at home, overseas government must be able to exert the full force of state power (Evans 2005: 138). By siding with Eyre and his use of martial law, the middle classes believed that they were upholding the constitution and integrity of the law and at the same time reinforcing its claims of universal application.

However, the Second Reform Act did not stop the rise in working-class mob violence.

These were turbulent years, for if the final passage of the Reform Bill had ended one source of trouble, there were others to take its place. Riot and murder were the order of the day. In Ireland and in England, the Fenians continued to make their raids; during 1867 and 1868, special constables were enlisted by the thousands to defend England

---

[14] Fenians were people associated with the Irish Republic Brotherhood committed to bringing about an independent Irish Republic free of British control. It was a term used by the English to refer to anyone who expressed Irish nationalist sentiment, and so was not limited to those who actually were Irish or members of the Brotherhood.

against Fenian assaults. Religious riots [between Protestant and Catholic] were taking place in Birmingham, and there were frequent reports of trade union murders emanating from the industrial midlands. These last particularly shocked the middle classes. (Semmel 1969: 144)

Violent demonstrations escalated middle-class fears of the 'lawless rabble', the vast 'unwashed' of unrespectable urban poor occupying the slums of London and the factory-towns of middle England. Industrial slum-dwellers, Irish Catholic activists, rebellious Jamaican ex-slaves—all were lumped together in the public's imagination, which was driven by a very real fear for its own safety. The majority of the middle and upper classes regarded—to varying degrees—these groups of unacceptable people as ignorant, greedy, lazy, uncivilized, biologically inferior and inherently dangerous (McVeigh and Rolston 2009).

CONCLUSION

Reflecting on the general mood of the English middle classes, Mathew Arnold, a poet-critic, wrote to his mother in late 1867 about the riots and demonstrations in the streets:

> You know I have never wavered in saying that the Hyde Park business eighteen months ago was fatal, and that a Government which dared not deal with a mob, of any nation or with any design, simply opened the floodgates to anarchy. You cannot have one measure for Fenian rioting and another for English rioting, merely because the design of the Fenian rioting is more subversive and desperate: what the State has to do is put down *all* rioting with a strong hand, or it is sure to drift into troubles. (cited in Semmel 1969: 141)

Mounting fears of enemies within British society as well as beyond its shores helps to explain why the English middle classes shifted their loyalty to side with a conservative and traditional elite against the working classes (and hence against the Jamaica Committee). Fear of the 'floodgates of anarchy' crystallized into a core belief that law and state authority must be reinforced and rarely questioned. Hence it was strongly argued that demands for political and civil rights by the working classes, as well as by Irish and native colonial subjects, must be rejected in the best interests of Britain's security and collective society. In the next chapter this fear of anarchy—and its relationship to prevailing religious and racist discourses—is examined in the context of the 1886 Chicago Haymarket riots. These riots occurred when tens of thousands of working-class people, many of them immigrants, took to the streets demanding basic rights such as the right to vote, a minimum wage, education, and an eight-hour workday. Following the legal logic established by the Eyre controversy, which upheld the state's right to massacre blacks in its colonial periphery, the Haymarket riot and trial is a legal landmark in the United States for establishing the precedent that imposing martial law at home is also justifiable under certain conditions. The focus in the next chapter is on exploring just what these conditions were.

Recommended Reading

Carretta, Vincent (2005) *Equiano The African: Biography of a Self-Made Man.* Georgia: University of Georgia Press.

Cooper, Frederick and Ann Laura Stoler (eds) (1997) *Tensions of Empire: Colonial Cultures in a Bourgeois World.* Berkeley: University of California Press.

Davis, David Brion (2006) *Inhuman Bondage: The Rise and Fall of Slavery in the New World.* Oxford, New York: Oxford University Press.

Desmond, Adrian and James Moore (2009) *Darwin's Sacred Cause: How a Hatred of Slavery Shaped Darwin's Views on Human Evolution.* Boston: Houghton Mifflin Harcourt.

Evans, Julie (2005) *Edward Eyre, Race and Colonial Governance.* Dunedin, New Zealand: University of Otago Press.

Gilroy, Paul (1991) *'There Ain't no Black in the Union Jack': The Cultural Politics of Race and Nation.* Chicago: University of Chicago Press.

Gould, Stephen Jay (1996) *The Mismeasure of Man.* Revised and expanded version. New York: WW Norton.

Hall, Catherine (2002) *Civilizing Subjects: Metropole and Colony in the English Imagination, 1830–1867.* Oxford: Polity.

Hobsbawm, Eric (2003, first published 1975) *The Age of Capital, 1848–1875.* London: Abacus.

Hochschild, Adam (2005) *Bury the Chains: Prophets and Rebels in the Fight to Free an Empire's Slaves.* Boston: Houghton Mifflin.

Kostal, Rande W (2005) *A Jurisprudence of Power: Victorian Empire and the Rule of Law.* New York: Oxford University Press.

Pitts, Jennifer (2005) *A Turn to Empire: The Rise of Imperial Liberalism in Britain and France.* Princeton: Princeton University Press.

Williams, Eric (1994) *Capitalism and Slavery.* Chapel Hill: University of North Carolina Press.

Wise, Steven M (2005) *Though the Heavens May Fall: The Landmark Trial that Led to the End of Human Slavery.* Cambridge, MA: Da Capo Press.

5

Demanding the Eight-Hour Workday (1886)

I N ENGLAND, in the latter half of the nineteenth century, middle and upper class people joined forces to support the rule of law and the right of the government to exercise violence against those who were seen as posing a threat to society. Many people were alarmed by the 'lawless' mobs of factory workers and poor inner-city dwellers who took to the streets demanding social and economic equity. In the context of working-class resistance, law functioned as a symbol of state legitimacy, a means to impose rules and implement order, and a tool to defend the economic interests of English industrial society. The middle and upper classes clung to the legal system as security against what they saw as impending anarchy and chaos. That it could be used to implement martial law, and justify the massacre of innocent blacks in far-away colonial outposts such as Jamaica (chapter four), was considered by many English people as ultimately an acceptable cost in ensuring control and sustaining the economics of capitalism and imperialism.

In this chapter, we cross the Atlantic to the United States to focus on the Chicago Haymarket riots of 1886, which took place approximately 20 years after the Morant Bay riots in Jamaica. The Haymarket riots followed what started off as a peaceful demonstration on May 1st, attended by some 80,000 workers marching through the streets of Chicago, calling for labor reforms and in particular an eight-hour workday. A few days later, things turned ugly when police stepped in to deal with a struggle over the crossing of a picket line by 'scabs', and four workers were killed. On 4 May a protest rally was organized. As it was drawing to a close, a bomb was thrown and a policeman was killed. In the ensuing panic, police opened fire and seven more policemen and at least four workers were killed. In the wake of the violence, the Mayor of Chicago declared martial law and ushered in a reign of terror which resulted in the rounding up of many workers and a trial the following year of eight men who had direct or indirect links to the rally (*Spies v People*). Ultimately, five men were condemned to death, one of whom committed suicide; the remaining four were hanged.

Seven years after the trial, the Chicago Governor, John Peter Altgeld, officially pardoned the eight defendants and declared them to be innocent victims of a biased trial. This was a public acknowledgement of what many already knew—that the imposition of martial law, harsh treatment of suspects by the police, and subsequent trial involved gross violations of law and justice. The Haymarket trial is considered a legal landmark in the development of modern Anglo-American law; it was a dramatic instance in which discourses about religion and race provided the rationale and justification for a denial of basic legal rights to working-class demonstrators. The riot and trial established a precedent in American legal history where the declaration of martial law and the denial of basic civil and political rights in the name of combating domestic 'terrorism' were considered an appropriate course of action by politicians, lawyers and mainstream society.

Interestingly, the Morant Bay uprising in Jamaica discussed in the previous chapter engendered a legal logic whereby it was deemed acceptable that basic justice should be done away with, and martial law imposed, in order to prevent the possibility of black violence against whites in a colonial outpost. This legal logic crossed the Atlantic, drawn upon, and taken one step further in the case of the Haymarket riots, where it was deemed acceptable by the majority of Americans to deny legal rights at home in one of the major urban centers of industrial capitalism. How did this flagrant denial of due process become acceptable in the United States? And why, given the open acknowledgement of bias and discrimination by the Chicago Mayor seven years after the event, has this pattern of extreme legal manipulation reoccurred throughout modern US legal history in contexts that sustain racial, religious, class and gender discrimination? Occurring as it did at the dawn of the 'Red Scare', the miscarriage of justice in *Spies v People* acts as a landmark precedent in a US tradition of extra-judicial lawlessness that stretched from this case through 100 years of labor turmoil, two World Wars, McCarthyism, Cold War, and the War on Terror (Darian-Smith 2007).

The Haymarket Riots of 1886

The events of the Haymarket riot have been recorded in a number of historical accounts.[1] May 1, 1886 was designated the start of a nationwide strike calling for an eight-hour workday. Around the country perhaps half a million workers, of 'all colors and nationalities', joined in the public demonstration. In Chicago, 80,000 workers marched peacefully down Michigan Avenue led by two prominent anarchists, August Spies and Albert Parsons. Anarchists in this period represented a range of political views and philosophies, but held in common a general belief in cooperation and mutual aid against the forces of a repressive

---

[1] Various books have been written about the Haymarket riot and its historical significance (see David 1936; Foner 1986; Roediger and Rosemont 1986; Nelson 1988; Avrich 1984). Most recently, James Green has published an excellent book, *Death in the Haymarket* (2006). For a particularly thorough account of the organized labor movement from the time of the Haymarket riots up to the 1960s, see Tomlins 1985.

government. Chicago had a reputation as a city full of anarchist organizations, and among the city's large population of immigrants from Poland, Germany, Bohemia and elsewhere there were men and women sympathetic to anarchist and socialist calls for labor reform emanating from England, France and other European nations. Many of these activists were Catholic; a few declared themselves to be atheists. These perspectives on faith rubbed up against the dominant Protestant social ethics of the period.

While Chicago's May Day parade was peaceful, two days later on 3 May the workers' mood quickly changed when a large crowd of lumbermen gathered at the McCormick Harvester Machine Co plant to rally against scab laborers. As the crowd forced the strikebreakers to retreat into the factory at the end of the day, the police were called and shots were fired, killing one worker immediately and causing another three to die later of their injuries. August Spies had been present at the rally and witnessed the police attack. Without delay, Spies and other activists printed off 20,000 circulars, in both English and German, calling for an early morning meeting the following day (4 May) in Haymarket Square to 'avenge this horrible murder'. At 7: 30 am around 3,000 protesters gathered. The speakers, August Spies, Albert Parsons and Samuel Fielden, addressed the crowd and called on them to take action against the government. As the rain came down, the crowds dispersed, leaving only around 200 workers listening to Fielden.

Mayor Carter Harrison, who had stood listening to the speeches, left the meeting and stopped in at the local police station about half a block away to tell Captain Bonfield to call off the police since the meeting was peaceful and nearly over. In direct opposition to the Mayor's orders, Bonfield ordered his 180 men to march into the market, surround the workers, and disperse the crowd. 'Seconds later a spluttering bomb flew through the air and exploded in front of the police, killing one instantly and wounding over seventy. The remaining police regrouped and emptied their revolvers into the panic-stricken protesters, wounding many, at least one fatally' (Foner 1986: 30; see Figure 23). It is estimated that about 60 police were wounded in the incident, and at least the same number of civilians. A total of 11 people died, eight of them policemen. No one saw who had thrown the bomb or where it came from. According to George Brown, an eye-witness:

He [Fielden] started to finish his speech when there was a movement of the crowd, which forced me back and up onto the pavement. From this position I could see over the heads of those in the street, and to my astonishment I saw a great company of police, with their revolvers drawn, rushing into the crowd which parted to make way for them. The captain commanded the meeting to disperse. Fielden leaned forward and said to the officer: 'This is a peaceable meeting, and you have no right to interfere'. Up to this time there had been no disorder of any kind. Now something occurred on the side of the street farthest from me, and the police captain called out, 'Arrest that man,' and instantly the police began firing into the people … something went quite high over my head which looked like a lighted cigar: in the semi-darkness only the lighted fuse showed. This was the bomb. It exploded in the midst of the police. I raised myself up as well as I could in the dense pack of the crowd, and looking past the wagon I saw a confused, writhing, squirming mass of policemen on the ground. (cited in Roediger and Rosemont 1986: 75)

Figure 23. Depiction of the Haymarket riots, 1886. © Chicago Historical Society.

Fear and hysteria descended over Chicago. Mayor Harrison declared martial law, then ordered widespread police dragnets. State Attorney General Julius Grinnel advised the police to disregard regular procedures as they made their raids of homes and union offices, where they tortured and abused hundreds in an attempt to find incriminating evidence. Thirty-one people were indicted, and eight selected for trial. Of those eight, only two had been present at the Haymarket riot, but all were declared 'guilty by association'. Those eight were August Spies, Albert Parsons, Louis Lingg, Adolph Fischer, George Engel, Oscar Neebe, Samuel Fielden, and Michael Scwab. Along with two US citizens, five were German immigrants, and one was a US citizen of German descent. The newspapers made much of the racist implications, calling the defendants 'foreign savages', the 'offscourings of Europe' and 'the lowest stratum found in humanity's formation' (cited in Roediger and Rosemont 1986: 93).

The Trial of the Chicago Martyrs

The trial of the defendants was set for 21 June 1886. Judge Joseph E Gary appointed a special bailiff to select the jurors; those selected were managers, salesmen, businessmen, and even a relative of a police officer who had been a victim of the Haymarket bombing. It was clearly a jury deeply prejudiced against those involved in any form of labor agitation. The defendants were charged not with murder or bomb-throwing, but with conspiracy. As declared by Attorney General Grinnell in his summation:

> Law is on trial. Anarchy is on trial. These men have been selected, picked out by the grand jury and indicted because they are the leaders. They are no more guilty than those thousands who follow them. Gentlemen of the jury: convict these men, make examples of them, hang them and you save our institutions, our society. (Foner 1986: 34)

The jury declared the men guilty and sentenced them all to death by hanging, apart from Oscar Neebe. After the defense appealed, the Illinois Supreme Court acknowledged faults in the trial but it upheld the verdict. A further appeal was made to the United States Supreme Court but the court refused to hear it. The execution date was set for 11 November 1887. Calls for clemency were made by labor movements across the United States as well as movements based in Britain, Germany, France, Holland, Russia, Italy and Spain. American intellectuals joined the trade unionists in petitioning for clemency, and William Dean Howells, a well-known novelist and literary critic, called the verdict 'the greatest wrong that ever threatened our fame as a nation' (*New York Tribune*, 6 November 1887). Partly in response to local and worldwide pressure, on 10 November, the day before the execution, the sentences of Fielden and Schwab were converted from death to life imprisonment. The next day, Lingg committed suicide in his cell, and Parsons, Engel, Spies and Fisher were hanged (Figure 24). Spies' last words on the scaffold were: 'There will be a time when our silence will be more powerful than the voices you strangle today.'

Seven years after the execution, on 26 June 1893, a day after the Haymarket Martyr Monument was dedicated before a crowd of 8,000 in Chicago, Governor John Peter Altgeld officially pardoned the eight defendants. Altgeld declared all eight to be innocent victims of a biased trial. As argued since by one historian:

> A biased jury, a prejudiced judge, perjured evidence, and extraordinary and indefensible theory of conspiracy, and the temper of Chicago led to the conviction. The evidence never proved their guilt ... No valid defense can be made for the verdict. (David 1936: 489)

Figure 24. The Law vindicated: four of the Chicago anarchists pay the penalty for their crime. *Frank Leslie's Illustrated Newspaper*, 19 November 1887. © Chicago Historical Society.

RELIGION: LAW AS FAITH

The 80,000 people who met to march on the streets of Chicago in 1886 were joined by half a million or so people marching in similar demonstrations across the United States. For decades these working-class laborers had repeatedly been promised legal reform and an acknowledgement of their basic legal rights to a minimum wage and reasonable working conditions. Such promises had rung hollow for years. Working men, women and children had struggled on in increasingly desperate conditions. In 1873, an economic slump occurred in what came to be known as the Great Depression; it lasted for over 20 years. The Depression forced industrialists to lay many workers off, then pursue policies that increased the hardships endured by the working classes.

At the same time as workers were facing a hostile legal system and their economic conditions deteriorated dramatically, the elite 'robber barons' of capitalism appeared to be enjoying ever more luxurious lifestyles. This was the period known as the Gilded Age (1877–90), when industrialists and financiers such as Cornelius Vanderbilt, John D Rockefeller, Andrew Carnegie, Henry Flagler, and

JP Morgan flouted their wealth in ostentatious style and grandeur. These later decades of the nineteenth century saw a massive socioeconomic chasm forming between the elite rich and the masses of impoverished poor—as is the case in the current phase of neo-liberalism that began in the later twentieth century (Harvey 2007).

Given this history of escalating conflict between rich and poor, what is surprising is that the march in Chicago started out as a peaceful demonstration with the aim of effecting legal reform. This peaceful intent suggests that while many poor people felt that society was ignoring their needs and that the judiciary and legal system were hostile to their pleas, there was also a widespread understanding that appealing for legal reform was the appropriate course of action. This peaceful political agenda stands in stark contrast to the bloody revolutions that had occurred the previous century with the American War of Independence of 1776, the French Revolution of 1789, workers' revolutions across Europe in 1848, and the short-lived Paris Commune of 1871 which resulted in at least 20,000 public executions of working-class people, and which had occurred only 15 years earlier.

In the United States in the late nineteenth century, the working classes were extremely disgruntled with exploitative industrialists, but yet not willing to give up on the legal system itself. Respect for law, and specifically property rights, was seen as the bulwark of democracy and emblematic of the new American nation as epitomized in the US Constitution and the Bill of Rights. This belief in the ideals of justice as promulgated through the legal system was reinforced by the fact that many of the working classes had witnessed—if not participated in—the horrifying and bloody American Civil War, which occurred only 20 years earlier (1861–65). The Civil War was a war about justice and freedom, and the rule of law had emerged triumphant in abolishing slavery. Moreover, the Reconstruction Amendments to the Constitution that were devised between 1865 and 1870—the Thirteenth, Fourteenth and Fifteenth Amendments—underscored the value of law in bringing about real change.[2] The Fifteenth Amendment gave voting rights to all men, regardless of 'race, color, or previous condition of servitude' (women's suffrage was not achieved until 1920). Granting male workers a mass franchise suggested that they were not entirely shut out of the processes of government and were in fact recognized members of American civil society (this mass franchise did not occur in Britain until the passing of the Representation of the People Act in 1918). So, despite the desperate plight of the American working classes, most people maintained a degree of faith in law and the legal system to ultimately acknowledge their rights and implement justice.

---

[2] The Thirteenth Amendment (proposed and ratified in 1865) abolished slavery. The Fourteenth Amendment proposed in 1866 and ratified in 1868 included the Privileges or Immunities Clause, Due Process, and Equal Protection Clauses. The Fifteenth Amendment, ratified in 1870, granted voting rights regardless of 'race, color, or previous condition of servitude'.

Law, Rationalization and Industrial Capitalism

A cultural faith in the primacy of law speaks to Max Weber's writings on the decline of religion in the modern era—what he called 'disenchantment'. According to Weber, irrational superstition (religion) was replaced by the growth of rational reason as the guiding principle that dictated and explained people's interactions and social relations. At the political level, rationalization helped established bureaucracies and state institutions such as the military, the police, the educational system, and the law courts. At the economic level, Weber noted that the Protestant ethic, in combination with formal-rational legal systems and bureaucracies, contributed to the rise of modern western capitalism. This argument is most famously set forth in Weber's *The Protestant Ethic and the Spirit of Capitalism* (1904–05) where he argued that there was an affinity between Calvinist ethics and capitalist aspirations to accumulate wealth. Once capitalism was firmly established, the importance of a Calvinist spiritual and material philosophy was no longer necessary.

Weber did not imply a causal model where formal, codified and predictable legal rules brought about capitalism. Rather, he suggested that 'the formal rationalization of law came about under the influence of a mixture of economic, cultural, political and legal conditions' (Deflem 2008: 47).[3] Since these conditions did not exist in the same way in all modern societies, Weber conceded comparative affinities and dissimilarities between European legal systems (such as in Germany), whose legal principles tend to be more rational in that they are codified and written down, and Anglo-American legal systems, which tend to rely more heavily on precedent and judicial interpretation (see Likhovski 1999; also Trubek 1972; Ewing 1987: 489). Despite these differences, Weber saw as important in the growth and spread of industrial capitalism among all western societies the increasing reliance on rational legal rules. The rules of law allowed for predictability, risk calculability, and contractual enforcement. As Weber noted in *The Protestant Ethic and the Spirit of Capitalism*, of undoubted importance for the success of capitalism 'are the rational structures of law and administration ... of a calculable legal system and of administration in terms of formal rules' (Weber 1904: 25).

The Rise of the Legal Profession

As Weber was very much aware, the rational structures of law and administration in the modern nation-state depended to a great degree on the rise of the legal profession, which included lawyers, judges, and a range of legal experts and legal educators (Weber 1922; Tamanaha 2006). These agents of the law, with their

---

[3] In this way he differed from Marx, who saw law as an instrument of capitalism.

specialized training and rules of legal practice, helped to reinforce the notion that law operated autonomously and independently, free of influence and corrupting power.

In England, the legal profession had enjoyed prestige and considerable power since medieval times. However, it was not until the nineteenth century, with the establishment of the Law Society in 1832, that the profession took seriously the need to standardize legal practices and legal education throughout England and Wales (Sugarman 1995). The Law Society set up its offices near the Inns of Court, the legal precinct in central London. The Inns of Court were the professional associations that supervised the education and training of barristers (who traditionally represent clients in court, as distinct from solicitors/attorneys who advise clients). These Inns—Lincoln's Inn, Gray's Inn, the Inner Temple and Middle Temple—date from the fourteenth century, and historically provided offices and domestic chambers for the barristers. To this day, each Inn maintains a library, a dining hall, and a chapel which is served by preachers and clergy of the Church of England. Members of the Inner and Middle Temples jointly use the Temple Church, which was consecrated in 1185 and was historically the place where solicitors awaited their clients for consultation (Brand 1992). Throughout the eighteenth century, all the Inns and particularly the Middle Temple provided legal training to students from the American colonies. Historians have determined that approximately 20 per cent of the signatories of the US Constitution were trained at the Middle Temple (Bucklin Society website).

Despite many early American lawyers receiving their training in London, and the relatively strict rules of practice that existed there, the legal profession in the United States prior to the Civil War was rather haphazardly organized. US legal practice was intrinsically a parochial affair; each state had its own legal rules and procedures. Hampering any efforts to standardize the legal profession at the national level were local elites anxious to maintain local control over legal and political activities in their home cities and states. Lawyers typically came from the upper, well-educated classes, worked in private practice, and were keen to see that the profession remain overwhelmingly white, male and Protestant. Given that in the pre-Civil War period, it was virtually impossible for a woman or a person from a racial or religious minority to enter the legal profession, the Protestant male white upper classes held a firm monopoly on legal practice (Konefsky 2008).

However, in the post-Civil War economy with the growth of industrial capitalism and the increasing demands made upon the law to manage corporate expansion, the legal profession was forced to accommodate a more urban, industrial and geographically interconnected clientele. During this period the idea of the law firm 'was slowly taking shape' (Konefsky 2008: 91). Also taking shape within the legal profession was a more instrumental perspective on law. Brian Tamanaha, in his grounding-breaking book *Law as a Means to an End: Threat to the Rule of Law*, argues that in the latter half of the nineteenth century lawyers, judges, legislators and politicians gradually began to perceive law as 'an instrument of power to advance their personal interests or the interests or policies of the individuals or groups they support'. Law was viewed as an empty vessel, 'to fill in, interpret, manipulate, and utilize ... to serve their own ends' (Tamanaha 2006: 1). Tamanaha explains that earlier debates among philosophers and lawyers in the sixteenth, seventeenth and eighteenth centuries about the intrinsic nature of law, its divine or natural authority, and its role since time immemorial in protecting liberty, justice and the good of society, were becoming overshadowed by an instrumental view of law that focused entirely on which laws advanced whose interests. Not coincidentally, an instrumental view of law was nurtured and supported by powerful industrialists (see also Hall and Karsten 2009: 246–67). According to the legal historian Morton Horwitz, by around 1850

> the legal system had almost completely shed its eighteenth century commitment to regulating the substantive fairness of economic exchange ... Law, once conceived of as protective, regulative, paternalistic and, above all, a paramount expression of the moral sense of the community, had come to be thought of as facilitative of individual desires and as simply reflective of the existing organization of economic and political power. (Horwitz 1977: 253)

Alongside lawyers' growing acceptance of an instrumental interpretation of law, the legal profession also started to rethink legal education. Legal professionals were keen to ensure that as a 'science' it was taught properly to appropriately qualified people. In 1870, Harvard University appointed Christopher C Langdell as dean of the law school, and a new era was established in terms of standardizing legal education in elite law schools. Langdell believed in a more formal understanding of and approach to law. He introduced the case method and published the first casebook on contracts in 1871 (Hall and Karsten 2009: 241). 'Langdell's revolution in legal education succeeded because it presented the law as a science, as an enterprise distinct from its old nemesis of politics ... and it also served well emerged corporate capitalism' (Hall and Karsten 2009: 242).

In tandem with the developments in law training and practice in the United States, new institutions such as bar associations were established to act as 'gate-keepers' of the profession. By imposing bar exams and requiring a law school degree, a hands-on practical apprenticeship with a lawyer was no longer deemed an acceptable route by which an aspiring lawyer could enter the profession. This meant that a person wishing to become a lawyer had to come from a socioeconomic background sufficient to support attendance and fees at a university. Moreover, bar associations sought to restrict women's entry to the legal profession, as well as African-Americans, Catholics, Jews and other racial and religious minorities. As the legal historian Robert Gordon notes, 'From the start the professionalization movement had mixed motives—high-minded civic reform combined with exclusion and scapegoating of ethnic newcomers, especially Jews from Eastern Europe' (Gordon 2008: 77). The massive influx of immigrants into the United States during the middle to later years of the nineteenth century (see below) helped to galvanize white nativist sentiments among lawyers keen to protect their burgeoning legal profession and preserve their political influence, particularly among wealthy industrialists. These gate-keeping tactics were not entirely successful. While women and minorities could be kept out of elite law schools, bar associations could not completely control other forms of legal education springing up across the country. For instance, in the early years of the twentieth century there emerged night schools and law degrees such as that offered by Suffolk Law School in Boston. These night schools served a less privileged clientele and became 'the quickest route into practice by immigrant lawyers' (Gordon 2008: 77).

Symbols of Law

The growth of the legal profession in the nineteenth century played a part in the expansion of industrial capitalism. In turn, corporate needs stimulated new legal instruments and innovations in contract, property and torts law. In this dovetail-ing of legal practice with corporate development, lawyers were becoming increas-ingly concerned with enhancing their public reputation and stature. Elite law schools, bar associations, standardized ethics and procedures and the growth of big city law firms all helped the legal profession to develop a more deliberate approach in deploying symbols of authority. As noted by Peter Goodrich, law embodies 'architecture, statuary, dress, heraldry, painting and insignia—gold rings, rods, coifs, seals and rolls—which provide popular consciousness with a Justice that can be seen and remembered' (Goodrich 1996: 96). Historically, these symbols of law, reminiscent of formal religious rituals, were seen in the long gowns and wigs traditionally worn by lawyers, and echo the habits and clerical garb of religious elders. These symbols also appeared in the ritual and rhetoric of court proceedings, again evoking ceremonial practices found in many formal religions.[4]

Perhaps the most explicit use of authoritative legal symbolism deployed by the legal profession was in the architectural surroundings and space of legal adjudica-tion itself. In both Britain and the United States in the mid-nineteenth century, as populations in towns and cities expanded and court business increased, 'courts came increasingly to be held in permanent locations and the trend toward custom-built courthouses began' (Mulcahy 2007: 388). Most of these courtrooms followed a basic layout that had existed in Europe since the fifteenth century, which placed the judiciary on a high platform rather like priests, with the areas below being designated for court officials, defendants, advisors, and the watching public.

---

[4] 'The aesthetics of authority offered by law, is, in many ways, similar to the aesthetics of authority found in religious practices. Robes, rituals and grandiose buildings are common to both, as are esoteric texts and specialized methods of interpretation. Also common to both religion and law are ritualistic appeals to the traditions and legitimacy of institutional hierarchies. Law, like religion, is tethered to its metaphysical transcendental sources of authority' (Butler 2003: 210).

The building of national courts provided an important opportunity for states to communicate the majesty of law to their public. Many western legal professions began to demand centralized national courts that would reinforce a sense of law's pristine splendor and exclusiveness from the melee of everyday activities. In the late nineteenth and early twentieth centuries, calls to find an appropriate place to house the US Supreme Court resulted in the building of the court in Washington, DC in 1937 (Figure 25). Modeled on the Temple of Diana at Ephesus, its neo-Classical architecture deliberately recalled a religious shrine, underscoring simultaneously the sacredness and timelessness of the American legal system, despite its relatively recent founding. The imposing building deliberately set out to inspire the visitor who ascends the staircase, dwarfed and inconsequential against the monumentality of the marble colonnade. As Piyel Halder has noted, this architecture was necessary because 'law continues to demand faith':

> The elegance of legal architecture provides the background against which justice is seen to be done; it advertises itself as a select and exclusive space in which a monopoly over the administration of justice according to rational precepts is supposed to reign. These ornamental features not only demarcate a discrete place; they also surround and attempt to seal legal discourse, defining its codified dimensions by marking off what may properly be articulated in the solemnity of law's majesty and mood. (Halder 1999: 135; see also Halder 1994; Mohr 1999)

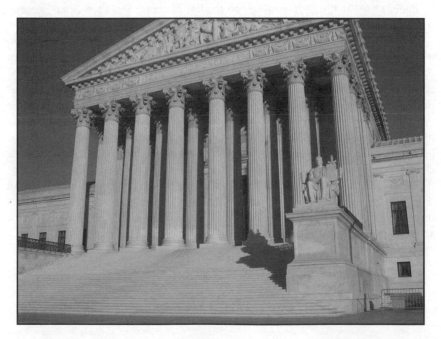

Figure 25. Supreme Court of the United States, Washington, DC. Built 1937. Photograph by Duncan Lock, 2004.

Thinking about law as faith helps to explain the effectiveness of law's power in modern democratic societies. In the second half of the nineteenth century, the increasing prominence of law as an ideological frame through which to explain social and political relationships coincided with a decline in the importance of religion which in pre-modern societies had been the glue that typically held them together. Alongside this decline in the significance of formal religion in civil society, Anglo-American legal professionals consciously deployed sacred symbols to enhance their public stature and reputation. These professionals were very much aware that law's power draws upon the interconnections and analogies between law and religion, despite the claim that law and religion occupied separate—if not mutually exclusive—spheres.

Historically, it appears that Anglo-American societies needed to believe that law (like religion) is somehow transcendental, existing above the fray of power, politics and personal ambition. The social need to believe in the authority of an objective legal system, untainted by self-interest, was (and remains) a central ideological tenet in the growth of state nationalism and the development of western capitalism. The supposed neutrality of law, and law's apparent accessibility to all, are potent democratic myths that allow people to overlook society's asymmetries of power and structural inequities.[5] Hence the potency of the rags-to-riches fairytale—a story that depends intrinsically upon denying the very existence of inequalities determined on the basis of a person's race, class, gender, sexuality and religious faith.

In American society in the latter half of the nineteenth century the widespread willingness, even the need, of ordinary people to believe in the rule of law as an objective system of determination and arbitration persisted, despite gross socio-economic disparities. People wanted to think of law in traditional terms, 'as protective, regulative, paternalistic and, above all, a paramount expression of the moral sense of the community' (Horwitz 1977: 253). However, the public's interpretation of the law contrasted with the instrumental view of law that was increasingly adopted and implemented by the legal profession and the corporate clients it typically served. As is explored in the rest of this chapter, the instrumental approach to law ultimately prevailed. Significantly, discourses of race and religion were aggressively mobilized by those in power to justify why labor laws should not be reformed and working-class people should be denied access to law and prevented from exercising their basic civil and political rights.

---

[5] Moreover, these myths assume that each individual is personally responsible for their relative economic successes and failures. In the 19th century, it was widely believed that people ended up in the poorhouses because of their own moral shortcomings and lack of work habits. In the 21st century we see an equivalent attitude in Anglo-American societies' treatment of homeless people, who supposedly are on the streets because they refuse to work.

RACE: RACIALIZING LABOR

In Europe's early modern period, a person's religion, more than their race, provided the line demarcating difference between people. One's religious affiliation provided the primary ideological lens through which the world was viewed and explained, and social relations justified. Hence in England, discrimination was typically determined—other than by gender—on the basis of one's religious affiliation. In terms of employment and occupation, Catholics, Jews and nonconformists such as Methodists and Presbyterians (and a very small number of other religious minorities such as Muslims then living in England) were prevented throughout the eighteenth and into the nineteenth century from entering politics, working in the civil service, and entering professions such as law and medicine.

England's system of legal discrimination based upon a person's religious affiliation gradually began to loosen up in the early 1900s. Catholics and Jews were finally allowed to run for election to the House of Commons, in 1828 and 1858 respectively. However, despite formal recognition of religious minorities' legal right to occupy certain positions of status and gain employment in certain fields, social discriminatory practices endured for many more decades. These exclusionary strategies helped to maintain England's socioeconomic class system by keeping religious minorities out of social clubs, universities, sporting events and so on. In the labor force, throughout the nineteenth century and well into the next, priority was given to white Anglican males seeking employment, be these for lucrative jobs in the banking and finance sector, poorly paid jobs in domestic service, skilled placements in wool mills, coal mines or steel industries, or unskilled jobs on factory floors.

One consequence of the loosening up of legal discrimination based on religious affiliation was that the historical emphasis on religion rather than race as the primary indicator of social difference began to shift. As religious minorities gained a degree of legal recognition and fought the open contempt that English society expressed toward them, race rather than religion took center stage as the discourse justifying enduring social discrimination. This shift in emphasis from religion to race suggests two phases by which discrimination was justified. The first used the institutions of religion and faith; the second used the institutions of secularism and learning. In England and the United States in the mid-nineteenth century, racist language emerged in the form of pseudo-scientific theories of social evolution derived from Darwin's biological theories and polygenism proposed by people such as Louis Agassiz and Samuel George Morton. These various theories, picked up by Herbert Spencer and others interested in anthropology and the study of humankind, sought to explain why white men were 'naturally' superior to people of darker skin tone.

As discussed in chapter four, these various pseudo-scientific theories were very attractive in mainstream English society; they justified in scientific terms supposedly devoid of class and religious bias widespread expressions of contempt for minorities, be they Jamaican blacks, indigenous Australians, Native Americans, Jews, or Irish Catholics. For example, popular discourse in the second half of the nineteenth century, as communicated through political cartoons, songs, novels and plays, began to emphasize the genetic predisposition of the Irish to laziness, barbarity and stupidity. In this way, contempt of Irish Catholics began to be framed not so much in terms of intolerance of Catholicism as intolerance of Irish racial inferiority. Race began to provide the primary language of bigotry and exclusion. Conveniently, it followed that no matter how much English society recognized the legal rights of Catholics, Catholics could—and perhaps should— continue to be socially discriminated against on the basis of their biological inadequacies.

This discursive shift from religion to race was picked up and reinforced by some of the very people marginalized by mainstream society. An intriguing example is Benjamin Disraeli (1804–81), who wrote popular political novels such as *Coningsby* in 1844, and more importantly served in the British government for 30 years as a Conservative Party member and was twice elected Prime Minister. Disraeli was born a Jew but apparently converted at the age of 12 and practiced Anglicanism throughout his life, hence his ability to enter politics. According to the historian Adam Kirsch, Disraeli played a prominent role in redefining Judaism as a matter of race rather than religion and so reshaped the basis of anti-Semitism in English society (Kirsch 2008). In his many novels, Disraeli stressed the intellectual superiority of Jews as a distinct human race and unfortunately reinforced popular racist assumptions and the appeal of the eugenics movement (see below).

Labor Politics in Nineteenth-Century America

In the United States the interconnections between religion and race played out somewhat differently than in Britain. Certainly a militant Protestantism helped to forge a sense of American national identity against Catholic France and Spain in the early years of colonial settlement. However, as John Higham has noted, the American Revolution was 'accompanied by a growing religious toleration and secular democracy' which largely 'suspended the wars of the godly' (Higham 2002: 6). This is not to say that religion was not an issue—the exploitation and abuse of slave and native populations were considered to be justified on the basis of their non-Christianity. However, in America visual markers of skin tone and hair color showed social difference in immediately accessible ways and the prominence of the transatlantic African slave trade certainly played a part in shaping an overt form of domestic racial politics. Throughout the early years of the Republic, issues of race emerged as a central concern and a prominent mechanism by which discrimination and specifically the exploitation of imported African slaves could be deemed acceptable.

In the years prior to and following the Civil War, American nationalism was to a large degree forged on the claim that it embraced peoples from a wide range of

European ethnic backgrounds and ancestry. Of course this ideal was opposed by nativist groups, such as the Know-Nothing movement in the 1840s and 50s which sought to establish a distinctly Anglo-Saxon Protestant notion of American identity (Higham 2002). However, ultimately these nativist movements could not compete with the dominant myths of US nationalism, which proclaimed that it was a land of freedom and possibility, a distinctly different nation from the European countries its immigrant citizens had deliberately abandoned. Charles Darwin himself promoted this way of thinking in *Descent of Man*, when he wrote in 1871 that 'the wonderful progress of the United States, as well as the character of the people, are the results of natural selection', and that the nation's superiority was due to the 'energetic, restless, and courageous men from all parts of Europe' and in particular the northern European Anglo-Saxons (Gossett 1997: 312).

This rhetoric of relative inclusiveness—at least with respect to peoples from Europe—was reinforced by the needs of industrial capitalism. Immigrants were needed to populate the vast lands and provide the wage labor necessary to build railways, work farm equipment and staff factory floors, as well as to meet consumers' needs, manifest in the swell in mass production. In this expanding economic climate, immigrants were warmly embraced. This warmth toward foreigners was particularly strong in the immediate post-Civil War years when people of all backgrounds had fought side by side in the Union army, united by abolitionist fervor. In 1864, in an effort to encourage migration to the United States, Congress went so far as to revise an eighteenth-century law, authorizing 'employers to pay the passage and bind the services of prospective migrants' (Higham 2002: 14).

In the decades following the Civil War, cracks began to appear in this populist rhetoric of a united American society. Anti-foreigner sentiment bubbled to the surface, much of it linked to the increasing competition for jobs in the 1870s and 80s as the country experienced an economic depression (see Jacobson 1998). 'Unlike earlier slumps of the great secular boom, this one did not seem to end' (Hobsbawm 2003: 62). Labor unrest, striking unions, and in some cases bloody violence between ethnic groups competing for jobs began to destabilize the apparent confidence of the so-called Gilded Age.

These cracks began many years earlier with anti-Chinese agitation on the west coast. In the wake of gold being discovered in California in 1848 and 1849, waves of gold diggers, called 'forty-niners', rolled into California from across the United States as well as from Australia, Europe, Latin America and Asia. In particular the Chinese population, which by 1852 numbered approximately 25,000, caused alarm with their distinctly different social and religious customs. A popular sentiment began to emerge that the Chinese, like Native Americans, would never be assimilated into American 'white' society because of their racial difference and, by implication, intellectual and cultural inferiority. In his classic history of race in America, Thomas Gossett notes that the early justifications for exclusion were based on pseudo-scientific racial profiling:

> As early as 1854, the Chinese in California were barred from testimony in the courts in cases involving whites. The reasoning of the Supreme Court of California in arriving at this decision was that since the Indians were not allowed to testify in the courts against whites and since the Chinese and Indians were of the same race, the Indians having many centuries ago come from China, the law which applied to the Indians should also apply to the Chinese. (Gossett 1997: 290)

By the later years of the nineteenth century, as the economic depression led to ever-increasing competition for jobs amongst minorities across the country, popular antagonism toward the Chinese grew. In 1888 and 1892 exclusion acts were implemented against Chinese immigrants and from that time on there were severe restrictions on their ability to come to the United States. These acts and other related legislation targeting the Chinese were strongly endorsed by labor organizers and the American Federation of Labor who were anxious to eliminate all competition for jobs.

Conflict over jobs escalated with the influx of freed blacks into the labor force both before and particularly after the Civil War. The Freedmen's Bureau was set up to help free blacks adjust to their new social position and specifically help in supervising labor contracts and entering the workforce. But the difficulties faced by blacks seeking fair and equal treatment from white employers were enormous. The Reconstruction era was plagued by what WEB Du Bois later called 'a labor problem of vast dimensions'. The great disappointment was that the rhetoric of legal equality, as exemplified in the Fifteenth Amendment, did not in fact provide social equality for blacks or other minorities. In disarmingly poetic language, Du Bois encapsulated the moment when he wrote: 'Thus Negro suffrage ended a civil war by beginning a race feud. And some felt gratitude toward the race thus sacrificed in its swaddling clothes on the altar of national integrity; and some felt and feel only indifference and contempt' (Du Bois 1903: 13, 28).

As blacks sought waged jobs in the thousands, the racializing of the American labor force became increasingly intense. In Noel Ignatiev's provocative book *How the Irish Became White,* the author explores some of the ways in which this racializing of labor occurred. By focusing on the large number of Catholic Irish who emigrated to the United States and faced strong competition from blacks for jobs in manual labor, Ignatiev shows the gradual process whereby the Irish came to declare themselves 'white' in order to differentiate themselves socially, culturally and politically from blacks, and in the process gain access to better jobs. Blacks, on the basis of their skin color alone, did not have this option available to them and so were perpetually left behind to fight the next group of incoming European immigrants until that group, like the Irish, adopted the cultural capital of whiteness (see Jacobson 1998; Roediger 2007: 133–66; Roediger 2005). According to Ignatiev:

> On the docks, the Irish effort to gain the rights of white men collided with the black struggle to maintain the right to work; the result was perpetual warfare. Black workers had traditionally been an important part of the waterfront work force in New York,

Philadelphia, and other Northern cities, as well as Baltimore, Charleston, New Orleans, and other Southern ports. By the 1850s the New York waterfront had become an Irish preserve; few black men could find work on the docks except during strikes under police protection, and even Germans were unwelcome. (Ignatiev 1995: 120)

Competition for jobs was further exacerbated by the enormous waves of immigrants pouring into the eastern seaboard throughout the 1860s, 70s and 80s, first passing through New York's Castle Garden Immigration Depot at Battery Park and, after 1892, processed through the more isolated Ellis Island. Between 1865 and 1873, 200,000 immigrants arrived at the port of New York alone (Hobsbawm 1975: 62). Most of these came from southern and eastern Europe, as opposed to earlier waves of immigration from northern and western Europe. Poles, Hungarians, Italians, Serbians, Greeks and Slavs all challenged the racially hierarchical labor system as well as the American Catholic establishment, which at the time was dominated by 'Irish, and to a lesser extent, German-Americans' (Fisher 2008: 70). These waves of immigrants were depicted in popular novels, magazines, newspapers and songs as ignorant, deceptive, untrustworthy, thieving and lawless (Figure 26).

Figure 26. 'The inevitable result to the American workingman of indiscriminate immigration', c 1881, James Albert Wales. Printed with permission from Special Collections and Archives, Georgia State University Library.

In the later years of the nineteenth century a shift in racial rhetoric emerged. The earlier romanticization of American nationalism forged out of an eclectic racial mix began to be downplayed, while the theme of invading foreigners threatening an American way of life was played up. This fear of foreigners, which escalated in the 1880s, 1890s and into the early decades of the twentieth century, was premised on the racial assumption that foreigners were intellectually, morally and culturally inferior and that their co-mingling (miscegenation) threatened the blood-lines of true Americans. Thus underlying many white Protestants' concern that the United States was becoming a nation of mixed races—what the Jewish playwright Israel Zwangwill coined 'the great melting pot' in 1908—was alarm at the dilution of Anglo-Saxon racial stock.

The Eugenics Movement

The shifting rhetoric of race and the role played by racialization in nineteenth-century labor politics cannot be divorced from the rise of the eugenics movement in the United States and its powerful influence on all aspects of society, including the labor force. The movement was firmly established by the last decade of the nineteenth century and enjoyed considerable success well into the 1920s. It has a complicated history, with different advocates drawing upon different kinds of statistical and biological data to prove their theories, as well as proposing a variety of solutions to what they regarded as the major concerns associated with genetic reproduction. Many fascinating books have been written on the British and United States eugenics movements and their scientific and intellectual histories (see Gould 1996; Carlson 2001; Barkan 1992; Ordover 2003).

A brief discussion of the eugenics movement will provide a context for the social and political backdrop against which the Chicago Haymarket riots of 1886 took place and how discourses of religion, race and rights played out. While the first eugenics-driven legislation was not put in place until a decade after the Haymarket riots, when the state of Connecticut passed marriage laws preventing 'imbecile or feeble-minded' people from marrying in 1896, mainstream society's receptiveness to the ideas of the eugenics movement had been brewing from the 1880s. These eugenics-inspired understandings of race informed the gross injustices and denial of legal rights to foreigners that were tolerated by the majority of Americans in the trial of the Haymarket rioters. Such understandings also reinvigorated white nativist and supremisist groups such as the Ku Klux Klan, which enjoyed a second revival in 1915 and with its anti-Catholic, anti-Semitic and anti-Communist rhetoric thrived, particularly in the south.

At its core, the eugenics movement set out to classify human beings on the basis of blood and genetic ancestry. This classification system was used to identify people with particular hereditary abnormalities such as diabetes, deafness, color blindness and mental retardation. It was also used to identify large bodies of people based on their supposed racial ancestry, grouping them by skin color, shape of eyes, size of brain, and so on. These identifications led to a variety of 'solutions', ranging from denial of legal rights such as refusing a person employment or citizenship, to more extreme denials that involved bodily processes such as forced sterilization, institutionalization in mental homes, and mass extermination (Nourse 2008; Lombardo 2008). These various solutions highlight how the eugenics movement differed from the pseudo-scientific social evolutionary theories proposed earlier by theorists such as Spencer, Haeckel, Agassiz and Morton. Most evolutionary theorists thought that inferior races would either catch up with superior races and assimilate, or alternatively simply die out. Unlike supporters of eugenics, social evolutionary thinkers did not push for explicit state policies to intervene and 'manage' human reproduction. Herbert Spencer, in fact, argued the opposite—that governments should take a laissez-faire approach and deny any assistance or charitable help to the impoverished. That being said, the racism explicit in social evolutionary models did provide the basis for discriminatory programs such as the establishment of reservations for Native Americans and the removal of indigenous children from their homes in the US, Canada and Australia (see Smith 2005; Roberts 2008).

One of the first proponents of eugenics was the English born mathematician Francis Galton, a cousin of Charles Darwin.[6] Galton was interested in, among other things, the artificial breeding of livestock and plants to promote particular traits or qualities. Drawing upon statistical data Galton argued that traits of intelligence and genius, which he regarded as hereditary, could be promoted through selective breeding to create superior humans. Coining the word 'eugenics' in 1883 in his book *Inquiries into the Human Faculty and its Development*, Galton declared his interest in exploring all the influences that 'give to the more suitable races or strains of blood a better chance of prevailing speedily over the less suitable' (Galton 1883: 17 fn 1). The following year, Galton set up an Anthropometric Laboratory in London and set about collecting measurements such as height, weight and foot length from over 9,000 people. 'Working with these data, Galton sought, and found, a confirmation of the existence of what is known in statistics as the normal, Gaussian distribution: the familiar bell-shaped curve' (Shipman 1994: 115). For his statistical contribution to understanding hereditary traits, and for supplying a scientific (though flawed) basis for human breeding, Galton was knighted by King Edward VII in 1909.

Galton's ideas about eugenics were warmly embraced in the United States in both scientific and popular circles. His ideas also resonated strongly with the conservative political agendas of the middle and upper classes, who were increasingly alarmed by the social unrest in the major industrial cities where high unemployment and squalid urban slums threatened the great economic engine of

---

[6] It seems that Charles Darwin was not totally convinced by Galton's theories, though he did not actively oppose them either. In a further ironic and somewhat horrifying twist, Darwin's son, Leonard Darwin, served as president of the Eugenics Society in England from 1891 to 1928. In 1926 he wrote the book *The Need for Eugenic Reform*, which he dedicated to his father (Shipman 1994: 121).

industrialization. Eugenics-inspired rhetoric about the innate intellectual and moral limitations of new immigrants conveniently negated any political need to address social reform such as better housing, education and health programs for illiterate and impoverished immigrants. Racially charged language blamed the poor themselves for their plight. According to the early twentieth century historian Frederick Jackson Turner, new immigrants counteracted the 'upward tendency of wages' and encouraged the 'sweatshop system'. Moreover, Turner argued that Jews were 'a race capable of living under conditions that would exterminate men whom centuries of national selection had not adapted to endure squalor and unsanitary and indecent conditions of a dangerously crowded overpopulation' (Gossett 1997: 292–93).

It was one thing for politicians to use ideas of racial inferiority to justify abandoning new immigrants to the tenement squalor of inner-city neighborhoods such as Little Italy and Chinatown in New York. But it was quite another when the slum dwellers threatened the nation's greatness and its core moral character as law-abiding and civilized citizens, strengths derived from its Anglo-Saxon ancestry. Illustrating that the rhetoric of eugenics was firmly established in well-educated circles by 1907, John R Commons, an economist at the University of Wisconsin, noted: 'The peasantry of Europe today is in large part the product of serfdom and of that race-subjection which produced serfdom. How different from the qualities of the typical American citizen whose forefathers have erected our edifice of representative democracy' (Gossett 1997: 293). This view was upheld by many others, including Josiah Strong, a Protestant clergyman and founder of the Social Gospel movement who maintained, among other things, that Anglo-Saxons had a duty to 'civilize and Christianize' due to their racial superiority. In clinical language reminiscent of eugenics philosophy, Strong argued, 'There is now being injected into the veins of the nation a large amount of inferior blood every day of every year'. Furthermore, argued Strong in 1898, 'the foreign population, as a whole, is depressing our average intelligence and morality in the direction of the dead-line of ignorance and vice' (Gossett 1997: 294).

Not only did mainstream society regard new immigrants as threatening the moral fiber and character of white 'native' Americans, more profoundly the newcomers threatened the stability and status quo of the laissez-faire capitalist system. It should be remembered that during this period the United States was experiencing a significant economic depression (1873–96). Industrialists were forced to lay many people off work and unemployment rates sky-rocketed. In response, strikes organized through trade unions became one of the primary means by which workers attempted to oppose their blatant exploitation and mistreatment. Against growing unrest within the desperate working classes, capitalists fought back by turning to the legal system and pushing for tougher legislation that criminalized working-class protest and specifically attacked the leaders of trade unions, who were seen as inciting violence and insurrection.

In this context, the eugenics movement provided further ammunition for angry industrialists, who, along with the alarmed middle and upper classes, stressed that working-class radicalism derived from the lawlessness of new immigrants. In the words of General Francis A Walker, a professor of economics and history at Yale, new immigrants had 'proved themselves the ready tools of demagogues in defying the law, in destroying property and in working violence'. More significantly, being of inferior 'peasant' stock, the new immigrants did not have the same faith in and respect for law as white 'native' Americans, whose Teutonic ancestry had 'descended from the tribes that met under the oak-trees of old Germany to make laws and choose chieftains' (cited in Gossett 1997: 302–03).

Mainstream society was not surprised that unruly and rebellious unions and labor organizations were often led by 'lawless' foreigners, and that these activists were typically labeled in the newspapers and pamphlets as 'revolutionaries', 'socialists' and 'anarchists'. In the rousing words of Chauncey Depew, conservative politician and director of numerous railway corporations, 'the ranks of anarchy and riots number no Americans. The leaders boldly proclaim that they come here not to enjoy the blessings of our liberty and to sustain our institutions but to destroy our government, cut our throats, and divide our property' (Gossett 1997: 298–99). Fear of declining industrial profits, fear of anarchy and lawlessness, fear of losing a national Protestant identity, fear of Catholics, Jews and other religious minorities, fear for the safety of one's person and family—all combined in the public imagination to create a powerful wave of reactionary xenophobic emotion.

RIGHTS: WORKERS VERSUS LAISSEZ-FAIRE CAPITALISM

The Haymarket rioters, and their demands for legal reform and specifically an eight-hour workday, represented one side in a bitter battle between laborers and capitalists that had been brewing in industrial societies throughout the nineteenth century. During this period, extreme tensions emerged between the working classes and the more conservative middle and upper classes over the poor's lack of health, education, minimum wage, and job opportunities. The central problem was extraordinarily harsh labor conditions in which men, women and children were forced to work up to 16 hours a day in mills, mines and factories in order to make enough money simply to survive. This was an era of explicit laissez-faire capitalism, an economic philosophy espoused by the theorist Adam Smith and others who argued for the principle of free trade with very little intervention or regulation by the state. In his book *An Inquiry into the Nature and Causes of the Wealth of Nations* (1776), Smith argued that laissez-faire capitalism was supported by the concept of utilitarianism, in which everything should be rationalized and have a pragmatic function. It followed that if a person is allowed to exercise rational self-interest and seek economic prosperity, this will provide for the general betterment of society (Smith 1776). Both laissez-faire capitalism and the concept of utilitarianism regarded economic profit as the paramount goal and rationale for all social behaviors and policies. In this prevailing intellectual climate, neither industrialists nor governments felt any obligation or need to defend workers' basic legal rights to a minimum wage, maximum length of working day, reasonable labor conditions, or wage compensation in the event of injury or death.

Charles Dickens' novels and journal installments were read avidly in England and the United States. In many of these writings he passionately criticized the social injustices faced by England's poor. In the novel *Hard Times* (1854), Dickens sought to expose the terrible working conditions of laborers and reprimand the owners of factories, mills and mines for their corrupt and immoral exploitation of the lower classes. In the novel *Oliver Twist* (1839), Dickens wrote about the impact of workhouses on an orphan boy who was forced onto the streets of urban London to be brought up by criminals and thieves. Drawing on his own experience working in a boot-polish factory at the age of 12, where he was forced to work up to 10 hours a day, Dickens used his writings to expose the shortcomings of an English society preoccupied with progress as measured by economic profit, and which tolerated the explicit abuse of one's fellow citizens, including children. Karl Marx and Friedrich Engels, who were also very much involved in critiquing the capitalist system and exposing the plight of the working classes in works such as the *Communist Manifesto* (1848), appreciated the writings of Dickens and other Victorian novelists. According to Marx in a newspaper article on the English middle classes, Dickens 'issued to the world more political and social truths than have been uttered by all the professional politicians, publicists and moralists put together' (*New York Tribune*, 1 August 1854).

In England, the plight of the working classes slowly began to change with the First Reform Act (1832) and Second Reform Act (1867), which considerably increased the proportion of the male population entitled to vote. These electoral advances in turn aided the passing of legislation that spoke specifically to labor issues, such as the Master and Servant Act of 1832 and the Trade Union Act of 1871. The reforms were the result of increasing pressure exerted by unions and workers' organizations on government to enact legislation that reined in some of the unfettered power of capitalists and their explicit denial of workers' rights. The 1871 Trade Union Act was very important in that it effectively removed all legal obstacles barring the right of workers to strike. Up to this point, trade union members were criminalized for restraining free trade and were liable to imprisonment (Hobsbawm 1975: 122–42). While these labor reforms went some way to alleviating the growing poverty among the working classes, it would take many more years before regulatory practices were adequately implemented and enforced in Britain. In particular, harsh labor laws that discriminated against religious minorities such as Catholics and Jews existed well into the twentieth century.

In the United States, labor agitation had been brewing throughout the nineteenth century, but it had assumed a particular racial and religious trajectory in the wake of the abolition of slavery and the unique nationalist challenges presented by the hundreds of thousands of largely Catholic immigrants seeking employment. Accordingly, 'On one side of the gulf are the business and professional people, mostly native-born and Protestant. On the other is the working class, nearly all of it foreign in background, much of it Catholic, and the rest convinced that Protestantism serves only the well-to-do' (Higham 1995: 39–40).

Robert Hunter, a wealthy social reformer, wrote extensively of the horrifying conditions of the working classes in Chicago and New York (Figure 27). Importantly, he highlighted the incredible socioeconomic divide between the working classes and the robber barons of the Gilded Age. Hunter's many books, including *Tenement Conditions in Chicago* (1901), *Poverty* (1904), *Socialists at Work* (1980) and *Violence and the Labor Movement* (1914), and his proposed solutions such as a living wage, unemployment insurance, safety regulations in the workplace and workers' compensation, had a significant influence on twentieth-century American labor laws. In moving language Hunter brought home to middle and upper class Americans the harsh realities of the exploited poor:

> On cold, rainy mornings, at the dusk of dawn, I have been awakened, two hours before my rising time, by the monotonous clatter of hobnailed boots on the plank sidewalks, as the procession to the factory passed under my window. Heavy, brooding men, tired, anxious women, thinly dressed, unkempt little girls, and frail, joyless little lads passed along, half awake, not one uttering a word as they hurried to the great factory. From all directions thousands were entering the various gates—children of every nation of Europe. (*Poverty* 1904)

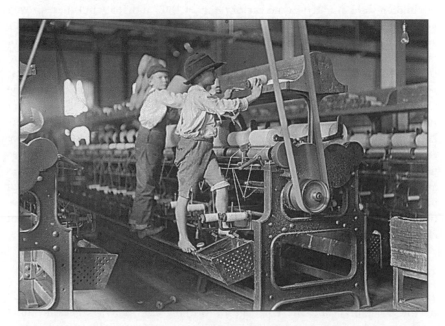

Figure 27.   Photograph of child workers, 1909. Bibb Mill No 1, Macon, GA. By Lewis Hine for the National Child Labor Committee.

One factor that helps to explain why labor politics and reform played out differently in England and the United States is, as argued by the historian William Forbath, that each country had a distinct court and constitutional system. In England parliament had the final word over the judiciary, and so legislative reforms in the later decades of the nineteenth and early twentieth centuries adopted a more class-based collective platform that invoked the rhetoric of centralized state welfare. In the United States, the more fragmented federal system led to an 'absence of a strong administrative state apparatus' (Forbath 1992: 211). Party politics in each state relied upon more localized systems of patronage that strongly resisted moves toward centralized federal labor reform. These localized bureaucracies and the political elite were keen that power remain in the hands of 'native' Protestants who occupied all prominent judicial positions. In this context of a relatively weak federal government and congress, 'the courts held greater sway over the interpretation, administration and enforcement of labor laws ... and during the 1880s and 1890s the state and federal courts were more likely than not to strike down the very laws that labor sought most avidly. By the turn of the century, judges had voided roughly sixty labor laws' (Forbath 1992: 209, 211; see also Tamanaha 2006: 44–52).

The structural differences between England, with its dominant parliament, and the US, with its dominant judiciary, can be illustrated by comparing the two countries' laws on child labor. In England, attempts to regulate the working hours of children were initiated in the Factory Acts of 1802 and 1819, but these proved to be ineffectual. Not until the Act of 1847 were the working hours of both adults and children limited to 10 hours a day. This legislation was enforced by the use of factory and mine inspectors, who as government officials held enforcement and rule-making powers (Forbath 1992: 209). In the United States, there were far fewer inspectors and they enjoyed no special powers. Moreover, laws limiting the working hours of children such as that introduced in 1892 by the Governor of Illinois, John Peter Altgeld (the same governor who pardoned the eight Haymarket defendants a year later), were quickly challenged, then overturned by the courts. So, despite increasing social concern at the horrors of child labor, it was not until 1916 that the Keating-Owen Child Labor Act was passed by Congress and signed into law by President Woodrow Wilson. This, however, was ruled unconstitutional by the Supreme Court. It was only in 1938, with the introduction of the Fair Labor Standards Act, upheld by the Supreme Court in 1941, that child labor was outlawed once and for all in the United States.

The Haymarket Affair

Throughout the 1880s union-organized strikes were increasingly declared illegal by the US courts, and the language of working-class activists became more desperate and radical. Among new and old immigrants, as well as among many educated social reformers such as Robert Hunter, there was widespread frustration at the perceived inadequacies of the American governmental system in effecting enduring labor reform. Victories in the form of legislation were short-lived as the industrial elite, in alliance with state and federal judiciary, quickly stepped in to overturn any laws that sought to alleviate the plight of the poor.

The trial of *Spies v People* unfolded in a period of intense labor frustration, provoking an outpouring of public emotion both in support of the indicted activists and in protest against them. The mainstream press resorted to sensationalism and highlighted prevailing stereotypes of radical immigrants that dovetailed with a eugenics philosophy. As mentioned above, five of the defendants were German and another was of German descent. Controversially, one of the defendants, Albert Parsons, was married to Lucy Parsons, a labor organizer and former slave with black, Mexican and Native American ancestry. Together the defendants were depicted as immoral outsiders and in their animalism arguably sub-human. 'The villainous teachings of the Anarchists bore bloody fruit', reported *The New York Times*, and the rioters, 'led by two wiry, whiskered foreigners', were filled with 'cruel heartlessness' (6 May 1886). The *Chicago Tribune* described the eight defendants as 'arch counselors of riot, pillage, incendiarism and murder', and other papers called them 'cutthroats', 'fiends', 'thieves', 'assassins', and 'bloody monsters' (Avrich 1984: 393). 'Long-haired, wild-eyed, bad-smelling, atheistic, reckless, foreign wretches, who never did an honest hour's work in their lives … crush such snakes … before they have time to strike' (cited in Higham 1995: 55).

Some critics of the Haymarket riot explicitly expressed their horror in terms of eugenics theory. One writer stated that anarchy is a 'blood disease' from which the English have never suffered. 'I am no race worshipper but if the master of this continent is subordinated to or overrun with communist and revolutionary races, it will be in grave danger of social disaster' (cited in Higham 1995: 138). Reverend Theodore T Munger, an advocate of social evolutionary theory, saw in the Haymarket affair 'anarchism, lawlessness … labor strikes, and a general violation of personal rights such as the Anglo-Saxon race has not witnessed since Magna Carta'. Munger was a strong supporter of restricting immigration 'so that the physical stock shall not degenerate' and 'the strong, fine strain [shall be kept] ascendant' (Higham 1995: 138). This sort of racial thinking was reflected in the popular press, such as *Frank Leslie's Illustrated Newspaper*, in which an anarchist was depicted as smaller in stature than upstanding Americans, irrational and crazy in his jumping on smoking bombs, monkey-like in his antics (Figure 28).

Even greater than the fear of racial degeneration was the fear of immigrant lawlessness. As the historian John Higham notes, 'No nativist image prevailed more widely than that of the immigrant as a lawless creature, given over to violence and disorder' (Higham 1995: 55). The American legal system provided a core institutional frame by which the moral worth of righteous citizens and their unique national identity could be measured. In this context, the conservative middle classes and industrial elite were appalled by the threat of working-class violence and its challenge to the rule of law. Images circulated in the public

UNCLE SAM (TO LABOR PARTY REPRESENTATIVE).—" *You did splendidly, my boy, for a first attempt ; but, for your own good and that of the country, get rid of that dangerous companion of yours as soon as possible.*"

Figure 28.   Uncle Sam (to Labor Party Representative): 'You did splendidly, my boy, for a first attempt, but, for your own good and that of the country, get rid of that dangerous companion of yours as soon as possible.' *Frank Leslie's Illustrated Newspaper*, 13 November 1886. With permission from Special Collections and Archives, Georgia State University Library.

imaginary of darker-skinned barbaric hordes, ungrateful and untrustworthy, and above all un-American in their sacrilegious disregard for law and order, freedom and liberty. In this racially charged environment it was widely felt that the full arm of the law was needed in order to keep foreigners in check. The scale of potential lawlessness justified, in the minds of many Americans, the lack of due legal process resulting from a biased jury and a failure to provide any evidence in the *Spies v People* trial. At stake was the future of the country. As declared by Attorney General Grinnell in his summation at the trial, 'convict these men, make examples of them, hang them and you save our institutions, our society' (Foner 1986: 34).

Reflecting on this travesty of justice, what the trial highlights is the lengths to which late nineteenth century middle and upper classes were prepared to go to protect their sense of Protestant white national identity, as well as their right to exploit the working classes and take advantage of a laissez-faire capitalist system. These lengths included the use of martial law, denial of due process, racial profiling, abuse of extra-judicial authority, and the manipulation of facts in order to prosecute and condemn the leaders of the movement. These gross injustices were written out of the legal records, though publicly acknowledged by the Governor who pardoned the indicted men seven years after the trial. In short, discourses about religion and race coalesced to provide justification for the gross illegalities associated with the *Spies v People* trial—a trial which has been characterized as one of the most serious miscarriages of justice in United States history.

Radicalizing and Co-opting May Day

The deaths of the Haymarket defendants galvanized an international labor movement as no previous event had. Two years after the Haymarket affair the International Labor Congress was held in Paris. A year later, on 1 May 1890, the First International Workers Day was held and thousands marched around the world in support of working-class demands for an eight-hour day. In London alone it was said that between 350,000 and 500,000 workers marched in what *The Times* described as the 'greatest demonstration of modern times' (5 May 1890). Frederick Engels, in his preface to the fourth German edition of the *Communist Manifesto*, wrote enthusiastically about the hundreds of thousands of workers who had demonstrated in so many countries:

> As I write these lines, the proletariat of Europe and America is holding a review of its forces: it is mobilized for the first time as One army, under One flag, and fighting for One immediate aim: an eight-hour working day, established by legal enactment ... The spectacle we are witnessing will make the capitalists and landowners of all lands realize that today the proletariat of all lands, are in very truth, united. If only Marx were with me to see it with his own eyes! (Foner 1986: 55)[7]

A year later, in preparation for May Day 1891, enthusiasm for the labor movement grew as thousands of workers and union groups planned mass demonstrations and strikes. The issue of the eight-hour workday was still central to the platform, but by this stage other demands had been added, such as the freeing of political prisoners, the right to political organization, and the end of colonial oppression. Members of the suffragette movement, spurred on by the militant resistance of their 'sisters' in Britain, became increasingly active, calling for the vote to be extended to women and minorities (Mayhall 2003; Harrison 2000). In an interview in *The People*, Samuel Gompers, President of the American Federation of Labor, announced:

---

[7] Karl Marx died on 14 March 1883, in conditions of extreme poverty. However, Marx's daughter, Eleanor Marx Aveling, was very much involved in these events.

May 1st of each year is now looked upon by organized wage-workers and the observing public as a sort of new Independence Day upon which they will every year strike a blow for emancipation and steadily weaken the shackles of wage slavery. (*The People*, 26 April 1891)

However, while the celebration of May Day became popular over the decades among labor organizations in many countries, in the United States concerted efforts were made by those in power to prevent further class organization and what was labeled anti-capitalist agitation. Through the early years of the twentieth century, it became an increasing economic and political necessity for the US government, as well as industrial and corporate interests, to radicalize the image of the labor movement, distort its agenda, and whip up public opposition against it. This was achieved relatively easily by using newspapers and pamphlets to underscore the links existing between labor groups and socialist and communist organizations. And since many labor organizers were immigrants and new to the United States, it was easy to fuel nationalist fears of invading foreigners. As early as the 1910s, first President Theodore Roosevelt and then President Woodrow Wilson warned of 'hyphenated Americans', who, the latter argued, had 'poured the poison of disloyalty into the very arteries of our national life. Such creatures of passion, disloyalty and anarchy must be crushed out' (Kennedy 1980: 24).

The government, in cooperation with corporate America, denigrated and denounced labor demands by fueling the growing Red Scare and general fears of Bolshevik activism that emerged in the wake of the Russian Revolution of 1917.[8] The result was a growing distrust of organized labor, which in turn became increasingly militant given the lack of substantive changes to labor laws. Conflicts, sometimes violent and bloody, occurred between labor activists and government agencies throughout World War I and into the 1920s and 30s, such as the Palmer Raids on the radical left which took place in the years 1919–21 (see Gage 2009). When the stock market crashed in 1929, leaving millions of people unemployed, starving and destitute, the need to quell civic protest intensified further. At the 1930 May Day parade in New York, a crowd of 100,000 gathered to demonstrate 'while machine guns appeared on top of low buildings and their muzzles tilted downward to the Square' (Foner 1986: 110).

But the most explicit and systematic silencing of domestic labor demands for just pay and conditions came with Harry Truman's initiation of the Cold War in the late 1940s and the second wave of the Red Scare under McCarthyism. By once again mobilizing fear outward against foreign peoples and their 'anti-American' ideologies, the powerful elite, backed by legal authority, could avoid having to deal with structural injustices and the exploitation of minorities and the poor built into the domestic capitalist system. In March 1947 Truman ordered a full-scale 'loyalty investigation' and his frenzy to ascertain who was a potential

---

[8] In 1919, both the Communist Party and the Communist Labor Party were formed in the United States, and in the following year 'over 6,000 men and women were arrested by federal agents, and 556 aliens, though convicted of no crimes, were deported' (Foner 1986: 92–93).

threat to the United States spilled over into legislation regulating labor. Under the 1947 Taft-Hartley Act, the power of employers was increased and the power of trade unions further limited. In an explicit conflation of terrorist fears with business interests, the Act forced union officials to swear that they did not have any allegiance to communist ideologies or belong to the Communist Party. Labeling labor movements as communist meant that labor demands could be dismissed. Since 1947, mainstream media in the United States has linked May Day to the Communist Party and in so doing silenced potential public demonstration by labor organizations against the inequalities leveled primarily at the working class and in particular women, children and racial minorities. As noted by the historian Donna Haverty-Stacke, 'the marginalizing of May Day became central to the construction of a new form of popular American nationalism' appropriate to the political culture of the Cold War. This new American nationalism was built on 'an anticommunist consensus and extolled the promise of democracy and the free market' (see Haverty-Stacke 2009: 223).

CONCLUSION

In 1955, in an explicit move to co-opt May Day, President Dwight Eisenhower declared 1 May to be 'Loyalty Day' and in 1958 Congress passed this resolution into law. That same year, Eisenhower also proclaimed 1 May to be 'Law Day' in an effort to 'strengthen our great heritage of liberty, justice, and equality under the law'.[9] While today very few people actually observe either Loyalty Day or Law Day on 1 May, the 1958 proclamations, intended to rewrite May Day's symbolism, demonstrate the lengths to which the government was prepared to go in a larger effort to fight both internal and external Cold War threats to the American way of life. Since the 1950s and the decline of the Red Scare, there have been very few May Day labor marches in the United States. While hundreds of thousands of people take to the streets each year on this day around the world and celebrate the courage and achievements of the Haymarket rioters, ironically in the United States, the birthplace of this achievement, the day typically passes without comment, recognition, or even much media coverage of the global demonstrations (Haverty-Stacket 2009).[10] Hundreds of thousands march, but for what reasons most Americans cannot remember.

Despite major efforts to erase or 'paper over' the Haymarket affair, the lawless extra-judicial circumstances of the case which included lack of due process,

---

[9] A few years earlier, in 1954, Eisenhower signed into law the resolution that made 'In God We Trust' the national motto of the United States; the phrase first appeared on paper currency in 1957.

[10] However, 1 May was chosen by immigrant groups in 2006 as the day for a massive general strike across the United States to protest against the increasingly harsh penalities imposed on illegal immigrants and heightened security at the US-Mexican border (Haverty-Stacke 2009: 1–2). In the *New York Times* and other major news media, it was said that the boycott was 'timed to coincide with International Workers' Day', which is apparently one of the few known instances of the day being mentioned by this name in the US press in the last 30 years.

torture, coercion, racial profiling, guilt through association, and the manipulation of media and political processes, have resurfaced periodically in the twentieth and early twenty-first centuries. These cyclical appearances of legally authorized injustices suggest a greater structural context for the sanctioning of lawlessness. In many ways, the Haymarket riot and trial stand as a landmark and predecessor to the use of extra-judicial authority invoked in subsequent times of national crisis to combat communism in the late 1910s, during World War II, in the 1950s under McCarthyism, and throughout the Cold War era. More recently, extra-judicial authority has been used to combat Islamic-fundamentalism in the Gulf Wars and in the post-9/11 War on Terror. This was most recently evidenced by the former Bush administration justifying the stripping of habeas corpus protections from those deemed to be terrorists under the Military Commissions Act of 2006, despite the Supreme Court deciding a few months earlier in *Hamdan v Rumsfeld* that the federal government did not have authority to set up special military commissions, and that these commissions were illegal under the Geneva Convention and the Uniform Code of Military Justice. In all these cases public consciousness has been influenced by particular discourses on religion and race that have been nurtured and strategically mobilized. Whether the enemy is labeled an irrational anarchist, a godless communist or an Islamic fundamentalist, it is the threat to the American way of life (which often involves a critique of laissez-faire capitalism) that has consistently been invoked to create an environment of fear and xenophobia, to deny legal rights to civilians, and to justify governmental and judicial lawlessness in the name of fighting domestic 'terrorism'.

Recommended Reading

Du Bois, WEB (1903) *The Souls of Black Folks*. New York: Bantam Books (1989).

Gage, Beverly (2009) *The Day Wall Street Exploded: A Story of America in its First Age of Terror*. Oxford: Oxford University Press.

Gordon, Robert W (2008) 'The American Legal Profession, 1870–2000', in Michael Grossberg and Christopher Tomlins (eds), *The Cambridge History of Law in America, Vol III*. Cambridge: University of Cambridge Press, pp 73–126.

Green, James (2006) *Death in the Haymarket: A Story of Chicago, the First Labor Movement and the Bombing that Divided Gilded Age America*. New York: Pantheon.

Hall, Kermit L and Peter Karsten (2009) *The Magic Mirror: Law in American Society*. 2nd edn, Oxford: Oxford University Press.

Higham, John (2002) *Strangers in the Land: Patterns of American Nativism, 1860–1925*. New Brunswick: Rutgers University Press.

Ignatiev, Noel (1995) *How the Irish Became White*. New York: Routledge.

Lombardo, Paul A (2008) *Three Generations, No Imbeciles: Eugenics, the Supreme Court, and Buck v Bell*. Baltimore: Johns Hopkins University Press.

Jacobson, Matthew Frye (1998) *Whiteness of a Different Color: European Immigrants and the Alchemy of Race*. Cambridge, MA: Harvard University Press.

Roediger, David R (2007) *The Wages of Whiteness: Race and the Making of the American Working Class.* Revised edn,
New York: Verso.
Rourse, Victoria (2008) *In Reckless Hands: Skinner v Oklahoma and the Near-Triumph of American Eugenics.* New York: WW Norton.
Tamanaha, Brian Z (2006) *Law as a Means to an End. Threat to the Rule of Law.* Cambridge: Cambridge University Press.
Weber, Max (1904) The Protestant Ethic and the Spirit of Capitalism. London: Routledge (1992).

6

Civilizing Native Americans—The Dawes Act (1887)

I N CONTRAST TO Irish, Polish, Hungarian, Italian and Greek foreigners
coming to the United States, Native Americans were not a threat in the sense
that they challenged the authority of industrialists to exploit the poor, or
competed with white working classes for limited jobs. Nor by the later decades of
the nineteenth century were Indians considered much of a threat to law and
order. Rather, the prevailing religious and racial attitudes at the time demanded
that natives, seen by most as racially inferior remnants of some sort of prehistoric
age, be simply left alone to die out or alternatively be forced to assimilate into a
dominant Protestant Christian society.

The legal landmark explored in this chapter is the General Allotment Act (the
Dawes Severalty Act) of 1887. For the first time under this Act the federal
government dealt with Indians and tribes collectively. This was an explicit
rejection of the former system of specific treaty negotiations between the
government and each federally-recognized tribe that had been widely used in the
nineteenth-century reservation era up until the passing of the Suspension of
Treaty-Making Act in 1871. The Dawes Act was expressly designed as a way to
'civilize' Indians and assimilate them into American society by granting individual Indians plots of land and forcing them to exercise western legal rights of
property ownership. So, unlike the mobilization of religious and racist discourses
to justify the denial of basic legal rights to working classes explored in the
previous chapter, the Dawes Act is an example of a reversed strategy whereby
granting legal rights was seen as a mechanism to compel the assimilation of
native peoples. The degree to which natives were deemed 'competent and
capable' to exercise their property rights determined the degree to which they
were considered assimilated. In other words, under the Dawes Act property
rights—more specifically the deemed competency to exercise those rights—was
the mechanism employed to resolve the ambiguous racial and religious status of
native peoples. The criteria for 'competency' were that Indians act, dress, speak
and work the land like non-Indians in singular nuclear-family units, which in
turn suggested a renunciation of tribal customs and 'heathen' spiritual practices.

The Dawes Act is considered a landmark in the history of Anglo-American law precisely because it was one of the first deliberate instances where a government, under the banner of granting individual property rights to marginalized people, could then make null and void legal rights held in common by Indians as members of specific tribes. The Act is also considered a landmark because while it was seen as a huge mistake and reversed in 1934, its ramifications and consequences continue to shape Indian and non-Indian relations in contemporary US society.

The Dawes Act was the culminating legislation in an era of blatant colonial abuse and legal manipulation of Indian peoples' claim to tribal territories and sovereign self-government. It legally endorsed cultural stereotypes of native peoples (ie lazy, unproductive, inept) that continue to be evoked in mainstream media and underscore today's prevailing cultural attitudes toward Indians. Moreover, it set out the means by which Indian identity was legally determined by affirming the use of blood quantum measures to determine who was an 'authentic' Indian for the purposes of being allotted land. To this day this psuedo-scientific western schema is used as evidence of Indian identity, and continues to be the cause of bitter social, political, economic and legal conflict within and between tribes, as well as between those deemed Indian and non-Indian. Lastly, and perhaps most profoundly, the Dawes Act took away tribal sovereign land from tribes. As a result, many tribes have not been able to reclaim their formal status as federally recognized tribes,[1] and so have been unable to receive social service benefits, such as health and education, to which they were entitled under former treaty arrangements.

The General Allotment Act (the Dawes Severalty Act) 1887

The bitter violence between native peoples and settler communities that intermittently flared up in the eighteenth and nineteenth centuries had dramatically diminished by the 1880s. The Battle of Little Big Horn in 1876, also known as Custer's Last Stand or the Battle of Greasy Grass Creek, was the last real victory for tribal communities. In this battle, Crazy Horse and Sitting Bull led a Lakota-Northern Cheyenne combined force to victory against the US Army's Seventh Cavalry Regiment, resulting in the deaths of hundreds of soldiers. This dramatic defeat precipitated fierce retaliation by the federal government. The army was expanded to deal with the remaining Indian resistance: reservation boundaries were redrawn to allow for greater white settlement, and within a few years the Sioux nation lay defeated and broken. The last of the Indian Wars was

---

[1] Today there are 562 federally recognized tribes, but many people who identify as being Native American do not belong to federally recognized tribes. As a consequence, these people do not qualify for most of the social services, health, education and other opportunities provided by the government for tribal members based on former treaties and federal trust responsibilities.

declared to be the Wounded Knee Massacre in South Dakota in 1890, which was prompted by the shooting of Sitting Bull, and left over 200 Lakota Sioux men, women and children dead.

For the majority of Americans who lived in the industrial cities of the eastern seaboard, the Wounded Knee Massacre in 1890 symbolized the final resistance of native peoples to the encroachment of white settlers. In a profound sense, the massacre was the final act in an era of enormous westward expansion driven by pioneers seeking to set up homesteads and farmland. In the same year as the massacre, the US census bureau reported that as a result of much western settlement, the frontier line no longer existed. The historian Frederick Jackson Turner responded to this pronouncement in an essay entitled *The Significance of the Frontier in American History* (1893), in which he concurred that the frontier was indeed 'closed'. Evidence used by Turner to support his thesis included the density of settlers per square mile and the evident taming of formerly savage Indians. According to Turner, America had once been a virgin continent where civilization (Europeans) met and ultimately conquered savagery (Indians). The collision between Europeans and Indians took place at the frontier, which was a fictitious geographical site that slowly moved from east to west as pioneers began to settle, farm, and tame the wild lands. Conquering nature, and by implication the native peoples who inhabited the wild frontier, was a central theme and mission for the new white American nation and its escalating nationalist spirit. This encounter with savagery, Turner argued, helped to forge the unique temperament and traditions of Americans. Building on Alexander De Tocqueville's earlier great work *Democracy in America* (1835), in which De Tocqueville expounded upon the vast expanse of open land and large landholdings in the United States which helped to make Americans very different in their social and political organization from the class-based Europeans they had left behind, Turner saw the frontier as central to the American character. 'Frontier America' became a central motif in understanding and explaining the rugged individualism, defense of personal freedom, sense of egalitarianism, and suspicion of government that many commentators since Turner have pointed to as indicators of the 'exceptional' American spirit.

Turner's claim that the Indians had been 'tamed' was in a sense true. Apart from last-ditch battles such as Wounded Knee, by the end of the nineteenth century Indian resistance to white settlers was sporadic and eventually virtually non-existent. Many native peoples had been spiritually, morally and physically devastated by the disease and destruction wrought by westward-bound pioneers. Tribal communities had been split and kinship networks dissipated. Disparate groups of native peoples were relegated to far-away reservations on poor lands with few resources such as running water. Under such conditions, it was generally believed by white Americans that most natives were rather pathetic, obsolete reminders of some sort of prehistoric age. This attitude is reflected in the soft-focus ghostly photographs of native peoples taken by Edward S Curtis (Figure 29). Hired by JP Morgan in 1906 to record the last of the 'vanishing'

Indians, Curtis inscribed in the introduction to the first volume of *The North American Indian*: 'The information that is to be gathered ... respecting the mode of life of one of the great races of mankind, must be collected at once or the opportunity will be lost.'

Figure 29.   Indians in a Piegan Lodge, c 1911, Edward S Curtis. This photograph depicts Little Plume and his son, Yellow Kidney, seated on the ground inside a lodge, with a tobacco pipe between them. 'According to Curtis's written caption – "The picture is full of suggestion of the various Indian activities" – occupations represented by medicine bundles, a buffalo-skin shield, and deerskin harnesses for horses' (Wakeham 2008:98). However, a comparison of the photo above with a subsequent version of it published in *The North American Indian* shows that Curtis touched up the second photograph by removing the alarm clock, and superimposing a rustic basket in its place. Curtis was anxious to present Native Americans as timeless and culturally pristine, unaffected by the devastating impact of colonialism. The clock was evidence of contact between Indians and non-Indians and so was erased. © United States Library of Congress.

Against this belief in the racial inferiority of Indians that signaled their inevitable decline, and morally justified their forceable removal to remote reservations under the Indian Removal Act (1830), concerted efforts were made by some humanitarian groups to 'save' the Indians. This mission was fueled by reports issued by the Bureau of Indian Affairs in the 1870s which suggested that Indians were not going to die out and that in fact some tribes had actually increased their numbers (Banner 2005a: 263). Given that the 'Indian problem' was not going to go away as many had hoped, attitudes shifted toward a policy of assimilating Indians into modern society. It is in this context that the Dawes Act, named after Republican Senator Henry L Dawes of Massachusetts, who sponsored the landmark legislation, must be understood. Driven by a belief in assimilation, the Dawes Act was conceived as a deliberate strategy to break up tribal communities and networks and give Indians their own plot of land to farm and become self-sufficient—to give Indians the same opportunities as had been granted white homesteaders and settlers. Many of those involved in promoting the Act were well-intentioned eastern humanitarians, and many were members of groups such as the Indian Rights Association, the Indian Protection Committee, and Friends of the Indians. These people, along with a few outspoken Native Americans, believed that granting land to Indians was the first step in making Indians 'civilized' members of modern society. Specifically, the racial stereotypes of Indians as lazy and ambitionless would be countered by granting Indians land and instilling in them the values of progress, self-sufficiency and 'rugged individualism' which Turner had articulated in his 'Frontier Thesis'.

A strong supporter of assimilation was Alice Cunningham Fletcher, an early ethnographer who greatly admired native peoples and led the group Friends of the Indians. Fletcher fought tirelessly for Indians to be granted citizenship and keenly promoted the Dawes Act, which under section 6 allowed an Indian to claim citizenship and 'all the rights, privileges, and immunities' associated with citizenship if he or she 'has voluntarily taken up ... his residence separate and apart from any tribe of Indians therein, and has adopted the habits of civilized life'.[2] That Indians had no choice but to be subject to the Dawes Act and 'to the laws, both civil and criminal, of the State or Territory in which they may reside' was irrelevant to Fletcher. In Fletcher's opinion, the very subjugation of Indians by US law was the essential key in liberating them. 'The Indian may now become a free man; free from the thralldom of the tribe; freed from the domination of the reservation system; free to enter the body of our citizens. This bill may therefore be considered as the Magna Carta of the Indians of our country' (Mark 1988: 118). Senator Dawes pushed this sentiment further by linking the ownership of property with being civilized. To be civilized, Dawes argued, was to 'wear civilized clothes ... cultivate the ground, live in houses, ride in Studebaker wagons, send children to school, drink whiskey [and] own property'.

---

[2] In this way the requirement for US citizenship was effectively 'the repudiation of native religions and ways of life, and acceptance of American middle-class Christianity with its attended customs' (Smith 1997: 318–19). Note that Native Americans were not granted citizenship until 1924, when Congress passed the Indian Citizenship Act.

The Real Motives behind the Dawes Act

At first the Dawes Act seemed a generous federal plan since it acknowledged the right of individual Indians to own plots of land and encouraged them to take up farming and agricultural practices in the same way as white settlers. However, in reality the Act conveniently provided the legal mechanism to make null and void all former treaties establishing self-governing Indian sovereign tribes on reservations. On this basis Senator Henry Moore Teller took a minority position and argued against the Dawes Act, which, he asserted, would result in the breaking up of tribal lands. In a congressional report in 1881 Teller insightfully noted that Indians already had legal systems that recognized property rights in the use of land and so did not need or would not benefit from the allotment process. He declared:

> The real purpose of this bill is to get at the Indian lands and open them up to settlement. The provisions for the apparent benefit of the Indians are but the pretext to get at his lands and occupy them ... If this were done in the name of greed, it would be bad enough; but to do it in the name of humanity, and under the cloak of an ardent desire to promote the Indian's welfare by making him like ourselves where he will or not, is infinitely worse. (cited in O'Brien 1989: 78)

Despite some resistance to the Dawes Act at the time of its passing, it quickly came to represent prevailing attitudes toward native peoples. A few years later, in 1890, the Commissioner of Indian Affairs, Thomas J Morgan, noted that 'It has become the settled policy of the Government to break up reservations, destroy tribal relations, settle Indians upon their own homesteads, incorporate them into the national life, and deal with them not as nations or tribes or bands, but as individual citizens' (Morgan 1890). Under the Dawes Act reservation land held 'in the entirety' by a tribe was broken up into separate plots to be held 'in severalty' by individuals. Furthermore, the Act held that the President of the United States was authorized to take any reservation or part of a reservation deemed 'advantageous for agricultural and grazing purposes' and allocate that land to individual Indians. This meant that a maximum plot of 160 acres could be allotted to heads of families, with single adults over 18 receiving a maximum plot of 80 acres and children receiving 40 acres. The land was held in trust for Indians for 25 years. This meant that native peoples could not sell or give away their lands away until that period had passed, though this time constraint was reduced in subsequent amendments.

The remaining 'surplus' lands would be bought by the federal government on terms it considered 'just and equitable', and resold to white settlers, railways companies, cattle ranchers and later on to oil and gas industries, creating a checkerboard of Indian and non-Indian landholdings (Biolsi 2001; Stremlau 2005: 277; Banner 2005a: 285). Needless to say, the surplus land redistributed to whites was typically of better quality, with greater access to water and mineral resources (Figure 30). Proceeds from the sale and leasing of these leftover lands

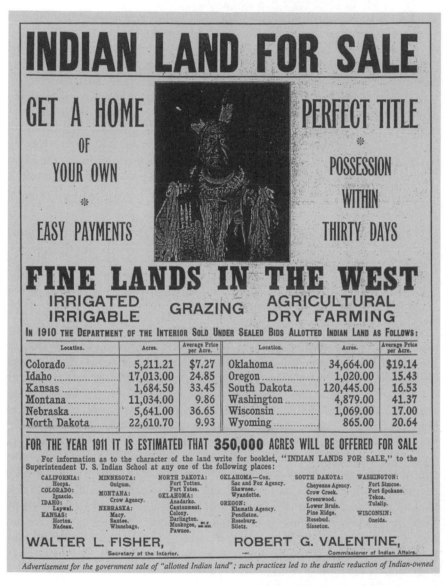

INDIAN LAND FOR SALE

GET A HOME
OF
YOUR OWN
❋
EASY PAYMENTS

PERFECT TITLE
❋
POSSESSION
WITHIN
THIRTY DAYS

FINE LANDS IN THE WEST
IRRIGATED
IRRIGABLE
GRAZING
AGRICULTURAL
DRY FARMING

In 1910 THE DEPARTMENT OF THE INTERIOR SOLD UNDER SEALED BIDS ALLOTTED INDIAN LAND AS FOLLOWS:

Location.	Acres.	Average Price per Acre.	Location.	Acres.	Average Price per Acre.
Colorado	5,211.21	$7.27	Oklahoma	34,664.00	$19.14
Idaho	17,013.00	24.85	Oregon	1,020.00	15.43
Kansas	1,684.50	33.45	South Dakota	120,445.00	16.53
Montana	11,034.00	9.86	Washington	4,879.00	41.37
Nebraska	5,641.00	36.65	Wisconsin	1,069.00	17.00
North Dakota	22,610.70	9.93	Wyoming	865.00	20.64

FOR THE YEAR 1911 IT IS ESTIMATED THAT **350,000** ACRES WILL BE OFFERED FOR SALE

For information as to the character of the land write for booklet, "INDIAN LANDS FOR SALE," to the Superintendent U. S. Indian School at any one of the following places:

CALIFORNIA: Hoopa.	MINNESOTA: Onigum.	NORTH DAKOTA: Fort Totten. Fort Yates.	OKLAHOMA—Con. Sac and Fox Agency. Shawnee.	SOUTH DAKOTA: Cheyenne Agency. Crow Creek.	WASHINGTON: Fort Simcoe. Fort Spokane.
COLORADO: Ignacio.	MONTANA: Crow Agency.	OKLAHOMA: Anadarko.	Wyandotte.	Greenwood.	Tekoa. Tulalip.
IDAHO: Lapwai.	NEBRASKA: Macy.	Cantonment. Colony.	OREGON: Klamath Agency.	Lower Brule. Pine Ridge.	WISCONSIN: Oneida.
KANSAS: Horton. Nadeau.	Santee. Winnebago.	Darlington. Muskogee, ^{etc.} Pawnee.	Pendleton. Roseburg. Siletz.	Rosebud. Sisseton.	

WALTER L. FISHER,
Secretary of the Interior.

ROBERT G. VALENTINE,
Commissioner of Indian Affairs.

Advertisement for the government sale of "allotted Indian land"; such practices led to the drastic reduction of Indian-owned

Figure 30. Poster advertising the sale of Native American lands, 1911. Issued by the Bureau of Indian Affairs.

would then be held in trust by the Department of the Interior, which oversaw the Bureau of Indian Affairs, for the 'education and civilization' of Indians. Through these imposed practices, the Dawes Act provided the legal mechanism for the federal government to strip Indians of much of their tribal territories and satisfy the pressure from white settlers to have access to arable farming land. The Act's recognition of Indians as American citizens conveniently allowed both federal and state governments to manage Indians by bringing them within the jurisdictional authority of western law.

This process of allotment proved to be culturally, politically and economically disastrous for the Indian tribes (Charlot 1999). In cultural terms, personally owned farming plots represented a very different understanding of one's relationship to land to that held by most Native Americans. Individual property rights over a spatially defined piece of land was not the norm among Indian communities; rather they exercised rights to particular uses and resources associated with a piece of land. As the legal historian Stuart Banner has pointed out:

> A person [ie Indian] might, for example, have a right to farm a given strip of land during the growing season, the right to pasture a certain number of animals in a certain field during certain times of the year, the right to gather wood from a given forest, and so on. Between the fifteenth century and the nineteenth century, this functionally organized system of property rights was gradually transformed into the spatially organized system we know today, in which individuals and families own zones of land and are understood to command all the resources within that zone. (Banner 2005a: 258)

Land held by individual Indians disrupted the idea of community-based tribal lands and created spatial distance between kinship groups. This had a devastating impact on cultural customs and spiritual practices, many of which depended on group involvement. Traditional gender roles were shattered and social relations between men and women were forced to change. Prior to the Act, women were the agriculturalists and men the hunters and warriors; under the Act men were forced to farm and women were forced to retreat to the domestic sphere, in the process losing much of their social and political power (Olund 2002: 157).

The allotment system also broke up traditional political systems of tribal governance and heralded the declining significance of indigenous systems of law and control. It forced Indians to work in a western legal system, which was largely inaccessible and prejudicial to their needs. As legally recognized rights-holding citizens, they were left vulnerable to being legally discriminated against and legally managed. This dismantling of tribal legal and social relations was predicted by former interior secretary Carl Schurz when he wrote, 'when the Indians are individual property owners their tribal cohesion will necessarily relax, and gradually disappear. They will have advanced an immense step in the direction of the white man's ways' (cited in Banner 2005a: 268).

The economic impact of the Dawes Act, in addition to other indignities, led to the tribes losing huge parcels of land. To what degree the scale of land loss was foreseen at the time of the Act's passing is hard to determine, though Senator Henry Moore Teller, an opponent of the Dawes Act, declared, 'when thirty or forty years have passed and these Indians shall have parted with their title, they will curse the hand that was raised professedly in their defense to secure this kind of legislation' (cited in Banner 2005a: 270). And indeed, between 1887 and 1934 indigenous communities lost 86 million acres, more than half their landholdings (Banner 2005a: 257). This land loss occurred in a number of ways. Some reservation lands were bought directly by the federal government and resold to white settlers. Other lands originally allotted to Indians were eventually leased or sold to white settlers. This happened because, as American citizens subject to the 'laws, both civil and criminal, of the State or Territory', many Indians had to pay property taxes for the first time. Since the government provided the new Indian farmers with very little in the way of training, ploughs, seeds and equipment, most failed miserably at the task. For those who did learn to farm, the 80-acre plots were typically too small to grow self-sustaining crops. Unable to pay taxes, many impoverished Indians were forced to sell their plots to white settlers and in turn work under them at very low wages simply in order to survive.

The Meriam Report (1928)

The disastrous impact on Indian communities perpetrated under the Dawes Act was revealed in the Meriam Report, which was published 40 years later. The report, issued by the Institute for Government Research (later to rename itself the Brookings Institute, Banner 2005a: 288) was officially entitled *The Problem of Indian Administration*. It was requested by the Secretary of the Interior, Hubert Work, who along with many others was concerned that the assimilation of Native Americans into mainstream society had not occurred at the same rate as it had for European immigrants. A survey team, led by the technical director Lewis Meriam, was charged with collecting information about the 'conditions among the Indians'. The final report, over 800 pages in length, contained a wealth of information on Indian health, education, economic development, social life, living conditions, and legal rights. In straightforward and uncompromising language the Meriam Report stated:

> Several past policies adopted by the government in dealing with the Indians have been of a type which, if long continued, would tend to pauperize any race ... When the government adopted the policy of individual ownership of the land on the reservations, the expectation was that the Indians would become farmers ... It almost seems as if the government assumed that some magic in individual ownership of property would in itself prove an educational civilizing factor, but unfortunately this policy has for the most part operated in the opposite direction ... Frequently the better sections of the land originally set apart for the Indians have fallen into the hands of the whites, and the Indians have retreated to the poorer lands remote from markets. (Meriam Report 1928 ch1: 3–4)

Ultimately the Meriam Report blamed the lack of governmental management in Indian affairs for the 'vicious circle of poverty and maladjustment' faced by most native peoples, and recommended that Congress supply $250,000 a year to establish a Division of Planning and Management of the Indian Service. The Meriam Report provided important evidence to support reform proposals, and helped to bring about the Indian Reorganization Act of 1934 (the Indian New Deal), which set out to reverse the Dawes Act and provide for tribes' return to self-government.

RELIGION: MISSIONARIES AND HEATHENS

The Meriam Report found that granting individual property rights to Indians would not 'magically' make them civilized and becoming assimilated into white non-Indian society. The Report also condemned other government policies relating to native people, particularly the pervasive trend to place Indian children in boarding schools and missionary outposts away from parents and family. 'The belief', stated the Report, 'has apparently been that the shortest road to civilization is to take children away from their parents insofar as possible to stamp out the old Indian life'. In language compassionate and yet still racist, the Report noted that while Indian communities have 'many objectionable features' a better strategy is not to attempt to destroy these features but rather attempt an 'educational process of gradual modification and development'. In particular, the Report suggested that the government and missionaries should 'take a sympathetic attitude toward Indian ways, Indian ethics, and Indian religion' (Meriam Report 1928: 9–10).

This call for sympathy toward the spiritual practices of native peoples directly confronted dominant attitudes that had existed in both England and America in one form or another for well over 200 years. These colonial-settler attitudes regarded non-Christian Indians as being brutish, beastly and inhuman. On that basis, they were justifiably the subjects of discrimination and even genocide (see chapter two). From the sixteenth century on, some Europeans even thought that Indians were man-eating cannibals who consumed the flesh of their enemies in revengeful, ritualistic ceremonies. Gruesome tales of blood lust circulated in travel diaries, merchants' records, and missionary accounts and provided a titillating backdrop to the common European understanding of the New World. While no concrete evidence existed to support the claim of cannibalism, nonetheless some colonists used the myth to justify deliberately killing or passively ignoring the disease, poverty and starvation that afflicted many Native Americans (on cannibalism see Jahoda 1999: 97–112; Pagden 1993; Lestringant 1997; Barta 1997).

In contrast to seeing Indians as inhuman beasts, in the second half of the eighteenth century some French Enlightenment philosophers and intellectuals idealized the notion of the 'noble savage' and praised native peoples for their apparently egalitarian societies devoid of class and religious divisions. Jean-Jacques Rousseau believed in the equality of all peoples, who, he argued, before becoming tainted with greed and selfishness had lived harmoniously in a pristine state of nature devoid of social and economic hierarchies. This romantic idealization of indigenous peoples often dovetailed with progressive thinkers who fought against slavery. For instance, Voltaire, in his satirical novel *Candide* (1759), combined idealized visions of natives living in bliss in Eldorado (ch XVII) with biting criticism of colonialism, slavery and the sugar trade (ch XIX). Across the Channel, English intellectuals, such as the poet and artist William Blake, while a unique thinker in his own right, nonetheless represented a relatively widespread pro-abolition movement which regarded both Africans and native peoples as equal in many ways to white Europeans. In one of his engravings Blake depicted a family of indigenous Australians in a comparatively dignified way, the mother and children presented with familiar Caucasian facial features and the father bearing a modest smile (Figure 31). Respect for indigenous peoples, albeit often based on a romanticized image of their harmonious social relations, crossed the Atlantic to the New World and, as we saw in chapter four, informed some of the American revolutionaries such as Benjamin Franklin, Thomas Jefferson and Thomas Paine.

Figure 31. *A Family of New South Wales,* 1792, engraving by William Blake after a sketch by Governor Phillip Gidley King. From John Hunter, *An Historical Journal of the Transactions at Port Jackson and Norfolk Island,* London, 1793. Etching and engraving (NGV 40), P8–1974, National Gallery of Victoria, Melbourne.

However, romanticized views of indigenous peoples were dismissed by the vast majority of European settlers living in north and central America. Despite the various motives behind exploration and conquest by Spanish, Dutch, French and English settlers, and the diverse ways in which each nation set up its colonial outposts, by the early 1700s they all held similar attitudes toward the native peoples they encountered (Darian-Smith 2003: 20–21). By the mid-1700s, these European attitudes had crystallized into a predominantly shared set of beliefs that indigenous peoples were wild, apelike savages without religion, culture, law or government. Reflecting an attitude typical of the time, the German scholar Meiners stated in 1773:

> The Americans are unquestionably the most depraved among all the human, or human-like creatures of the whole earth, and they are not only much weaker than the Negroes, but also much more inflexible, harder, and lacking in feelings …one will nonetheless feel, and be astonished, that the inhabitants of a whole continent are so closely related to dumb animals, (cited in Jahoda 1999: 21–22)

Making Indians Christian

The belief that Indians were wild and savage non-Christians marked their difference from mainstream society. This belief informed US federal and state government policies towards native peoples which either sought to wipe them out altogether or move them further west onto distant reservations, as exemplified by the Indian Removal Act of 1830 and the subsequent establishment of reservations in the mid-nineteenth century. Against this policy of extermination or isolation, there emerged a shift in the nineteenth century among some white Americans who believed that natives, despite being racially and socially inferior, could be 'civilized' and eventually assimilated. And it was argued that one of the most effective methods for assimilation was implementing new educational practices, which were funded in part by the federal government and to a large degree by Christian missionaries. By educating Indians 'properly', which in effect meant eradicating their pagan religions and converting them to Christianity, moves could be then made toward civilizing and assimilating them into white society. Individual ownership of land was seen as both a cause and consequence of Christian conversion. Only a Christian, it was argued, understood the true value of working the land for profit, and, as argued by the Revolutionary General Benjamin Lincoln approximately 100 years before the Dawes Act, an Indian could not be converted to Christianity until he understood his 'own situation, as it regards an exclusive right to the soil' (cited in Banner 2005a: 260).

In an attempt to 'save' native peoples, the US Congress passed the Civilization Fund Act in 1819 which established resources for the explicit purpose of promoting the 'civilization' of Native Americans through the power of schooling. This policy was aggressively pushed by Thomas McKenney, the first head of the Office of Indian Affairs, who argued that within one generation, Indians could be converted and civilized if they were forced to attend white missionary schools

(Spring 2007: 22–24). Throughout the nineteenth century, Protestant and Catholic churches in conjunction with federal and state authorities established a variety of missionary schools on reservations (on the conflicts between these churches see Prucha 1979). Many of these missions were required under imposed treaty agreements.

Then, in the late 1870s, off-reservation industrial boarding schools were also established with the specific intention of removing young Indian children from their families and homelands and disconnecting them from their heritage and traditions. The off-reservation boarding schools followed a long-standing model of forced cultural acculturation that had first been implemented by Reverend Eleazer Wheelock a century earlier (Axtell 2001: 174–88). Wheelock was known for converting Samson Occom, a Mohegan, and on the basis of this 'success' raised sufficient funds to establish Dartmouth College in 1769. According to Dartmouth's Charter, the school was established to educate English youth and 'to encourage the laudable and charitable design of spreading Christian knowledge among the savages of our American wilderness' (Dartmouth Charter 1769). The first nineteenth century off-reservation industrial boarding school was the Carlisle Industrial Training School in Pennsylvania, founded in 1879 by Richard Henry Pratt. The school was based on an earlier project Pratt had developed, a prison school for Indian prisoners of war at Florida's Fort Mansion prison. Pratt's desire was to 'kill the Indian and save the man'. In language evoking baptism, Pratt announced that he wanted to immerse 'Indians in our civilization and when we get them under [hold] them there until they are thoroughly soaked' (cited in Spring 2007: 32).

In addition to large off-reservation boarding schools for native children, Indian day schools were opened on reservations. These were cheaper to run than boarding schools and more acceptable to Indian communities, who often resisted their children's removal. Public schools were also opened up that could accommodate the growing number of white children as well as Indian children on allotted lands. Together all of these schools in the later decades of the nineteenth century—church run, government run, residential or day—sought to impose the values of 'disciplinary' Christianity. And in the process of making good Christians, the schools were also to make good American citizens. As Reverend AJ Lippincott declared at a Carlisle Indian School commencement, 'Let all that is Indian within you die! … You cannot become truly American citizens, industrious, intelligent, cultured, civilized until the Indian within you is dead' (cited in Adams 1995: 274). Thus in the 1887 *Annual Report of the Commissioner of Indian Affairs,* it was ordered that only English could be spoken in Indian schools. Two years later, the Commissioner of Indian Affairs, Thomas Morgan, issued 'Instructions to Indian Agents in Regard to Inculcation of Patriotism in Indian Schools'. These instructions dictated that the American flag was to be flown outside each Indian school, and all efforts made by teachers to instill duty and loyalty to the US government. In order to build patriotism, particular holidays were celebrated such as Washington's birthday, the Fourth of July, Thanksgiving, Christmas, and the anniversary of the day the Dawes Act was signed into law (Spring 2007: 33). No mention was to be made of native culture, customs, religion, songs, stories, law, or forms of government.

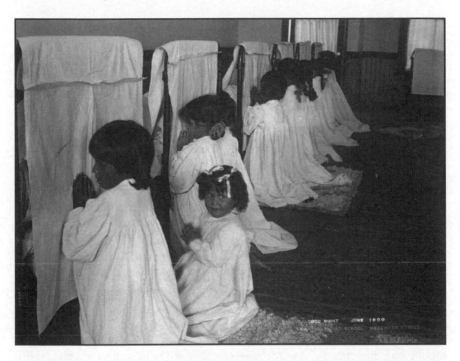

Figure 32. Little girls praying beside their beds, Phoenix Indian School, Arizona. Photographed by Messinger, June 1900. American Indian Select List number 162, courtesy of the National Archives, USA.

The effect of the boarding schools on native communities was devastating. The systematic removal of young people to off-reservation boarding schools contributed to a breakdown of kinship networks and internal tribal relations and often destroyed the ritual succession of customs from one generation to the next. Many young Indians suffered terrible emotional and physical hardship as a result of being removed from their loved ones, forced to speak in English and abandon their native names, wear uniforms, conform to strict rules, and being subject to harsh punishments. Large numbers of Indians were converted to Christianity, often under duress (Figure 32). As argued by the historian Michael Coleman, 'Christian proselytizing suffused the educational effort during these decades … For most secular as well as missionary educations, "civilization" was inconceivable unless grounded in Christian—especially Protestant—values' (Coleman

2007: 115). It has been estimated that by the end of the nineteenth century there were at least 20,000 Indians registered in 148 boarding schools, 25 of which were federally funded (Mihesuah 1996: 41).[3]

Criticism of Indian Boarding Schools

Investigations into boarding schools in the early decades of the twentieth century exposed the terrible conditions in which most Indian children existed. The Meriam Report of 1928 was scathing in its assessment of these boarding schools, stating 'frankly and unequivocally' that:

> ... the provisions for the care of Indian children in boarding schools are grossly inadequate ... The outstanding deficiency is in the diet furnished the Indian children, many of whom are below normal health. The diet is deficient in quantity, quality and variety. ... The major diseases of the Indians are tuberculosis and trachoma. ... The medical service rendered the boarding school children is not up to reasonable standard ... Next to dietary deficiencies comes overcrowding in dormitories. The boarding schools are crowded materially beyond their capacities. (Meriam Report 1928: 7)

The day-to-day existence of most of these schools depended upon the labor of the children. They were forced to work long days both at their schoolwork and in washing, cooking, sewing, carpentry and farming. Many children were 'loaned' to local farmers at the weekends and during the summer months to continue their education and provide cheap labor for local white communities. This practice, called the 'outing system' by Pratt at the Carlisle School, was widely practiced among boarding schools. The Meriam Report noted with respect to child labor:

> Those above the fourth grade ordinarily work for half a day and go to school for half a day ... [this] makes the day very long, and the child has almost no free time and little opportunity for recreation. ... The question may very properly be raised as to whether much of the work of Indian children in boarding schools would not be prohibited in many states by the child labor laws ... (Meriam Report 1928: 7)

By the time the Meriam Report was published, support for the Indian boarding school system had declined dramatically, both among government agencies and among the general public. Training children only in skills that had no relation to their Indian culture was deemed inappropriate, both for children who eventually returned to their tribes and who were often considered outcasts, and for those who

---

[3] These boarding schools and their goals of assimilation were not limited to the United States. A similar system existed in Canada, known as the residential school system (Lawrence 2004), as well as in Australia, where many Aboriginal children were removed from their clans in an attempt to educate and assimilate them (Beresford and Omaji 1998: Pierce 1999; Jacobs 2009). These children are often called 'the lost generations' or 'the stolen generations'. For a powerful and moving dramatization of these events see the film *Rabbit-Proof Fence* (2002), based on true stories as told by Doris Pilkington Garimara in her book *Follow the Rabbit-Proof Fence* (2001).

tried to use their skills in white society but without support, with the result that they were unable to compete competitively and often failed dismally.

It was clear that many of the Indian schools were not effective in assimilating Indians into white society and—like the allotment system—needed to be drastically reformed. In subsequent years the curriculum in Indian schools was broadened to include aspects of native cultures, but reform initiatives made during the Indian New Deal under the Commissioner of Indian Affairs, John Collier (1933–45), were overshadowed by the outbreak of World War II.

Legacy of the Dawes Act

Despite the problems associated with boarding schools, attendance levels increased during the twentieth century. It is estimated that in 1973, 60,000 Native American children were enrolled in some type of boarding school. Many of these schools closed in the 1980s and 90s as a result of a turn toward community schools rather than boarding schools. That being said, according to the Bureau of Indian Affairs, in 2007 there were still 9,500 Indian children living in Indian boarding schools. These boarding schools included 45 on-reservation, 7 off-reservation, and 14 other peripheral schools (Bureau of Indian Affairs 2008).

I am not suggesting that today's Indian boarding schools are the same as the boarding schools set up to assimilate native peoples between 1879, the year Pratt established the Carlisle Indian School, and 1928 when the Meriam Report soundly condemned these schools for their 'grossly inadequate' practices. Today's schools have different goals and curricula, and employ different educational practices. However, the very existence of Indian boarding schools as a method of education exclusive to native populations derives from federal policies toward Indians implemented under the Dawes Act over a century ago. The Dawes Act explicitly set out to assimilate Indians into mainstream society, and was central in granting legal and institutional support to the then prevailing dominant attitudes about native peoples in the United States. These dominant attitudes called for the implementation of off-reservation Indian boarding schools, and the legacy of those attitudes lives on, albeit implicitly, in the continuance of Indian boarding schools today.

Even after the Dawes Act was overturned and Indian boarding schools—which had prohibited the practice of native religions—were condemned, native religious practice and expression was still severely curtailed by US state and federal laws. This curtailment occurred despite growing sympathy for native culture which grew in the 1920s and 30s and is reflected in the Indian Reorganization Act of 1934. Finally, in 1978, the American Indian Religious Freedom Act was passed, which set out the basic right of all native peoples to practice their own religions 'including but not limited to access to sites, use and possession of sacred objects, and the freedom to worship through ceremonials and traditional rites'. While the 1978 Act is considered a foundational piece of legislation, it did not adequately empower Indians with a mechanism to enforce their rights to freedom of spiritual expression. After years of conflict and tension, the Native American Free Exercise of Religion Act was passed in 1993 which made it legal for peyote[4] to be used for ceremonial purposes by the Peyote Indians. However, there is still much controversy over the government's failure to protect sacred sites and to provide for Native Americans to practice their religions in jail in the same way as other ethnic or religious groups are allowed. In the twenty-first century, many native peoples still do not enjoy the same rights as others in American society to practice freedom of religion.

The legacy of the Dawes Act lives on in many ways besides religious oppression. In the following sections we will discuss its enduring consequences in determining race and identity issues for Indians today, as well as in the determination of Indians' legal rights, particularly with respect to the rights of tribes as self-determining sovereign nations.

RACE: DETERMINING THE RACE WITHIN

As discussed in chapter five, the eugenics movement, in conjunction with social evolutionary theories, had been developing in Britain and the United States throughout the 1800s. By the later decades of the nineteenth century, the eugenics movement was firmly entrenched in the United States as the dominant 'scientific' theory explaining differences between people. Proponents of eugenics claimed that a person's blood ratios and genetic lineage matched up to a classificatory system. The darker the tone of a person's skin, for instance, the greater the proportion of Indian blood versus Euro-American blood is presumed. Blood quantum—the quantity of blood from a particular race—was the method most commonly used to calculate a person's racial identity and, by implication, their social, intellectual and moral worth. Of course blood quantum cannot be physically ascertained—people do not actually have percentages of different blood that correlate to different races in their bodies. The concept of race is a social reality, not a biological one. Nevertheless, despite the fictional basis of blood quantum theory, many people believed (and still do today) that a person's blood could be rationally broken down into racially distinct components. Not only did blood quantum ratios provide a convenient explanation for social, legal, economic and physical disparities between humans, it also determined a person's 'fitness' for assimilation into American society (Garroutte 2003).

With respect to the US government's management of the 'Indian Problem', eugenics came to play a significant role. From the 1820s, the federal government had embarked on an aggressive policy of treaty negotiations with Indians in

---

[4] A small, spineless, dome-shaped cactus (*Lophophora williamsii*) native to Mexico and the southwest United States. It has buttonlike tubercles that are chewed fresh or dry as a narcotic drug by certain Native American peoples. It is also known as 'mescal'.

exchange for the use and appropriation of tribal lands (see Washburn 1971; Biolsi 1995). These treaties invariably obliged the federal government to provide a variety of ongoing services to Indians such as health, education, clothing and farming equipment that were intended to help native populations adjust to their diminished access to resources and tribal landholdings. The Statutes at Large Act of 1818 held that each Indian nation was to have a federal agent appointed who would act as a liaison and oversee the proper administration of the services provided. Throughout the century, the cost of the agents and the scale of these commitments became increasingly burdensome (Jaimes 1992: 125).

In an effort to limit the government's obligations and reduce the financial burden involved, the Department of the Interior increasingly turned to the blood quantum or 'degree of Indian blood' method as a way of identifying who could, or could not, qualify for government services. Not only did an Indian have to be from a federally recognized tribe with a treaty agreement in place, that person had to prove blood ties of a sufficient strength (usually one-half Indian) in order to meet the criteria. For many people, it was very difficult to prove their genealogical tree given the decimated Indian populations through genocide and disease, forced relocation of tribes from the eastern states to those in the west, and in some cases the amalgamation of parts of tribes into new political entities. From the perspective of the federal government, the blood quantum method proved to be effective in keeping the number of eligible Indians to a minimum, so much so that by the early 1900s

the eugenics mechanism of the blood quantum had already proven itself such a boon in the federal management of its Indian affairs that it was generally adapted as the 'eligibility factor', triggering entitlement to any federal service from the issuance of commodity rations to health care, annuity payments, and education benefits. If the government could not repeal its obligations to Indians, it could at least act to limit their number, thereby diminishing the costs associated with underwriting their entitlements on a per capita basis. Concomitantly, it must have seemed logical that if the overall number of Indians could be kept small, the administrative expenses involved in their service programs might also be held to a minimum. Much of the original impetus toward the federal preemption of the sovereign Indian prerogative of defining 'who's Indian', and the standardization of the racist degree-of-blood method of Indian identification, derived from the budgetary considerations of a federal government anxious to avoid paying its bills. (Jaimes 1992: 126–27)

The Dawes Act and Eugenics Policies

The blood quantum method of identification was used effectively by federal agents implementing the Dawes Act and in the allotment of land plots to individual Indians. As noted above, Indians were deemed eligible only if they could prove that one-half or more of their blood was Indian blood from one recognized tribe, and this identification had to be documented and then recorded on official registries or rolls. Many Indians failed the test, either because they were unable to prove their genealogical ancestry or because they had mixed tribal ancestry that did not amount to half blood from one tribe. For Indians from non-federally recognized tribes there was no mechanism for proving their legal 'authenticity' at all. In addition to these problems of proof, some Indians refused to cooperate with federal agents and declined to have their names entered on official rolls. For all those whose names did not appear on rolls, land allotment and social services of any kind were denied, and most were forced to move away from their communities and families without any compensation or assistance. For those who did pass the blood quantum test and were granted allotments, there were no guarantees that their children would also be legally recognized as 'authentic' Indians. This sense of unpredictability was heightened by the close proximity of Indians to white settlers on adjacent landholdings, and the increasing birth rate of interracial children.

From the perspective of the federal government, any difficulties in proving blood quantum eligibility only meant that more land was 'leftover', to be parceled out to the large numbers of white settlers anxious to take up landholdings on former Indian reservations. Relying upon a blood quantum system was a win-win situation for the government, both reducing its obligations to federally recognized Indians under earlier treaties and enabling it to make a profit by selling or leasing reservation land to non-Indians. But there was also a more sinister aspect to the blood quantum requirements imposed by the federal government, which directly related to eugenics theory. This was the understanding that pure full-blood Indians would become rarer and rarer, given the natural 'dilution' of blood ratios as a result of increasing intermarriage between Indians from various tribes, and between Indians and non-Indians. In the words of one scholar, 'Set the blood quantum at one-quarter, hold to it as a rigid definition of Indians, let intermarriage proceed as it had for centuries, and eventually Indians will be defined out of existence. When that happens, the federal government will be freed of its persistent "Indian Problem"' (Limerick 1987: 338).

Given the prevalence and authority of eugenics theory in the later part of the nineteenth century when the Dawes Act was passed and implemented, it is hard to argue that the federal government was unaware of the long-term implications of the blood quantum criteria as a means of legally eliminating the concept of 'authentic' Indians. While the wording of the Dawes Act does not mention blood quantum, the federal agents employed to implement the Act applied blood quantum standards in making their rolls of 'qualified' Indians. The government was, implicitly or explicitly, investing in eugenics as a particular method of measuring race and modeling racial difference. Hence the recent allegations made against the historian Ward Churchill for falsely claiming that blood quantum was required under the Act take too literal a position, and arguably these allegations are spurious and politically driven (Churchill 2005).

The Enduring Legacy of Blood Quantum

While it is possible to place US governmental endorsements of eugenics theory in the historically racist context of the late nineteenth and early twentieth centuries, it is almost impossible to understand why a theory of eugenics informs contemporary methods of determining Indian identity today. In short, despite widespread denunciation of eugenics theory, particularly in reference to the role it played in justifying the horrors of World War II, blood quantum still plays a part in the legal determination of who qualifies as Indian in US jurisdictions and courts in the twenty-first century. As the scholar Circe Sturm has noted:

> Racial ideologies are particularly problematic for Native-American communities, of which the Cherokees are one prominent example. For instance, the federal government through the Bureau of Indian Affairs (BIA) continues to use blood quantum as both a metaphor and measure of 'Indian' identity to manage tribal enrolments and determine eligibility for social services. Native Americans who wish to receive benefits such as health care, housing, and food commodities must meet a biological standard, usually set at one-quarter or more Indian blood, and must also present a certificate degree of Indian blood (CDIB) authenticated by their tribe and the BIA. (Sturm 2002: 2)

Most Native American organizations and movements are fully aware of the sinister implications of blood quantum policies and the extent to which such criteria control their legal access to social services, educational opportunities, health, food, and a wide variety of programs and opportunities informed by affirmative action. In a petition to the Bureau of Indian Affairs entitled 'Blood Quantum Does Not Determine Identity', the authors Christine Rose and Lawrence Sampson write:

> Not only is this racist economics in action but it is also blood quantum genocide. By allowing America to determine who is Indian, simply because the government doesn't want to be held accountable, to their word, by meeting their obligations, we allow the US government to legislate Indians out of existence. (www.petitiononline.com/0001/petition.html, accessed 18 March 2010)

Individuals, too, are sensitive to the problems of blood quantum, such as Orrin Lewis, a mixed heritage tribal member of the Cherokee Nation, who strongly argues that blood quantum criteria should be done away with:

> Basically, there are four problems ... One, it puts pressure on Indians not to marry white people or their children will lose their heritage, and that bothers a lot of people. Two, it means that if some of your ancestors aren't in the records, you can be denied being an Indian. Three, it's wrong for outsiders to tell you if you can or can't belong to an ethnic group. Nobody makes African-Americans prove their entire family line and apply for some governmental Certificate of Degree of African Blood before they can get a scholarship from the NAACP or put 'Black-owned' on their business if they want to. And four, most disturbingly: it guarantees the extinction of the American Indian. By this standard, white is the default, and everyone is approaching whiteness. Someone who is 1/8 Indian is considered white, and that is the end of their Indianness—they are

white and their children will be white, forever. On the other hand, I am 1/8 white, but that doesn't mean that's the end of whiteness in my line. It keeps sitting there, just as it has since the nineteenth century when my white ancestors entered my family. Eventually one of my descendants will marry a white person again and hah! We will be 1/4 white. A person can get more white, but not more Indian. Do you see what I mean? Every generation, there are fewer people this system thinks are full-bloods, and all the blood quantums get smaller. (www.native-languages.org/blood.htm)

Despite widespread recognition of the archaic and arbitrary nature of blood quantum criteria to determine native identity, this process is still widely used not only by government organizations and agencies but by Indian tribes as well. According to a 1997 survey, approximately two thirds of all federally recognized tribes use some form of blood quantum criteria and one-quarter blood degree is the most common minimum requirement in order to establish legal citizenship of a tribe. The remaining tribes typically require that a person show direct lineal descent from another tribal member in order to be enrolled (Garroutte 2003: 15; see also Fitzgerald 2007: 185–224; Sturm 2002).

Technically, almost all tribes can determine their own legal rules ascertaining tribal identity and membership. This principle was determined in the case of *Waldron v United States* in 1905, and later confirmed in the case *Martinez v Santa Clara Pueblo* in 1978. However, despite the legal principle that tribes are free to determine their own criteria for enrollment, this does not necessarily mean that they are free to abandon blood quantum standards. The Indian Health Service Act, for instance, requires that an applicant obtain a Certificate of Degree of Indian Blood before they can receive care. Under these circumstances, tribes must retain ancestral records since to do otherwise might effectively deny tribal members access to federally sponsored programs. In other words, tribes may be technically free to determine their own rules of citizenship, but in practical and material terms exercising this sovereign right may not be a viable option. As a result:

> federal policy has set off a ridiculous game of one-upmanship in Indian Country: 'I'm more Indian than you' and 'You aren't Indian enough to say (or do, or think)' that have become common assertions during the second half of the twentieth century. … It has established a scenario in which it has been perceived as profitable for one Indian to cancel the identity of her/his neighbor as a means of receiving his/her entitlement. Thus, a bitter divisiveness has been built into Indian communities and national policies, sufficient to preclude our achieving the internal unity necessary to offer any serious challenge to the status quo. At every turn, US practices vis-à-vis American Indians is indicative of an advanced and extremely successful system of colonization. (Jaimes 1992: 136)

In the early years of the twenty-first century, tribal, state and federal government concern over who qualifies as Indian has taken on a new dimension and intensity. For the first time, the US government introduced into the 2000 census the option for a person to self-identify as belonging to more than one race. One result of this was that the number of people checking 'Indian' doubled from the figure in the 1990 census. The reasons for many more people self-identifying as Indian are complicated. One factor that has become important in recent decades is the introduction of casinos on some Native American reservations. In a number of cases, these casinos have made huge profits, which have then been divided among officially recognized tribal members. If somebody cannot prove their tribal ancestry, they are not eligible to receive any revenue. As a result, there has been a rapid rise in the number of people now claiming to be 'Indian' and demanding rights to profit-sharing (Darian-Smith 2003). Unfortunately, this has led to increasing internal conflicts within tribes. Somewhat ironically, we are witnessing a renewed reliance by some tribal governments on blood quantum standards and colonial records for proof of ancestry. The Catawba tribes of South Carolina, the Paiutes of Nevada, and the Tigua of Texas have all debated the rules of blood quantum and tribal membership in the past decade. Probably the most dramatic and well-publicized case of this sort is the Cherokee Freedmen controversy, which involves descendants of black freed slaves—formerly made citizens of the Cherokee Nation in an 1866 treaty between the federal government and the Cherokee National Council—claiming their right to be reinstated as enrolled Cherokee citizens. This case has been heard in numerous tribal and federal courts for over 20 years and there does not appear to be a ready solution in sight. In a statement applicable to the Cherokee and other tribes, Eva Marie Garroutte writes:

> A number of them [tribes] have been sifting through their membership records and adjusting—sometimes repeatedly—the requirements for citizenship. Some have made their citizenship criteria more stringent, and some have made them less so. Some have closed their rolls altogether so that no new tribal citizens are accepted. Some have even disenrolled, or revoked the membership of, significant numbers of former tribal citizens, charging that they do not meet necessary criteria. The bitterness and anger associated with these decisions frequently reach alarming proportions. (Garroutte 2003: 6)

RIGHTS: LIMITING NATIVE SOVEREIGNTY

The Meriam Report of 1928 severely denounced the Dawes Act for its treatment of native peoples. One of the Report's major criticisms was the 'legal aspects of the Indian Problem', and the confusion that existed over which legal jurisdiction Indians were governed by. Drawing on the quaint phrasing of an earlier Idaho decision, the Report noted that the situation could be characterized as 'government in spots' (Meriam Report Ch XIII). The spottiness existed because in some cases state and federal laws applied, while in other cases local Courts of Indian Offenses, which were tribunals made up of Indian judges, prevailed. Rightly, the Report felt that these myriad laws and adjudicating bodies created uncertainty and confusion.

In order to deal with the legal confusion, the Meriam Report envisaged a 'transitional period' in which local tribunals would be gradually phased out as Indians became better educated about health, property, farming, and western-style family life. It was hoped that eventually local jurisdictions could be done away with altogether as Indians became sufficiently assimilated 'to warrant the extension to them of the state laws'. So, while the Report strongly denounced the Dawes Act, it did not denounce its ultimate goal, which was to assimilate Indians into white society and have the dominant legal system control their activities and conduct (Meriam Report Ch I: 13–14, Ch XIII). The strategies and means employed to achieve this goal differed between the Dawes Act and the Meriam Report but the overall objective remained the same.

According to the Report, one necessary element in achieving this objective was that non-Indians should be more respectful of native peoples and their legal rights.

> In the execution of this program, scrupulous care must be exercised to respect to the rights of the Indian. This phrase 'rights of the Indian' is often used solely to apply to his property rights. Here it is used in a much broader sense to cover his rights as a human being living in a free country. Indians are entitled to unfailing courtesy and considera-tion from all government employees. … [This] will necessitate more understanding of and sympathy for the Indian point of view. … The Indians have much to contribute to the dominant civilization, and the effort should be made to secure this contribution, in part because of the good it will do the Indians in stimulating proper race pride and self respect. (Meriam Report Ch I: 14)

Despite the paternalistic tone of this passage, it nonetheless marks a shift from the 1870s to the 1920s in the dominant ways of thinking about Indian people and their engagement with American law. White society was becoming more sympa-thetic to the plight of the Indian. This shift occurred slowly over the decades, fueled by works such as Helen Hunt Jackson's controversial report *A Century of Dishonor* (1881), which recorded the government's violation of treaty contracts and general disregard for the human rights of Indian communities. While controversial, *A Century of Dishonor* had little impact on politicians or the public. In contrast to the report, Hunt's novel *Ramona*, published a few years later, was an instant success. Originally entitled *In The Name of the Law*, the novel featured a half-Indian/Scottish illegitimate girl and her handsome and courageous Indian husband, Alessandro. Drawing on the novelty of the central characters, the book made accessible to the general public a tragic and heroic love story describing the brutal exploitation of native peoples by white society (see Phillips 2003).

In the context of increasing public sympathy for the plight of Indians in the early decades of the twentieth century, the Meriam Report recognized that an individual Indian does have legal 'rights as a human being' and that it is the government's responsibility to respect them and nurture a sense of those rights in Indians through education and social services. It is important to note, however, that underlying this acknowledgement of indigenous rights as they pertain to an individual is the presupposition of non-recognition of Indian rights as they pertain to his or her tribal collectivity. In other words, the Meriam Report followed the trajectory established under the earlier Dawes Act to grant individual Indians western property rights (and the legal right to be taxed that accompanied such proprietary ownership) as a mechanism to break up tribal units and tribal ways of self-government. As such, the Report could only go so far in recognizing a native person's engagement with the American legal system and could not endorse the concept of collectively-based tribal sovereignty.

The Marshall Trilogy

The Meriam Report's rejection of the concept of tribal sovereignty based in the collective rights of a tribal community is hardly surprising. In addition to US federal political policies explicitly aimed at breaking up tribal communities, in the legal system there had been a steady qualifying of the concept of tribal sovereignty throughout the nineteenth century. This qualification was most famously articulated in the three opinions of Chief Justice John Marshall expressed in the US Supreme Court decisions now often referred to as the Marshall Trilogy: *Johnson v M'Intosh* (1823), *Cherokee Nation v Georgia* (1831) and *Worcester v Georgia* (1832) (see Wilkinson 1987 who first referred to the cases as a trilogy). Together these cases—though plagued by inconsistencies such as Chief Justice Marshall's depiction of Indians as weak and dependent in *Johnson* and strong and independent in *Worcester*—'identified the contours of American Indian law as they remain in the modern era' (Fletcher 2006: 628–29).

It is essential to appreciate that the three cases were decided in the context of increasing unrest in southern states and threats of their secession from the Union. One of the claims made by southern states was that they—not the federal government—had ultimate authority over tribes within their territories. Chief Justice Marshall, a committed federalist, was keenly aware of what was at stake and throughout his decision-making, and often by rather circuitous reasoning, he affirmed federal powers over state powers. Not coincidentally, a year after *Johnson v M'Intosh* was decided, the Bureau of Indian Affairs was officially established, definitively formalizing the federal government's role of overseeing Indian issues and in particular native lands held in trust.

Much has been written on these three cases and I give only a brief description here for the purposes of discussing the concept of native sovereignty as well as the limitations of that legal status (see Robertson 2007). In the first of the cases, *Johnson v M'Intosh*, Chief Justice Marshall argued that Indians did have original title to their lands prior to the arrival of white settlers but this status changed after 'discovery' of America by Europeans.

> They [Indians] were admitted to be the rightful occupants of the soil, with a legal as well as a just claim to retain possession of it, and to use it according to their own discretion; but their rights to complete sovereignty, as independent nations, were necessarily diminished, and their power to dispose of the soil at their own will, to

whomsoever they pleased, was denied by the original fundamental principle, that
discovery gave exclusive power to those who made it.

Relying upon the Doctrine of Discovery, Marshall argued that since the English
discovered America, Indians could not alienate or give away land title to any
other entity other than the American government, which had assumed title from
the English after the War of Independence. As a result, the United States held title
in tribal lands and Indians had a right of occupancy only. Hence only the federal
government—not state governments—could grant land title to a third party.
However, as Stuart Banner has compellingly argued, the *Johnson* case went
against colonists' and settlers' long-standing recognition of Indians holding
collective property rights in tribal land. Banner writes, 'The idea that Indians
possessed only a right of occupancy in their unsold land was a concept that was
only three decades old in 1823. English law had included no such concept, nor
had American law before the 1790s. Unsold Indian land had once been thought
to be owned by Indians' (Banner 2005a: 179). Notwithstanding this historical
reality, Marshall's ruling in the *Johnson* case swept away the formerly recognized
collective legal property rights of Indians and formally established the Doctrine
of Discovery in federal Indian law.

The concept of Indian sovereignty was further eroded in *Cherokee Nation v
Georgia* (1831). Despite growing dissent among the Supreme Court judges, the
final decision held, in the words of Chief Justice Marshall, that tribes are not
'foreign states' as envisaged under the American Constitution, but rather 'domestic dependent nations' in 'a state of pupilage'. In short, a tribe's relationship to the
United States resembles that of a 'ward to his guardian'. Chief Justice Marshall
went on:

> They [tribes] look to our government for protection; rely upon its kindness and its
> power; appeal to it for relief to their wants; and address the president as their great
> father. They and their country are considered by foreign nations, as well as by ourselves,
> as being so completely under the sovereignty and dominion of the United States that
> any attempt to acquire their lands, or to form a political connexion with them, would
> be considered as an invasion of our territory, and an act of hostility. These considera-
> tions go far to support the opinion, that the framers of the constitution had not the
> Indian tribes in view, when they opened the courts of the union to controversies
> between a state or the citizens thereof, and foreign states.

A year later, *Worcester v Georgia* was decided in what seems to be an about-turn
by the Supreme Court. The majority opinion held that despite tribes being
'domestic dependent nations' as determined in *Cherokee Nation*, they still operated as 'distinct political communities, having territorial boundaries, within
which their authority is exclusive, and having a right to all the lands within those
boundaries, which is not only acknowledged, but guaranteed by the United
States'. In this decision Chief Justice Marshall was determined to make it clear
that states—here the state of Georgia—could not nullify federal law by imposing
state laws on tribal reservations and in this case intervene in the domestic

governance of the Cherokee Nation. In strong and clear language, Marshall argued that as a distinct nation with well-marked boundaries, 'the laws of Georgia can have no force, and … the citizens of Georgia have no right to enter, but with the assent of the Cherokees themselves, or in conformity with treaties, and with the acts of congress'.

The *Worcester* case unequivocally held that tribal communities did have exclusive and sovereign control over their reservation lands. Unfortunately, though, as legal scholar Matthew Fletcher notes, 'There had not been a stronger statement of respect for the legal authority of Indian tribes—and there has not yet been one like it since' (Fletcher 2006: 647). Nor did the *Worcester* case help the victorious Cherokees, given that within the decade they had been driven from their lands and forced to relocate in Oklahoma, enduring what is known as the Trail of Tears. During this long march westward, over 4,000 Cherokee and many other native peoples similarly forced to relocate died from starvation, exposure or disease. Fletcher goes on to argue that not only did the finding in the case of *Worcester* not help the Cherokees at the time the decision was made, the case continues to be deemed irrelevant or ignored by the modern Supreme Court. As a result, 'tribes still cannot sue states without their consent. Tribes don't even have the right to sue under the federal civil rights statutes. … In general, when an Indian tribe argues that *Worcester* compels a certain result in their favor, the Court rebuffs them' (Fletcher 2006: 647–48).

Native Sovereignty in the Twenty-First Century

Ambiguities and inconsistencies with respect to the legal concept of native sovereignty continue to undermine Indian and non-Indian relations to this day. 'The United States has sometimes recognized and supported tribal sovereignty; at other times, it has acted to deny, diminish, or even terminate their sovereign status. … [T]ribes can never be assured that they will receive an impartial hearing' (Wilkins 2008: 244). Most justices and lawyers would probably agree, albeit perhaps reluctantly, with Clarence Thomas's assessment that 'Until we begin to analyze these questions honestly and rigorously, the confusion I have identified will continue to haunt our cases' (*United States v Lara* (2004), No 03–107). However, despite general confusion in federal and state Indian law over the meaning of native sovereignty, there do appear to be recognizable trends in judicial interpretation. Typically US courts interpret the concept of native sovereignty to accord with the institutional interests of the state to the detriment of tribal interests. These interpretations stress that tribes do not hold inherent sovereign power and are only qualified to exercise any form of self-government because, by virtue of their status as 'wards', that right has been delegated to them by the United States. As Thomas Biolsi notes, the court's idea of tribal sovereignty is 'limited, in fact, to the point that it does not make logical sense to many Indian people, is not really sovereignty at all from their point of view, and can only be understood as bespeaking a profoundly racist view of Indians on the part of Congress, the courts, and white people in general' (Biolsi 2005: 243).

It is true that today some tribes exercise a relatively high degree of independence within the jurisdictional boundaries of their reservations, and a reasonable number have their own system of government, rules and courts. The Indian Reorganization Act of 1936, which came to be known as the New Deal for Indians, went some way to preventing the sale of reservation land and encouraging tribal self-management. While well intentioned, the 1936 Act did not fulfill its promise and in most cases western-style courts and constitutions were imposed on tribes (O'Brien 1989: 82). Today, as in the past, tribal communities are not considered to be exercising rights of self-government by virtue of an inherent tribal sovereignty. As 'domestic dependent nations' within state and federal governments, these communities exist within overlapping and interdependent jurisdictions and political and economic networks. Tribes and their members are governed by a wide range of native and non-native legal systems and are subject to more laws than any other people in the United States. As a result the legal boundaries of reservations are extremely porous and the concept of native sovereignty extremely tenuous.

In recent years, conflict over the legal concept of native sovereignty has become intensely politcal. This is primarily due to the rising presence of casinos on Native American reservations (Darian-Smith 2003, 2002). Technically, a tribe can only build a casino if it is a federally recognized tribe and can assert sovereignty over a specified reservation territory. The degree to which a tribe has sole sovereign control over its reservation land is what is now being hotly contested. If one argues that tribes are merely 'domestic dependent nations', then it follows that activities on their reservations should be subject to state law. Accordingly, revenues from Indian-owned casinos should be subject to state taxation and all sorts of other state regulations and controls. However, if one argues that tribes have sovereignty over their delegated reservation land, then it follows that they should not be forced to comply with state laws, taxation, zoning regulations, environmental standards and so on. Tribes, in other words, can operate their enterprises without direct state control. Given that Indian tribes generated US $25.9 billion in gross gaming revenues in 2008, according to the National Indian Gaming Association, these battles over the limits of native sovereignty have become highly politicized and controversial.

Opponents to Indian-owned casinos are quick to argue that tribes that do not have to comply with the dominant state legal system are receiving 'special rights' or special privileges (Dudas 2005, 2008; Goldberg-Hiller and Milner 2003). This line of argument conveniently ignores the history of colonial oppression out of which these rights emerged (Darian-Smith 2003). As the anthropologist Jessica Cattelino has remarked with respect to the Seminole tribe, 'no one bothered them so long as they were poor and selling trinkets, but once they started making money they came under harsh public scrutiny and were subject to new stereotypes and resentments from non-Indians' (Cattelino 2007, 2008). At a deeper level, opponents of Indian-owned casinos resent the capacity of tribes to act as a collectivity under differently applied legal rules, and the explicit challenge this poses to the idea of a homogenous, modular political system substantiated through the idea of one set of laws applicable to all US citizens. To put it another way, a more robust concept of native sovereignty makes explicit what has always been sought to be hidden in the United States and other modern democratic countries: that there are varying degrees and zones of sovereignty 'so as to benefit some citizens systematically and, just as systematically, to disempower or otherwise harm other citizens …' (Biolsi 2005: 241).

CONCLUSION

In the first decade of the twenty-first century, the rhetoric of 'government-to-government' has been used by both Republican and Democrat politicians in the United States to evoke an inclusive sense of equality between Indian and non-Indian communities. Indeed, in the early months of President Obama's administration, an explicit attempt was made to respect the notion of tribal sovereignty and encourage the input of Native Americans in the new administration's strategies and policies. Yet to what degree Obama's understanding of tribal sovereignty accords with native peoples' understanding of tribal sovereignty remains to be seen. Native communities are rightly optimistic but wary given that on the US domestic scene federal courts have up to this point honored a profoundly limited notion of tribal sovereignty.

On the international scene, recent events have not presented an encouraging scenario for Native Americans. Under former president George W Bush, the United States—along with Australia, Canada and New Zealand—refused to vote in favor of the United Nations Declaration on the Rights of Indigenous Peoples in September 2007 (Australia subsequently endorsed the Declaration in 2009). This refusal was seen by the other 143 countries that did support the Declaration as a stark example of British settler societies' inability to deal conceptually with their colonial histories of indigenous subjugation and exploitation, and come to terms with the collective rights of native peoples which are expressly affirmed in the Declaration. The position on the UN Declaration taken by the United States is enormously disappointing but, sadly, not unexpected. The legacy of the Dawes Act—despite being widely condemned as a piece of legislation—lives on in many ways, including most obviously the practice of denying that certain legal rights can be held in common by native communities.

Recommended Reading

Banner, Stuart (2005a) *How the Indians Lost Their Land: Law and Power on the Frontier.* Cambridge: The Belknap Press of Harvard University Press.
Barta, Roger (1997) *The Artificial Savage: Modern Myths of the Wild Man.* Translated by Christopher Follett. Ann Arbor: University of Michigan Press.

Biolsi, Thomas (2001) *Deadliest Enemies: Law and the Making of Race Relations on and off Rosebud Reservation.* Berkeley: University of California Press.

Cattelino, Jessica R (2008) *High Stakes: Florida Seminole Gaming and Sovereignty.* Durham, NC: Duke University Press.

Darian-Smith, Eve (2003) *New Capitalists: Law, Politics and Identity Surrounding Casino Gaming on Native American Land.* Belmont, CA: Wadsworth (Case Studies in Contemporary Social Issues).

Dudas, Jeffrey R (2008) *The Cultivation of Resentment: Treaty Rights and the New Right.* Palo Alto: Stanford University Press.

Garroutte, Eva Marie (2003) *Real Indians: Identity and the Survival of Native America.* Berkeley: University of California Press.

Goldberg-Hiller, Jonathan and Neal Milner (2003) 'Rights as Excess: Understanding the Politics of Special Rights' 29 *Law & Social Inquiry* 1075.

Jahoda, Gustav (1999) *Images of Savages: Ancient Roots of Modern Prejudice in Western Culture.* London: Routledge.

Lawrence, Bonita (2004) *'Real' Indians and Others: Mixed Blood Urban Native Peoples and Indigenous Nationhood.* Lincoln: University of Nebraska Press.

Robertson, Lindsay G (2007) *Conquest by Law: How the Discovery of America Dispossessed Indigenous Peoples of their Lands.* Oxford: Oxford University Press.

Sturm, Circe (2002) *Blood Politics: Race, Culture, and Identity in the Cherokee Nation of Oklahoma.* Berkeley: University of California Press.

Washburn, Wilcomb E (1971) *Red Man's Land/White Man's Law: A Study of the Past and Present States of the American Indian.* New York: Charles Scribner's Sons.

Wilkins, David E (2009) *Documents of Native American Political Development: 1500s to 1933.* Oxford: Oxford University Press.

Wilkinson, Charles F (1987) *American Indians, Time, and the Law: Native Societies in a Modern Constitutional Democracy.* New Haven: Yale University Press.

III

Religion, Race and Rights in a Global Era

7

Nuremberg's Legacy (1945–49)

A N ENORMOUS AMOUNT has been written about World War II and the subsequent Nuremberg trials, which sentenced prominent military and political leaders of the Nazi regime for violations of the laws of war. Existing literature includes extraordinary first-hand accounts of the trials (Harris 1954; Taylor 1992; Sonnenfeldt 2006), analyses of the trials' legitimacy in international law (Biddiss 1995), discussions of the differences and similarities between the Nuremberg trials and the Tokyo War Crimes Tribunals (Brackman 1987; Totani 2008), histories of the trials (Persico 1995; Conot 1983; Tusa and Tusa 1983), and countless examinations of Nuremberg's impact and significance in the twentieth century, particularly with respect to international law (Ehrenfreund 2007; Wilke 2009). Despite this vast body of extant literature, it is necessary to revisit the Nuremberg trials once again because no examination of contemporary Anglo-American law can avoid engaging with its legacy. The Nuremberg trials heralded a new era in the recognition of human rights, state accountability, and an acknowledgement of collective worldwide responsibility for crimes against humanity. This legacy can be seen in the unfolding of postwar events throughout the 1940s and 50s, and in more recent decades with the prosecution of individuals such as the former leader of Serbia Slobodan Milošević, former Rwandan Prime Minister Jean Kambanda, and former Iraqi dictator Saddam Hussein. Most recently, we can see Nuremberg's legacy materialize in the new International Criminal Court, which was set up in 2002 to prosecute war crimes and crimes against humanity.

The Nuremberg trials were a landmark in the evolution of modern Anglo-American law, and international law more generally. As noted by the former US judge Norbert Ehrenfreund, 'the ideas spawned at Nuremberg—new concepts of justice and human rights—have spread across much of the world' (Ehrenfreund 2007:xvi). Nuremberg established the right to prosecute a person for participating in aggressive acts of war, war crimes, crimes against humanity and genocide, even if such acts were carried out under order. No one can be legally excused if one's behavior constitutes a violation of universally accepted wartime rules, such as not to take the life of defenseless citizens or engage in torture. The trials qualified the long-standing concept of state sovereignty in international law, which for centuries leading up to the 1940s had basically accepted a government and a government's agents as having exclusive control over citizens within its jurisdiction. After Nuremberg, the concept of an individual's immunity from international scrutiny and accountability with respect to war crimes was forever altered. The degree to which this accountability has in fact been enforced is a separate question and falls beyond the scope of this chapter.

The Nuremberg trials underscored the legal viability—if not universally accepted legitimacy—of a joint judgment by multiple states. Drawing upon a team of prosecutors and judges from the major Allied powers (Britain, the Soviet Union, France and the United States), the trials established the precedent of collective judicial collaboration. This was an important historical breakthrough given the reluctance of some Allied powers, in particular the United States, to establish an international tribunal to prosecute German war criminals after World War I (see Willis 1982). The trials helped to lay the legal and symbolic groundwork for the United Nations, which was set up concurrently in 1945 with the UN's principal judicial organ, the International Court of Justice (ICJ) in The Hague. The Nuremberg Principles, which set out guidelines as to what constitutes a war crime, were recognized by the UN General Assembly and adopted in the 1948 Universal Declaration of Human Rights. The Declaration established an international human rights regime and, along with other Geneva Conventions, laid down the rules 'governing war between states, differentiating legal conduct from illegal and criminal acts in war' (Henkin 1993: 607). The Declaration is one of the central instruments of international law today and has influenced—in various ways and to varying degrees—all domestic national legal regimes.

Here, I give only a brief account of the first of the Nuremberg trials, which was held between 1945 and 1946 and involved charges against 22 prominent Nazi leaders and six Nazi organizations. I do not go into any detail in respect of the 12 subsequent trials, which were presided over by US judges and ran until 1949 (see Marrus 1997: 93–106), or the concurrently held Tokyo War Crimes Tribunal which dealt specifically with the prosecution of Japanese leaders (1946–48). I use the first Nuremberg trial, which at the time was followed closely by a large international audience, as a marker and reminder of both the potential for human depravity and more disturbingly the ordinariness of the men who committed such atrocities, which Hannah Arendt famously coined in reference to the 1961 trial of Adolf Eichmann 'the banality of evil'. What the Nuremberg trials as a whole revealed about what people can do to others reverberated throughout the subsequent decades of the twentieth century, and to this day pervades all discussions of contemporary war and warfare.

My overall goal is to move beyond the revelations of horror at Nuremberg, which have been discussed at length elsewhere. I approach the trials as an historical watershed to reflect more expansively upon the differences in thinking in Britain and the United States in the decade immediately following World War II. As public spectacle, the Nuremberg trials brought home to many, and in particular Americans where television and newspaper coverage of the trials was extensive, the power of a political/religious ideology in the implementation of racist practices. The dovetailing of religion and race both in the Nazi Aryan ideology and in the Nazi rationalization of the persecution of minorities, particularly Jewish populations, highlighted for many the complex layering and blurring between these two categories. A central question that hovered in the public consciousness was this: were Jews victimized on the basis of their religious practices or their ethnicity? One result of the Nuremberg trials was that conceptualizations of religion and race became more nuanced and people were forced to see that at times the concepts were intimately interconnected. While today we often take for granted the connections between religion and race, it was the events of Nuremberg that first made this apparent in very accessible terms to broad cross-sections of citizens internationally. A further aspect of the Nuremberg trials—and one that should not be downplayed—is that it acts as a harrowing reminder to modern, western, democratic and supposedly secular nations that matters of religion and race were still central to the social and political interrelations of European peoples.

Nuremberg Trial of the Major War Criminals (November 1945–October 1946)

Stories of wartime atrocities and horror on an unprecedented scale filtered out of Germany and its occupied territories in the later years of World War II. By 1942, plans were being made by the Allied powers to develop a common policy to deal with the German leaders once the war was over. But despite a general agreement between Joseph Stalin, Franklin D Roosevelt and Winston Churchill that war crimes must be prosecuted, there was division and uncertainty about how best to proceed. According to Michael Marrus, 'London and Washington were reluctant to move too quickly—unwilling to give too much voice to the governments in exile, opposed to diverting warmaking resources into retaliatory exercises, fearing German vengeance in the event of a too aggressive policy against war criminals, and uneasy about working with the Soviets on the issue' (Marrus 1997: 19–20).

By 1943, Britain seemed to favor summary execution without trial of the Nazi leaders, the Soviets seemed to be leaning towards establishing an international tribunal to try these leaders, and the United States was anxious not to declare its postwar policies and exacerbate tensions among the Allied forces, although of course it could not sit on the fence indefinitely. In January 1945, the US Secretary of War, Henry Stimson, the Secretary of State, Edward Stettinius Jr, and the Attorney General (and later American judge at Nuremberg) Francis Biddle, wrote a memorandum to Roosevelt in an effort to convince him against summary execution. Concerned with ensuring that justice was to be both done and seen to be done, this document essentially set out US policy on how to deal with captured German leaders. The three men recommended the following:

> After Germany's unconditional surrender the United Nations could, if they elected, put to death the most notorious Nazi criminals, such as Hitler or Himmler, without trial or hearing. We do not favor this method. While it has the advantages of a sure and swift disposition, it would be violative of the most fundamental principles of justice,

common to all the United Nations. This would encourage the Germans to turn these criminals into martyrs, and, in any event, only a few individuals could be reached in this way.
We think that the just and effective solution lies in the use of the judicial method. Condemnation of these criminals after a trial, moreover, would command maximum public support in our own times and receive the respect of history. The use of the judicial method will, in addition, make available for all mankind to study in future years an authentic record of Nazi crimes and criminality. (cited in Marrus 1997: 30)

President Roosevelt died suddenly in April 1945, less than a month before Germany's unconditional surrender. He was succeeded by Harry Truman, who as a former judge firmly believed in the notion of a fair trial. Under President Truman the US position solidified in favor of a trial. However, while the Soviet Union, Britain and France agreed in theory with the US plan to establish a war crimes tribunal, it would take many months of negotiations to thrash out the actual details of procedure. The Allied powers were in uncharted legal waters since laws and legislation had to be drafted to fit the crimes charged and penalties had to be agreed upon. More challenging still was moving beyond the attitude that a trial was unnecessary given the obvious responsibility of the Nazis for the death of millions of people.

In an effort to counter this reluctance, the United States assembled a huge team of lawyers (numbering in the hundreds) and 'drove the decision-making', putting more human and material resources into formulating how the tribunal would proceed than the other Allied powers together (Marrus 1997: 39). Robert Jackson, chief prosecutor for the United States, fought long and hard for a trial based on due process and judicial fairness, and finally won the opposition over. By arguing that even a person suspected of committing the most monstrous of crimes still deserved a fair trial, Jackson set in motion a decision that 'was a turning point in the history of law, igniting a revolution in the law of nations. It changed the way we perceive justice, even the way we perceive each other' (Ehrenfreund 2007: 13). Nuremberg was a turning point, because while today we take it for granted that everyone deserves a fair trial, this proposition 'wasn't so obvious in 1945' (Ehrenfreund 2007: 13–14).

Jackson convinced the other Allied powers to hold the tribunal in Nuremberg, not in Berlin which is what the Soviets desired. Nuremberg was finally agreed upon primarily because its Palace of Justice and attached prison were left largely intact despite extensive Allied bombing (Figure 33). Moreover, Hitler had staged huge propaganda rallies in Nuremberg, and so it was a symbolically important site on which to bring the Nazi leaders to justice. Of economic importance, and not to be discounted in a war-ravaged Europe, Nuremberg was in the American zone, which meant that the US would pay most of the costs associated with the trials. Jackson also convinced everyone that the US and British adversarial legal system, which allowed for defense lawyers and cross-examination, should be used over the judge-centered inquisitorial system used by the French and the Soviets.

Figure 33. View of Nuremberg in Ruins, 1945, at the time of the Nuremberg trials. The twin-spired Lorenz Church is visible in the distance. The statue to the right is of Kaiser Wilhelm I on horseback. Printed with permission of the United States Holocaust Memorial Museum, Washington, DC. The views or opinions expressed in this book and the context in which they are used, do not necessarily reflect the views or policy of, nor imply approval or endorsement by, the United States Holocaust Memorial Museum.

The Charter of the International Military Tribunal, signed by the Allied representatives on 6 August 1945, set out the laws and procedures that would govern the Nuremberg trials.

Finally, Jackson managed to persuade the Allied powers to agree on the four charges against the Nazi leaders. Each of these charges was to be assigned to the four prosecution teams, with the US assigned to count 1, the British to count 2, and the French and Soviets to share counts 3 and 4. The four charges were:

1. Conspiracy to Wage Aggressive War;
2. Waging Aggressive War;
3. War Crimes (violation of the rules and customs of war such as mistreating prisoners and enemy civilians);
4. Crimes Against Humanity (including torture and genocide of people on the basis of racial grounds, ie what is now called the Holocaust).

The first two counts (together known as crimes against peace) were not officially recognized as crimes in international law before World War II and so were subject to the criticism that they were invented after the fact. The Russians in particular were uncomfortable with these counts given their own culpability as former allies of Germany in the invasion of Poland and signatories of the Nazi-Soviet pact of August 1939. Against the position that aggressive warfare was not a crime under international law, Jackson argued in his *Report to the President* of 6 June 1945 that these acts had been recognized as crimes since time immemorial (Marrus 1997: 43). Moreover, during the trial Jackson and his assistant, Sidney Alderman, were keen to show that international customs established in the inter-war years, particularly with respect to the 1928 Kellogg-Briand Pact, held that states did not have the right to wage aggressive war as an instrument of premeditated national policy.

There is no doubt that without Robert Jackson's belief in the importance of a trial and his unwillingness to back down on the form of the charges themselves, in particular the charge of 'conspiracy', the first Nuremberg trial would not have achieved the same results and arguably might not have been held at all. Jackson was not much liked by the Allied prosecutors and judges and was considered by some to be ill-equipped for the task and at times ill-tempered. However, in his opening address for the United States at Nuremberg (Figure 34), Jackson eloquently spoke for all concerned when he stated:

> The privilege of opening the first trial for crimes against the peace of the world imposes a grave responsibility. The wrongs which we seek to condemn and punish have been so calculated, so malignant, and so devastating, that civilization cannot tolerate their being ignored, because it cannot survive their being repeated. That four great nations, flushed with victory and stung with injury stay the hand of vengeance and voluntarily submit their captive enemies to the judgment of the law is one of the most significant tributes that Power has ever paid to Reason. (cited in Marrus 1997: 79)

The Nuremberg War Crimes Tribunal went on for a year and involved 403 open sessions and 94 witness examinations, processed thousands of German documents, and generated mountains of transcripts, many of which were transcribed into four languages. Broadcasts of the trial were made twice daily on German radio (Judt 2006: 53). Throughout the proceedings the world learnt about the internal organization and structure of the Nazi regime, the progressive clampdown on minorities and in particular Jewish populations through the Nuremberg Laws and related measures, and the horrors perpetrated by the Third Reich on millions of people through eye-witness accounts. One such account was given by Marie Claude Vaillant-Couturier, a decorated member of the French Resistance who had been held in concentration camps for three years. As she presented her testimony the shocked courtroom fell silent:

> We saw the unsealing of the cars and the soldiers letting men, women, and children out of them. We then witnessed heart-rending scenes; old couples were forced to part from each other, mothers made to abandon their young daughters, since the latter were sent to the camp, whereas the mothers and children were sent to the gas chambers. All of these people were unaware of the fate awaiting them. They were merely upset at being separated, but they did not know that they were going to their death. To render their welcome more pleasant at this time—June-July 1944—an orchestra composed of

Figure 34. US Chief Prosecutor Robert H Jackson delivers his opening speech, 21 November 1945. Printed with permission of the United States Holocaust Memorial Museum, Washington, DC.

internees, all young and pretty girls dressed in little white blouses and navy blue skirts, played during the selection, at the arrival of the trains, gay tunes such as "The Merry Widow", the "Barcarolle" from the Tales of Hoffman, and so forth …

At Auschwitz there were eight crematoriums but, as from 1944, these proved insufficient. The SS had large pits dug by the internees, where they put branches, sprinkled with gasoline, which they set on fire. Then they threw the corpses into the pits. … One night we were awakened by terrifying cries. We discovered, on the following day, from the men working in the Sonderkommando—the "Gas Kommando"—that on the preceding day, the gas supply having run out, they had thrown the children into the furnaces alive. (cited in Marrus 1997: 155–56)

217

The first Nuremberg trial concluded in October 1946. Against the looming possibility of Cold War, and in the wake of the devastation resulting from the nuclear bombs dropped by the US on Hiroshima and Nagasaki two months earlier, the Allied powers declared judgment. In words reflecting American optimism in the rule of law and the country's confidence in newly forged international institutions, President Truman declared on 27 October 1946, 'I have no hesitancy in declaring that the historic precedent set at Nuremberg abundantly justifies the expenditure of the effort, prodigious though it was. This precedent becomes basic in the international law of the future' (cited in Ehrenfreund 2007: 106). After months of defendant testimony and defense summations, on 1 October 1946 the 21 defendants filed into the Palace of Justice to receive their verdicts. One defendant, Martin Bormann, was declared dead by his lawyer and not available to hear the case against him. At the final count, 18 defendants were convicted on one or more counts and three men were found not guilty (though immediately after the trial these three men were tried in German courts for alleged violations of German law; see Conot 1983: 498–99). Eleven defendants were sentenced to hang, including Goering, who committed suicide by swallowing a cyanide pill hours before the scheduled execution on 16 October 1946.

Much criticism has been aimed at the Nuremberg trials, both at the time they were held and in subsequent years. But, despite its flaws and inconsistencies, the trials showed that four different countries with different legal rules and procedures, policies, customs and languages could come together and create an effective international tribunal. This in itself was a remarkable achievement considering that the Soviet Union and the United States and Britain were at this time in the early stages of what would quickly escalate into the Cold War standoff. Winston Churchill, it should be remembered, delivered—while the first Nuremberg trial was still in process—his famous 'Iron Curtain' speech in March 1946 in Fulton, Missouri. In this speech he called for world peace and an Anglo-American alliance against the expansionist aspirations of the Soviets. Moreover, the trials can be seen as a triumph for setting 'a standard for a fair trial and respect for the rights of the accused' no matter how terrible the charges (Ehrenfreund 2007: 106). The presumption of a person's innocence until proven guilty was established as a norm in a much publicized international legal forum. In the context of postwar Europe, when many people, understandably, sought some sort of revenge for the horrors of war, this was remarkable.

RELIGION: CONFRONTING RELIGIOUS PLURALISM

When the New York stock market crashed on Black Tuesday, 29 October 1929, the United States was immediately hit hard. As the economic collapse reverberated around the world, other countries felt the impact at different times and to different degrees. Australia, for instance, where the export of wheat, wool and meat was the mainstay of the economy, suffered very badly. When global prices crashed its unemployment figures in turn peaked at 29 per cent in 1932. However despite Australia's and other countries' significant economic hardships, perhaps no western country other than the US, and certainly no European country, suffered as badly from the outbreak of the Great Depression as Germany. While Gustav Stresemann, Chancellor of the Weimar Republic, had led Germany well in the recovery process after World War I and as a result brought the country a measure of stability and prosperity, his death in 1929 coincided with the outbreak of the Great Depression. Amidst spiraling economic decline, the withdrawal of US recovery loans, and unemployment figures at 30 per cent, German social and political life became extremely volatile.

In these dire circumstances, Hitler's National Socialist Party (the Nazis) provided a ray of hope and optimism for many people (Burleigh 2001). While Hitler had led the Nazi party since 1921 and endured two years of imprisonment for his failed Munich Beer-Hall *Putsch* in 1923, it was not until 1929 that the party really became a significant political force. With the outbreak of the Great Depression, Nazi party membership soared. Men desperate for wage-paying employment swelled the ranks of Hitler's brown-shirted Storm Troopers (Sturmabeilung or SA). Some members of the general voting public too began to see a future in Hitler's extreme nationalist ideology. In the July 1932 elections, the Nazis took 230 seats in the Reichstag elections, 100 more seats than the second-ranked Socialists. Once in power, Hitler moved quickly and on 23 March 1933, he ensured the passing of the Enabling Act, which granted him dictatorial power until 1937. A year later, on 30 June 1934, Hitler sent in his personal troops, the Schutzstaffen (SS) and the Gestapo (secret police), to assassinate any lingering political opposition. Known as the 'Night of the Long Knives', the purge resulted in the deaths of approximately 100 SA leaders and other potential opponents on the radical right.

Hitler's hold on the country became absolute as he centralized the government and seized authority over law courts and law enforcement. In cultural terms all views that opposed a racist-nationalist agenda were censored and all art, music, radio and books that did not endorse this view were destroyed (Steinweis 2001). Schools taught Aryan and anti-Semitic myths, and all children between the ages of 10 and 18 were forced to join Hitler Youth. Rallies, marches and propaganda spectacles were staged at Nuremberg and elsewhere. The Nuremberg Laws were passed in September 1935, outlawing marriage and sexual intercourse between Germans and Jews and stripping Jewish people of citizenship. Jews and other minorities, including the disabled, homosexuals, and Romi and Sinti (gypsies), stepped up efforts to flee the country.

Nazism and Christianity

What did ordinary Germans do to stop the rise of Hitler? To what degree did people resist or ultimately collude in the rise of Nazi power? What role did established German churches and church leaders—both Protestant and Catholic—play in the development of the Third Reich? While historical accounts written in the 1960s and 70s suggest little support of Nazism from traditional churches (ie Conway 1968), these assessments have been re-examined in recent decades. Today there exists a growing body of research suggesting that some Christian churches and specific church leaders colluded, albeit not necessarily intentionally, in Hitler's rise to power. In short, some church leaders were more sympathetic to Nazi ideology with respect to anti-semitism, anti-socialism, anti-feminism and anti-homosexuality than had previously been appreciated. As noted by the historian Richard Steigmann-Gall:

> We have come to realize with growing empirical certainty that many Christians of the day believed Nazism to be in some sense a Christian movement. Even in the later years of the Third Reich, as anti-clerical hostility grew, churchmen of both confessions [Protestant and Catholic] persisted in their belief that Nazism was essentially in conformity with Christian precepts. (Steigmann-Gall 2003: 5)

This reassessment of the relationship between Nazism and Christianity goes against long-standing assumptions about the divide between them. Until very recently, it was accepted that while the Nazis may have cynically exploited the trappings and symbolism of Christianity for purposes of political expediency, they were nonetheless ideologically anti-Christian. This perspective can be seen in the pre-war political cartoon drawn by Philip Zec, where Nazi barbarity is vividly represented by a gorilla manipulating the Christian cross to form a swastika (Figure 35). Zec was a well-known, and at times controversial, political cartoonist in Britain whose work was published for many years in the *Daily Mirror*. He was one of the first to criticize fascism and the Nazi regime in the 1930s, a time when many other commentators were willing to lampoon but not openly condemn the rise of Hitler (see Zeman 1984; Taylor 2001: Zec 2004).

The sense that Nazis were non-Christian persisted throughout the war years, with Karl Barth writing in 1943 that Christianity was separated 'as by an abyss from the inherent godlessness of National Socialism' (cited in Steigmann-Gall 2003: 4). Hannah Arendt, writing in 1945, declared that the spiritual roots attributed to Nazism 'owe nothing to any part of the Western tradition, be it German or not, Catholic or Protestant, Christian, Greek, or Roman … On the contrary, Nazism is actually the breakdown of all German and European traditions' (Arendt 1945: 108–09). Echoing Arendt, François de Menthon, the French chief prosecutor at the first Nuremberg trial, argued that Germany had retreated from Christianity, re-adopting an earlier state of primitivism. Note the distancing strategy used by Menthon in the rhetorical question he presented to the court in his opening statement:

Figure 35. *The New Christianity. 100% Aryan.* Philip Zec, *Daily Mirror,* 16 May 1941.

How can we explain how Germany, fertilized through the centuries by classic antiquity and Christianity, by the ideals of liberty, equality, and social justice, by the common heritage of western humanism to which she had brought such noble and precious contributions, could have come to this astonishing return to primitive barbarism? ... In the middle of the century Germany goes back, of her own free will, beyond Christianity and civilization to the primitive barbarity of ancient Germany. She makes a deliberate break with all universal conceptions of modern nations. The National Socialist doctrine, which raised inhumanity to the level of a principle, constitutes, in fact, a doctrine of disintegration of modern society. (cited in Marrus 1997: 92–93)

Over the decades, the assumption of the divide between Nazism and Christianity has been reinforced again and again by scholars, analysts and ordinary people trying to make sense of the horrors perpetrated by the Nazis. The assumption reflects a concerted effort to distance modern nations and modern western societies from the holocaust and to deny that any Christian could behave as the Nazis did. Against this assumption, Steigmann-Gall in his controversial and compelling book *The Holy Reich* has asserted that 'Nazism was not the result of a "Death of God" in secularized society, but rather a radicalized and singularly horrific attempt to preserve God *against* secularized society' (Steigmann-Gall 2003: 12). Steigmann-Gall goes on to ask, why is it that scholars are prepared to accept a certain sympathy toward Nazism by some Protestant and Catholic churchmen, but unable to think that the opposite may also have been true, that some Nazis were sympathetic to Christianity and may even have regarded Nazi ideology as a Christian movement?

Whether one agrees with Steigmann-Gall or not, declaring Nazism antithetical to Christianity was, and remains, a mechanism that attempts to convince us of the uniqueness of the horrors of World War II and at the same time reassure us that they could never happen again. Of course, subsequent genocides, such as those that occurred in Cambodia, Rwanda and Bosnia in the second half of the twentieth century, belie these claims. Still, in the wake of World War II, in Europe, America and the rest of the world, Nazi leaders were widely regarded as diabolical and barbaric animals with no ability to relate to Christian ethics and values, especially with respect to valuing human life. A recent example of this attitude was expressed by Pope Benedict XVI in a visit to the Middle East in May 2009. Recalling memories of a visit to the death camp at Auschwitz, the pope blamed the horrors of the Holocaust on 'a godless regime that propagated an ideology of anti-semitism and hatred' (*New York Times*, 16 May 2009: 5).

Religion in Britain in the Postwar Years (late 1940s–mid-1950s)

Prior to World War II, Britain suffered great poverty and high unemployment in the interwar years marked by the depression. Coinciding with economic decline, Britain experienced a wave of moral conservatism; there was a marked rise in puritan austerity and a revival of evangelical religious practices. This was most obviously manifest in the prohibition movement immediately following World War I, which placed restrictions on the sale and consumption of alcohol and reinforced a social obsession with purity of mind and spirit. However, as the economy picked up in the mid-1930s, there was a shift away from church-based practices. This move was particularly noticeable among men who were members of veteran groups, where the camaraderie of fellow soldiers more adequately satisfied a spiritual need than conventional church attendance (Brown 2006: 125–26). Sunday was no longer seen as a mandatory day of quietness and penitence. 'For millions of working-class families it was a day for digging in the garden, visiting relatives, or snoozing over the *News of the World*' (McLeod 1984: 66). As historian Callum Brown has observed, 'In many respects, the inter-war years were when British Christianity became like an old sofa—relaxing, unpretentious, and less demanding on the user' (Brown 2006: 139).

Following World War II and into the 1950s there was once again a renewal of conservative values in both Britain's popular culture and official policy. In material terms, shortage was pervasive, with government rationing of furniture until 1948, clothes until 1949, petrol until 1950, and food until 1954 (Brown 2006: 180; Kynaston 2007; Zweiniger-Bargielowska 2000). In keeping with material restrictions, personal austerity in the form of discipline and self-control were also highly valued. Girls were to be shielded from the influences of American culture, and in particular the seductive practices of American servicemen who had money and access to goods (such as silk stockings and chocolate) to tempt young women. Extra-marital activity was publicly condemned and it was strongly expected that both men and women should be virgins at marriage. Women were encouraged to return to the home and child-raising duties—after having worked in factories and elsewhere during World War II—and a renewed domestic ideology ensured that women's liberation was deferred until the 1960s. Above all there was widespread concern with social respectability, particularly among women, who were 'compelled to conform to "respectability" through the everyday use of religious platitudes and homilies that "controlled" behaviour in the communities' (Brown 2006: 186).

Perhaps not surprisingly in this drab postwar era many British people, especially women and the young, reacted enthusiastically to the crusades of the Reverend Dr Billy Graham. Graham was a southern US Baptist, who first came to England in 1946 and held 360 meetings in 27 cities over a period of five months (Brown 2006: 189). He returned to London in 1954 and again in 1955 to advertise new moral crusades against communism, socialism and secularism. Graham made Hollywood films such as *Oil Town, USA* in 1946 which conveniently coincided with his arrival in London. For many British people, bowed down by postwar austerity, Graham's appeal lay in his novel and exciting glitzy movie-star persona. Accompanied by another popular movie star, the cowboy Roy Rogers and his horse Trigger, Graham put on extravagant shows to huge audiences of many thousands in football stadia and public spaces (Figure 36). These mass services deliberately set out to appeal to all classes people from all walks of life in a calculated effort to establish an American-style British Christianity:

> The sense of Hollywood and celebrity was immediately unusual to British churchgoers more accustomed to the cold, dark pews of the British church. The services were also very different from the norm. They were introduced by gospel-style hymn-singing by mass choirs of up to 3,000 men and women, bedecked in white dresses and black suits, making a stark moral backdrop. (Brown 2006: 193–94)

By the end of Graham's 1954 and 1955 crusades in London and Glasgow, he had been seen live by over three million people. Unfortunately, English and Scottish enthusiasm for Graham did not translate into British businesses contributing financially to his militant Christianity campaign against the threat of communism (Brown 2006: 193). Among ordinary churchgoers, Graham did not fare too well; 'church membership figures peaked in 1956, and then fell' (Brown 2006: 195). It seems that while millions attended Graham's shows, he in fact had

Figure 36.   Billy Graham speaking in Trafalgar Square, London, 1954. Original caption:
'Bible in hand, American evangelist Billy Graham speaks to a crowd of intent listeners
packing London's Trafalgar Square. In England on an extreme preaching marathon, Graham
is currently drawing overflow crowds to Harriday Arena.' © Bettmann/Corbis.

very little impact on the steady decline in church attendance in Britain from the
mid-1950s on. Nor could Graham prevent the secularist movement from gaining
momentum and popularity. Driven primarily by disaffected youth who were fed
up with being respectable, the secularist movement burst onto the British scene
in the 1960s.

Religion in the United States in the Postwar Years (late 1940s–mid-1950s)

The United States, like Britain, was anxious to reaffirm its identity as a Christian
nation in the wake of the Nuremberg trials. However, unlike Britain, US efforts in
proving its moral superiority went much further and a widespread crusade of
evangelical militant Christianity was embarked upon, as epitomized by church
leaders such as Billy Graham (see Miller 2009). I am not suggesting that as a
result of World War II and Nuremberg the wider US population suddenly
attended church as a means of asserting their Christian devotion. On the
contrary, the vast majority of Americans professed to attend church regularly
prior to the outbreak of the war, and between '1926 [and] 1950, church

membership nationwide grew 59.8 per cent, while the population went up just 28.6 per cent' (Feldman 2005: 147). What is interesting to note about the United States—in contrast to Britain—is that promotion by political progressives of a growing secular society was firmly rejected by mainstream America. In the United States anti-religious sentiment was increasingly seen as unacceptable, and when it did become apparent, it was often associated with intellectuals and university elite.

In the United States in the 1940s and 50s, belief in a Christian God was essential in order to be considered patriotic and truly American (a situation that arguably still exists in the United States today). National identity and belief in God were inseparable in the public consciousness. Part of this sensibility was linked to the function of churches in society. Churches provided the site for social networking and leisure, and many offered a variety of events such as such as women's leagues, bowling teams, and teen group activities (Feldman 2005: 164). Membership of a church, in other words, provided an essential sense of belonging to a local community. This sensibility developed at the national level through the emergence of an inclusive liberal Christianity that did not clearly identify with any one specific church. This nonsectarian Christianity enabled religion and science to be reconciled (a conflict which had erupted in the Scopes Monkey Trial in Tennessee, 1925—see Larson 1997; Lambert 2008: 104–29). Moreover, it allowed for reconciliation between the evangelical moderates and fundamentalists, as well as the full range of Christian denominations. This amorphous notion of Christianity was supported by all classes of society, promoted in schools, and endorsed by public officials and politicians. As the historian Noah Feldman has noted, 'mid century polls showed that nearly all Americans professed to believe in God. Politicians publicly espoused the importance and value of religious affiliation, which they expressly associated with the "American way of life"' (Feldman 2005: 164).

The coalescence of a generic Christianity with US national identity was underscored by Cold War politics which erupted in the immediate post-1945 period. Fear of a communist takeover was rife in the United States and western Europe. Outside of Stalinist Russia, communist influence was beginning to play a significant role in China, Greece and Iran, while communist parties had already come to power in Romania, Albania, Romania and Yugoslavia. A Soviet-dominated eastern bloc was forming, and events such as the Berlin Blockade in 1948 which forced the US to airdrop supplies into non-Soviet sectors of Berlin, the forming of NATO in 1949, the testing by the Soviet Union of an atomic bomb in 1949, and the invasion of South Korea by Soviet-supported North Korea in 1950 all contributed to the sense of an impending new world war.

In western countries, and in particular the United States, the common propagandist theme was that communists, like Nazis, were non-Christian, or even worse, 'godless'. In contrast, Americans were spiritual people and almost unanimously Christian. Nowhere was the linking of national identity, patriotism and religious affiliation as explicit as in the inquiries, hearings and investigative proceedings associated with Senator Joseph McCarthy and conducted in a period known as the Second Red Scare. The rise of McCarthyism tapped into a long-standing practice in the United States of conservatives labeling liberal reforms as 'communist' or 'anarchist'—a trend first evident in the late nineteenth century, as discussed in chapter five with respect to immigrant laborers and the Haymarket riots of 1886. This kind of derogatory labeling again emerged in the later years of World War I with fears of a Bolshevik revolution in the US, and reappeared in the 1930s in political conservatives' open criticism of the Roosevelt administration and its New Deal policies (Fried 1990; Brinkley 1995). Not surprisingly, this trend endures to this day, with some conservative Republicans calling the current US President Barack Obama, who favors social and economic reform, a 'socialist' and asserting that he has 'communist connections'.

McCarthyism lasted from the late 1940s through to the late 1950s. Through such bodies as the House Committee on Un-American Activities, the Senate Internal Security Subcommittee and the Civil Service Commission Loyalty Review Board, many people were accused of being communists or sympathetic to communism. These accusations were often determined on the basis of evidence collected by the illegal and unethical activities of the FBI, orchestrated by its director J Edgar Hoover. Blacklists were drawn up and certain groups were targeted, such as those associated with the Communist Party and trade unions, and those involved in Hollywood and the film industry. It has been estimated that up to 12,000 people lost their jobs, and hundreds were imprisoned (Schrecker 1998). Many more were publicly harassed and bullied, particularly if they were suspected of homosexuality (D'Emilio 1998). Against the backdrop of McCarthyism and fears of a godless communist influence, Americans were anxious to reaffirm their Christian spiritualism, patriotic nationalism and democratic righteousness in the Cold War clash. In 1954 Congress added to the United States' pledge of allegiance the words 'under God', and in 1956 officially declared that the national motto was 'In God We Trust'.

Creating the Judeo-Christian Myth

In the United States, the Nazi regime's persecution of Jews as revealed in detail during the Nuremberg trials produced a unique reaction in mainstream society. In conjunction with the growing militant Christianity that was gathering momentum in the 1940s and 50s, a large number of Americans began expressing greater sympathy toward American Jews and Judaism. This in turn required that the narrative of the United States as a non-sectarian Christian nation be re-drafted to include Jewish people. It also required a re-memorializing of US history since anti-semitic attitudes had been both widespread and tolerated in the later decades of the nineteenth century and throughout the years leading up to World War I. By the 1950s, Jews were no longer seen as poor immigrant slum dwellers. In the postwar era Jews occupied a substantial presence in industry and financial sectors, in elite universities, and in the production of popular culture through music, film and literature. This was particularly the case in major centers such as New York, Los Angeles and Chicago. One result of the emerging respectability of American Jews in the 1950s was that United States 'heritage was reinvented as inclusive: America had been built, it was now increasingly said, on Judeo-Christian roots' (Feldman 2006: 166; Butler et al 2008: 342–44).

The invention of a Judeo-Christian heritage was even more remarkable considering that American Jews in the 1950s constituted approximately only 4 per cent of the population, with 68 per cent declaring themselves Protestant, 23 per cent Catholic, and 5 per cent admitting no religious preference (Herberg 1960: 47). And, as mentioned above, nearly all Jews lived in major urban centers, which meant that the majority of Christian Americans did not know or engage with any Jewish people. This geographical distancing made the inclusive myth easier to swallow, since it had very little immediate impact on ordinary social relations. One person who was instrumental in selling the myth to the American public was Will Herberg, a Jew and former Communist Party member who later denounced Marxism and turned to religious conservatism. In 1955 Herberg wrote the bestselling book *Protestant—Catholic—Jew: An Essay in American Sociology*, where he set out the unique characteristics of what he called the 'common religion' of American society underpinning democracy and the 'American Way of Life'. Using language that made his argument hard to reject, Herberg wrote that this common religion is

> a faith that has its symbols and its rituals, its holidays and its liturgy, its saints and its sancta; it is a faith that every American, to the degree that he is an American, knows and understands ... It is not a synthetic system composed of beliefs to be found in all or in a group of religions. It is an organic structure of ideas, values and beliefs ... undergirding American life and overarching American society despite all indubitable differences of region, section, culture, and class. (Herberg 1960: 77, 78–79)

The inter-faith movement in the United States had been on the rise since the 1920s, when the National Conference on Christians and Jews was established. By the 1950s, notes Herberg, the tripartite inter-faith movement had become 'something that increasingly commends itself to the American mind as intrinsically right and proper because it is so obviously American and so obviously all-inclusive of the total American community' (Herberg 1960: 243). Of course Herberg glossed over the presence of any additional religions, such as Hinduism, Buddhism and Islam. For Herberg and the American majority, the embracing of religious pluralism could only go so far and other faiths were implicitly rejected. Also rejected was the embracing of atheism; the 'interfaith venture' between Protestants, Catholics and Jews was united in its intolerance of non-believers. By positing true Americans as spiritual, Herberg set up the justification for the inter-faith movement's 'hatred' of 'godless communists', an emotion that was on the surface extremely uncharitable and unchristian. Herberg had this to say:

Americans feel they *ought* to love their fellow men despite differences of race or creed or business interest; that is what the American Way of Life emphatically prescribes. But the American Way of Life almost explicitly sanctions hating a member of a 'dangerous' political party (Communists and fascists are obviously meant here) or an enemy of one's country, and therefore an overwhelming majority avow their hate. (Herberg 1960: 76)

Not all of American society bought into the Judeo-Christian myth. While open expressions of anti-semitism were no longer publicly acceptable in the postwar period, anti-semitic practices did not entirely go away, particularly outside urban environments. Even among Jewish communities, who arguably had the most to gain by widespread acceptance of the myth, there was some skepticism and opposition. The theologian and novelist Arthur A Cohen in *The Myth of the Judeo-Christian Tradition* (1970), and later the extremely well-respected historian Jacob Neusner in *Jews and Christians: The Myth of a Common Tradition* (1991), both questioned the rationale for blurring religious differences between Jews and Christians. Cohen argued that the myth was invented for political reasons and was fueled by fears of a common enemy. Rather than 'patching-over' the distinct histories and cultures and faiths associated with Judaism and Christianity, the future, wrote Cohen perceptively, lies in recognizing that 'This is a time ... when men must speak *out* of their differences and *over* the chasm that separates them' (Cohen 1970:xxi). Neusner reinforced this perspective by asserting: 'Only when we recognize difference can we appreciate points shared in common' (Neusner 1991:xi).

Today, claims of a Judeo-Christian American heritage are relatively weak. The warm alliance articulated in the postwar period has not been easy to maintain over the intervening decades, particularly with the tensions accumulating between some Jewish and evangelical churches. Still, references to a Judeo-Christian American heritage increased in the 1980s and 90s in tandem with the rise of the conservative right (Hartmann et al 2005). And in the wake of 9/11 the term has again been revitalized by conservative Jewish and evangelical communities in an attempt to unite the US population against the terror of an Islamist threat, as well as the perceived perils of secularism and multiculturalism. As the historian Jon Butler has pointed out, the term 'functioned as a code for exclusion', implying that 'Christians and Jews were the "true" Americans and that everyone else—Hindus, Buddhists, Muslims, Sikhs, Taoists, humanists—professed beliefs outside the mainstream' (Butler et al 2008: 343). Liberal critics of the 'Judeo-Christian' term, such as law professor Stephen M Feldman, have argued that there is not a common heritage. On the contrary, Feldman argues, Christianity has historically incited anti-semitism. The supposed separation of church and state in the founding of the United States did not result in the equal treatment of all religions but in fact privileged Protestant Christianity over all other faiths (Feldman 1998).

Whatever one thinks today in the ongoing culture wars between conservatives and progressives, in the 1950s the 'Judeo-Christian' narrative was widely supported by American politicians as well as ordinary people on both sides of the political divide. The narrative served a number of purposes. First, it helped to distinguish and distance the United States from the German atrocities of World War II by declaring America a spiritual nation in contrast to the non-believing Nazis. Second, the narrative was easily adapted to fit the unfolding Cold War context and used widely in American propaganda against godless communists. Third, the inclusive Judeo-Christian narrative allowed for more open discussion about the separation of church and state. As I discuss below, since society could relax in the knowledge that it was religiously inclusive, greater opportunities arose for the legal profession and courts to push a more secular agenda. This was critical for the burgeoning civil rights movement led by Martin Luther King Jr and others. Fourthly, and perhaps most importantly, a belief in a Judeo-Christian tradition reassured Americans that their country was a land of democracy and freedom, a place that refused to tolerate discrimination on the basis of one's religion, ethnicity or race (or business interests—see the Herberg quote above).

The public affirmation of American liberty and inclusiveness was essential given that the United States in the immediate postwar era was still deeply racist and socially and economically segregated, particularly in the south. Declaring the country inclusive veiled the truth about its deeply problematic racial politics. Even among those who professed to embrace religious pluralism, be it in terms of an inclusive Christianity, as with Billy Graham's militant evangelicalism, or in terms of an inclusive interfaith spirituality, as espoused by Will Herberg's claim to a Judeo-Christian American tradition, when it came down to issues of race these men's rhetoric of brotherly love lacked substance. For all of Graham's critique of segregation and his calling for racial harmony he hesitated to openly support the civil rights movement (see Miller 2009). Likewise, Herberg, while embracing an inter-faith democracy, nonetheless railed against Martin Luther King Jr and the civil rights movement. Herberg wrote an article in the *National Review* in 1965 in which he revealed that his primary concern was the threat to law and order rather than the racist practices the activists protested against. Evoking apocalyptic imagery of 'anarchy and chaos', Herberg argued:

> For years now, the Rev Dr Martin Luther King and his associates have been deliberately undermining the foundations of internal order in this country. With their rabble-rousing demagoguery, they have been cracking the 'cake of custom' that holds us together. With their doctrine of 'civil disobedience,' they have been teaching hundreds of thousands of Negroes—particularly the adolescents and the children—that it is perfectly alright to break the law and defy constituted authority if you are a Negro-with-a-grievance; in protest against injustice. And they have done more than talk. They have on occasion after occasion, in almost every part of the country, called out their mobs on the streets, promoted 'school strikes,' sit-ins, lie-ins, in explicit violation of the law and in explicit defiance of the public authority. They have taught anarchy and chaos

by word and deed—and, no doubt, with the best of intentions—and they have found apt pupils everywhere, with intentions not of the best. Sow the wind, and reap the whirlwind. (Herberg 1965: 769–70)

RACE: RETHINKING RACE

Eugenics theory, a pseudo-scientific racial theory based on blood lines, was discussed in chapter five with respect to US attitudes toward European immigrants in the later decades of the nineteenth century, and in chapter six with respect to the US treatment of Native Americans. The Nuremberg trials revealed that eugenics was also employed by Hitler in his efforts to create an Aryan or Nordic master race. More specifically, this form of scientific racism was used to justify the Nazi regime's population programs, which sought to eliminate hereditary diseases and deformities through sterilization, and its medical experimentation on those held in prison and later concentration camps. Ultimately it was the rationale for the 'final solution' that sought to exterminate Jews and other ethnic and religious minorities.

At the core of eugenics theory is the concept of biologically determined racial categories of people. Eugenics informed Hitler's policies and formed the basis of his legal reforms targeting Jews and other minorities. For instance, in 1931 the Race and Settlement Office was formed to ensure that SS personnel (the 'elite' military unit of the Nazi party) married 'suitable' spouses of Aryan stock. Another explicit example is the Nuremberg Laws of 1935, which were based on a pseudo-scientific understanding of blood quantum. Under the Nuremberg Laws, as shown visually in Figure 37, people who could prove that they were descended from four German grandparents (white circles) were considered to have 'German blood', while Jews were defined as those who were descended from three or four Jewish grandparents (black circles), who in turn were defined as members of a Jewish religious community. People of both German and Jewish heritage were considered to be of 'mixed' blood. The Nuremberg Laws declared both Jews and most people of mixed blood to be non-citizens, and prohibited intermarriage and all sexual relations between people deemed to be of different races because such activity was thought to dilute the true Aryan German stock.

Karl Brandt was Hitler's personal doctor, responsible for the Nazi regime's policies on population control and racial hygiene. At the Nuremberg trials, Brandt's defense lawyer entered into evidence a book in an attempt to mitigate his case by showing that Nazi racial policies were not unique to the Third Reich. The book, entitled *The Passing of the Great Race,* had been written in 1916 by an American, Madison Grant, and had enjoyed considerable support in the United States throughout the 1920s and 30s, though it was publicly condemned by many academics, including the economist Gunnar Mydral and the leading German-American anthropologist Franz Boas. In any case, the book was the first non-German book to be translated and published by the Nazi press and had clearly

Figure 37. Chart used to explain the Nuremberg Laws, 1935. At the top of the first column, the four white circles indicate four white grandparents of 'German blood'. The chart shows progressive ratios of mixed blood, with 'Jewish blood' represented as black circles. The furthermost right column depicts four Jewish grandparents.

been influential in the shaping of Nazi racial policies. When it was entered into evidence, the US lawyers at Nuremberg were mortified. The book, arguably, had helped to shape Nazi policies and was an uncomfortable reminder for many Americans back home of some of the similarities between German and US thinking on racial identification and management through programs such as sterilization and segregation (see Nourse 2008; Lombardo 2008).

Race in Britain—pre- and post- World War II

Prior to World War II, many people emigrated from Britain to Australia, Canada and the United States in search of greater opportunities. This left a deficit in labor pools, and in the postwar period Britain was forced to actively encourage immigration to its shores to help restore the war-torn country, rebuild its industries and infrastructure, and feed its citizens. Demands for raw materials were exacerbated by the reduction of its overseas colonial territories, with the independence of India in 1947, and Burma and Ceylon (Sri Lanka) in 1948. Many of the people who came to Britain in the postwar period were originally from its former colonies. In 1948, 547 migrants from Jamaica arrived at Tilbury, a docktown just outside London, on the old troop ship *The Windrush*, ushering in a new era in British race relations. Within 10 years there were approximately 210,000 'coloured colonial immigrants' living in Britain (Therborn 1995: 41). By 1970 the number of non-white residents numbered 1.4 million, although a third of these people were born in Britain.

The growing presence of former colonial subjects in Britain, many of whom were forced to take poorly paid unskilled jobs, created intense social and cultural tension and conflict. Prior to the arrival of *The Windrush* there had been race riots in Liverpool, where up to 8,000 blacks had set up marginal residential communities in the south of the city around the docks (Hesse 2000: 100). As the primary slave-trading port in the eighteenth century, Liverpool had a long history of cultural tensions between its white and black populations. With the abolition of the slave trade in 1807, the port city became home to a small population of seafaring blacks. Over the years this black community endured various forms of discrimination, and in the 1940s many were deliberately excluded from working on British ships by white seaman fearful of competition and losing their jobs. In 1945, 'over a period of three days, white mobs … laid siege to different hostels and clubs that catered for Black seamen … When the police intervened to restore order, they used the opportunity to inflict violence and arrest mostly Black people' (Hesse 2000: 101). Incidents similar to the 1945 Liverpool race riot became much more common and widespread with the arrival of substantial numbers of immigrants from the West Indies, India and Pakistan after 1948. The presence of new immigrants resulted in large-scale conflicts in cities including London, Birmingham, Manchester, Nottingham and Liverpool throughout the 1950s and 60s (Gilroy 1991; Hall 1990).

One such conflict occurred in Bristol in 1963. A 60-day boycott of the Bristol Bus Company was staged to demand that the public company employ blacks and Asians as bus drivers. On 28 August 1963, the Bristol Bus Company was forced to lift the color ban, the same day as Martin Luther King Jr presented his famous 'I have a Dream' speech to 250,000 civil rights supporters on the steps of the Lincoln Memorial in Washington, DC. One year later, the UK Race Relations Act 1964 was passed, making racial discrimination a legal offence. However, in Britain, as in the United States with the passing of the Voting Rights Act (1965), racism did not stop overnight. Many minorities suffered terrible, often insidious, forms of racial discrimination for decades. A notable example is Bernie Grant, who was born in Guyana and in 1963 at the age of 19 arrived in Britain to engage in a blue-collar work program sponsored by the British government. He quickly became active in trade unions and the Labour Party, and went on to become a local Council leader and eventually Member of Parliament for Tottenham in 1987. Reflecting on his life, Grant noted:

> When I arrived [in Britain] there were still the signs on the windows—no blacks, no Irish, no dogs, no children. Then there was the Race Relations Act of 1964 which outlawed all that. But what I found was that the problem lay in this institutional racism, hidden policies which you found in housing, in education and so on. There would be a policy which said that to get a house you needed such and such connections with the

borough. Then they would define 'connections' as having your family living there for three generations or whatever. It was moving the goalposts, and it meant that black families hadn't a hope of getting a house. There were many policies in education that discriminated against black people. It was easy enough to deal with overt racism; you could fight the people concerned and that would be the end of it. The institutionalized variety just kept going. So I became involved with a lot of anti-racist work. (Bernie Grant Archives, Middlesex University, www.berniegrantarchive.org.uk)

Race in the United States—Jim Crow and Racial Segregation

Following the Civil War in 1865 and the failure of the Reconstruction era to bring equality to emancipated black populations, tensions between blacks and southern whites steadily intensified. Southern landowners were fed up with having to treat their former slaves with civility. The impact of a long economic depression that began in the 1870s contributed to the breakdown of social relations between blacks and whites. Towards the end of the nineteenth century laws were put into place that explicitly discriminated against blacks. These laws became known as 'Jim Crow laws' and many remained in force until 1965, when the Voting Rights Act was passed.

Jim Crow laws were grounded in the concept of racial segregation and legally endorsed and aggressively enforced through the 'separate but equal' doctrine that was upheld by the US Supreme Court in the landmark *Plessy v Ferguson* decision of 1896. In this case Homer Plessy, a man of fair skin tone and deemed 'one-eighth negro', bought a first class train ticket and refused to leave the 'whites only' car and sit in the 'colored only' car. The Supreme Court held that Louisiana's segregated public transport was constitutional. As a result, many states enacted similar legislation institutionalizing segregation with respect to public transport as well as a full range of laws that impacted all aspects of black people's lives, including where blacks could sit in a movie theater, what water fountain they cold drink from, what jobs they could accept, and of course where their children could attend school. By the 1920s, there was segregated housing, education, transport, health facilities, churches, jails and jobs. As late as the 1940s, blacks who enlisted in the US army—to fight against Nazi racism—were segregated from their fellow white US soldiers. It would not be until 1948, after World War II and with the first Nuremberg trial complete, that President Harry S Truman banned segregation in the American armed forces.

Institutionalized racism permeated American society in the first half of the twentieth century and was justified by a widely accepted eugenics theory of biologically determined race. Eugenics theory made public lynching of blacks acceptable, and made being a member of the Ku Klux Klan respectable. Racism justified through pseudo-scientific eugenic explanations was mapped onto a popular understanding of a hierarchy of races, which positioned white males at the top with other 'races' ranked beneath, typically according to deepening skin tone. Under this rubric, it was generally believed that blacks were intellectually, morally and socially inferior, and therefore prone to criminal activity and debauchery. This kind of thinking justified US anti-miscegenation laws prohibiting mixed-race marriage, sterilization programs targeting mentally and physically challenged non-white populations, and segregation laws that cordoned off 'deficient' blacks (and Native Americans) from white communities.

At the Nuremberg trial, when Karl Brandt's lawyer entered into evidence the book *The Passing of the Great Race* in order to show that the United States, like Nazi Germany, practiced racial discrimination, it was a moment of extreme shame for all Americans. While the US never went as far as the Nazis in applying eugenics to identify, manage and ultimately exterminate racially and ethically diverse people, there were indisputable parallels between German laws in the interwar and WWII years and US laws of the Jim Crow period (see Kühl 1994; Lombardo 2002; Tucker 2002). The revelation of the disquieting parallels at Nuremberg prompted postwar re-evaluations of segregation back in the United States (Ehrenfreund 2007: 131). Nuremberg forced many politicians, lawyers, civil rights activists and ordinary Americans to rethink the country's legal and social relationship with its own racial minorities, and in particular the generally accepted institutionalized racism directed at blacks. But the trial did more than lead to comparisons being made between Germany and the United States; it also suggested that there was a need to rethink ideas about race itself. By drawing attention to the fact that many Jews looked indistinguishable from non-Jewish Germans, Nuremberg demonstrated that the concept of race needed to accommodate complex interconnections between religion, culture and ethnicity that may or may not correlate to the color of a person's skin. The Germans' persecution of Jews, in other words, brought to the fore new questions that left many people asking, particularly in the United States where black/white racial politics dominated, were Jews targeted because of their religion, because of their culture, or because of their race?

WEB Du Bois

Arguably no US intellectual was more responsive to and influenced by the Nazi persecution of Jews and the culminating impact of the Nuremberg trials than the African-American WEB Du Bois. When World War II broke out in 1939, Du Bois was already a renowned scholar, journalist and civil rights activist. He was the first African-American to receive a PhD from Harvard University in 1895, had been a founding member of the National Association for the Advancement of Colored People (NAACP) in 1909, was involved in establishing the Pan-African international movement, and was one of the first to write critically and accessibly about US race relations as seen through the eyes of a black person. He wrote many books and novels, the most well-known probably being *The Souls of Black Folk* (1903). The book was important on a number of fronts; its title deliberately linked Christianity with African Americans in an effort to make blacks appear more 'human' to a white society. The book was also written in an accessible poetic style that would appeal to a general audience.[1] Du Bois wrote another strategically important book which highlighted the positive impact of black emancipation on US race relations, called *Black Reconstruction* (1935).

In the early 1930s, Du Bois was not overly engaged with rumors emerging out of Europe of German persecution of Jews and other minorities. Of course he found these activities abhorrent and unacceptable, but in his mind they did not compare with the injustices perpetrated by whites against blacks back home. In *The Crisis*, published in May 1933, Du Bois declared, 'It seems impossible in the middle of the twentieth century a country like Germany could turn to race hate as a political expedient. Surely, the experience of American is enough to warn the world ...' (cited in Brackman 2000: 59). Moreover, Du Bois did not see the persecution of Jews in Germany and the persecution of blacks in America as analogous. Jews, argued Du Bois, were victimized because of their relatively high social-economic status in the interwar years as well as for reasons of religion and community. In contrast, blacks in America were subject to color prejudice which was justified in pseudo-scientific biological theories such as eugenics.

With the passing of the Nuremberg Laws in 1935, Du Bois became aware of the scale and enormity of the anti-Jewish persecution, and as a result became even more outraged. According to Du Bois, Nazi anti-semitism 'surpasses in vindictive cruelty and public insult anything I have ever seen; and I have seen much. ... There has been no tragedy in modern times equal in its awful effects to the fight on the Jew in Germany. It is an attack on civilization, comparable only to such horrors as the Spanish Inquisition and the African slave trade' (cited in Brackman 2000: 65). In 1936, Du Bois was also forced to rethink his understanding of race. Like his fellow scholars Gunnar Mydral and Franz Boas, he had long opposed the notion of scientific racism based upon eugenics theories (Degler 1991; Taylor 1981; Liss 1998). However, while Du Bois rejected biological essentialism he 'remained committed to a race-centered analysis, but with race redefined as a construct of class and culture within and across nations' (Brackman 2000: 77; see also King 2004: 40–45). In the context of Jewish persecution, Du Bois had to refine his thinking on race and racial discrimination yet again in order to appreciate that religion and shared community were also vital elements, alongside skin tone, in creating and demarcating racial categories and identities.

During this period Du Bois also began to view German anti-semitism and American racism against blacks as emerging out of the same historical phenomenon. Specifically, Du Bois located these racist practices in an historical continuum and interpreted the German atrocities of World War II as an outcome of

---

[1] Du Bois' concept of the 'double consciousness' of blacks remains to this day a significant contribution to understanding the politics of race in the United States (Du Bois 1903: 29).

an earlier phase of European colonialism which witnessed the degradation and oppression of native peoples and gave rise to the modern theory of race (King 2004: 47). According to Du Bois:

> There was no Nazi atrocity—concentration camps, wholesale maiming and murder, defilement of women or ghastly blasphemy of childhood—which the Christian civilization of Europe had not long been practicing against colored folk in all parts of the world in the name of and for the defense of a Superior Race born to rule the world. (cited in King 2004: 47)

Du Bois' linking of German anti-semitism with former histories of colonialism was a reoccurring theme in his writings. For Du Bois, the pain and suffering imposed on others at the margins of empire set up the psychological and cultural conditions in which violence and suffering could re-emerge in the European/American center. This linking of domestic racism with global racism was a truly significant insight and contribution to the rethinking of race, and was the intellectual underpinning of Du Bois' earlier work in the Pan-African movement that took him to international conferences in London and elsewhere. Du Bois interpreted the US history of slavery and racism as part of a global system of oppression that linked all Africans in a common community, hence 'the United States was living not to itself, but a part of the strain and stress of the world' (cited in Kaplan 2002: 175). As the historian Richard King has noted, 'By widening the field of concern from the United States to Europe and, then, to Africa and beyond, Du Bois's work suggested that the American dilemma was also a European and a global one' (King 2004: 470). Du Bois was able to bring this message forcefully home to the American public by capitalizing on the widespread interest in the horrors revealed by the Nuremberg trials and highlighting the analogous experiences suffered by both Jews and blacks. Reflecting on his three visits to the Warsaw Ghetto, Du Bois wrote, 'the race problem in which I was interested cut across lines of color and physique and belief and status and was a matter of cultural patterns, perverted teaching and human hate, which reached all sorts of people and caused endless evil to all men' (Du Bois 1952: 46).

In the immediate post-World War II period Du Bois' notion of a globally interconnected system of racism and oppression resonated with the increasingly intense self-determination and independence movements appearing in European colonies such as British governed India, Burma, Egypt, Iraq and Malaya; French governed Algeria, Lebanon, Syria and Indochina; and Dutch governed Indonesia. Du Bois, a strong advocate of human rights both in the United States and overseas, was essential in galvanizing national and international support for the recognition of human rights for all peoples, including minorities and indigenous populations. He was instrumental in establishing the Pan-African Congress, which held a series of five meetings between 1919 and 1945. The last was held in Manchester, England, a locus which was already the site of racial tensions between whites and blacks. At the fifth Congress the pan-African movement dovetailed with postcolonial movements to create a much wider front against western imperialism. The Congress was symbolically and politically important: it involved not only black Africans, but also Afro-Caribbeans and Afro-Americans in the common call for independence from imperial control and demands for recognition of human rights. It helped to develop 'pan-Africanism strategically as a political movement on three continents: Western Europe (especially Britain), the Americas (eg the Caribbean and the United States), and Africa (especially West Africa)' (Hesse 2000: 107).

In June 1945, Du Bois acted as a consultant in discussions to establish the UN Charter in San Francisco, a meeting attended by 50 nations determined to set up an international organization which was to be responsible for the prevention of future violence. At this historic meeting, Du Bois, along with many others, forcefully argued that recognizing human rights around the world was essential for securing world peace (see Lauren 2003: 177–98). Du Bois declared that the proposed UN Charter should:

> make clear and unequivocal the straightforward stand of the civilized world for race equality, and the universal application of the democratic way of life, not simply as philanthropy and justice, but to save human civilization from suicide. What was true of the United States in the past is true of world civilization today—we cannot exist half slave and half free. (cited in Lauren 1983: 21)

Then, in 1947, Du Bois, as a researcher for the NAACP, presented to the UN a petition titled 'An Appeal to the World: a Statement on the Denial of Human Rights to Minorities in the Case of Citizens of Negro Descent in the United States of America and an Appeal to the United Nations for Redress' (Lauren 2003: 218–19; Lewis 2000). In this document, Du Bois pointed out that visitors to the United States, and in particular international delegates of the UN, are 'always liable to insult and to discrimination; because they may be mistaken for Americans of Negro descent'. He went on to argue that discrimination against blacks in the US cannot be 'persisted in, without infringing upon the rights of the peoples of the world' (Du Bois 1947: 13). While the petition may not have had the immediate impact Du Bois and other NAACP leaders had hoped for, it was nonetheless crucial in highlighting the universal dimensions of racial discrimination and in turn building international support for the UN's Universal Declaration of Human Rights, which was issued the following year.

RIGHTS: IMPLEMENTING HUMAN RIGHTS

The Nuremberg trials, both directly through international media detailing Nazi activities, and indirectly by influencing politicians and activists such as Du Bois, played an important role in helping to bring about the Universal Declaration of Human Rights. As argued below, this declaration is unequivocally the twentieth century's most important legal document affecting issues of racial discrimination. It forever changed international and domestic humanitarian law and social, economic and political relations within and between states and geo-political regions. That being said, in the immediate postwar decade significant problems in implementing and enforcing the Universal Declaration of Human Rights prevailed. In contrast to this relative failing of the Declaration to set up an enforceable international human rights regime in the 1950s, the Declaration had an enormous impact on the national politics and laws of the United States. This was largely due to the unforeseen consequence of the Nuremberg trials on US domestic jurisdiction.

Postwar International Relations and the Universal Declaration of Human Rights

Establishing the United Nations under the 1945 UN Charter, and the UN's subsequent issuing of the Universal Declaration of Human Rights in 1948, represented a new understanding of the interconnections between nations across the world. The thrust of this new understanding was twofold. It qualified the concept of state sovereignty. As demonstrated by both world wars, the domestic problems of any one country affected its neighboring nations and regions. Countries could not prevent their internal problems spilling out across geopolitical boundaries. This appreciation of the artificiality of state boundaries altered, at least in theory, the long-standing international doctrine that a government holds prerogative sovereign control over its domestic populations. Under the new international rubric, it was strongly argued that the UN should be able to intervene economically or militarily on behalf of the international community to prevent a country suppressing freedom of speech, denying due process, or persecuting targeted communities. During discussions of the Commission to Study the Organization of Peace prior to establishing the UN Charter it was declared:

> Now, as a result of the Second World War, it has become clear that a regime of violence and oppression within any nation of the civilized world is a matter of concern for all the rest. It is a disease in the body politic which is contagious because the government that rests upon violence, will, by its very nature, be even more ready to do violence to foreigners than to its own fellow citizens, especially if it can thus escape the consequences of its acts at home. The foreign policy of despots is inherently one that carries with it a constant risk to the peace and security of others. In short, if aggression is the key-note of domestic policy, it will also be the clue to foreign relations. (cited in Lauren 2003: 175)

Despite wide support for the UN Charter, not all national representatives were willing to cede ultimate authority over their domestic jurisdictions to an international organization. Some western nations, and especially those with overseas colonies or oppressed minorities within its borders such as South Africa, were openly critical of the new international community's agenda. In response to concerns about the overriding powers of the UN, Article 2(7) was included in the Charter.

Article 2(7): Nothing contained in the present Charter shall authorize the United Nations to intervene in matters which are essentially within the domestic jurisdiction of any state or shall require the Members to submit such matters to settlement under the present Charter; but this principle shall not prejudice the application of enforcement measures under Chapter VII.

While Article 2(7) appeased some state representatives, it should be noted that it cannot override the powers of the UN's Security Council as set out in Chapter VII of the Charter. These executive powers are arguably the most important element of the whole document. Under Article 42 the Security Council can 'take such action by air, sea or land forces as may be necessary to maintain or restore international peace and security. Such action may include demonstrations, blockade, and other operations by air, sea, or land forces of the Members of the United Nations' (see www.un.org/aboutun/charter). The Security Council's mandate to prevent war, even if it required international intervention in a country's domestic jurisdiction, was reflected in the first two charges brought against Nazi leaders at the Nuremberg trials, which together accused the men of 'crimes against peace'.

The second major development in international relations was a newfound appreciation that in order to secure world peace, fundamental basic human rights must be protected around the world. In other words, peace could not be secured simply by dividing up the spoils of war between victorious allies. The failure of the League of Nations and Treaty of Versailles in 1919, in which the victorious Allied powers negotiated the terms of post-World War I peace, including forcing Germany to accept full responsibility, underscored the need to rethink how best to secure future peace. In short, 'peace defined exclusively and narrowly in terms of deterrence among the Great Powers in a geopolitical balance of power would no longer suffice' (Lauren 2003: 174). New ways of thinking broadened the concept of peace to become a 'people's peace' in which human rights, including the protection of civil and political rights and rights to self-determination, featured prominently. The UN Charter's signatories were keen to underscore that all peoples, of whatever religion, race, ethnicity, nationality, gender or language, would be equally protected. In the famous opening lines of the Charter it was declared that the UN was 'to save succeeding generations from the scourge of war', and 'to reaffirm faith in fundamental human rights, in the dignity and worth of the human person, in the equal rights of men and women of nations large and small'.

Upon the passing of the UN Charter, groups such as the NAACP, the Pan-African Congress and the Indian Rights Association immediately called for action. Amidst heated debate, both philosophical and moral, among UN delegates about the implementation of the Charter there developed a common purpose—the establishment of an international bill of rights. Over the next two years, hundreds of meetings and discussions took place to thrash out the terms and methods of developing such a bill of rights. Eleanor Roosevelt was a central figure in this endeavor, working tirelessly and graciously with the UN Commission on Human Rights to draft a document acceptable to all parties. Some delegates were not happy with the Universal Declaration of Human Rights. For instance, Poland, the Soviet Union, South Africa and the United States all objected to varying degrees. The president of the American Bar Association declared that the Declaration was revolutionary in the development of international law, presenting a serious threat to the principle of national sovereignty and the right of states to govern their own domestic jurisdictions. Still, as the historian Paul Gordon Lauren has argued:

> despite the fact that they came from a wide variety of backgrounds and had a wealth of differences between them, the overwhelming majority of delegates at the United Nations were determined to do something that had never been done before: create a declaration of universally accepted norms or standards of human rights, developed after full consideration of the philosophies, cultures, and political systems of the world, and designed to establish what Eleanor Roosevelt described as a common standard valid 'for all peoples and all nations' …
>
> Finally, at four minutes before midnight on 10 December 1948, Herbert Evatt of Australia, serving as the president of the General Assembly, announced that the time had come for the entire membership of the United Nations to cast their votes. Acutely sensing that they were about to make history, conveyed by excited murmurings throughout the normally solemn chamber of the Palais Chaillot, each delegate watched for the votes of others with anticipation and prepared to cast their own. In the end, the president announced the final vote: forty-eight in favor and eight abstentions. Not one country opposed. In the midst of spontaneous rejoicing, the delegates arose and gave Eleanor Roosevelt a standing ovation. Then they and the members of the news media alike left the large assembly hall to announce that the United Nations had just proclaimed a vision on behalf of all peoples in the world to be known as the Universal Declaration of Human Rights. (Lauren 2003: 227, 229)

The years immediately following 1948 were difficult in terms of implementing and enforcing the Universal Declaration of Human Rights. Initially, things seemed to go very well and the following year saw the adoption of the Convention on the Prevention and Punishment of the Crime of Genocide, as well as the revision of the existing Geneva Conventions and the adoption of a new fourth Geneva Convention, which spelled out the protection of civilians in times of war. Inspired by the Universal Declaration, the European Convention on Human Rights was declared in 1950. Despite these significant victories in international law, the implementation of the Declaration itself was increasingly stalled, mainly because of the growing tensions between the Soviet Union and the United States, the polarization of international relations between a communist east and capitalist west, and the growing demand of newly independent nations in Asia, Africa and the Middle East for involvement in human rights discussions (Judt 2006: 213–37; Burke 2010). In this environment of mounting tension and conflict, both the Soviet Union and the United States—ironically—shared a fear of UN intervention in their domestic affairs and resented any qualification of their national sovereignty.

The politics of the Cold War brought what has been called the 'Deep Freeze' to international human rights (Hajjar 2005). In the United States the American Bar Association was openly hostile to the Genocide Convention, and the Daughters of the American Revolution publicly condemned Eleanor Roosevelt. American business entrepreneurs were scared of a communist takeover through radical labor organizations and unions, media outlets were fearful of communist propaganda infiltrating social relations, and ordinary white Americans, especially those from the midwest and south, were scared that their world based on racial segregation and oppression of minorities would be challenged. McCarthyism and the blacklisting of communist sympathizers (see above) further whipped up public anxiety about godless and violent Russians insidiously infiltrating the 'American way of life'. Attempts were made to stop the US participating in an international human rights regime. While ultimately unsuccessful, these attempts halted the development of international human rights law for many years. For instance:

> Republican Senator John Bricker decided to introduce legislation demanding that the United States withdraw from all treaties having anything to do with human rights. 'My purpose,' he declared, 'is to bury the so-called covenant on human rights so deep that no one holding office will ever dare to attempt its resurrection.' He described it as 'completely foreign to American law and tradition' and as nothing less than a 'UN Blueprint of tyranny.' Bricker then stridently announced: 'I do not want any of the international groups, and especially the group headed by Mrs Eleanor Roosevelt, which has drafted the covenant of Human Rights, to betray the fundamental, inalienable, and God-given right of American citizens enjoyed under the Constitution. That is really what I am driving at.' (cited in Lauren 2003: 237)

Nuremberg's Legacy of Rights

Nuremberg's legacy on the international legal scene hit a roadblock in the immediate postwar decade as the Declaration became entangled in the politics of the Cold War. Within Britain, Nuremberg underscored the horrors of racist practices among the general population and arguably fostered a public consciousness with respect to racism and discrimination. But it is hard to trace a direct link between the aftermath of the Nuremberg trials and emerging civil rights activism within Britain in the postwar period. In contrast, on the US domestic scene the Nuremberg trials had an immediate, profound and largely unforeseen impact. There is an explicit connection between Nuremberg and the emergence of the American civil and politics rights era of the 1950s and 60s, which forever erased all legal justifications of racial segregation and white discrimination against blacks.

Some scholars, such as Gerald Rosenberg in *The Hollow Hope: Can Courts Bring About Social Change?* (2008), have argued that the American Supreme Court has in fact had very little impact on social issues. According to this perspective, despite the perennial hand-wringing about politically driven judicial appointments to the Supreme Court, the ultimate weight of such appointments matters little. Rosenberg argues that if the Court is to accomplish significant change, there must also exist sufficient precedent for change, and the Court's decision must also have widespread support from congress and citizens. Without these other legal, political and social conditions already in place, courts in and of themselves are relatively powerless. The Supreme Court does not effect social change; it can only affirm and endorse it.

Whether one agrees or not with this rather controversial argument, the facts are that the lead prosecutor for the American team at Nuremberg, Robert Jackson, did return to the United States and was involved—as a judge sitting in the Supreme Court—in landmark decisions relating to the implementation of political and civil rights. The most important of these cases was *Brown v Board of Education* (1954), a NAACP-sponsored test case that consolidated five different claims seeking relief from school segregation. Arguing for the plaintiffs before the Supreme Court was Thurgood Marshall, later appointed the first African American Supreme Court Judge in 1967. Marshall forcefully presented his case, arguing:

> Why, of all the multitudinous groups in this country, [do] you have to single out the Negroes and give them this separate treatment? It can't be because of slavery in the past, because there are very few groups in this country that haven't had slavery some place back in the history of their group. It can't be color, because there are Negroes as white as drifted snow, with blue eyes, and they are just as segregated as the colored man. The only thing it can be is an inherent determination that the people who were formerly in slavery, regardless of anything else, shall be kept as near that state as possible. (*Brown v The Board of Education of Topeka, Kansas*, 347 US 483 (1954))

Much to the surprise of the general public and the legal community, the Supreme Court unanimously held in *Brown* that racial segregation in public schools was unconstitutional and violated the Fourteenth Amendment. The era of Jim Crow laws was on the way, albeit slowly, to being dismantled.

There has been much debate about the effectiveness of the *Brown* decision in changing racial relations (Patterson 2002; Kluger 2004). Especially in the south, there was bitter and at times bloody resistance to the bussing of black students into white neighborhoods. Such resistance included shutting down white schools rather than accept black students, and politicians personally blocking black students' access to schoolrooms (Figure 38). Despite the widespread unenforceability of the desegregation doctrine, the *Brown* case nonetheless helped to unleash a sequence of public demonstrations such as the bus boycott in 1955, the lunch counter sit-ins in 1961, and the Birmingham civil rights demonstrations in 1963. At Birmingham, Martin Luther King Jr wrote his famous 'Letter from a

Figure 38. Dorothy Counts, the first black student to attend Harry Harding High School in Charlotte, North Carolina, USA, maintains her composure amidst shouting, gesticulating white students, 4 September 1957. Dorothy was taunted, spat upon, had rubbish and rocks thrown at her, and was ignored by teachers and other students. Fearing for her physical safety, her father removed her from the school after only four days. AP Photo/Douglas Martin, © Desegregation. Dorothy Counts 1957 570904081.

Birmingham Jail', declaring that 'One has not only a legal, but a moral responsibility to obey just laws. Conversely, one has a moral responsibility to disobey unjust laws … All segregation statutes are unjust'.

Brown was not the first case to argue against segregation, but it is widely regarded as the case that launched the civil rights movement and which ultimately ushered in the Voting Rights Act of 1965 and technically ended African-American disenfranchisement. *Brown* is a landmark decision on many fronts. Ian Haney Lopez, a renowned law and race scholar, has argued:

> The single greatest difference between what we might term pre- and post-*Brown* racial jurisprudence is that, generally speaking, since *Brown v Board of Education* declared in 1954 that separate conditions are inherently unequal, our nation's laws have moved from using explicit racial categories in an oppressive manner toward using these explicit racial categories to ameliorate racial discrimination. (Lopez 1996: 112)

How is the *Brown* case linked to Nuremberg? The decision reflected many Americans' growing sense that racial discrimination was morally wrong. This increased sensitivity of whites to black injustices had, arguably, been brewing for some years but was brought to the fore of public consciousness by the media surrounding the Nuremberg trials. The revelations of Nazi atrocities and explicit parallels suggested by the German defendants between the treatment of Jews in Europe and the treatment of blacks in the United States highlighted issues that many in the United States had not questioned or thought about before. Moreover, the Supreme Court's citing in *Brown* of the work of social scientists such as Gunnar Mydral, who rejected scientific racism, underscored the unacceptability of a eugenics-based theory, at least with respect to supporting segregation.

Another important factor in the *Brown* decision was the rise in the United States of what Noah Feldman has called 'legal secularism'. By this term Feldman refers to the gradual reframing of the role of the Supreme Court and its emerging reluctance to prescribe dominant views in politics, nationalism or religion or 'force citizens to confess by word or act their faith therein' (cited in Feldman 2005: 157). In the case of *West Virginia State Board of Education v Barnette* (1943) the Supreme Court held that Jehovah's Witnesses could not be forced to salute the American flag or sing the Pledge of Allegiance since it violated their religious code. According to the Court, 'Public education' must be 'faithful to the idea of secular instruction and political neutrality', and therefore 'will not be partisan or enemy of any class, creed, party or faction' (cited in Feldman 2006: 157).

The Supreme Court's decision-making in *Barnette* was in part informed by the growing Jewish community in the United States who had fled Europe in the later years of World War II. This growing community, particularly in major cities such as New York, underscored the existence of a vulnerable religious minority that needed—and deserved, after being persecuted by the Nazis—legal protection. The growing tolerance in the US for non-Christian religious faiths (ie Judaism) in the immediate postwar years helped to give rise to legal secularism, characterized by the Court shedding its mantle of protector of the Christian Protestant faith and taking up the role of defender of the rights of certain religious minorities. According to Feldman, legal secularism was driven primarily by issues of religion. Nonetheless it was a movement essential for the Court's arriving at its subsequent decisions on race. The Court's emerging sense of its role as defender of religious liberties translated into being the defender of political and civil liberties too—as reflected in the overriding sentiment of the Court in *Brown* (Feldman 2006: 183).

There is a more specific connection between Nuremberg and *Brown* in addition to the shift in public attitudes about religion and race that occurred in American society in the postwar decade, some of which had been shaped by the events of World War II. Robert Jackson, the chief US prosecutor and a major legal and intellectual force at Nuremberg, was also one of the presiding judges in the Supreme Court in the *Brown* decision. While it has been argued that Jackson was initially going to dissent in the *Brown* case on legal technicalities (Schwartz 1996: 96), there can be no doubt that Jackson abhorred the idea of segregation for humanitarian reasons. In 1950, while pondering his legal position with respect to segregation, Jackson wrote to the legal scholar Charles Fairman, 'You and I have seen the terrible consequences of racial hatred in Germany. We can have no sympathy with racial conceits which underlie segregation policies ... I am clear that I would support the constitutionality of almost any Congressional Act that prohibited segregation in education' (cited in Ehrenfreund 2007: 136). Later, in Jackson's unpublished concurrence of May 1954, he again argued that desegregation was necessary as a political and social imperative. Jackson noted that conditions had changed in the 1950s, and the erroneous 'factual assumptions' that 'there were differences between the Negro and the white races' could no longer be tolerated (Jackson 1954; Tushnet and Lezin 1991). In Jackson's private words and public deeds the impact of Nuremberg is evident. According to the historian James Sheehan:

> Nuremberg produced a graphic record of horrors of the systematic torture and genocide undertaken by that regime. Widespread dissemination of that appalling record increased American sensitivity to racial injustice and to other endemic infringements of civil liberties. Pictures of southern sheriffs attacking peaceful civil rights protestors bear an undeniable resemblance to pictures of SS troopers attacking Jews. Whatever Justice Jackson took from his experiences at Nuremberg, the force of these analogies, even if unspoken, became a factor in the awakening of the judiciary in the 1960s to the need for enhanced protection of human rights in the United States. (cited in Ehrenfreund 2007: 137)

CONCLUSION

Despite the immediate worldwide euphoria over the adoption in 1948 of the Universal Declaration of Human Rights, particularly among developing nations and those seeking independence from colonial control, the goodwill and optimism that the Declaration generated was short-lived. International humanitarian law was not widely recognized by the United States and other western nations until the late 1980s. As a result, human rights did not play a significant part in international law for many decades. The primary setback was the prevailing politics of the Cold War, which in turn severely hampered the ability of UN agencies to implement normative standards and protect against human rights violations. As a consequence, genocide and crimes against humanity have periodically occurred in sites around the world since 1949, and one could arguably claim that the Universal Declaration of Human Rights has made very little difference.

While riddled to this day with enforcement problems, the Universal Declaration of Human Rights, emerging as it did in the wake of the Nuremberg trials, has always played a highly symbolic and psychological role in international relations. Even when the Declaration's enforceability is seriously in question, it has nonetheless functioned as an essential reminder of future goals. Together, Nuremberg and the Declaration heralded a new era in international humanitarian law, institutionalizing both the concept of state accountability for crimes against humanity and the corollary principle of international responsibility for protecting the inalienable civil, political, economic, social and cultural rights of all people. And in the context of the United States, Nuremberg and the Declaration together had a profound influence on domestic legal and social policies with respect to religious and racial minorities.

What the Nuremberg trials did was to demonstrate 'the tragedy and horror of war to our generations and future generations with *concrete factual evidence*' (Yasuaki 1986: 50). Less concretely, but perhaps just as importantly, the trials also presented 'a world order promise by the allies to the future' (as stated by Richard A Falk, a leading expert in international law). In other words, the trials exemplified a worldwide commitment to change which played out in postwar social and political life in Europe, the United States and around the world. As pointed out by William J Bosch:

Even when the last person who experienced the war is dead, men will return to the Nuremberg court because it was a test of men's basic concepts of law, politics and morality. Nuremberg is significant not so much because of what happened once and for all in 1946 in a Bavarian city, but because of what it has become for many men—sign and symbol of greater realities. (cited in Ehrenfreund 2007: front matter)

Recommended Reading

Brown, Callum G (2006) *Religion and Society in Twentieth-Century Britain*. Harlow: Pearson Longman.

Burleigh, Michael (2001) *The Third Reich*. New York: Hill and Wang.

Butler, Jon, Grant Wacker and Randall Balmer (2008) *Religion in American Life: A Short History*. Oxford: Oxford University Press.

Du Bois (1952) 'The Negro and the Warsaw Ghetto', in Phil Zuckerman (ed), *The Social Theory of WEB Du Bois*. Thousand Oaks, CA: Pine Forge, pp 45–46.

Ehrenfreund, Norbert (2007) *The Nuremberg Legacy*. New York: Palgrave Macmillan.

Gilroy, Paul (1991) *'There Ain't No Black in the Union Jack': The Cultural Politics of Race and Nation*. With a new foreword by Houston A Baker Jr. Chicago: University of Chicago Press.

Judt, Tony (2006) *Postwar: A History of Europe Since 1945*. Harmondsworth: Penguin.

Kluger, Richard (2004) *Simple Justice: The History of Brown v Board of Education and Black America's Struggle for Equality*. New York: Vintage.

Kühl, Stefan (1994) *The Nazi Connection: Eugenics, American Racism, and German National Socialism*. New York: Oxford University Press.

Lewis, David Levering (2000) *WEB Du Bois: The Fight for Equality and the American century, 1919–1963*. New York: H Holt.

Lopez, Ian F. Haney (1996) *White By Law: The Legal Construction of Race*. New York: New York University Press.

Marrus, Michael Robert (1997) *The Nuremberg War Crimes Trial, 1945–46. A Documentary History* (Bedford Series in History and Culture). Boston: Bedford Books.

Neusner, Jacob (1990) *Jews and Christians: The Myth of a Common Tradition*. New York: Trinity Press International and SCM Press.

Patterson, James T (2002) *Brown v Board of Education: A Civil Rights Milestone and its Troubled Legacy* (Pivotal Moments in American History). Oxford: Oxford University Press.
Steigmann-Gall, Richard (2003) *The Holy Reich: Nazi Conceptions of Christianity, 1919–1945*. Cambridge: Cambridge University Press.

8

Democracy, Neoliberalism, and the New Crusades

A L-QAEDA'S ATTACKS on the United States on 11 September 2001 marked, both materially and symbolically, the beginning of the new millennium, and in the United States opened up a 'yawning chasm of fear' (Toope 2006: 237).[1] In the first decade of the twenty-first century, public confidence in the invincibility of the west has waned. In the US, and to a lesser degree in Britain, people's lives have become more insecure, and there is a palpable sense of vulnerability that did not exist in the 1990s when western nations rode high on the euphoria of a Cold War victory over communism (Gusterson and Besteman 2009). Fears of terrorist threats from without relate to a sense of inadequate national security and permeate political debate about immigration, citizenship, and civil and political liberties.

The attacks of 9/11 resulted in two wars, one against Afghanistan, which began in 2001, and one against Iraq, beginning in 2003. The wars, led by the US and supported militarily by Britain and the 'Coalition of the Willing', are together referred to as the War on Terror. In this chapter I focus on the War on Terror to reflect upon the interconnections between military aggression, economic aggression, and gender and race aggression that underlie the US imperialist agenda. In linking corporate policies within the United States to the country's imperialist military practices overseas, I argue that the economic philosophy of neoliberalism that has dominated western financial policies for the past 30 years also informs the War on Terror's underlying economic rationale. In other words, the attacks of 9/11 and the subsequent War on Terror should be analyzed in historical context, and not be treated as discrete stand-alone events. Together they should be seen as linked to prior international relations that include, among other things, the occupation of Afghanistan in 1979 by the Soviet Union, the financing of anti-communist resistance by the United States and Britain in the 1980s and

---

[1] The attacks of 9/11, as well as the subsequent bombings in Madrid on 11 March 2004 which killed 191, and in London on 7 July 2005 which killed 56 people, have forever altered the political, cultural and social landscape of Europe and the United States. Though unlike the United States, Europe has experienced terrorist activity and bombings perpetrated by groups such as the Provisional IRA and the Basque organization ETA in Spain throughout the second half of the twentieth century.

90s (Coll 2004; Crile 2003), and, more generally, increasing economic disparities in recent decades between a global north and global south.

Neoliberalism has dominated western financial policies for over 30 years, and to a large extent informs the practices of the contemporary global political economy (Harvey 2007; Sands 2005: 117–42). Neoliberalism refers to economic and political strategies that protect corporate property rights and encourage free market activities. Neoliberalism developed as a critique of John Maynard Keynes' macroeconomic theory that had dominated economic strategies since the 1930s and the New Deal, and which argued that fiscal policy should play a greater role in mediating market forces (Skidelsky 2009). Against this thinking, neoliberalism argues for economic strategies of privatization and deregulation, which ultimately favor business interests over individuals' access to health services, education, safety, and regulated work conditions (Harvey 2007).

Neoliberalism appeals to the political philosophy of neoconservatism, which typically argues against centralized power and government oversight and regulation. Neoconservatism is a complex political and economic philosophy that has historically drawn supporters from both the left and right of the political spectrum. Under US President Ronald Reagan and British Prime Minister Margaret Thatcher, neoconservatives were given official government positions and their philosophy dominated domestic and foreign policies in the 1980s and 90s. Neoconservatives gained even more prominence under both Bush administrations, and to a lesser degree under Prime Minister Tony Blair. The British journalist and political commentator John Kampfner writes:

> The neo-cons of Britain and the US share an adoration of the free market. They see the Anglo-Saxon economic model of low-wage labour costs and flexibility as an international paradigm. They harbour an instinctive fondness for large corporations—their moral and economic beneficence—and hold in disdain or contempt European-style collectivism and trade union rights. (Kampfner 2003)

In defense of corporate interests, neoconservatives on both sides of the Atlantic argue for the necessity of using military force to impose, in the name of democracy, free market economies around the world.

Together the economic strategies of neoliberalism and the political philosophy of neoconservatism have contributed to furthering the economic division between a global north and a global south. To what degree the international prominence of neoliberalism and neoconservatism correlate to a rise in religious fundamentalism and terrorist activity leading up to the 9/11 attacks is a highly debatable issue. Nonetheless, despite the discomfiture such a question may give rise to, it is worth pursuing if we are going to begin to understand why there has been a surge in religious fundamentalism/extremism in recent decades, why it continues to flourish in developed and developing nations, and what this means in terms of national and international security.

In thinking about the relationship of neoliberalism, neoconservatism and terrorist activities, I focus on the enormously successful Wal-Mart company as emblematic of the USA's neoliberal/neoconservative corporate culture. Wal-Mart is widely hailed by financial analysts and business people as the most successful economic enterprise in American history. Against this exalted position, I explore the internal workings of Wal-Mart, and in particular criticisms made of the company's discriminatory labor practices with respect to its economically vulnerable employees, and especially women employees. In 2001, a few months before the attacks of 9/11, the class action *Dukes v Wal-Mart Stores Inc* was brought by 1.6 million women employees against the company for denying them appropriate pay and promotions.[2] Wal-Mart's corporate practices illustrate the limits of democracy in the US with respect to providing equal economic and social rights for all, and underscore women's deeply entrenched inequity in the American workforce. The *Dukes* case also speaks, albeit indirectly, to a corporate culture that condones the exploitation of women overseas. Wal-Mart, as well as many other multinational corporations, is involved in practices of global capitalism that includes the outsourcing of manufacturing and taking advantage of cheap and largely unregulated overseas labor pools in developing nations. Outsourcing is a central feature of neoliberal economic polices and effectively allows western-based companies to exploit and abuse people economically, especially women and children.

The limits of democracy with respect to women under neoliberal policies point to the hypocrisy inherent in the public stance taken by the Bush administration and the 'Coalition of the Willing' in the war with Afghanistan, and against the Middle East more generally. As part of the US and British propaganda machine surrounding the War on Terror in 2001, the rhetoric of liberation targeted, among other things, 'vulnerable' Muslim women. The governments' focus on women expediently highlighted the undemocratic nature of Islamic fundamentalists, who, it was argued, failed to recognize women's human rights by keeping them in the home, uneducated, veiled and, in some cases, subjecting them to stone-throwing and other 'barbaric' customs. A western vision of bringing democracy to Muslim women[3] through the War on Terror presented a clear and unquestionable goal that had widespread appeal across religious and secular communities in many countries around the world. The rhetoric of 'saving brown women' also effectively evoked paternalist responsibilities on the part of the US and other western countries (Abu-Lughod 2002; Cooke 2002, 2006; Ayotte and Husain 2005; Jarmakani 2008).

Against this backdrop of western representations of oppressed Muslim women and the role these played in promoting the War on Terror, we need to remember that a large segment of US corporate practice ostensibly denies many women equality in the workplace and fails to recognize their full economic and social

---

[2] This case continues to wind its way through the courts and as of early 2010 has not yet been determined.

[3] The term 'Muslim women' is a gross over-generalization, but this was how women were characterized in public debate and media.

rights (see below). Wal-Mart can also be read as emblematic of much that the non-western world detests about advanced industrial nations—their greed and their internal hypocrisies and failure to reflect upon the limits of democracy within their own national jurisdictions. The irony is that in galvanizing support for a war against 'evil' Islamic fundamentalists, the Bush administration mobilized images of subjugated Afghani, and later Iraqi, women who 'need' the west's recognition of their basic human rights.

The Wal-Mart Empire

Wal-Mart Stores Inc is a US-based corporation, highly revered in the United States and around the world for its size, efficiency and profitability. *Fortune 500* has repeatedly ranked it the most profitable company in the country, ahead of corporate giants such as BP, Toyota and Exxon Mobile. The first Wal-Mart store was opened in 1962 by Sam Walton, the son of a farmer, who grew up in Missouri. The history of Wal-Mart lends itself to the capitalist myth that anyone can make money if they try hard enough—the romanticized rags-to-riches fairytale. Indeed, Walton, in his 1992 autobiography *Made in America*, suggests that this was the case with respect to his success, glossing over the fact that his wife came from a wealthy family (Walton 1992: 43).

Walton proved to be a very good manager and the Wal-Mart company incorporated in 1969 and quickly expanded. By 1980, the company owned 272 stores in 11 states. By 1987 there were 1,198 stores, which brought in sales of $1.5 billion and employed 200,000 'associates'. By 2005, the company had expanded to become the world's largest corporation. It had 3,800 stores in the US, 2,800 subsidiary stores in other countries around the world including Britain (operating under the name ASDA), China, Mexico, Argentina, Brazil, South Korea, Canada, El Salvador, Guatemala, Honduras and Puerto Rico, and its sales amounted to $312.4 billion. In 2009, according to the Wal-Mart website:

> Walmart serves customers and members more than 200 million times per week at more than 8,159 retail units under 55 different banners in 15 countries. With fiscal year 2009 sales of $401 billion, Walmart employs more than more than 2.1 million associates worldwide. A leader in sustainability, corporate philanthropy and employment opportunity, Walmart ranked first among retailers in Fortune Magazine's 2009 Most Admired Companies survey. ... Saving people money to help them live better was the goal that Sam Walton envisioned when he opened the doors to the first Walmart more than 40 years ago. Today, this mission is more important than ever to our customers and members around the world. We work hard every day in all our markets to deliver on this promise. (walmartstores.com/AboutUs)

Between 1985 and 1988, *Forbes* magazine ranked Sam Walton the richest man in the United States. In 1992, President Bush awarded Walton the Presidential Medal of Freedom, the highest civilian award in the US, for his work in the retail industry (Gross 1997: 283). In 1998, six years after his death, Walton was named one of the hundred most influential people in the twentieth century by *Time* magazine. The Business College at the University of Arkansas is named in his honor. However, despite widespread admiration for Walton and his business model, which included innovative technology and marketing strategies (Lichtenstein 2009), over the past decade Sam Walton and his Wal-Mart empire have been soundly criticized. These criticisms have stemmed from a number of sources, including labor unions objecting to Walton's efforts to block employees from union participation, local communities resistant to Wal-Mart displacing local businesses, and grassroots activists objecting to Wal-Mart's strategies of outsourcing to take advantage of largely unregulated, non-unionized labor pools overseas (Cummings 2007; Bair and Bernstein 2006; Bonacich and Wilson 2006: 233–34; Lichtenstein 2009).

Sam Walton's successful business practices have had to be adapted in recent decades to accommodate new economic, political and cultural realities. In the early period of Walton's operations in the 1960s and 70s, nearly 10 per cent of American workers were farmers, and 'this percentage was considerably higher in those southern and mid-western states in which Wal-Marts were first located' (Shelley et al 2006: 207). In this early period, Wal-Mart stores appeared almost solely in such rural communities. However, with the end of the Cold War, Walton's death in 1992 and the transition in the US from an industrial economy to a service-sector economy during the 1980s and 90s, Wal-Mart's strategies for locating new store sites has been driven by partisan politics rather than a rural customer-base. The figures on store locations are startling. In the conservative state of Arkansas, the site of Wal-Mart's corporate headquarters, there are 32 stores for every million state residents. In the more progressive states of New York, New Jersey and California, there are fewer than five stores per million residents (Shelley et al 2006). Today, Wal-Mart stores are heavily concentrated in Republican voting communities, and 'hiding behind the façade of commodity fetishism lurks a distinct and deeply conservative politics, often religious in nature. Wal-Mart's politics emerges in terms of what it chooses or refuses to sell, its censorship of certain materials, the careful way it encourages people to "buy American" yet rely heavily on foreign imports' (Warf and Chapman 2006: 178; see also Bianco 2006: 239–54). Not surprisingly, Wal-Mart is associated with 'cultural conservatism that is linked with the contemporary Republican party ... and cultural conservatives are much more likely to shop at Wal-Mart' (Shelley et al 2006: 211).[4]

Critics of Wal-Mart's policies and practices have produced an industry in books attacking the company and its business model (Vance and Scott 1994; Brunn 2006; Fishman 2006; Bianco 2006; Lichtenstein 2006, 2009; Morteon

---

[4] Despite the majority of its American customer base sharing a conservative political perspective, as Wal-Mart expands its operations out of small-town America into major city centers, and into major international markets in Britain, Germany and China, it has had to tone down its implicit Christian message and sell products that have a wider appeal to metropolitan, multicultural and secular customers (Bianco 2006: 254).

2009). These books highlight some of the drastic policies used by Wal-Mart to guarantee low prices, such as paying minimal wages to its employees, providing limited health care packages to its employees,[5] denying employees overtime pay, refusing to allow employees to take standard rest periods and lunch breaks, locking employees in stores overnight, hiring illegal immigrants, violating labor laws with respect to children, pressurising employees not to join unions by shutting down unionized stores, and knowingly allowing their overseas suppliers to use sweatshop and prison labor (Cummings 2007; Bair and Bernstein 2006; Bonacich and Wilson 2006: 233–34; see also Ritzer 2000: 123–45).

Criticisms of Wal-Mart have been accompanied by a flood of lawsuits against the corporation on a wide number of issues. But perhaps no case has received more publicity and attention than *Dukes v Wal-Mart Stores Inc.* As mentioned above, this is a lawsuit brought by a former Wal-Mart employee, Betty Dukes, against the company for discriminating against women in denying them appropriate pay and promotions (Figure 39). Dukes argued that Wal-Mart violated Title VII of the Civil Rights Act (1964), which protects workers from discrimination on the basis of sex, race, religion or national origin. Dukes' lawyers argued

Figure 39. Wal-Mart protest in Utah, 14 July 2005. Photograph taken by Joey Caputo.

[5] 'Human Rights Watch calculated that in 2002, Wal-Mart spent only about three-quarters as much on *all* benefits per covered worker as other major retailers averaged for their covered workers' health cover alone' (Moreton 2009: 72–73).

that Wal-Mart's employees are 72 per cent women, but only 34 per cent of its managers are women, a figure considerably lower than its major competitors. The lawyers argued that Wal-Mart endorsed an internal culture of discrimination in which it was widely accepted among male managers that any woman making demands would be given less desirable jobs, ignored or overlooked for promotions, and generally targeted for its 'Open Door Policy'—an internally understood euphemism for being fired. These biased practices were experienced by many women, and arguably more so by women of color. According to Judge Martin Jenkins of the US District Court in 2004, the *Dukes* case, like *Brown v Board of Education* which 50 years earlier had declared school segregation unconstitutional, was 'historic' and served 'as a reminder of the importance of courts in addressing the denial of equal treatment under the law whenever and by whomever it occurs' (cited in Moreton 2009: 49). In the words of Lisa Featherstone, a well-respected freelance journalist, Wal-Mart, and the company Enron, 'are grim symbols of the greedy pursuit of profits at the expense of human beings, including their own employees' (Featherstone 2004: 11).

Despite Wal-Mart's explicit discrimination against women, many employees and customers remain intensely loyal to it, perplexing many of the company's critics. Customers may be prepared to turn a blind eye to these activities if they continue to be offered very cheap products. However, it is less easy to understand why long-exploited employees, who are paid low salaries and receive minimal benefits, continue to defend Wal-Mart's unfair practices. The limited opportunities for finding a job somewhere other than at Wal-Mart does not adequately account for such loyalty. One explanation lies in Wal-Mart's hiring practices, which include hiring relatives of employees and preferring 'high school graduates, whose ideals it could mold into utter loyalty to the company, primarily through intensive training seminars' (Vance and Scott 1994: 163). Another explanation is the effective system of myths promoted and sustained by Sam Walton and his subsequent company directors. These myths deliberately appeal to small-town rural Americans, and promote the image that the stores serve ordinary people, many from working-class backgrounds. To its employees, the Wal-Mart culture claims that its 'associates' form a collective family, where hard work and dedication are rewarded (Walton 1992). Moreover, it claims to be family-oriented and supportive of traditional family values, a very appealing message to its predominantly female workforce from lower socioeconomic backgrounds. In reality, according to the plaintiffs in the *Dukes* case, Wal-Mart does not reward hard work and commitment as promised, nor does it support families: child-care is not provided, wages are so low that paying for private child-care is out of the question, and working hours are not sufficiently flexible to accommodate family needs (Featherstone 2004; Ehrenreich 2000: 121–92).

RELIGION: EXPLOITING GOD

Religion played a large part in the economic success of Sam Walton's Wal-Mart empire (Moreton 2009). Walton astutely recognized that by presenting himself as a spiritual man he would be able to maximize profits. An appeal to evangelical spirituality, wrapped up in traditional 'family values', worked well among the farming communities that Walton specifically targeted as his first customers. He built up the myth that he was personally religious, and that the company he ran was a Christian company (in fundamentalist and evangelical terms). This was relatively easy in the bible-belt region of his company headquarters in Benton-ville, Arkansas, and in the rural and small-town settings of many of his stores. 'Employees constantly mention that Sam Walton was a family man and devout Christian', writes Lisa Featherstone, 'although in real life he was neither—he did not have strong religious belief and rarely went to church' (Featherstone 2004: 62; Moreton 2009: 90).

One of Walton's biggest hurdles was to convince white rural Protestants that consuming material goods was a celebration of their faith, rather than a denial of frugality, self-control and discipline that had come to characterize an ascetic Protestantism as defined by Max Weber in *The Protestant Ethic and the Spirit of Capitalism* (1905). In an effort to encourage material consumption, Walton took advantage of a regional evangelical revival, playing down luxury and consumer desire in his thrifty stores, which resembled warehouse rather than opulent department stores, and playing up a Christian-based ethos of service (Moreton 2009: 89). This service mentality made it ethically acceptable for women custom-ers, many of whom were also mothers, to buy goods on behalf of their family, and Wal-Mart employees interpreted their job as serving these women customers in pursuit of such consumption. Referring to the book *To Serve God and Wal-Mart* by Bethany Moreton, the economist Robert Frank writes:

> Walton and his fellow executives quickly recognized the economic advantage of weaving specific strands of the Ozark region's fundamentalist belief system into their corporate strategy. At the heart of that strategy was the company's emphasis on the Christian concept of 'servant leadership'. In other parts of the retail sector, the servitude demanded of retail clerks was typically experienced as demeaning. But by repeatedly reminding employees that the Christian servant leader cherishes opportunities to provide cheerful service to others, Moreton argues, Wal-Mart transformed servitude from a negative job characteristic into a positive one. (Frank 2009)

Walton's evocation of evangelical Christianity and family values was particu-larly effective up until the late 1980s and early 1990s. Many women sought employment at Wal-Mart precisely because it claimed to be a family-oriented business with conservative values that did not seek to elevate women above the traditional role relative to men as family leaders and breadwinners. In this context, many women did not question the company's policy 'of reproducing the social relationships characteristic of fundamentalist Christian households in the workplace ... the company salved the egos of the men by celebrating a patriarchal idea of a "Christian manliness". The women, for their part, were only too happy to adopt the prescribed submissive role' (Frank 2009; see Moreton 2009: 100–25).

While the emphasis on family values and Christian spirituality may have varied from store to store and region to region, there is no denying the presence of a pervasive spiritual commonality among Wal-Mart's employees and customers throughout the 1970s and 80s. By the 1990s, 'for the nation at large, the company came to function as a sort of after-hours megachurch. "If you want to reach the [Christian population] on Saturday, then you do it in Wal-Mart", declared Ralph Reed, then executive director of the Christian Coalition' (Moreton 2009: 90). Wal-Mart's appeal to a Christian employee and customer base has endured to a large extent into the twenty-first century, at least within stores located in the United States. Among the *Dukes* plaintiffs, many of the women attend church and pride themselves on their spirituality. These women feel particularly disillusioned and betrayed by the company's unfair treatment of them, 'more so than if they'd been ill treated by a "non-Christian" company' (Featherstone 2004: 61).

In 1985 Walton decided to spread his financial business model—and its expedient reliance on evangelical religious and social culture—into Central America (Moreton 2009: 222–47). This move was driven by his desire to combat communism, encourage the spread of capitalism in the region, and open up potential production sites and consumer markets. Walton set up scholarships and established the 'Walton Scholars' program whereby students from Central American countries would come to the United States and attend religious schools in Arkansas. According to Walton in his autobiography:

> When we learned that the then Soviet Union and Cuba had programs to teach their values to kids from other places, we decided Americans ought to be doing the same sort of thing with our values. We want kids to learn about the tremendous potential of the free enterprise system and to see for themselves what all the advantages are of a stable, democratic government. Who knows, maybe one day some of them will be running Wal-Marts or Sam's Clubs in Honduras or Panama or Guatemala—or even Nicaragua. (Walton 1992: 236)

Alumni from Walton's religious colleges took with them the 'specific business culture of the Christian service sector', and many eventually wound up working for major *Fortune 500* companies such as Coca-Cola, Compaq, Colgate-Palmolive, Procter & Gamble, and Pepsi (Moreton 2009: 243). Moreton writes:

> In the post-Cold War era of economic globalization, the Walton Scholars helped create the new common sense of globalization. The positive inputs many brought home included technical skills, a pro-market orientation, an activist Christian faith, and personal relationships in Arkansas and the larger evangelical world. The impact of these contributions was magnified by the extreme situation to which they returned. In Guatemala and El Salvador especially, a generation of the educated Left had been decimated, hundreds of thousands of civilians wiped out, tens of thousands more

tortured into submission by US-backed regimes … The Walton Scholars offered new student leaders to take the place of that generation. Their Christian business educations in Arkansas linked them to a specific vision of globalization with direct roots in Wal-Mart's own stores and offices. Their hearts and minds were won to the free-trade gospel while singing in chapel, surrounded by people who trusted and cared for them. (Moreton 2009: 247)

Walton proved to be most skilful in exploiting evangelical Christianity to maximize company profits through specific polices toward female employees, and in expanding his business strategies overseas to maximize profits from a growing international network. That these policies did not always work effectively, as evidenced by Wal-Mart having to close its stores in South Korea and Germany in 2006, does not diminish the extraordinary power and effectiveness of his evangelical economic mission.

Corporatism, Politics and Religion

Walton's effective joining of evangelical religiosity with neoliberal economic strategies proved to be very successful in building his vast national and international corporate empire. But such a combination is not necessary for capitalist policies and practices to be economically successful. In advanced industrial countries such as Britain, Germany, France, Australia and Canada, which have all implemented a neoliberal agenda over the past 30 years, evangelical and fundamentalist Christians have not played a role in these countries' economic success.

In contrast, during this same period in the United States evangelicals emerged to become the country's dominant religion, with a prominent presence in mainstream society and politics (Jewett 2008: 282). In this context, combining neoliberal economic policies with evangelical religion proved to be—as evidenced by the financial successes of Wal-Mart—an enormously profitable arrangement. The alignment of neoliberalism and religion became explicit in US national politics in the late 1970s, with the founding of Jerry Falwell's 'moral majority' as a political movement. At this time, the Republican Party began to court the theologically conservative Christian movement (often referred to as the theocons) for its own political and economic ends (Linker 2006; Jewett 2008: 262–64). 'From then on the unholy alliance between big business and conservative Christians backed by the neo-conservatives steadily consolidated, eventually eradicating all liberal elements from the Republican Party, particularly after 1990' (Harvey 2007: 50; Sharlet 2008). Under Bush Senior's administration, this coalition led to a steady insertion of references to God in government policy, as well as the Republican Party's aggressive support of the religious right's negative position on issues such as same-sex marriage, abortion, stem-cell research, euthanasia, and supplying contraceptives to developing nations. In return, the religious right stood behind the political conservatives. It should not be forgotten that evangelicals and fundamentalists played a decisive role in the presidential elections of 2000 and 2004, and that 'without their support the Republicans would not have won' (Jewett 2008: 282; Linker 2006).

There are disturbing similarities between Sam Walton and George W Bush in their manipulation of ordinary people's religious sensibilities. Walton explicitly drew on evangelical and fundamentalist values in his business strategies in order to maximize profits. Evangelicalism made attractive a 'family values' philosophy and service mentality that promoted male managerial authority and women's submissiveness. This in turn correlated economically to denying women promotions and benefits and paying them lower wages. At the national level, Bush, and the members of his inner circle, explicitly exploited evangelical and fundamentalist values to further their power base in Washington, DC, with the ultimate goal of reaping economic benefits by means of the neoliberal polices of privatization and deregulation.

At the international level, the utilization of religion is evident in Walton's criticism of Soviet communism in the 1980s during the Cold War, and Bush's military War on Terror in the Middle East since 2001. While these actions are of vastly different import and consequence, in both cases each man dressed up a money-making agenda by referencing a missionary crusade to spread democracy and freedom around the world. Within the Republican Party, attracting religious affiliates to support an international political and economic agenda was the express purpose of conservative think-tanks and private organizations of the 1980s and 90s (George 2008). The Project for the New American Century (PNAC), established in 1997, was one of these organizations. PNAC was important for building coalitions between the political right and the religious right, and for articulating an explicit agenda in international relations. PNAC's 1997 Statement of Principles reads:

> As the 20th century draws to a close, the United States stands as the world's preeminent power. Having led the West to victory in the Cold War, America faces an opportunity and a challenge … we need to accept responsibility for America's unique role in preserving and extending an international order friendly to our security, our prosperity, and our principles. Such a Reaganite policy of military strength and moral clarity … is necessary if the United States is to build on the successes of this past century and to ensure our security and our greatness in the next. (http://www.newamericancentury.org/statementofprinciples.htm)

The Republican Party's economic agenda was expressly spelled out in September 2003 when the US-appointed transitional government, the Coalition Provisional Authority, promulgated four orders that were later to become law in Iraq. These orders were hailed by *The Economist* as a 'capitalist dream' that fulfills 'the wish list of international investors', while they were condemned by the Iraq Governing Council's interim Trade Minister, Ali Abdul-Amir Allawi, as 'free market fundamentalism' (Docena 2003). The orders included:

> 'the full privatization of public enterprises, full ownership rights by foreign firms of Iraqi businesses, full repatriation of foreign profits, the opening of Iraq's banks to

foreign control, national treatment for foreign companies, and the elimination of nearly all trade barriers'. The orders were to apply to all areas of the economy, including public services, the media, manufacturing, services, transportation, finance, and construction. Only oil was exempt (presumably because of its special status as revenue producer to pay for the war and its geopolitical significance). The labor market, on the other hand, was to be strictly regulated. Strikes were effectively forbidden in key sectors and the right to unionize restricted. (Harvey 2007: 6)

The US-led War on Terror has managed to establish neoliberal free market strategies in the very war zones it seeks to control and manage. As the above quote makes clear, tightly regulating labor and at the same time privatizing and deregulating all sectors of revenue making was an explicit government policy. In this context, the War on Terror can arguably be seen as a making-money venture for multinational corporations. The most obvious example of this war-for-profit strategy is the Halliburton controversy, which exploded in 2003. Halliburton is a US-based company that specializes in oilfield management and extraction and was granted contracts to perform work in Iraq. The controversy surrounded allegations that Halliburton did not bid competitively for these contracts, but received them because of ties to US vice president Dick Cheney, who had been the CEO of Halliburton from 1995 to 2000. The allegations eventually led to criminal investigations by the Federal Bureau of Investigation (FBI) and the US Department of Justice.

In contrast to the unethical money-making agendas of corporations in respect of the war in Iraq, among ordinary people in the United States and the 'Coalition of the Willing' the war was essentially about liberating Iraqi people from the burdens of authoritarian governance and helping them in their quest to improve their quality of life. In the early years of the war, Americans in particular were willing to overlook controversies such as Halliburton in their favorable response to the crusading rhetoric and logic of liberation evoked by the Bush administration.

Crusading in the Public Imagination

'Crusade' is a suggestive and versatile word, meaning different things to people of different faiths at various times (Hillenbrand 2004; Maalouf 1989). In simple terms it means an engagement in religious warfare, or what are often called 'holy wars', and evokes the multiple crusades that were waged by Catholic Europe against the Islamic world as early as 1095. The ostensible aim of the medieval crusades was to secure the Christian kingdom against Muslim territories, and recover control of Palestine and specifically Jerusalem which was revered by Christians as a site of pilgrimage and devotion. In reality, the geopolitics of the crusades involved securing land, money and trading networks for the papacy as well as for European knights, lords and mercenaries (Runciman 1987; Tyerman 2006). Eventually Muslim forces mobilized and pushed back against the crusaders to regain control of Jerusalem in 1187, though the strongholds of Tripoli and Acre were not regained by the Muslims until 1291.

In the United States, the idea of crusading has morphed into a long-standing historical narrative that speaks deeply to the country's nationalist spirit. This narrative has existed since the seventeenth century, when the puritan colonists first migrated to New England. The puritans drew heavily on the books of Revelation and Matthew to support their view that they were a chosen people, sent to the New World to establish a 'new Jerusalem' and 'city upon a hill' (Luke 12: 48). In the words of the puritan Reverend John Winthrop in his 1630 sermon 'A Model of Christian Charity', 'we must consider that we shall be as a city upon a hill. The eyes of all people are upon us'. This sense of purpose imbued the puritans with what they saw as a mission to build a new city and government based on rules that accorded with their scriptural beliefs (Witte 2006: 143–68; Witte 2007: 277–320).

Over the course of 300 years, the puritan image of a 'city upon a hill' was tempered by US social and political change, and modified by the country's geographic and demographic growth. In terms of political power, Washington, DC became the new 'city upon a hill' in 1790, and the strict laws enforced by the puritan New England colony were expanded to accommodate a range of religious and cultural perspectives. Still, the image of building a special city, with its essential feature of being ordained by God, has endured and remains an enormously powerful symbol for many American people. President Ronald Reagan, in his farewell speech to the nation in 1989, drew a contemporary image of the 'city upon a hill' when he declared:

> I've spoken of the shining city all my political life, but I don't know if I ever quite communicated what I saw when I said it. But in my mind it was a tall proud city built on rocks stronger than oceans, wind-swept, God-blessed, and teeming with people of all kinds living in harmony and peace, a city with free ports that hummed with commerce and creativity, and if there had to be city walls, the walls had doors and the doors were open to anyone with the will and the heart to get here.

The notion of being a chosen people building a new city in a new land, watched over by God, is a theme that is called to mind again and again in the standardized myths of the United States' past. It was a central theme in the nineteenth century concept of manifest destiny, which held that Americans had a sacred duty and obligation to expand westwards across the North American continent. It also underscores the concept of American exceptionalism, which first emerged in Alexis de Tocqueville's *Democracy in America*, published in 1835. De Tocqueville was enchanted with the apparent lack of social and class barriers in the United States, and his writings helped to nurture the idea that the country was one of unprecedented opportunity and freedom. The United States, so goes the myth, is unique among nations and the only country to truly embrace democracy, liberty and the rule of law.

The notion that Americans are specially chosen by God implies that violence and militarization can be used, if necessary, to achieve God's will. If one is on a sacred mission, presumably one has divine authority to wield force to implement that mission. As has been discussed throughout this book, over the centuries the sense of building a unique 'city upon a hill' helped to justify violence within the United States against native peoples, enslaved Africans, and immigrants from China—all deemed in various ways to be non-Christian, barbaric, and ultimately deserving of retribution.

Crusading in International Relations

Looking outward, beyond the conquest of US domestic territories, crusading imagery has remained a central impulse informing US foreign policy. It has justified the country's missionary zeal to intervene in overseas countries and regions in the name of Christian liberation and democracy, while at the same time imposing its imperial agendas (Stephanson 1995; Jewett 2008). In the late nineteenth century, the notion of America's sacred duty to defend freedom provided the logic for overseas military occupations such as those occurring in Hawaii (1893), Puerto Rico (1898), the Philippines (1899) and Cuba (1899). This dual sensibility of defending Christianity and freedom resurfaced repeatedly through the second half of the twentieth century, framing and explaining the Cold War and its battles against non-Christian communists. It helped to justify the domestic purging of US citizens under McCarthyism in the late 1940s and 50s, and overseas military interventions into Korea in 1950 and Vietnam in the late 1960s (Jewett 2008; Brewer 2009; Albright 2006: 23–24).

Envisaging one's country as a crusading nation is not unique to the United States. The idea that western industrial nations are somehow involved in a civilizing mission to bring democracy and freedom to the world was invoked in World War I. British clergy played up the German alliance with the Muslim Ottoman Empire, and deployed the term 'crusade' to rally their constituencies. In 1916, British Prime Minister David Lloyd George declared, 'Young men from every quarter of the country flocked to the standard of international right, as to a great crusade' (Hillenbrand 2004: 204). This rhetoric became more explicit in World War II. The British-led military expedition to North Africa in late 1941 was called 'Operation Crusader', and proved to be the first victory for the Allied powers over Germany.

However, with the bombing of Pearl Harbor, which provoked the United States into joining the Allied powers in December 1941, crusading rhetoric increased, as did its overtly religious tone. The day after Pearl Harbor, US General Dwight D Eisenhower addressed Congress, declaring, 'No matter how long it may take us to overcome this premeditated invasion, the American people, in their righteous might, will win through to absolute victory' (8 December 1941).[6] After the war, Eisenhower published a memoir entitled *Crusade in Europe*. According to the historian HW Brands Jr, 'Eisenhower emerged from [World War II] convinced of America's moral preeminence', with 'an ideology of unquestioning righteousness ... the product of a conflict in which the world neatly divided into camps of good and evil' (Brands 1988: 195–200). Another historian, Ira Chernus, has noted that Eisenhower's 'crusading, his alarmism, and his approach to military strategy all reflected his tendency to view military issues in terms of the religious tradition most typical of crusades: the apocalyptic tradition' (Chernus 1997: 603).

Victory in 1945 redefined international relations. The US suffered relatively few military casualties, and, unlike its European allies, none of war's conse-quences in terms of disrupted infrastructure or on-going distress among its civilian populations. The US's crusading mission was seen as an enormous success, leaving it an undisputed political and economic super-power. The popular perception in the US was that its armies had swooped into Europe and won the war, making it the morally righteous leader of the west. In short, it was widely believed that the world had been saved by God's intervention; he had led the American people in a crusade across the sea to fight on behalf of the good and the free. This simplistic interpretation of the Allied victory underpinned the facile but popular belief that the world could be divided into 'good' and 'evil'—a sensibility that endures in political and popular culture to this day. The historian Robert Jewett summarizes the crusading imagery and its apocalyptic theme in US history as follows:

> New England Puritans had an apocalyptic view of history and believed they could create a faithful theocracy that would play a decisive role in the final drama of world history. They believed that with the successful completion of the war by the saints against Satan's agents, the thousand-year kingdom promised by the book of Revelation would appear. Evil would be defeated and Satan disabled for a millennium, while the saints would rule the peaceable kingdom. The Great Awakening, the French and Indian War, the American Revolution, the 'post-millennial republic', and the wars from 1860 to 1945 continued to be conceptualized in millennial terms although the biblical founda-tions of Puritanism were gradually forgotten. Reformulated over and over again through American religious history, these millennial ideas surfaced in President Bush's rationale of a war to rid the world of evil. (Jewett 2008: 293; see Hall 2009)

Selling the War

The twenty-first century's War on Terror illustrates that crusading imagery and the theme of moral righteousness continue to permeate US foreign policy and

---

6   Eisenhower explicitly referred to being involved in a crusade on a number of occasions, writing to a boyhood friend on 7 April 1943: 'It seems to me that in no other war in history has the issue been so distinctly drawn between the forces of arbitrary oppression on the one side, and, on the other, those conceptions of individual liberty, freedom and dignity, under which we have been raised in our great Democracy ... I do have the feeling of a crusader in this war' (cited in Chernus 1997: 597).

popular belief (Rhodes 2005). For many people across the world, but particularly in the United States, the events of 9/11 were seen in religious terms, as attacks on Christianity by a non-Christian terrorist organization. George W Bush used the term 'crusade' when, only five days after 9/11, he stepped out of his helicopter declaring, 'We need to be alert to the fact that these evildoers still exist. We haven't seen this kind of barbarism in a long period of time. This is a new kind of evil. This crusade, this war on terrorism is going to take a while.' Bush was later reprimanded and forced to apologize for this controversial reference to medieval holy wars, which offended and alarmed many in the Islamic world (Lyons 2001).

While Bush's use of the term 'crusade' was widely criticized in the media, and he refrained from using it again, throughout his presidency he and the 'theocons' who supported his policies blurred the line between religion and politics (Linker 2006). Bush often referred to the war—and his role as a 'divinely appointed' leader in it—in biblical terms (Fineman et al 2003). In public appearances and policy speeches he constantly drew upon the comparison between good Americans and evil others. This rhetoric resonated widely with the American public. As mentioned above, in recent decades in the United States evangelicals have emerged to become the nation's dominant religion and they enjoy a disproportionately powerful presence in political circles. 'In 1999, a poll conducted by *Newsweek* found that 40 per cent of Americans—more than 100 million people— "believe that the world will end, as the Bible predicts, in a battle between Jesus and the antichrist". Nineteen per cent of the respondents believe that the Antichrist is alive today. Thirteen per cent believed in the "Rapture"' (Albright 2006: 136). In this context, the rhetoric of good versus evil holds powerful symbolism and scriptural authority, bringing to mind the Book of Revelation and a coming apocalyptical millennium which is central in many evangelical teachings. According to Bush's former speech-writer, David Frum, this rhetoric was central to the War on Terror (Fineman et al 2003). Conveniently, the words 'good' and 'evil' were easily interchangeable with 'civilized' and 'uncivilized', or 'us' and 'them'. In the wake of 11 September 2001, an overwhelming sensibility of 'good, civilized, us' overlaid a surge of patriotic vitriol as millions of American people reacted angrily to the outside world while concurrently clinging to images of US nationalism.

Of the many patriotic commodities that have profited 9/11 merchants, the most ubiquitous and abused has been our own national trademark, 'old glory', the American flag. According to published statistics, the total amount of American flag sales in 2001 reached $51.7 million, a record profit. Ironically, according to the same statistics, 67 percent of those flags were manufactured in China ... and when Americans went shopping for flags they turned to Wal-Mart, which sold 116,000 American flags on September 11, 2001. (Heller 2005: 16–17)

Within the United States in the immediate wake of 9/11, Bush's religious language, crusading imagery and nationalist demands for retribution were widely accepted by both conservatives and progressives. Going to war was largely seen as necessary to fight al-Qaeda and ensure national security, as well as to rescue oppressed Afghans, especially Afghan women. War would also, the Bush administration argued, ensure self-rule and self-determination. In short, among a diverse range of people with a variety of political and religious perspectives, the military response to the events of 11 September 2001 was supported because it was seen as a defense of modernity and its core themes of progress, democracy and the rule of law. To refuse to help the oppressed peoples of Afghanistan meant turning one's back, in effect, on the concepts of representative government and individual legal rights—concepts that have developed over the past 400 years to become the hallmarks of modern Anglo-American law.

Outside the United States, invoking religion in the name of war increasingly caused discomfort and raised many questions (Odone 2001; Lincoln 2006; Hobsbawm 2007: 115; see Figure 40). Around the world, as well as within more progressive constituencies in the United States, there emerged growing reticence about the impending war with Iraq throughout 2002, leading up to the invasion in March 2003. More and more people were viewing US policy as an attempt to 'revive the apocalyptic terrors of the Cold War, when they no longer have any plausibility, by inventing "enemies" that legitimize the expansion and use of its imperial power' (Hobsbawm 2007: 137). During this period relations between the US and other members of the UN Security Council became strained. The US, along with Britain and Spain, felt that UN Resolution 1441, which called for Iraq to disarm and give up its weapons of mass destruction, had not been adequately addressed. UN inspectors in Iraq found no such weaponry, and diplomacy between the UN, US and Britain began to break down. Among those critical of the march to war, it was felt that the planned pre-emptive military intervention in Iraq amounted to a US-led 'holy war' (Albright 2006: 160). In Britain, Rupert Cornwell, a journalist for the national newspaper *The Independent*, summarized the position of many members of the UN Security Council and other European nations:

> Mr Bush's Christian fervor only confirms suspicions that the looming war with Iraq is indeed a 'crusade' against Muslims, exactly as Osama bin Laden suggests. For world-weary Europe the Presidential language evokes mirth and queasiness in equal measure. A European leader who spoke in such terms would be laughed off the stage. An American one who speaks this way only increases the fear that the simplicities of faith, and a habit of seeing a hideously complicated world in a black-and-white, good or evil fashion, are a recipe for disaster. (Cornwell 2003)

Figure 40. *Join Our Crusade.* © Project for the OLD American Century

RACE: 'SAVING BROWN WOMEN'

Racializing the Enemy

The crusading rhetoric of war in terms of 'good' and 'evil' requires the making of a public enemy. Drawing on long-standing narratives of west against east, the United States and its allies have been complicit in constructing and nurturing racist images of a Middle Eastern enemy (Qureshi and Sells 2003). With respect to the War on Terror, the Islamic menace 'has replaced the red menace, and the "evil empire" of the cold war has become the less eloquent, but just as deadly, "evil doers" of the Arab and Muslim world' (cited in Steuter and Wills 2008: 30).[7]

The War on Terror taps into an orientalist discourse that has deep historical roots in European colonialism. Orientalism denotes western depictions of eastern peoples and cultures in the eighteenth and nineteenth centuries (Said 1979). Orientalist imagery developed in conjunction with western imperial expansion into Asia, and typically presented dark-skinned eastern people in an unfavorable and biased light. Orientalist attitudes can be seen in European paintings of half-dressed women in harem settings, pagodas and pavilions in quasi-Chinese or Japanese style, and operas and plays that often highlighted the silliness or perversity of foreign peoples. Together these elements amounted to widespread European fascination in and also condemnation of the east, which was ultimately thought of as homogenous and inferior, and at its core antithetical to the 'civilized' west (Said 1979; Breckenridge and van de Veer 1993; Kabbani 1994; Jarmakani 2008).

Orientalist imagery, while developing historically out of European colonial ventures, crossed the Pacific to inform an American perspective of the east (Little 2001; Klein 2003). Orientalism frames the War on Terror, just as historically it framed US and British relations with the Middle East throughout the twentieth century, particularly during World War II and the Cold War period. Orientalist attitudes help to dehumanize and demonize the enemy as morally, culturally and religiously deficient by nature. It is this process of 'othering' the enemy, of damning a group or community on the basis of what is deemed their intrinsic nature, that sustains the simplistic logic of hate necessary for warfare. The enemy is not identifiable by what they do, but by who they are. As Edward Said has noted:

> Much of what one reads in the media about Islam represents the aggression coming from Islam because that is what 'Islam' *is*. Local and concrete circumstances are thus obliterated. In other words, covering Islam is a one-sided activity that obscures what 'we' do and highlights instead what Muslims and Arabs, by their flawed nature, are. (Said 1997: xxii)

One of the more obvious ways of 'knowing' the enemy is to focus on issues of race, which create immediate visual markers of difference. In the War on Terror, in common with most modern wars of the twentieth century, racism has been important in creating a homogenous, easily identifiable adversarial target (Keen 1986). Focusing on a person's identity rather than their actions has been legally sanctioned through security legislation such as the US Patriot Act (2001), UK Terrorism Acts (2000, 2006), Australian Anti-Terrorist Act (2005), Canadian

---

[7] Bruce Lawrence has argued that then as now, 'there is no Muslim enemy. In the eleventh century the First Crusades constructed him to cover spurious conquests and wanton killings. In the twenty-first century, the New Crusades reconstruct him to cover global asymmetrics and moral blunders. Both sets of crusaders are zealots' (cited in Steuter and Wills 2008: 30).

Anti-Terrorism Act (2001), French 2006 Law, and German Anti-Terrorism Package (2001 and its 2006 supplement). Together these instruments have intensified surveillance of 'Muslim-looking' or 'Arab-looking' people in North America and Europe, and in many cases have granted the legal basis for suspending people's rights and detaining them without counsel or representation, sometimes for months, as was the case in the Guantanamo Bay detention camp. These acts have, in effect, legalized racial profiling and other race-based discriminatory practices. As international relations scholar Sherene Razack reminds us:

> race thinking becomes embedded in law and bureaucracy so that the suspension of rights appears not as a violence but as the law itself. Violence against the racialized other comes to be understood as necessary in order for civilization to flourish, something the state must do to preserve itself. (Razack 2008: 9)

It may come as no surprise that in the United States and in many European countries, public opinion polls indicate that large numbers of people support racial profiling and see little wrong with denying citizenship to immigrants, or removing passengers from airplanes, on the basis of their ethnic appearance or nationality. Together these security acts have been significant in nurturing the rise of anti-Muslim racism in western nations in the post-9/11 era. Human Rights Watch, Amnesty, and other 'watchdog' organizations have published report after report detailing human rights abuses stemming from racial profiling. One such report, *Ethnic Profiling in the European Union: Pervasive, Ineffective, and Discriminatory,* published by the Open Society Justice Initiative, summarizes the situation in Europe thus:

> Since the 9/11 attacks in the United States, 32 per cent of British Muslims report being subjected to discrimination at airports. Police carrying machine guns have conducted identity checks on 11-year-olds at German mosques. Moroccan immigrants have been called 'moro de mierda' ('Arab shit') by Spanish police. The personal data of 8.3 million people were searched in a massive German data mining exercise which targeted— among other characteristics—people who were Muslim, and which did not identify a single terrorist. These are examples of ethnic profiling by police in Europe—a common, longstanding practice that has intensified in recent years. Evidence from countries across the European Union shows that police routinely use generalizations about ethnicity, religion, race or national origin in deciding whom to target for identity checks, stops, and searches. Contemporary concerns about terrorism underlie a rising interest in ethnic profiling in Europe, which many see as an effective way to identify terrorist suspects. (*Ethnic Profiling* 2009)

Stereotypes of the enemy, and the legal endorsement of racial and ethnic profiling on the basis of these stereotypes, are common in times of war (Keen 1986). In World War II, the Japanese and German internment camps in the United States are testament to people's extreme reactions when they feel that they are surrounded by enemies and possible harm. After the bombing of Pearl Harbor in 1941 the US Congress passed Executive Order 9066, which was subsequently upheld by a majority opinion in the Supreme Court in *Korematsu v*

United States (1944). As a result of Executive Order 9066, approximately 120,000 American civilians of Japanese descent were relocated to camps without due process or legal representation for the duration of the war (Muller 2007). In the Civil Liberties Act of 1988, Congress acknowledged that the internment of Japanese-Americans was based on 'race prejudice, war hysteria, and a failure of political leadership'.

Unfortunately, we do not always learn from our mistakes, and recognizing internment camps, and other race-based practices of discrimination, as an extreme abuse of political and legal power does not prevent future similar actions. For instance, on 26 November 2006, a radio talk-show host, Jerry Klein, played a hoax on his listeners when he invoked the horrors of Nazism by suggesting that all Muslims living in the United States should be identified by a distinctive arm-band or crescent-shaped tattoo. The suggestion caused his phone lines to jam up immediately with many callers agreeing with him. According to a Reuters report by Bernd Debusmann:

> The first caller to the station in Washington said that Klein must be 'off his rocker'. The second congratulated him and added: 'Not only do you tattoo them in the middle of their forehead but you ship them out of this country … they are here to kill us'. Another said that tattoos, armbands and other identifying markers such as crescent marks on driver's licenses, passports and birth certificates did not go far enough. 'What good is identifying them?' he asked. 'You have to set up encampments like during World War Two with the Japanese and Germans.' (Debusmann 2006)

'Saving Brown Women' Overseas

In the months and years immediately following 9/11, mainstream news media in the United States—and to a lesser degree in Britain and other western nations—presented biased coverage that helped to sustain racial stereotypes and racial profiling. Mainstream news media was essential in furthering the Bush administration's pro-war agenda, providing 'a receptive, largely uncritical audience amongst the corporate media's owners, editors, and reporters' (Dimaggio 2008: 26; Steuter and Wills 2008; Domke 2004). According to Amy Goodman of *Democracy Now!*, 'When George Bush said there were Weapons of Mass Destruction [in Iraq], he could not have done it alone … he needed an international apparatus to launder what he said, or to put the stamp of approval on it, and he had it in the US media. More powerful than any bomb or missile, the Pentagon has deployed the US media' (cited in Dimaggio 2008: 26).

The complicity of the news media in promoting a pro-war agenda was seen immediately in the days following 9/11 as the United States geared up to attack Afghanistan, which began in late 2001. At this early stage, the media was almost unanimously pro-war and took every opportunity to echo the Bush administration's crusading language and demonization of the enemy. One of the most powerful and dehumanizing media images of the enemy was to paint Al-Qaeda and Taliban terrorists—and by implication all Muslim and Arab men—as inherently violent towards women. This presentation of the woman-abusing enemy tapped into a well-established colonial rhetoric used by the British regime in nineteenth-century India, where it was widely accepted that 'civilized' Britons must save Indian women from practicing sati, the ritual of throwing oneself onto the burning funeral pyre of one's deceased husband (Spivak 1988; Abu-Lughod 2002: 784). More recently, public demonstrations involving French generals 'unveiling' Algerian women reinforced the notion of a European liberation of oppressed women (Abu-Lughod 2002: 785).

In the twenty-first century, western depictions of terrorists as woman-abusers served a number of purposes. It helped to convince those still unsure about waging war in Afghanistan that it was necessary. Whether people responded positively or otherwise to the overtly religious tone of Bush's war rhetoric, almost all Americans and many people around the world responded emotionally to the idea of freeing women (and children) from oppressive male Islamist terrorists (Figure 41). According to Miriam Cooke, the rescue paradigm relies on four stages:

> (1) women have inalienable rights within universal civilization, (2) civilized men recognize and respect these rights, (3) uncivilized men systematically abrogate these rights, and (4) such men (the Taliban) thus belong to an alien (Islamic) system. Imperial logic genders and separates subject peoples so that the men are the Other and the women are civilizable. To defend our universal civilization we must rescue the women ... The rhetoric of empire conceals race, ethnicity, and class so that gender becomes these Afghans' major defining characteristic. Politics in the era of US empire disappears behind the veil of women's victimization. (Cooke 2002)

This four-stage rescue paradigm helped to generalize the Islamic enemy. By talking about a homogenous category of third-world women needing to be saved, the notion of a homogenous male counterpart suppressing them was reinforced in the public consciousness.

The rescue paradigm was carefully orchestrated by the Bush administration and enthusiastically embraced by the news media. On 17 November 2001, after the fighting in Afghanistan had been largely successful and it looked as though the US might be able to pull out, the President's wife, Laura Bush, stood in for her husband in his weekly national radio address. She took the unprecedented opportunity of launching a worldwide campaign to focus on the brutality suffered by women and children at the hands of Al-Qaeda and Taliban terrorists.

> Laura Bush effectively became the voice of the US government on the subject of women's oppression in Afghanistan ... Moreover, the fact that she is a woman was undoubtedly the reason that she, rather than President Bush, delivered the speech on this topic; White House strategists likely assumed their audiences would be more apt to identify with a woman speaking on 'women's issues'. (Ayotte and Husain 2005: 123)

Mrs Bush unabashedly invoked the civilized/uncivilized binary that helps to justify war by distancing 'us' from 'them', declaring, 'Civilized people throughout the world are speaking out in horror not only because our hearts break for the

Figure 41. Two women in burqas and several children wearing a mix of western and traditional attire rush by, Afghanistan, 5 February 2009. Photograph taken by Staff Sgt Russell Lee Klika, US Army National Guard.

women and children in Afghanistan, but also because in Afghanistan we see the world the terrorists would like to impose on the rest of us' (cited in Cooke 2002: 470).

There is no question that women in Afghanistan suffered—and continue to suffer—under oppressive policies. Women have been denied access to education, to jobs outside the home, and at times are subjected to extreme physical violence and punishment, including the mandatory wearing of the burqa, the long garment covering a woman's entire body. However, the politics surrounding women in Afghanistan and other Muslim countries, and especially the 'politics of the veil', are extremely complex (Mernissi 1987; Mahmood 2005; Keddie 2007; Scott 2007; Jarmakani 2008; Razack 2008). Women's place in Afghan society is deeply embedded in its historical development, involving structural and institutional inequalities that include the involvement of European colonial powers in the region. As Lila Abu-Lughod reminds us, 'Islamic movements themselves have arisen in a world shaped by the intense engagements of Western powers in Middle Eastern lives' (Abu-Lughod 2002: 789).

Laura Bush's address to the nation calling on the world to save oppressed Afghani women served to silence more complicated questions of politics, economics and structural inequalities in the Middle East, particularly Afghanistan. Laura Bush helped to 'artificially divide the world into separate spheres— recreating an imaginative geography of the West versus East, us versus Muslims, cultures in which First Ladies give speeches versus others where women shuffle around silently in burqas' (Abu-Lughod 2002: 784). With her speech, the United States joined ranks with European powers that have appropriated images of oppressed third-world women for their own political agendas, masking their military interventions in terms of compassion and benevolence (Ayotte and Husain 2005: 116–17, 121, 122).

The Abuse of Women at Home

The political effectiveness of the distinction between western women (ie Laura Bush) and eastern women (ie those living in Afghanistan) relies on the presupposition that western women are liberated and free. In relative terms, it is not hard to make the case that women in the United States are better off than women in Afghanistan. Women in the US and other advanced industrial nations live in democracies and can vote, seek legal representation, own property, attend school, and wear almost whatever they want. Many of these reforms are relatively recent, and build upon the work of the suffragette movements of the late nineteenth and early twentieth centuries, particularly in Britain and the United States. These movements galvanized women, typically from middle and upper class backgrounds, into demanding equal treatment before the law. In many cases, mobilized political action took the form of public riots and demonstrations, often resulting in women being arrested and subjected to ridicule and even violence. Yet despite widespread resistance by mainstream male-dominated political parties, the various suffragette movements were central in obtaining the franchise—women were first granted the right to vote in New Zealand in 1893, Australia 1902, Canada 1917, Russia 1917, Britain 1918, Germany 1918, and the United States in 1920. In the years following, many legal and social advances have been made to instill equality for women. Particularly since the 1960s, women in western countries enjoy relative political, economic and social freedom.

That being said, it is undeniable that women in western societies, especially with respect to the labor force, are still discriminated against and full gender equality has not been achieved. Barbara Ehrenreich, in her book *Nickel and Dimed: On (Not) Getting by in America*, depressingly reveals the extent to which low-wage women are systematically exploited and subjected to uncivil and disrespectful treatment by employers, creating what she calls 'a culture of extreme inequality' (Ehrenreich 2000: 210–12). Unfortunately, conditions of inequity are not only prevalent among the working poor, and apply to women of all socioeconomic classes and backgrounds. Despite legislation such as the UK's Equality Act (2006) and the United States' Equal Pay Act (1963) and Title IX of the Education Amendments (1972), women have typically not been able to command equal wages and salaries. At the top end of the scale in terms of salary, prestige and power, women are still paid less than men for doing the same job, and are not well presented in managerial and leadership positions. According to the American Bar Association, in 2008 women made up almost half of all associates in law firms, but only 18.3 per cent of partners. Only 15 women run *Fortune 500* companies. At the lower end of the scale in terms of remuneration, women similarly receive less than men for doing the same job, and women from diverse ethnic backgrounds are by far the most discriminated against on the basis of both sex and race. According to the US Department of Labor in 2003, the median weekly earnings of white men were $715. White women earned 79 per cent of this amount, black women earned 68 per cent, and Hispanic women earned 57 per cent ($410) (US Department of Labor). These disparities become even more stark when illegal immigrant women are brought into the picture.

The US Department of Labor data reflects a division of labor between the sexes. Some men refuse to accommodate the particular needs of women entering the labor force who may be involved in child-bearing, family-caring and so on. Some women self-select to avoid entering jobs and professions typically identified as 'male' such as plumbers, firefighters, airplane pilots, doctors, lawyers, engineers, and scientists. However, the inequality of wages between men and women also involves more subtle forms of discrimination at work reflecting mainstream social and cultural values and attitudes (Lipman 2009). In most advanced industrial nations, labor markets devalue care-giving jobs such as nursing, teaching and social work, and at the same time reward male-dominated occupations with higher salaries and status. Perversely, in tough economic times, this has meant that more men, who occupy higher paying positions, have lost their jobs than women (Belken 2009). In addition to women working in devalued and underpaid employment sectors, feminist scholars note that many informal barriers prevent job equity:

> informal barriers create impediments and construct 'glass ceilings' that foil substantive equality. These artificial barriers to advancement include gender stereotypes about roles, abilities, and leadership styles: exclusion of women from informal networks of communication; a lack of company commitment to the advancement of women; and the absence of mentors. The subtle forms of bias—such as not having lunch or playing racquetball with a supervisor, and then not being considered a 'team-player'—may be difficult to see in everyday working life. Senior leaders may assume that 'women's emotions prevent them from managing effectively', or they may subscribe to deep normative standards that women should not exercise power over men. (Levit and Verchick 2006: 74)

Within the Wal-Mart company, sex and race discrimination have been rife for decades. Betty Dukes, the woman in whose name the *Dukes* sex discrimination class action has been submitted, has also filed claims of racial discrimination against Wal-Mart. But as Lisa Featherstone in her book on the *Dukes* case notes, while a few women have won lawsuits against the company for racial discrimination, on the whole Wal-Mart has dealt better with racial issues, and the 'company is plagued less by systemic racism than by systemic sexism' (Featherstone 2004: 39). Wal-Mart recognizes that it cannot ignore issues of racism and has responded reasonably promptly to allegations of racial bias. In recent years it has recognized the commercial advantages of hiring minorities and, for instance, using images of blacks in its campaigns against unions. Wal-Mart has 'populated the executive ranks in its "People Division" with numerous high-profile Latinos and African Americans' (Lichenstein 2009: 140). These positions have typically gone to men, such as Coleman Peterson, who is black, and served on the board of the National Association for the Advancement of Colored People. Coleman was Executive Vice President of human resources for Wal-Mart until 2004, and while in charge his primary objective was to find diverse people to implement the company's business strategies around the world. Not only does diversity hiring improve Wal-Mart's image as an equal opportunities employer, it also improves its economic profits in international markets.

For many black, Latino and other minority women working at Wal-Mart, opportunities for advancement and appointments to high-level managerial positions have not been so forthcoming. As the labor historian Nelson Lichetenstein has noted, Wal-Mart's historical record of hiring black women has not been good. To a large degree, this record reflects the company's early beginnings in the predominantly all-white Ozarks and the racial legacy of the region. The southern belt in which Sam Walton first established his Wal-Mart stores had in the early twentieth century experienced terrible racial discrimination as competition for jobs between blacks and whites escalated. In the 1910s and 20s, lynching and violence forced thousands of black residents to flee. When Walton began his career many years later in the 1960s he did not have to engage with many blacks at all, either as customers or potential employees (Moreton 2009: 77). And when Walton did open up stores in communities with black populations:

> he adopted the sales codes practiced by many southern white merchants following the passage of the civil rights laws. He hired few African Americans and then sought to keep them out of direct contact with white customers ... But as Wal-Mart opened stores in the Deep South, largely in the 1980s, the civil rights winds had ebbed. White customers were less reluctant to shop in an integrated store, and most African Americans saw the arrival of a local Wal-Mart as a sign of racial progress. (Lichtenstein 2009: 63)

In recent decades, Wal-Mart has substantially improved its record with respect to hiring minorities. By 2001, it could claim that it was the largest private employer of African Americans in the United States, which was not particularly difficult or surprising given that it was (and is) the country's largest employer, with a collective employee force of over 1.2 million. Today, Wal-Mart's hiring practices typically reflect the demographics of the community in which a particular store is located—if it is a largely black community, then a good ratio of its employees are black. Wal-Mart's current record of hiring minority women is a step in the right direction, but does not excuse the company for continuing to participate in sexual discrimination practices, as argued in the *Dukes* case. Moreover, Wal-Mart's hiring of minority women within the United States does not address the company's involvement in the exploitation and abuse of women in developing nations.

Abusing Women Abroad

Today, Wal-Mart imports the vast majority of the goods it sells in the United States. It has been estimated that 10 per cent of all China's imports to the United States are sold at Wal-Mart, and 'if Wal-Mart were a country, it would be China's fifth largest export market' (Featherstone 2004: 9–10). So, despite the long-standing claim that Wal-Mart sells only 'made in America' goods, 'at least 85 per cent of Wal-Mart products are made overseas, most of those in China, under sweatshop conditions, by workers, mostly women, who lack the right to organize' (Featherstone 2004: 53; Vance and Scott 1994: 110–11). In short, Wal-Mart takes full advantage, as do many other American-based companies, of outsourcing labor and reaping the financial benefits of largely unregulated, non-unionized labor pools in overseas countries (Bair and Bernstein 2006; Bonacich and Wilson 2006: 233–34; Lichtenstein 2009).

Women and children across the developing world, in what has come to be known as the global south, work to produce goods that are eventually sold in Wal-Mart stores. Of course men are also involved in producing such goods, but typically the majority of these workers are women and children. Unfortunately, women are often subjected to financial exploitation in terms of receiving meager wages as well as other forms of abuse. Many are held as indentured servants, meaning that if they leave before their employment contract has ended they risk imprisonment or criminal charges. Many live in perpetual fear of violent reprimands and forced abortions, and sleep in shared barracks rife with disease within barbed-wire compounds. One example of horrific labor conditions is discussed in a 1999 report on the Korean-owned Daewoosa factory in American Samoa. Over 200 Vietnamese women and men (90 per cent women) were shipped to this factory as 'guest workers' and held for two years under conditions of indentured servitude, sewing clothing for Wal-Mart, JC Penny, Target and Sears. The report reads:

> The labels read 'Made in the USA' since American Samoa is a US territory. However, the women were not even paid the already low $2.60 an hour minimum wage in Samoa. The women were beaten, sexually harassed, threatened with deportation and imprisonment, starved, forced to work 12 to 18 hours a day, seven days a week when rush orders came in, and made to live in crowded rat-infested dormitories. (National Labor Committee 2001: 1; 'Beatings and Other Abuses' 2001)

Knowledge about these 'labor camps' is widespread, and their practices are condoned by some politicians at the highest levels of government. In a disgusting display of power and corruption, the Republican Senator of Texas and later House Majority Leader, Tom Delay, prevented a worker-reform bill being heard in the US House of Representatives in 2000. The bill was aimed at putting an end to sweatshop conditions in factories in the US territory of the Northern Mariana Islands, which involved mostly immigrant employees from China, the Philippines, Sri Lanka and Bangladesh. Delay, working with lobbyist Jack Abramoff, paid off support for the bill and effectively shut down all attempts at government oversight of the abusive corporate practices. In an interview for the *Washington Post*, Delay described how the low-wage, anti-union conditions of the Marianas constituted 'a perfect petri dish of capitalism'. He went on, 'It's like my Galapagos island' (cited in Shields 2005).

In addition to Wal-Mart importing a great deal of its goods from Chinese factories and other smaller manufacturing sites in places such as the Marianas, many of the products it sells are made in Mexican maquiladoras (or maquilas)— factories that have sprung up in the thousands on the Mexico-US border. Most of these factories are 100 per cent foreign owned, many by US companies. The factories are allowed to import material and equipment duty-free under the Maquila Decree of 1989. The only stipulation is that goods produced in these factories must be exported.[8] Maquiladoras have been subject to a great deal of criticism for their substandard working conditions, limited and non-existent accident and pension compensation schemes, long-working hours, and failure to pay a minimum wage to their employees (Human Rights Watch 1996; Cravey 1998; Moffat 2006).

Wal-Mart's use of factories in China and Mexico involves outsourcing, which refers to a client company contracting with a supplier to buy goods produced in another location, typically with lower labor costs and lesser regulation and control over workers' wages and conditions. Outsourcing to poorer countries has become a hallmark of contemporary forms of corporate globalization and profit diversification. It is a practice that has been going on in the United States since the 1970s, starting off with low-tech items related to auto parts, toys and apparel, then moving into electronics and digital services. However, it did not become a formal business strategy until the late 1980s, and has only been brought to the attention of the general public in recent decades. Outsourcing became a political campaign issue in the 2004 US presidential election when democratic candidate John Kerry criticized companies that outsourced as a way of avoiding paying higher taxes. Polls taken at the time indicated widespread public disapproval of outsourcing, with 71 per cent of American voters believing that outsourcing hurt the economy, and 62 per cent agreeing that greater regulatory action should be taken against companies that transferred domestic jobs overseas (Zogby International poll 2004).[9]

It is difficult to glean from the 2004 statistical data the degree to which the American public appreciated the racial dimension of outsourcing jobs overseas.

---

[8] The Maquila Decree came into effect largely to encourage foreign investment in Mexico as a mechanism for dealing with the huge numbers of unemployed workers who had been forced to leave their temporary agricultural jobs in the US when the Bracero Program was formally dismantled in 1964.

[9] Given the world economic crisis that erupted in 2007–08 and rising unemployment statistics in the United States and elsewhere, public disapproval of outsourcing may have increased in recent years.

As stressed by race theorist Howie Winant, today's globalization is a 're-racialization of the world' (Winant 2004: 131). By this Winant means that we cannot talk about global interaction and interconnection, which have been enabled by new forms of technology, communication, international legal instruments and economic agencies such as the World Bank, without also speaking of the racial implications behind global processes. According to Winant:

> What have come to be called 'North-South' issues are also deeply racist issues. The disparities between the world's rich and poor regions, between the (largely white and wealthy) global North and the (largely dark-skinned and poor) global South have always possessed a racial character. They are the legacy of a half millennium of imperialism. (Winant 2004: 131)

If we take Winant's point seriously about a 're-racialization of the world', it becomes hard to reconcile the crusading rhetoric of George and Laura Bush in their media campaign to 'save brown women' with the neoliberal policies of unregulated markets that have allowed Wal-Mart and other corporations to participate in widespread mistreatment of women in the United States and around the world. It seems that on the one hand we get all worked up about fighting to alleviate the oppression of women overseas, but on the other hand we are quite apathetic that it goes on with respect to our mothers, sisters and daughters at home. Within advanced industrial nations, certain questions loom large: How is it possible not to see the incongruities and contradictions in such intolerable practices? More specifically, why aren't we saving women, and especially minority women, from corporate exploitation? Why isn't mainstream media jumping up and down, calling on us to rescue our own?

RIGHTS: THE CHALLENGES OF NEOLIBERALISM

Twentieth Century Developments in Human Rights

The concept of human rights (including political, civil, social and economic rights) has a long historical legacy. However, as discussed in chapter seven, human rights rhetoric did not have a significant international presence until the middle of the twentieth century with the emergence of independent nationalist movements and decolonialization in the 1940s and 50s, the worldwide media attention given the first Nuremberg trial in 1945–46, the establishment of the United Nations in 1945, the passing of the Universal Declaration of Human Rights in 1948, and the passing of the Geneva Conventions in 1949. Yet despite these monumental milestones, over the second half of the twentieth century the concept of human rights as it related to international law developed very slowly. For instance, the United States did not ratify the Geneva Conventions until 1986. The concept of human rights began to appear in international treaties such as the Convention on the Elimination of all Forms of Discrimination Against Women

(CEDAW) in 1979, and exerted modest pressure on shaping domestic legislation in a few countries, but it did not have a widespread impact at either the national or the international level (Merry 2006).

According to the legal scholar and practitioner Philippe Sands, it was not until the arrest of the former military dictator of Chile, Augusto Pinochet, in October 1998, while he was recuperating from surgery in a London clinic, that international law, and specifically the concept of universal jurisdiction, attracted widespread attention (Sands 2005: 4). In the media frenzy surrounding the trial of Pinochet in the House of Lords, a new legal consciousness was formed. Everyone—not just legal experts—wanted to know what gave states (ie Britain) the right to try a former leader of another country for crimes committed outside its jurisdiction; what were the rights, if any, of state leaders seeking immunity from their actions; and what were the rights of Pinochet's victims in their search for retribution and justice? The Pinochet case drew public attention to the international legal concept of universal jurisdiction with respect to human rights violations and crimes against humanity. This is the principle that all states have the authority to try an individual for crimes committed outside the geographical territory of the prosecuting state, on the basis that the crimes are an offense to the entire international community (see Falk 2009: 97–120). The Pinochet case also highlighted that state sovereignty is not absolute, and that an international legal regime requires, by definition, each nation to compromise some dimension of its capacity to govern itself. Pinochet was released from Britain in 2000, returned to Chile for trial, and placed under house arrest. He died from a heart attack in 2006, at which time hundreds of criminal charges were still pending against him in the Chilean Court of Appeals.

The idea of a court claiming transnational jurisdiction is not new. The International Court of Justice (ICJ) was established in 1945 under the UN Charter to deal with legal conflicts between states. In recent years it has been involved in a number of 'contentious cases' and advisory proceedings that have attracted widespread attention, such as its advisory opinion on the legal consequences of the construction of a wall in the Occupied Palestinian Territory in 2003. However, the ICJ tends to avoid highly politicized conflicts between nations because of the difficulties inherent in enforcing its rulings. More recently, the International Criminal Court (ICC) was established in 2002 to deal with the prosecution of individuals for genocide, crimes against humanity, and war crimes. As of October 2009, 110 states were members of the ICC, and a further 38 states had signed but not ratified it. The United States, along with China, Russia and India, is critical of the ICC, largely on the basis that it represents a breach of each nation's sovereignty. Together the ICJ and the ICC underscore the potential reach of an international human rights system to survey and bring to account the actions of both states and state leaders with respect to violations of human rights.

The US's opposition to the ICC represents a trend in its larger dealings with the UN and international legal obligations over the last 20 years. In the 1940s, the US and Britain showed commitment and leadership in bringing about an international legal regime, particularly with respect to laws governing economic flexibility and promoting the creation of markets. However, 'in the 1980s and 1990s a different and stronger voice emerged, reflecting an American and British approach which was considerably more skeptical about international rules and multilateralism' (Sands 2005: 13). As Sands notes:

> Well before 9/11, the United States had turned against many of the international rules which lay outside the economic domain, including some which had attracted very broad support. ... This was a return to American exceptionalism, an attitude which had periodically—and powerfully—dominated its thinking earlier in the century. We are different, said the neoconservatives; the rules cannot apply to us. ... And as this new approach emerged, Britain too found itself pulled in different directions. On the one hand, as a declining power with no empire to protect, it was more committed than ever to the international rule of law. On the other hand, it did not want to alienate its great friend and ally. (Sands 2005: 14–15)

Under the Bush administration, attitudes toward international law have been at best ambivalent, and at worst hostile. While some scholars question the extent of this hostility, there is no doubt that there has been an historical shift from the embracive commitment to international law given in 1945 by President Truman, and the attitudes expressed 60 years later under the Bush administration (Cerone 2007).

Human Rights in the Twenty-First Century

Within the US there is open distrust of international legal norms and treaties relating to human rights, which are interpreted as constraints on free market capitalism.[10] Conservative movements, such as the organization Concerned Women for America, have attacked CEDAW for promoting contraceptives for women and the decriminalization of prostitution in some developing nations (www.cwfa.org/main.asp). This attack on women's rights has been supported by a range of right-wing evangelical organizations, ultimately influencing US foreign policy with respect to charitable aid in developing nations. At the national level, the United States openly disregarded human rights standards in the later years of the twentieth century. As noted by Kenneth Roth, former Executive Director of Human Rights Watch:

> This refusal to apply international human rights law to itself renders US ratification of human rights treaties a purely cosmetic gesture. It allows the US government to pretend to be part of the international human rights system, but in fact does nothing to enhance

---

[10] This attitude is evident in other arenas of international law as well. For instance, the US refused to ratify the 1997 Tokyo Protocol governing global warming on the basis that it would harm the country's economy. Tellingly, this self-serving economic perspective has been rejected by the 187 other nations that have both signed and ratified the Protocol. What is more difficult to understand, because there is no obvious economic advantage, is why the US has failed to sign the UN Convention on the Rights of the Child (194 signatories in 2009), and the Mine Ban Treaty which seeks to eradicate landmines (156 states party to the treaty in 2009).

the rights of US citizens. ... Washington's cynical attitude toward international human rights law has begun to weaken the US government's voice as an advocate for human rights around the world. (Roth 2000: 349–53)

Events post-11 September 2001 substantiate the charge that the United States violates basic civil, political and social rights among its own citizens. The US is not alone on this front. As mentioned above, the UK Terrorism Acts (2000, 2006), like the US Patriot Act (2001), have endorsed the legalization of racial profiling and myriad other race-based discriminatory practices and violations of due process within their respective jurisdictions (Falk 2002). Many other countries have followed suit by introducing legislation similar to the US Patriot Act in an attempt to deal with their own issues of national security against terrorism.

Across Europe, governments are expanding police powers to detain, to wiretap, and to survey electronic communications. France now allows police to search private property with warrants; Germany has loosened regulations controlling wiretaps, the monitoring of e-mail, and access to bank records. More disturbing still are the many states using the specter of terrorism to launch frontal assaults on domestic opposition and upon claimants to self-determination. (Toope 2006: 241; Open Society Justice Initiative 2009)

The US, along with Britain, Canada, Australia and many other liberal democracies, apparently accepts the logic that creating greater security requires, by necessity, that human rights are compromised. However, the exact opposite is in fact the case; we need to protect civil and political rights in order to ensure successful and effective national security. To accept the first argument is to embark on a strategy of repressive governance. It may come as no surprise that many of the 'new-found allies' in the War on Terror, such as China, Egypt, Pakistan, Russia and Saudi Arabia, are officially recognized as 'egregious human rights violators' (Toope 2006: 241). These new alliances make it very difficult to take seriously the United States' claim to moral superiority as defender of liberty and leader of 'Operation Iraqi Freedom'.

Perhaps no issue more dramatically underscores the Bush administration's willingness to violate basic human rights than its treatment of 'enemy combatants' in prison camps such as Abu Ghraib in Iraq and Guantanamo Bay detention camp in Cuba. At these and other military camps, prisoners have been held for years without being expressly charged, and without adequate legal counsel. In addition to denying war prisoners due process, in 2004 the world was shocked by the scandalous accounts of physical, sexual and psychological abuses at Abu Ghraib (Hersh 2004; Harbury 2005; Greenberg and Dratel 2005). More images of horrific abuse surfaced in 2006 and again in 2009, with the US Congress banning the public release of the images in the latter case in the interests of national security. In 2007, it was reported that the Central Intelligence Agency (CIA) was using waterboarding on war prisoners, a particular form of torture long declared illegal in international humanitarian law. This report sparked a huge international scandal and the US was condemned for violating its constitutional and international obligations (*New York Times*, 4 October 2007; *The Guardian* (London), 5 February 2008). In 2009 it was revealed that the US government, and explicitly former Vice President Dick Cheney, had authorized the use of torture in 2002, a move that expressly and intentionally violated the international laws of war spelt out in the UN Geneva Conventions (Hajjar 2004, 2009).

The US-led War on Terror is tainted by its explicit violation of human rights and humanitarian laws as spelt out in the Universal Declaration of Human Rights and the Geneva Conventions. A three-year study conducted in 40 countries by a panel of eminent jurists convened by the International Commission of Jurists in 2009 found that the US and Britain's counter-terrorism practices have actively undermined international human rights standards, which prior to 9/11 were considered relatively robust. According to one commentator:

> A sober assessment of the political and legal status of human rights after September 11th leads to the conclusion that many governments, led by the administration of the most powerful state, are using the threat of global terrorism to undermine the fragile edifice of human rights law. Attacks on hard-won human rights gains are taking place in domestic and international contexts. The two contexts are linked. Undermining domestic human rights norms in liberal democracies, as well as authoritarian states, has the effect of further weakening international law norms, both through the degradation of customary law standards and through damaging reinterpretations of treaty law. Attacks on human rights are made possible by a media-fed climate of fear in America, which the governments of other states then use to justify repressive measures. They are also permitted by the hubris that guides the actions of the US administration, a hubris that inhibits critical self-assessment and that underplays the risks to America of claims to untrammeled state power made in the name of the war on terror. (Toope 2006: 245)

Human Rights and Neoliberalism

In the later twentieth and early twenty-first centuries, it appears that the commitment to democracy and protection of human rights as espoused by industrialized western societies is running up hard against an economic commitment to global free trade. Historian Eric Hobsbawm notes that the core problem is that free market logic is incompatible with democratic governance. He writes:

> The ideal of market sovereignty is not a complement to liberal democracy, but an alternative to it. Indeed, it is an alternative to any kind of politics, since it denies the need for political decisions, which are precisely decisions about common or group interests as distinct from the sum of choices, rational or otherwise, of individuals pursuing their private preferences ... Participation in the market replaces participation in politics; the consumer takes the place of the citizen. (Hobsbawm 2007: 104)

In the context of the War on Terror, we should pay careful attention to Hobsbawm's argument of the incompatibility of free markets and democratic principles. The War illustrates the lengths to which some western governments are prepared to go in compromising the ideals of liberal democracy as they relate to human rights with respect to both citizens and declared enemies. While it might have been impossible to predict the US government's 'behind-the-scenes' endorsement of torture, there were earlier indicators of widespread tolerance within governments and corporate businesses of lesser kinds of human rights violations in the workplace and elsewhere. Enormously successful companies such as Wal-Mart—whether we are willing to admit it or not—have been complicit in abusing their own women employees, as demonstrated by the *Dukes* case and other lawsuits, as well as endorsing economic strategies overseas that tolerate the abuse of women (and men) from poorer nations (National Labor Committee 2001: 1).

The prominence of neoliberal economic and political polices in western nations over the past three decades—which justify actions in terms of their financial profitability—help to make such abuses seem acceptable. In Britain, the implementation of neoliberalism is typically associated with Margaret Thatcher, who took up office as Prime Minister in 1979 with the explicit goal of breaking union power and freeing up markets to encourage entrepreneurialism. In the United States, the introduction of neoliberalism is associated with Ronald Reagan, who became president in 1981 and steadily implemented economic and legal reforms eliminating trade barriers and favoring international free markets. Neoliberalism has been the dominant ideology informing the government policies of both conservative and progressive administrations in Britain and the United States—and many other countries—for around 30 years (Sands 2005: 117–42; Harvey 2005).[11]

Neoliberalism has been largely implemented through the deregulation of constraints on the movement of capital, as well as the privatization of nationally owned enterprises and utilities such as the prison system, banks, state security, and electricity companies. The dominance of neoliberalism is linked to governments playing a reduced role in certain sectors, resulting in a decline of welfare services and legal protections for individual workers and citizens. This decline has been most evident in the United States, where employees' health cover has been steadily eroded under neoliberal policies, and union protections have been largely dismantled.

Among those supporting neoliberalism, what is often glossed over is that state governments have been co-opted to work on behalf of corporations, blurring the boundaries between state and corporate interests. States, in other words, are no

---

[11] An early proponent of unregulated laissez-faire capitalism was the philosopher and novelist Ayn Rand, who apparently wore a brooch in the shape of a dollar-sign to advertise her love of capitalism and correlative disgust of liberal social programs based on an altruistic belief in the idea of a common good. Rand's 1957 novel *Atlas Shrugged*, while not particularly well written or well received in her lifetime, was subsequently a bestseller among the conservative right in the 1990s (Burns 2009; Heller 2009). In recent years the book has again gained notoriety in the United States, with people such as conservative political commentator Rush Limbaugh apparently making frequent references to it on his radio show.

longer seen as upholding the ideals of democracy and defending individuals against greedy entrepreneurs, but work on behalf of corporations. According to David Harvey:

> The rolling back of regulatory frameworks designed to protect labour and the environment from degradation has entailed the loss of rights. The reversion of common property rights won through years of hard class struggle (the right to a state pension, to welfare, to national health care) into the private domain has been one of the most egregious of all policies of dispossession, often procured against the broad political will of the population. All of these processes amount to the transfer of assets from the public and popular realms to the private and class-privileged domains. (Harvey 2007: 161, 76)

This 'rolling back' represents a huge shift in the relationship between state, employer and employee, which in the past saw the state as a necessary intermediary between capitalist and worker because it could set regulatory limits on entrepreneurial exploitation, such as setting a minimum wage scale. The uncomfortable reality is that in the pursuit of the dollar in contemporary western society, the freeing up of the economy has come at the price of closing down the freedom of labor to negotiate better conditions and salaries.

It is no coincidence that Wal-Mart's business strategy of taking economic advantage of largely unrepresented and unregulated labor markets at home and abroad sit comfortably with the Republican Party's conservative political agenda and endorsement of global capitalism. The enormous success of Sam Walton's Wall-Mart empire is due in large part to the enabling economic and legal policies of neoliberalism, which allowed him to abuse his employees such that 1.6 million women are now seeking a class action against him for economic exploitation in the form of lost wages, benefits and promotions. The *Dukes* case represents an indictment of neoliberal practices and ideologies—a sentiment that ironically resonates with many contemporary terrorist organizations' criticism of the United States and other advanced industrial nations for their focused pursuit of global profits.

CONCLUSION

The *Dukes v Wal-Mart* case brings into sharp relief the limits of democracy in our own domestic arenas, where exploitation is tolerated and the human rights of our own mothers, daughters and sisters are denied. *Dukes* highlights that western nations are not intrinsically morally, legally or culturally superior when it comes to inequalities in society regarding women. Certainly, some countries hold a better record than others on this front, but no country or society is beyond reproach.

The abuse of labor permitted under a global free market economy over the past 30 years has not gone unnoticed in the global south and other less industrialized nations. By contrast, in wealthier countries that have benefited financially from such abuses, a prevailing apathy, if not denial, permeates. The degree to which the global south's anger with respect to economic abuse correlates to the rise of religious fundamentalism and terrorist activity leading up to the events of 9/11 and other terrorist attacks in places such as Spain, Britain and Indonesia is hard to ascertain. Presumably the two issues are linked, but exactly how is not clear. At this stage, all we can be sure of is that the US and other liberal democracies, in their focused pursuit of economic profit over recent decades, have been losing ground in their attempts to claim moral superiority over more repressive government systems. The War on Terror, which has seen the endorsement and deployment of torture by the United States and Britain, has escalated this loss.

Perversely, forfeiting the moral high ground may open up the possibility of new avenues of communication and reconciliation between countries and peoples. Recognizing that the 'west', like the 'rest', does not treat all of its citizens equally is perhaps the first vital step in shattering a deeply entrenched crusading logic that depends on simplistic binaries of good and evil, civilized and barbaric, lawful and lawless. In this context, the *Dukes* case is not only a testament to the flaws of unregulated global capitalism and the bravery of individuals who seek to challenge it, but also to the superficiality of historical binaries that seek to refute complexity and draw fast and easy distinctions between societies, economies, cultures, governments and religions.

Recommended Reading

Featherstone, Lisa (2004) *Selling Women Short: The Landmark Battle for Worker's Rights at Wal-Mart.* New York: Basic Books.

Greenberg, Karen J and Joshua L Dratel (eds) (2005) *The Torture Papers: The Road to Abu Grhaib.* Cambridge: Cambridge University Press.

Harvey, David (2007) *A Brief History of Neoliberalism.* Oxford: Oxford University Press.

Hobsbawm, Eric (2007) *Globalization, Democracy and Terror.* London: Little, Brown.

Lichtenstein, Nelson (2009) *The Retail Revolution: How Wal-Mart Created a Brave New World of Business.* New York: Metropolitan Books.

Lichtenstein, Nelson (ed) (2006) *Wal-Mart: The Face of Twenty-First Century Capitalism.* New York: New Press.

Little, Douglas (2001) *American Orientalism: The United States and the Middle East since 1945.* Chapel Hill: University of North Carolina Press.

Moreton, Bethany (2009) *To Serve God and Wal-Mart.* Cambridge, MA: Harvard University Press.

Razack, Sherene H (2008) *Casting Out: The Eviction of Muslims from Western Law and Politics.* Toronto: University of Toronto Press.

Said, Edward (1979) *Orientalism.* New York: Vintage.

Sands, Philippe (2005) *Lawless World: America and the Making and Breaking of Global Rules from FDR's Atlantic Charter to George W Bush's Illegal War.* New York: Penguin.

Seymour, Hersh (2004) *Chain of Command: The Road from 9/11 to Abu Ghraib.* New York: HarperCollins.

Steuter, Erin and Deborah Wills (2008) *At War with Metaphor: Media, Propaganda, and Racism in the War on Terror.* New York: Lexington Books.
Winant, Howard (2004) *New Politics of Race: Globalism, Difference, Justice.* Minneapolis: University of Minnesota Press.

Conclusion: The Resurgence of Faith

O
VER 40 YEARS AGO, on 8 April 1966, just before Easter, *Time* Magazine provocatively printed in bold red lettering on its front cover the question: Is God Dead? The cover caused public uproar in the United States. Many readers declared the question offensive; many others said it was appropriate in an increasingly secular age. The cover referred to an inside article written by John Elson on contemporary thinking on the issue of God. Elson's rather lengthy theological discussion was supplemented with data from 300 interviews conducted around the world by more than 30 *Time* foreign correspondents. Elson wrote, 'Secularization, science, urbanization—all have made it comparatively easy for modern man to ask where God is and hard for the man of faith to give a convincing answer, even to himself' (Elson 1966).

Today the question 'Is God Dead?' may strike the reader as somewhat anachronistic. In the United States, and to a lesser degree in Britain and other liberal democracies, the question of religion, both Christian and non-Christian, and the relative influence religion may have in social and political circles, has become a hot topic. In the post-9/11 world, references to God and Christian values are a constant theme in mainstream media. Moreover, there is a strident urgency in presenting Christianity as the 'sane' religion in contrast to the radical and irrational fundamentalism of 'terrorists'. Scholars and commentators, too, have bombarded the public with discussions about religion, its place in politics, and its rising prominence in international affairs. Books with titles such as *God is Back: How the Global Revival of Faith is Changing the World* (Micklethwait and Woolridge 2009) and *The Left Hand of God: Taking Back Our Country from the Religious Right* (Lerner 2006) have become the norm.

In Britain, and across Europe, religious issues have also taken center stage in recent years. Most notably there is widespread concern among white populations over the growing Muslim presence, as evidenced by the increasing number of mosques and other expressions of non-Christian faith in many major European cities. France has been consumed with the so-called headscarf controversy, and in 2004 the government banned girls from wearing headscarves when attending public schools (Scott 2007). While the ban did not expressly target Muslim schoolgirls, it is widely interpreted to be a direct attack on Muslim communities' freedom of religious expression. In November 2009, on the basis of a referendum, Switzerland banned the building of new minarets on mosques. Islamic faith is not the only contentious religious issue. In December 2009 in Britain, questions about a religious community's relationship to the state erupted in the highly controversial Jewish Free School (JFS) case decided by the UK's Supreme Court.[1] By a narrow 5–4 majority, the court held that an Orthodox Jewish school had violated the UK's Race Relations Act by using 'descent based criteria' as its basis for refusing to admit a non-Orthodox Jewish student (Scolding 2009). The legal decision ignited old debates about the role of the state in determining rights of religious association. Many Orthodox Jews (as distinct from Reform and Progressive Jews, a large number of whom are pleased with the decision, Romain 2009) are outraged at the state's claim that it should decide the criteria by which a person's religious faith is determined.

Given the amount of energy and discussion devoted to God in national and international politics, mainstream media and scholarly analysis, it is clear that God is not 'dead' in the twenty-first century. A 2009 report conducted by the University of Chicago entitled *Religious Change Around the World* confirms, unsurprisingly, that while religious faith and practices have changed over time, globally religion is still very much a central force in a great many people's lives (Smith 2009). The secularization thesis, that modernization, science and rationality will rid the world of its dependence on spiritual faith, has proven to be overly simplistic and grossly inadequate in explaining the enduring presence of multiple religions in the contemporary world. Whether people in liberal democracies are willing to acknowledge it or not, it now seems clear that religion and spiritual belief have always been at play in Anglo-European-American societies. The Enlightenment and so-called rise of reason in Europe during the seventeenth and eighteenth centuries may have modified or dampened levels of public religiosity, and even pushed certain public demonstrations of faith behind closed doors, but it did not eradicate the need to believe in God or some form of transcendent authority.

Similarly, understandings of race and manifestations of racial prejudice were not eradicated by the supposed rise of rational thought in Enlightenment Europe. In fact, the modern concept of race, with its basis in ethnic classificatory schemes and pseudo-scientific thought, is a product of the Enlightenment. In short, reason rationalized racism. So, despite the great strides towards equality and democracy made by the American and French Revolutions in 1776 and 1789, and formalized in the US Constitution and Bill of Rights and the French Declaration of the Rights of Man, racism has not been eliminated. Racial inequities and prejudices continue to exist in the contemporary west, and have arguably become even more complex in their intimate association with issues of faith and religion. Under various pieces of legislation enacted to confront

---

[1] *R(E) v Governing Body of JFS* [2009] UKSC 15.

terrorism in the wake of 9/11 in Britain, the United States and many other nations around the world, religious affiliation can stand in as an indicator of race, and racial profiling can mask religious discrimination. Legislation with respect to terrorism has deliberately blurred the relationship between religion and race. As a result, civil, political and human rights, including the right to habeas corpus and legal representation, are being compromised for people of particular faiths and skin-tones.

Against a backdrop of deeply embedded and enduring religious beliefs and racist practices, this book has attempted to chart the history of modern Anglo-American law in the modernist period. My general argument is that the discourses surrounding issues of religion, race and rights should be considered together in mapping the foundations and emerging characteristics of modern western law. This trio of forces challenges the enduring Enlightenment narrative of modern law embodying rationalism, pragmatism and objective universality. I argue that shifts in legal thinking experienced in Europe's modern period from the sixteenth through to the twenty-first century are intimately connected with dramatic upheavals in religious belief, and that these upheavals are in turn linked to political ideas about national identity that involve—amongst other things—interpreting cultural difference through a racist lens. One force does not causally affect another, but each shapes and is shaped by the others. Theological, political and legal reforms in the sixteenth century—as in subsequent centuries—developed as mutually constitutive belief systems, ideological positions and material practices.

I began the book with Martin Luther nailing his 95 Theses on the door of Wittenberg's castle church in 1517, which heralded the Reformation. The Reformation split the Christian world into Protestant and Catholic camps and forever redefined the cultural, social, political, military and economic landscape of Europe. Luther's criticism of the religious abuses of the Catholic Church and the canon law that supported it opened up opportunities for public critique, and helped to create social and political momentum for a dramatic change in western legal philosophy and practice. In arguing that people should take personal responsibility for their spiritual salvation, Luther also argued that people should take personal responsibility for their actions based on reason, not blind religious devotion to God as promoted by Catholicism. With respect to the threat to Europe from the 'infidel Turk', Luther did not argue that one should fight Muslims simply because the pope commanded it, as had been the case in former crusades, but rather because it was the appropriate action to take according to the direction of secular leaders. In other words, Luther's stress on the role of the individual was revolutionary in both religious and political terms, and, although largely unintentionally, his thoughts and teachings provided the impetus and conduit for radical legal change.

Radical legal change is further exemplified by the beheading of King Charles I by the English parliament in 1649, over 100 years later. In a public state trial, the king was declared a tyrant for claiming to rule by divine right and in the process failing to heed the demands of his elected parliamentarians. The beheading of Charles I established, once and for all, the capacity of the English aristocracy, gentry and merchants to stake a joint claim in the governance of the nation and establish their right as Anglo-Saxon, male and propertied individuals to partici-pate in law-making. Furthermore, I argued that this emerging sense of rights consciousness among Englishmen in the seventeenth century was intimately connected to English colonial expansion in the New World. The refining of English law to suit local colonial needs and practices underscored men's involvement—not God's—in the adaptation and enforcement of law and helped in the articulation of a secular state system back home.

Intellectually and politically, the beheading of Charles I paved the way for subsequent popular revolutions in America and France that were to champion a more democratic sharing of executive power. Thomas Paine's essay *Common Sense,* written on the eve of the American Revolution in 1776, and *Rights of Man,* written in the midst of the French Revolution in 1791, together promoted dramatic political change that helped to shape modern legal concepts of human rights and representative democracy (chapter 3). According to Paine, a person's perspective on religion, race, law and governance were inextricably linked. If one believed in religious tolerance, it was then possible to embrace an ideology of cultural diversity and be at least willing to think about equal legal and political rights for all people. Paine was not the first person to think in terms of democratic principles based on an individual's rights. However, he was original in his belief that such rights pertain to all humans regardless of their specific religious or spiritual belief system. Up until this time, most Europeans believed that a Christian God ruled supreme and political and legal rights were granted to individuals—if at all—only if one was of a certain faith, racial background and socioeconomic class, and male in gender. African slaves and native peoples encountered in the New World were not Christians and so were denied access to entitlement. Paine challenged this premise head-on, arguing that all peoples by virtue of their humanity should be shown respect and justice, and be treated equally. He was, in short, one of the first political thinkers and writers to talk in terms of human rights being applied universally.

Against the extraordinary breakthroughs in legal thought produced by the American and French Revolutions in the later eighteenth century, the nineteenth century was marred by bloody conflict and violent opposition to legal reform. The 1865 Morant Bay riot involving ex-slaves on the island colony of Jamaica ignited wider debates about slavery in Britain and the United States, occurring as it did only six months after the end of the American Civil War. In many ways the public debates raging in England over the legality of the blood shed in Jamaica can be interpreted as an intellectual civil war that tore English society in two. On one side were scientists, abolitionists and progressive thinkers such as Charles Darwin, Thomas Huxley and John Stuart Mill, and on the other were political and religious conservatives such as Thomas Carlyle, John Ruskin and, somewhat surprisingly, Charles Dickens. These men represented opposing viewpoints among the general public that pivoted largely on the issue of whether one could consider African people and their descendants human beings, and so capable of converting to Christianity.

Fueling the controversy were pseudo-scientific theories about race and racial hierarchies that flourished in the mid to later part of the nineteenth century. These theories were enormously popular and were deeply embedded in British and American national identities and consciousness, reinforcing ideas about the moral and intellectual superiority of western 'civilized' nations over inferior colonial subjects. Pseudo-scientific theories of race were put to political and economic use, justifying the exploitation and abuse of conquered colonial people in Africa, India, the Pacific and Asia. In the United States and Britain, social evolutionary theories of race also justified social, political and legal mistreatment of minorities at home. This connection was explicit in the US, where scientific racism provided a popular platform on which to build 'Jim Crow laws' against former slaves, legalize the labor exploitation of immigrants from Ireland and eastern and Mediterranean Europe, and justify the widespread abuse of Native Americans and the removal of their lands.

Industrialization in the nineteenth century brought a new sense of faith in law as a rational and objective enterprise. In a sense, faith in law replaced faith in God as the dominant mechanism explaining the world and one's place in it. As a logical system of thought, law was thought of as intrinsically fair and just. Moreover, thinking about law as a neutral system of order suggested that it was universal in its applicability, meaning that it could be transferred to overseas colonies and imposed on non-western cultures and societies. Faith in law meant that as a system of control it was beyond reproach, ostensibly operating above the melee of economic and political self-interest. This was essential given the connections between law and laissez-faire capitalist growth that were evident throughout the nineteenth century; connections that supported a range of new property, contract, tort and commercial rules that gave entrepreneurs an advantage over the vast working classes. In Britain and the US the industrial power elite helped to nurture faith in law among lay populations by building grand state court buildings and promoting the pomp and ritual of legal process.

However, by the early to middle decades of the twentieth century, the pretense that western law was neutral, objective and beyond critique could no longer hold among various sectors of English and US society. The self-determination movements erupting in the British colonies of India, Ceylon and Burma, and activist organizations' calls for the dismantling of Jim Crow laws in the United States, brought increasing public attention to the gross injustices that western law condoned with respect to non-white populations. Law was seen by minority groups both inside and outside the US and Britain as a tool of imperial power and control and a mechanism reinforcing racial inequality and oppression. The scholar and activist WEB Du Bois was very much involved in attacking the Jim Crow laws in the US, and concurrently establishing a Pan-African international movement. As news of Nazi atrocities against Jews and other minorities filtered out of Europe during World War II, Du Bois began to view German anti-semitism and American racism against blacks as emerging out of the same historical phenomenon. Specifically, he located these racist practices in a histori-cal continuum and interpreted the Nazi atrocities as an outcome of an earlier phase of European colonialism which witnessed the degradation and oppression of non-Christian native peoples and gave rise to the modern theory of race.

Further connecting US racism and Nazi atrocities was the notion of eugenics. In the early decades of the twentieth century, eugenics theory enjoyed consider-able appeal in the United States. It justified US anti-miscegenation laws prohib-iting mixed-race marriage, sterilization programs targeting mentally and physically challenged populations, and segregation laws that cordoned off 'defi-cient' blacks (and Native Americans) from white communities. At the Nuremberg trials in the wake of World War II, Karl Brandt, who had been responsible for the Nazi regime's policies on population control and racial hygiene, entered into evidence a book written by an American eugenicist, Madison Grant, called *The Passing of the Great Race* (1916). The book had enjoyed enormous popularity in the US in the interwar years, and it is thought that 1,600,000 copies had been sold by 1937. It was the first non-German book to be translated and published by the Nazi press and had clearly been influential in the shaping of Nazi race policies. The sight of the book was a horrifying moment for the United States lawyers at Nuremberg, who sought to distance themselves from Hitler's regime. Moreover, for many Americans back home it served as an uncomfortable reminder of the similarities between German and US thinking on racial identification and management through programs such as sterilization and segregation.

Out of the horrors revealed at Nuremberg came a new international legal order, determined never to let such atrocities occur again. In 1945 the United Nations was established, and in 1948 the Universal Declaration of Human Rights was issued. Together they represented a new understanding of the interconnec-tions between nations. The thrust of this new understanding was twofold. It qualified the concept of autonomous state sovereignty by declaring that under the new international rubric, the UN should be able to intervene economically or militarily on behalf of the international community to prevent a country from suppressing freedom of speech, denying due process, and persecuting targeted communities. The second major development was a newfound appreciation that in order to secure world peace, fundamental basic human rights must be protected around the world. In other words, peace could not be secured by simply dividing up the spoils of war between victorious allies; it must be broadened to include 'people's peace' in which human rights, including the protection of civil, political, religious and gender rights, should feature promi-nently. Unfortunately, the lessons learnt from the horrors of the Holocaust did not inform all countries equally. As Richard Falk has persuasively argued with respect to US foreign policy and leadership post-1945, the focus was primarily on Cold War politics and military preparedness, not on the criminal activities of Germany's past. Notes Falk:

To the extent that the Holocaust was considered by those involved in the inner circles of foreign policy, it was viewed as either irrelevant to the future because it was an anomaly of pathological politics, or inconvenient in relation to 'the new thinking' about Germany, not as a defeated enemy, but as a divided country that was the most dangerous flashpoint for the onset of World War III (Falk 2009:90–91).

In the twenty-first century the lofty goals promoted in the UN Universal Declaration of Human Rights have not been fully achieved. Certainly great advances have been made in human rights and humanitarian law, and the world is a better place in these areas than it was 50 years ago. The field of international human rights has been created to accommodate new ways of thinking about issues such as global poverty, health, violence and the environment that transcend conventional national/international political and legal frames (Stacey 2009; Fields 2003; Bob 2008; Baxi 2002). Such innovations are evident in the International Criminal Court (ICC), set up in 2002 to hear charges against individuals for genocide, crimes against humanity and war crimes. And innovations can be seen in the processes of decolonization and the rise of an ethos of national self-determination (Burke 2010), and in new UN documents such as the Declaration on the Rights of Indigenous Peoples of 2007, which speaks of collective human rights based on indigenous cultural affiliations, including rights to land, territories and resources.

However, despite these great advances in international law relating to human rights, there are also great obstacles. Arguably, the convergence of neoliberal economic strategies and neoconservative political strategies within western liberal democracies over the past 30 years has created an environment that seeks to block or diminish, rather than advance, human equality and freedom. When money is the primary motivation and justification for human activity, as demonstrated by American-based companies such as Wal-Mart, we face very serious challenges to the institutionalization of practices that protect human dignity. And when neoliberal economic strategies are backed up by military force, as is occurring in Iraq in the name of the War on Terror, human rights protection becomes extremely problematic.

In this context, Partha Chatterjee, a leading postcolonial scholar, writes despairingly about the future prospects for democracy:

The trends in global politics initiated by the United States following the events of September 11, 2001 have put new constraints on political society in most of the world. The imperial privileges that are now being asserted in carrying out the so-called 'war on terror', the arrogant disregard for established international laws and procedures, the abrogation of the civil rights of both citizens and foreign residents in the name of homeland security and, above all, the global spread of ubiquitous and infinitely malleable concepts of 'the terrorist' and 'those that sympathize with terrorism'—labels that can be attached to almost any individuals, groups, ethnicities, or nationalities whose political desires happen to draw the ire of ruling regimes and dominant powers—can have only a negative impact on popular politics. (Chatterjee 2004: 129)

Chatterjee sees powerful western nations that violate human rights and reject international legal norms as lowering the standards of world civility and granting legitimacy to violence more generally. Despite his despair, however, Chatterjee remains faintly optimistic about what may be happening among ordinary people on the ground, behind the scenes, set apart from media attention and political intervention.

> When violent and hateful mobilizations in political society can draw their legitimacy from the cynical deployment of state violence by those who claim to speak for the free societies of modernity [United States and Britain], the less glamorous projects of patient, humane, and democratic social transformation are liable to come under severe strain. One only hopes that while it is the former that is making most of the news today, history is being made through the latter endeavors. (Chatterjee 2004: 129–30)

I have argued throughout this book that seeking what Chatterjee calls 'patient, humane, and democratic social transformation' requires an appreciation of the connections and intersections linking understandings of religion, race and rights, be they within a local, national or international legal context. Anglo-American law is not intrinsically objective and value-free, and should not be thought of as a transferable commodity that can be taken overseas and easily established in different cultural settings. We must always remember that modern western law is informed by a specific set of historical circumstances and is shaped today, as much as it was in the past, by religious intolerance, racial violence and economic greed. However, the difficulty we face in acknowledging this truth is that it forces us to confront the enduring need of citizens of western nations to *believe in* the impartiality of the rule of law.

Bibliography

Abu-Lughod, Lila (2002) 'Do Muslim Women Really Need Saving? Anthropological Reflections on Cultural Relativism and its Others' 104(3) *American Anthropologist* 783.

Adams, David Wallace (1995) *Education for Extinction—American Indians and the Boarding School Experience 1875–1928*. Lawrence: University Press of Kansas.

Adams, Stephen (2001) *The Best and Worst Country in the World: Perspectives on the Early Virginia Landscape*. Charlottesville: University Press of Virginia.

Adamson, John (2009) *The Noble Revolt: The Overthrow of Charles 1*. London: Weidenfeld & Nicolson.

Albright, Madeline (2006) *The Mighty & The Almighty: Reflections on America, God, and World Affairs*. New York: Harper Perennial.

Altman, Andrew (1993) *Critical Legal Studies*. Princeton: Princeton University Press.

Anghie, Anthony (2005) *Imperialism, Sovereignty and the Making of International Law*. Cambridge: Cambridge University Press.

Anghie, Anthony, Bhupinder Chimni, Karin Mickelson and Obiora Okafor (eds) (2003) *The Third World and International Order: Law, Politics and Globalization*. Leiden: Brill.

Arendt, Hannah (1945) 'Approaches to the German Problem' XII/I *Partisan Review*, Winter. Reprinted in Hannah Arendt, *Essays in Understanding 1930–1954*. New York: Schocken.

Arvidsson, Stefan (2006) *Aryan Idols: Indo-European Mythology as Ideology and Science*. Chicago: University of Chicago Press.

Asad, Talad (2003) *Formations of the Secular: Christianity, Islam, Modernity*. Palo Alto: Stanford University Press.

Aughton, Peter (2002) *Endeavour: The Story of Captain Cook's First Great Epic Voyage*. London: Cassell.

Avrich, Paul (1984) *The Haymarket Tragedy*. Princeton: Princeton University Press.

Axtell, James (2001) *Natives and Newcomers: The Cultural Origins of North America*. New York: Oxford University Press.

Ayotte, Kevin J and Mary E Husain (2005) 'Securing Afgahan Women: Neocolonialism, Epistemic Violence, and the Rhetoric of the Veil' 17(3) *NWSA Journal* 112.

Bainton, Roland H (1995) *Here I Stand: A Life of Martin Luther*. New York: Penguin.

Bair, Jennifer and Sam Bernstein (2006) 'Labor and the Wal-Mart Effect' in Stanley D Brunn (ed), *Wal-Mart World: The World's Biggest Corporation in the Global Economy*. New York: Routledge, 99–114.

Baker, Sir John (2004) 'Human Rights and the Rule of Law in Renaissance England' 2(3) *Northwestern University Journal of International Human Rights*.

Banner, Stuart (2005a) *How the Indians Lost Their Land: Law and Power on the Frontier*. Cambridge: The Belknap Press of Harvard University Press.

Banner, Stuart (2005b) 'Why *Terra Nullius?* Anthropology and Property Law in Early Australia' 23(1) *Law and History Review* 95.

Barkan, Elazar (1992) *The Retreat of Scientific Racism: Changing Concepts of Race in Britain and the United States Between the World Wars*. New York: Cambridge University Press.

Barnes, Thomas Garden (ed) (2008) *Shaping the Common Law: From Glanvill to Hale, 1188–1688*. Palo Alto: Stanford University Press.

Barta, Roger (1997) *The Artificial Savage: Modern Myths of the Wild Man*. Translated by Christopher Follett. Ann Arbor: University of Michigan Press.

Bartolomé de las Casas (1974) *The Devastation of the Indies, a Brief Account*. Translated by Herma Briffault. Baltimore: Johns Hopkins University Press.

Baxi, Upendra (2002) *The Future of Human Rights*. Oxford: Oxford University Press.

Baxi, Upendra (2006) 'What May the "Third World" Expect from International Law?' 27(5) *Third World Quarterly* 713, special issue: *Reshaping Justice—International Law and the Third World*.

'Beatings and Other Abuses Cited at Samoan Apparel Plant that Supplied US Retailers' (2001) *New York Times,* 6 February.

Belken, Lisa (2009) 'The New Gender Gap' *New York Times Magazine*, 30 September 2009, pp 11–12.

Bell, Dean Phillip (2008) *Jews in the Early Modern World*. New York: Rowman & Littlefield.

Bell, Madison Smartt (2007) *Toussaint Louverture: A Biography*. New York: Pantheon.

Bellomo, Manilo (1995) *The Common Legal Past of Europe: 1000–1800* (Studies in Medieval and Early Modern Canon Law). Washington, DC: Catholic University of America Press.

Benton, Lauren (2002) *Law and Colonial Cultures: Legal Regimes in World History*. Cambridge: Cambridge University Press.

Beresford, Quentin and Paul Omaji (1998) *Our State of Mind: Racial Planning & the Stolen Generations*. Perth: Fremantle Arts Centre Press.

Berger, Peter L (1999) 'The Desecularization of the World: A Global Overview' in Peter L Berger (ed), *The Deseculariztion of the World: Resurgent Religion and World Politics*. Grand Rapids: William B Eerdmans, pp 1–18.

Berman, Harold J (1993, 2000 edn) *Faith and Order: The Reconciliation of Law and Religion*. Grand Rapids: William B Eerdmans.

Berman, Harold J (2003) *Law and Revolution, II: The Impact of the Protestant Reformations on the Western Legal Tradition*. Cambridge: The Belknap Press of Harvard University Press.

Bhandar, Brenna (2009) 'The Ties that Bind: Multiculturalism and Secularism Reconsidered' 36(3) *Journal of Law and Society* 301.

Bianco, Anthony (2006) *The Bully of Bentonville: How the High Cost of Wal-Mart's Everyday Low Prices is Hurting America*. New York: Currency.

Biddiss, Michael (1995) 'Victor's Justice? The Nuremberg Tribunal' *History Today,* May 1995, 40.

Biolsi, Thomas (1995) 'The Birth of the Reservation: Making the Modern Individual among the Lakota' 22(1) *American Ethnologist* 28.

Biolsi, Thomas (2001) *Deadliest Enemies: Law and the Making of Race Relations on and off Rosebud Reservation*. Berkeley: University of California Press.

Biolsi, Thomas (2005) 'Imagined Geographies: Sovereignty, Indigenous Space, and American Indian Struggle' 32(2) *American Ethnologist* 239.

Blanks, David R (1999) 'Western Views of Islam in the Premodern Period: A Brief History of Past Approaches' in David R Blanks and Michael Frassetto, *Western Views of Islam in Medieval and Early Modern Europe*. New York: St Martin's Press, 1–10.

Blanks, David R and Michael Frassetto (1999) *Western Views of Islam in Medieval and Early Modern Europe*. New York: St Martin's Press.

Bob, Clifford (2008) *The International Struggle for New Human Rights*. Philadelphia: University of Pennsylvania Press.

Bohnstedt, John W (1968) 'The Infidel Scourge of God: The Turkish Menace as seen by German Pamphleteers of the Reformation Era' 58(9) *Transactions of the American Philosophical Society* 1.

Bonacich, Edna and Jake B Wilson (2006) 'Global Production and Distribution: Wal-Mart's Global Logistics Empire (with special reference to the China/Southern California Connection)' in Stanley D Brunn (ed), *Wal-Mart World: The World's Biggest Corporation in the Global Economy*. New York and London: Routledge, 227–42.

Bovilsky, Lara (2008) *Barbarous Play: Race on the English Renaissance Stage*. Minneapolis: University of Minnesota Press.

Brackman, Arnold C (1987) *The Other Nuremberg: The Untold Story of the Tokyo War Crimes Trials*. New York: William Morrow.

Brackman, Harold David (2000) '"A Calamity Almost Beyond Comprehension": Nazi Anti-Semitism and the Holocaust in the Thought of WEB Du Bois' 88(1) *American Jewish History* 53.

Braddick, Michael (2008) *God's Fury, England's Fire: A New History of the English Civil Wars*. London: Allen Lane.

Brand, Paul (1992) *The Origins of the English Legal Profession*. Oxford: Blackwell.

Brands, HW Jr (1988) *Cold Warriors: Eisenhower's Generation and American Foreign Policy*. New York: Columbia University Press.

Brantlinger, Patrick (1990) *Rule of Darkness: British Literature and Imperialism, 1830–1914*. Ithaca: Cornell University Press.

Breckenridge, Carol A and Peter van de Veer (1993) 'Orientalism and the Postcolonial Predicament' in Carol A Breckenridge and Peter van de Veer (eds), *Orientalism and the Postcolonial Predicament*. Philadelphia: University of Pennsylvania Press.

Brewer, Susan A (2009) *Why America Fights: Patriotism and War Propaganda from the Philippines to Iraq*. Oxford: Oxford University Press.

Brinkley, Alan (1995) *The End of Reform: New Deal Liberalism in Recession and War*. New York: Vintage.

Brown, Callum G (2006) *Religion and Society in Twentieth-Century Britain*. Harlow: Pearson Longman.

Brunn, Stanley D (ed) (2006) *Wal-Mart World: The World's Biggest Corporation in the Global Economy*. New York and London: Routledge.

Bucklin Society, bucklinsociety.net/legal_profession.htm.

Bull, Hedley, Benedict Kingsbury and Adam Roberts (eds) (1990) *Hugo Grotius and International Relations*. Oxford: Oxford University Press.

Burgess, Glenn (1993) *The Politics of the Ancient Constitution: An Introduction to English Political Thought, 1603–1642*. Pennsylvania: Pennsylvania State University Press.

Burgess, Glenn, Rowland Wymer and Jason Lawrence (eds) (2006) *The Accession of James I: Historical and Cultural Conquences*. New York: Palgrave Macmillan.

Burke, Roland (2010) *Decolonization and the Evolution of International Human Rights.* Philadelphia: University of Pennsylvania Press.

Burleigh, Michael (2001) *The Third Reich.* New York: Hill and Wang.

Burns, Jennifer (2009) *Goddess of the Market: Ayn Rand and the American Right.* Oxford: Oxford University Press.

Buswell, James O (1964) *Slavery, Segregation and Scripture.* Grand Rapids: William B Eerdmans.

Butler, Brian E (2003) 'Aesthetics and American Law' 27(1) *Legal Studies Forum* 203.

Butler, Jon, Grant Wacker and Randall Balmer (2008) *Religion in American Life: A Short History.* Oxford: Oxford University Press.

Calavita, Kitty (2007) 'Immigration Law, Race, and Identity' *Annual Review of Law and Social Science* Vol 3: 1–20.

Cane, Peter (ed) (2008) *Law and Religion in Theoretical and Historical Context.* Cambridge: Cambridge University Press.

Carbado, DW (2002) 'Race to the Bottom' 49 *UCLA Law Review* 1283.

Carlson, Elof Axel (2001) *The Unfit: A History of a Bad Idea.* New York: Cold Springs Harbor Press.

Carlyle, Thomas (1850) 'Occasional Discourse on the Negro Question', reprinted in the USA as 'West India Emancipation' in *Commercial Review of the South and West*, June 1850, Vol VIII (Old Series), Vol II, No 4 NS, pp 527–538. Edited by JD De Bow, New Orleans.

Carretta, Vincent (2005) *Equiano The African: Biography of a Self-Made Man.* Georgia: University of Georgia Press.

Carswell, Donald (ed) (1934) *Trial of Guy Fawkes and Others (The Gunpowder Plot).* London: William Hodge.

Cattelino, Jessica R (2007) 'Florida Seminole Gaming and Local Sovereign Interdependency' in D Cobb and L Fowler (eds), *Beyond Red Power: Rethinking Twentieth-Century American Indian Politics.* Santa Fe: School of American Research Press, pp 262–279.

Cattelino, Jessica R (2008) *High Stakes: Florida Seminole Gaming and Sovereignty.* Durham: Duke University Press.

Cerone, John P (2007) 'Dynamic Equilibrium: The Evolution of US Attitudes toward International Criminal Courts and Tribunals' 18(2) *European Journal of International Law* 277.

Chakravarty, G (2004) *The Indian Mutiny and the British Imagination.* Cambridge: Cambridge University Press.

Charlot, Martin (1999) 'Farming and Futility' in Peter Nabokov (ed), *Native American Testimony: A Chronicle of Indian-White Relations from Prophecy to the Present, 1492–2000.* 2nd edn, New York: Penguin.

Charter of Dartmouth College, December 13, 1769, www.dartmouth.edu/~govdocs/case/charter.htm.

Chatterjee, Partha (2004) *The Politics of the Governed: Reflections on Popular Politics in Most of the World.* Delhi: Permanent Black.

Chen, David W (2001) 'Rehabilitating Thomas Paine, Bit by Bony Bit' *New York Times*, 30 March 2001.

Chernus, Ira (1997) 'Eisenhower's Ideology in World War II' 23(4) *Armed Forces & Society* 595.

Chimni, BS (2006) 'Third World Approaches to International Law: A Manifesto' 8 *International Community Law Review* 2.

Churchill (2005) en.wikipedia.org/wiki/Ward_Churchill_misconduct_issues.

Clarke, Peter (2001) 'The Growth of Canon and Civil Law Studies, 1070–1535' in Susan L'Engle and Robert Gibbs (eds), *Illuminating the Law: Legal Manuscripts in Cambridge Collections*. London: Harvey Miller, pp 22–38.

Clarke, Peter (ed) (2009) *The Oxford Handbook of the Sociology of Religion*. Oxford: Oxford University Press.

Cohen, Arthur A (1970) *The Myth of the Judeo-Christian Tradition*. New York: Harper & Row.

Coleman, Michael (2007) *American Indian Children at School, 1850–1930*. Jackson: University Press of Mississippi.

Coll, Steve (2004) *Ghost Wars: The Secret History of the CIA, Afghanistan, and Bin Landen, from the Soviet Invasion to September 10, 2001*. New York: Penguin.

Collingridge, Vanessa (2003) *Captain Cook: The Life, Death, and Legacy of History's Greatest Explorer*. London: Ebury Press.

Collins, Patricia Hill (1998) 'The Tie that Binds: Race, Gender, and US Violence' 21(5) *Ethnic and Racial Studies* 917.

Conot, Robert E (1983) *Justice at Nuremberg*. New York: Harper & Row.

Conway, JS (1968) *The Nazi Persecution of the Churches 1933–45*. New York: Basic Books.

Cooke, Miriam (2002) 'Saving Brown Women' 28(1) *Signs: Journal of Women in Culture and Society* 468.

Cooke, Miriam (2006) 'Women's Jihad before and after 9/11' in Daniel J Sherman and Terry Nardin (eds), *Terror, Culture, Politics: Rethinking 9/11*. Bloomington: Indiana University Press, pp 165–83.

Coolsaet, Rik (ed) (2008) *Jihadi Terrorism and the Radicalisation Challenge in Europe*. Aldershot: Ashgate.

Cooper, Frederick and Ann Laura Stoler (eds) (1997) *Tensions of Empire: Colonial Cultures in a Bourgeois World*. Berkeley: University of California Press.

Cooper, Helen M (1996) '"Tracing the Route to England": Nineteenth-century Caribbean Interventions into English Debates on Race and Slavery' in Shearer West (ed), *The Victorians and Race*. Hertfordshire: Scolar Press, pp 194–212.

Coquillette, Daniel R (1992) *Francis Bacon*. Palo Alto: Stanford University Press.

Cormack, Bradin (2007) *A Power to Do Justice: Jurisdiction, English Literature, and the Rise of Common Law, 1509–1625*. Chicago: University of Chicago Press.

Cornwell, Rupert (2003) 'In God He Trusts: How George Bush Infused the White House with a Religious Spirit' *The Independent* (London), 21 February, 15.

Cravey, Altha J (1998) *Women and Work in Mexico's Maquiladoras*. New York: Rowman & Littlefield.

Crenshaw, Kimberlé W (1989) 'Demarginalizing the Intersection of Race and Sex: A Black Feminist Critique of Antidiscrimination Doctrine, Feminist Theory and Antiracist Politics' *University of Chicago Legal Forum* 139.

Crenshaw, Kimberlé W (1991) 'Mapping the Margins: Intersectionality, Identity Politics, and Violence against Women of Color' 43(6) *Stanford Law Review* 1241.

Crile, George (2003) *Charlie Wilson's War: The Extraordinary Story of the Largest Covert Operation in History*. New York: Atlantic Monthly Press.

Cummings, Mark (2004) *The Carlyle Encyclopedia*. Madison: Fairleigh Dickinson University Press.

Cummings, Scott L (2007) 'Law in the Labor Movement's Challenge to Wal-Mart: A Case Study of the Inglewood Site Fight' 95(5) *California Law Review* 1927.

Cushing, John D (1977) *The Laws of the Pilgrims: A Facsimile edition of The Book of the General Laws of the Inhabitants of the Jurisdiction of new-Plimouth. 1672 & 1685.* Plymouth: Michael Glazier Inc in cooperation with the Pilgrim Society.

D'Emilio, John (1998) *Sexual Politics, Sexual Communities.* 2dn edn, Chicago: University of Chicago Press.

Dabydeen, David (1987) *Hogarth's Blacks: Images of Blacks in Eighteenth Century English Art.* Athens: University of Georgia Press.

Darian-Smith, Eve (1999) *Bridging Divides: The Channel Tunnel and English Legal Identity in the New Europe.* Berkeley: University of California Press.

Darian-Smith, Eve (2002) 'Savage Capitalists: Law and Politics Surrounding Indian Casino Operations in California' 26 *Studies in Law, Politics, and Society* 109.

Darian-Smith, Eve (2003) *New Capitalists: Law, Politics and Identity Surrounding Casino Gaming on Native American Land.* Belmont: Wadsworth (Case Studies in Contemporary Social Issues).

Darian-Smith, Eve (2007) 'Precedents of Injustice: Thinking about History in Law and Society Scholarship' 41 *Studies in Law, Politics, and Society* 61, special issue: *Law and Society Reconsidered.*

David, Henry (1936) *The History of the Haymarket Affair: A Study in American Social-Revolutionary and Labor Movements.* New York: Russell & Russell.

Davis, David Brion (2006) *Inhuman Bondage: The Rise and Fall of Slavery in the New World.* Oxford: Oxford University Press.

Day, David (1997) *Claiming a Continent: A New History of Australia.* Sydney: HarperCollins.

Debusmann, Bernd (2006) 'Radio Hoax Reveals US Anti-Muslim Sentiment in US, fear and distrust of Muslims runs deep' Reuters, 1 December.

Deflem, Mathieu (2007) 'Legal Profession' in George Ritzer (ed), *The Blackwell Encyclopedia of Sociology.* Oxford: Blackwell, pp 2583–84.

Deflem, Mathieu (2008) *Sociology of Law: Visions of a Scholarly Tradition.* Cambridge: Cambridge University Press.

Degler, Carol M (1991) *In Search of Human Nature: The Decline and Revival of Darwinism in American Social Thought.* New York: Oxford University Press.

Demerath, NJ (2001) 'Secularization Extended: From Religious Myth to Cultural Commonplace' in Richard K Fenn (ed), *The Blackwell Companion to Sociology of Religion.* Oxford: Blackwell, pp 211–28.

Derrida, Jacques (1990) 'Force of Law: The Mystical Foundation of Authority' 11 *Cardozo Law Review* 919.

Desmond, Adrian and James Moore (2009) *Darwin's Sacred Cause: How a Hatred of Slavery Shaped Darwin's Views on Human Evolution.* Boston: Houghton Mifflin Harcourt.

Diamond, Larry, Marc F Plattner and Daniel Brumberg (eds) (2003) *Islam and Democracy in the Middle East.* Baltimore: Johns Hopkins University Press.

Dillenberger, John (1999) *Images and Relics: Theological Perspectives and Visual Images in Sixteenth-Century Europe.* New York: Oxford University Press.

Dimaggio, Anthony R (2008) *Mass Media, Mass Propaganda: Examining American News in the 'War on Terror'.* Plymouth: Lexington Books.

Dixon, Scott C (2002) *The Reformation in Germany.* Oxford: Blackwell.

Docena, Herbert (2003) 'Will the Real Collaborators Please Stand Up?' *Asia Times*, 18 November.

Domke, David (2004) *God Willing? Political Fundamentalism in the White House, the 'War on Terror', and the Echoing Press.* Ann Arbor: University of Michigan Press.

Douzinas, Costas, Peter Goodrich and Yifat Hachamovitch (1994) *Politics, Postmodernity and Critical Legal Studies: The Legality of the Contingent.* Oxford: Routledge.

Du Bois, WEB (1903) *The Souls of Black Folks.* New York: Bantam Books (1989).

Du Bois, WEB (1947) *An Appeal to the World.* Prepared for the NAACP, New York.

Du Bois (1952) 'The Negro and the Warsaw Ghetto' in Phil Zuckerman (ed), *The Social Theory of WEB Du Bois.* Thousand Oaks: Pine Forge, pp 45–46.

Dudas, Jeffrey R (2005) 'In the Name of Equal Rights: "Special" Rights and the Politics of Resentment in Post-Civil Rights America' 39 *Law & Society Review* 723.

Dudas, Jeffrey R (2008) *The Cultivation of Resentment: Treaty Rights and the New Right.* Palo Alto: Stanford University Press.

Durston, Christopher (1995) *James I.* London: Routledge.

Dutton, Geoffrey (1982) *In Search of Edward Eyre.* Melbourne: Macmillan.

Dyck, Ian (ed) (1987) *Citizen of the World: Essays on Thomas Paine.* London: Christopher Helm.

Ehrenfreund, Norbert (2007) *The Nuremberg Legacy.* New York: Palgrave Macmillan.

Ehrenreich, Barbara (2001) *Nickel and Dimed: On (Not) Getting by in America.* New York: Metropolitan Books.

Eisenhower, Dwight D (1948) *Crusade in Europe.* London: W Heinemann.

Eisenstein, EL (1993) *The Printing Revolution in Early Modern Europe.* Cambridge: Cambridge University Press.

Ellis, Joseph E (2005) *His Excellency: George Washington.* New York: Vintage.

Elson, John (1966) 'Is God Dead?' *Time Magazine,* 8 April.

Erickson, Peter and Clark Hulse (eds) (2000) *Early Modern Visual Culture: Representation, Race, Empire in Renaissance England.* Philadelphia: University of Pennsylvania Press.

Evans, Julie (2005) *Edward Eyre, Race and Colonial Governance.* Dunedin: University of Otago Press.

Ewing, Sally (1987) 'Formal Justice and the Spirit of Capitalism: Max Weber's Sociology of Law' 21 *Law and Society Review* 487.

Falk, Richard (2002) *The Great Terror War.* New York: Olive Branch Press..

Falk, Richard (2009) Achieving Human Rights. New York: Routledge.

Falk, Richard A, Gabriel Kolko and Robert Jay Lifton (eds) (1971) *Crimes of War: A Legal, Political-Documentary, and Psychological Inquiry into the Responsibility of Leaders, Citizens, and Soldiers for Criminal Acts in Wars.* New York: Random House.

Featherstone, Lisa (2004) *Selling Women Short: The Landmark Battle for Workers' Rights at Wal-Mart.* New York: Basic Books.

Feldman, Noah (2005) *Divided By God: America's Church-State Problem – and What We Should Do About It.* New York: Farrar, Straus and Giroux.

Feldman, Stephen M (1998) *Please Don't Wish Me a Merry Christmas: A Critical History of the Separation of Church and State.* New York: New York University Press.

Fenn, Richard K (ed) (2003) *The Blackwell Companion to the Sociology of Religion.* Oxford: Blackwell.

Fields, A Belden (2003) *Rethinking Human Rights for the New Millennium.* Basingstoke: Palgrave Macmillan.

Fineman, Howard et al (2003) 'Bush and God' *Newsweek,* 10 March.

Fineman, Howard and Tamara Lipper (2004) 'The Gospel According to George' *Newsweek,* 28 April.

Fisher, James T (2008) *Communion of Immigrants: A History of Catholics in America.* Oxford: Oxford University Press.

Fishman, Charles (2006) *The Wal-Mart Effect: How the World's Most Powerful Company Really Works—and How It's Transforming the American Economy.* New York: Penguin.

Fitzpatrick, Peter (1992) *The Mythology of Modern Law.* London: Routledge.

Fitzpatrick, Peter (2004) '"We know what it is when you do not ask us": the unchallengeable nation' 8 *Law Text Culture* 263.

Fitzgerald, Kathleen J (2007) *Beyond White Ethnicity: Developing a Sociological Understanding of Native American Identity Reclamation.* Lanham: Lexington Books.

Fletcher, Matthew LM (2006) 'The Iron Cold of the Marshall Trilogy' 82(3) *North Dakota Law Review* 627.

Flood, John (1998) 'The Book in Reformation Germany' in Jean-Francois Gilmont (ed), *The Reformation and the Book* (translated by Karin Maag). Aldershot: Ashgate, pp 21–103.

Floyd-Wilson, Mary (2006) *English Ethnicity and Race in Early Modern Drama.* Cambridge: Cambridge University Press.

Foner, Eric (2005 revised edition) *Tom Paine and Revolutionary America.* Oxford: Oxford University Press.

Foner, Philip S (1986) *May Day: A Short History of the International Workers' Holiday 1886–1986.* New York: International Publishers.

Forbath, William (1992) 'Law and the Shaping of Labor Politics in the United States and England' in Christopher L Tomlins and Andrew J King (eds), *Labor Law in America: Historical and Critical Essays.* Baltimore: Johns Hopkins University Press, pp 201–30.

Forster, John (1875) *Life of Charles Dickens.* London: James R Osgood.

Foucault, Michel (1995) *Discipline and Punish: The Birth of the Prison.* 2nd edn, New York: Vintage.

Frank, Robert (2009) 'Nickel and Dimed' *New York Times Sunday Book Review*, 2 August, p 15.

Franklin, Julian H (2009) *Jean Bodin and the Rise of Absolutist Theory* (Cambridge Studies in the History and Theory of Politics). Cambridge: Cambridge University Press.

Fraser, Antonia (1996) *Faith and Treason: The Story of the Gunpowder Plot.* New York: Nan A Talese Doubleday.

Fried, Albert (1990) *Nightmare in Red: The McCarthy Era in Perspective.* Oxford: Oxford University Press.

Gage, Beverly (2009) *The Day Wall Street Exploded: A Story of America in its First Age of Terror.* Oxford: Oxford University Press.

Galenson, David W (1981) *White Servitude in Colonial America: An Economic Analysis.* Cambridge: Cambridge University Press.

Galton, Francis (1883) *Inquiries into Human Faculty and its Development.* London: Macmillan.

Garner, Steven (2003) *Racism in the Irish Experience.* London: Pluto.

Garroutte, Eva Marie (2003) *Real Indians: Identity and the Survival of Native America.* Berkeley: University of California Press.

Gay, Peter (1968) *The Enlightenment: An Interpretation. The Science of Freedom.* New York: WW Norton.

Geck, Elisabeth (1968) *Johannes Gutenberg: From Lead Letter to Computer.* Bad Godesberg: Inter Nationes.

Gentles, Ian (2009) 'The Politics of Fairfax's Army, 1645–9' in John Adamson (ed), *The English Civil War* (Problems in Focus). New York: Palgrave Macmillan, pp 175–201.

George, Susan (2008) *Hijacking America: How the Religious and Secular Right Changed What Americans Think.* New York: Polity.

Gilmont, Jean-Francois (1998) 'Printing at the Dawn of the Sixteenth Century' in Jean-Francois Gilmont (ed), *The Reformation and the Book* (translated by Karin Maag). Aldershot: Ashgate, pp 10–20.

Gilroy, Paul (1991) *'There Ain't No Black in the Union Jack': The Cultural Politics of Race and Nation.* With a new foreword by Houston A Baker Jr. Chicago: University of Chicago Press.

Goldberg-Hiller, Jonathan and Neal Milner (2003) 'Rights as Excess: Understanding the Politics of Special Rights' 28(4) *Law & Social Inquiry* 1075.

Golinski, Jan (1992) *Science as Popular Culture: Chemistry and Enlightenment in Britain, 1760–1820.* Cambridge: Cambridge University Press.

Goodrich, Peter (1996) *Law in the Courts of Love: Literature and Other Minor Jurisprudences.* New York: Routledge.

Goodrich, Peter (1999) 'The Iconography of Nothing: Blank Spaces and the Representation of Law in Edward VI and the Pope' in Costas Douzinas and Lynda Neal (eds), *Law and the Image: The Authority of Art and the Aesthetics of Law.* Chicago: University of Chicago Press, pp 89–114.

Gordon, Robert W (2008) 'The American Legal Profession, 1870–2000' in Michael Grossberg and Christopher Tomlins (eds), *The Cambridge History of Law in America, Vol III.* Cambridge: Cambridge University Press, pp 73–126.

Gordon, Shirley C (1998) *Our Cause for His Golory: Christianization and Emancipation in Jamaica.* Barbados: University of the West Indies Press.

Gorski, Philip S (2000) 'Historicizing the Secularization Debate: Church, State, and Society in Late Medieval and Early Modern Euorpe, ca 1300–1700' 65(1) *American Sociological Review* 138.

Gorski, Philip S (2003) *The Disciplinary Revolution: Calvinism and the Rise of the State in Early Modern Europe.* Chicago: University of Chicago Press.

Gossett, Thomas F (1997) *Race: The History of an Idea in America.* New York: Oxford University Press.

Gould, Stephen Jay (1996) *The Mismeasure of Man.* Revised and expanded version, New York: WW Norton.

Grabham, Emily, Davina Cooper, Kane Krishnadsas and Didi Herman (eds) (2008) *Intersectionality and Beyond: Law, Power and the Politics of Location.* Oxford: Routledge Cavendish.

Green, James (2006) *Death in the Haymarket: A Story of Chicago, the First Labor Movement and the Bombing that Divided Gilded Age America.* New York: Pantheon.

Greenberg, Karen J and Joshua L Dratel (eds) (2005) *The Torture Papers: The Road to Abu Grhaib.* Cambridge: Cambridge University Press.

Gross, Daniel (1997) *Forbes Greatest Business Stories of All Time.* New York: John Wiley.

Gusterson, Hugh and Catherine Besteman (eds) (2009) *The Insecure American: How we got here and what we should do about it.* Berkeley: University of California Press.

Hajjar, Lisa (2004) 'Torture and the Future' *Middle East Report,* May.

Hajjar, Lisa (2005) 'From Nuremberg to Guantanamo: International Law and American Power Politics' in Jeremy Brecher, Jill Cutler and Brendan Smith (eds), *In the Name of Democracy: American War Crimes in Iraq and Beyond.* New York: Metropolitan Books.

Hajjar, Lisa (2009) 'American Torture: The Price Paid, the Lessons Learned' *Middle East Report*, Summer.

Halder, Piyel (1994) 'In and Out of Court: On Topographies of Law and the Architecture of Court Buildings (A Case Study of the Supreme Court of Israel)' 7(20) *International Journal for the Semiotics of Law* 185.

Haldar, Piyel (1999) 'The Function of the Ornament in Quintillian, Alberti and Court Architecture' in Coustas Douzinas and Linda Nead (eds), *Law and the Image: The Authority of Art and the Aesthetics of Law*. Chicago: University of Chicago Press, pp 117–36.

Hall, Catherine (2000) 'The Nation Within and Without' in Catherine Hall, Keith McClelland and Jane Rendall (eds), *Defining the Victorian Nation: Class, Race, Gender and the Reform Act of 1867*. Cambridge: Cambridge University Press, pp 179–233.

Hall, Catherine (2002) *Civilizing Subjects: Metropole and Colony in the English Imagination, 1830–1867*. Oxford: Polity Press.

Hall, John R (2009) *Apocalypse: From Antiquity to the Empire of Modernity*. New York: Polity Press.

Hall, Kermit L and Peter Karsten (2009) *The Magic Mirror: Law in American History*. 2nd edn, Oxford: Oxford University Press.

Hall, Stuart (1990) 'Cultural Identity and Diaspora' in Jonathan Rutherford (ed), *Identity, Community, Culture, Difference*. London: Lawrence & Wishart.

Hamburger, Philip (2002) *Separation of Church and State*. Cambridge: Harvard University Press.

Hamilton, Malcolm (1995) *The Sociology of Religion: Theoretical and Comparative Perspectives*. 2nd edn, London: Routledge.

Hamor, Ralph (1615) *A True Discourse of the Present Estate of Virginia, 1615*. Reproduced in Edward Wright Haile (ed) (1998) *Jamestown Narratives*. Champlain: Roundhouse.

Hannaford, Ivan (1996) *Race: The History of an Idea in the West*. Baltimore: Johns Hopkins University Press.

Harbury, Jennifer K (2005) *Truth, Torture, and the American Way: The History and Consequences of US Involvement in Torture*. Boston: Beacon Press.

Hariot, Thomas (1972) *A briefe and true Report of the new found Land of Virginia*. The complete 1590 edition with 28 engravings by Theodor de Bry, after the drawings of John White and other illustrations. With a new introduction by Paul Huton of the British Museum. Mineola: Dover Publications.

Harris, Tim (2006) *Restoration: Charles II and His Kingdoms, 1660–1685*. New York: Penguin Global.

Harris, Tim (2008) *Revolution: The Great Crisis of the British Monarchy, 1685–1720*. New York: Penguin Global.

Harris, Whitney R (1954) *Tyranny on Trial: Evidence at Nuremberg*. Dallas: Southern Methodist University Press.

Harrison, Patricia G (2000) *Connecting Links: The British and American Woman Suffrage Movements, 1900–1914*. Santa Barbara: Praeger.

Hartmann, Douglas, Xuefeng Zhang and William Wischstadt (2005) 'One (Multicultural) Nation Under God? Changing Uses and Meanings of the Term "Judeo-Christian" in the American Media' 4(4) *Journal of Media and Religion* 207.

Harvey, David (2007) *A Brief History of Neoliberalism*. Oxford: Oxford University Press.

Havety-Stacke, Donna T (2009) *America's Forgotten Holiday: May Day and Nationalism, 1867–1960*. New York: New York University Press.

Hawkin, David J (ed) (2004) *The Twenty-first Century Confronts its Gods: Globalization, Technology and War*. Albany: State University of New York.

Hay, Denys (1957) *Europe: The Emergence of an Idea*. Edinburgh: Edinburgh University Press.

Hazlitt, William (ed) (1856) *The Table Talk of Martin Luther*. London: HG Bohn.

Hefelbower, SG (1918) *The Relation of John Locke to English Deism*. Chicago: University of Chicago Press.

Heller, Anne C (2009) *Ayn Rand and the World she Made*. New York: Nan A Talese Doubleday.

Heller, Dana (ed) (2005) *The Selling of 9/11: How a National Tragedy Became a Commodity*. New York: Palgrave Macmillan.

Helmholz, RH (2008) 'Western Canon Law' in John Witte Jr and Frank S Alexander (eds), *Christianity and Law: An Introduction. Cambridge*: Cambridge University Press, pp 71–88.

Herberg, Will (1960) *Protestant—Catholic—Jew: An Essay in American Sociology*. With a new introduction by Martin E Marty. Chicago: University of Chicago Press.

Herberg, Will (1965) '"Civil Rights" and Violence: Who Are the Guilty Ones?' *National Review*, 7 September.

Herman, Didi (2008) '"I do not attach great significance to it": Taking Note of "The Holocaust" in English Case Law' 17(4) *Social & Legal Studies* 427.

Hesse, Barnor (2000) 'Diasporicity: Black Britain's Post-Colonial Formations' in Barnor Hesse (ed), *Un/settled Multiculturalisms: Diasporas, Entanglements, Transruptions*. London: Zed Books, pp 96–120.

Heuman, Gad (1994) '*The Killing Time*': *The Morant Bay Rebellion in Jamaica*. Knoxville: University of Tennessee Press.

Hewitt, Steve (2008) *The British War on Terror: Terrorism and Counter-Terrorism on the Home Front Since 9/11*. London: Continuum.

Hibbitts, Bernard J (1992) 'Coming to Our Senses: Communication and Legal Expression in Performance Cultures' 41(4) *Emory Law Journal* 873.

Higham, John (1995) *Strangers in the Land: Patterns of American Nativism, 1860–1925*. New Brunswick: Rutgers University Press.

Hill, Christopher (1970) *God's Englishman: Oliver Cromwell and the English Revolution*. New York: Dial Press.

Hill, Christopher (1975) *Change and Continuity in Seventeenth-Century England*. Cambridge: Harvard University Press.

Hill, Christopher (1986) *Religion and Politics in 17th Century England* (Collected Essays of Christopher Hill, Vol 2). Amherst: University of Massachusetts Press.

Hillenbrand, Carole (2004) 'The Legacy of the Crusades' in Thomas F Madden (ed), *Crusades: An Illustrated History*. Ann Arbor: University of Michigan Press, pp 202–11.

Hirsch, Rudolf (1967) *Printing, Selling and Reading 1450–1550*. Wiesbaden: Otto Harrassowitz.

Hitchens, Christopher (2006) *Thomas Paine's Rights of Man*. New York: Atlantic Monthly Press.

Hobsbawm, Eric (2003) [1975] *The Age of Capital, 1848–1875*. London: Abacus.

Hobsbawm, Eric (2007) *Globalization, Democracy and Terror*. London: Little, Brown.

Hochschild, Adam (2005) *Bury the Chains: Prophets and Rebels in the Fight to Free an Empire's Slaves*. Boston: Houghton Mifflin.

Hocking, Jenny (2004) *Terror Laws: ASIO, Counter-Terrorism and the Threat to Democracy.* Sydney: University of New South Wales Press.

Hodgson, Carol M (2004) 'When I Go Home I'm Going to Talk Indian', www.twofrog.com/hodgson.html.

Hoffer, Peter Charles (1998) *Law and People in Colonial America.* Revised edn, Baltimore: Johns Hopkins University Press.

Hollis, Patricia (1980) 'Anti-Slavery and British Working-class Radicalism in the Years of Reform' in Christine Bolt and Seymour Drescher (eds), *Anti-Slavery, Religion and Reform: Essays in Memory of Roger Anstey.* Folkestone: Dawson, Archon, pp 294–318.

Holmes, Clive (2006) *Why Was Charles I Executed?* London: Hambledon Continuum.

Holmes, David L (2006) *The Faiths of the Founding Fathers.* Oxford: Oxford University Press.

Holmes, Richard (2009) *The Age of Wonder: How the Romantic Generation Discovered the Beauty and Terror of Science.* New York: Pantheon.

Horn, James (2006) *A Land as God Made it: Jamestown and the Birth of America.* New York: Basic Books.

Horwitz, Morton J (1977) *The Transformation of the Legal American Law, 1780–1860.* Cambridge: Harvard University Press.

Houston, SJ (1973) *James I Seminar Studies in History.* London: Longman.

Hsia, R Po-Chia (2004) 'A Time for Monsters: Monstrous Births, Propaganda, and the German Reformation' in Laura Lunger Knoppers and Joan B Landes (eds), *Monstrous Bodies/Political Monstrosities.* Ithaca: Cornell University Press, pp 67–92.

Hulsebosch, Daniel J (2006) 'The Ancient Constitution and the Expanding Empire: Sir Edward Coke's British Jurisprudence' in Glenn Burgess, Jason Lawrence and Rowland Wymer (eds), *The Accession of James I: Historical and Cultural Consequences.* New York: Palgrave Macmillan, pp 187–207.

Human Rights Watch (1996) *No Guarantees: Sex Discrimination in Mexico's Maquiladora Sector*, 1 August 1996, B806, www.unhcr.org/refworld/docid/3ae6a7f110.html (accessed 8 December 2009).

Hunt, Lynn (2008) *Inventing Human Rights.* New York: WW Norton.

Ignatiev, Noel (1995) *How the Irish Became White.* New York: Routledge.

Ishay, Micheline (2008) *The History of Human Rights: From Ancient Times to the Globalization Era.* 2nd edn, Berkeley: University of California Press.

Jackson, Robert (1954) *Memorandum by Mr Justice Jackson.* 15 May, brown file, Robert H Jackson Papers, Library of Congress.

Jacobs, Margaret D (2009) *White Mother to a Dark Race: Settler Colonialism, Maternalism, and the Removal of Indigenous Children in the American West and Australia, 1880–1940.* Lincoln: University of Nebraska Press.

Jacobson, Matthew Frye (1998) *Whiteness of a Different Color: European Immigrants and the Alchemy of Race.* Cambridge: Harvard University Press.

Jahoda, Gustav (1999) *Images of Savages: Ancient Roots of Modern Prejudice in Western Culture.* London: Routledge.

Jaimes, M Annette (1992) 'Federal Indian Identification Policy: A Usurpation of Indigenous Sovereignty in North America' in M Jannette Jaimes (ed), *The State of Native America: Genocide, Colonization, and Resistance.* Boston: South End Press, pp 123–38.

Jarmakani, Amira (2008) *Imagining Arab Womanhood: The Cultural Mythology of Veils, Harems, and Belly Dancers in the US.* New York: Palgrave Macmillan.

Jenkin, Louis et al (1993) *International Law.* St Paul: West Publishing Co.

Jensen, De Lamar (1975) *Confrontation at Worms: Martin Luther and the Diet of Worms. With a complete translation of the Edict of Worms.* Utah: Brigham University Press.

Jewett, Robert (2008) *Mission and Menace: Four Centuries of American Religious Zeal.* Minneapolis: Fortress Press.

Jewett, Robert and John Shelton Lawrence (2003) *Captain America and the Crusade Against Evil: The Dilemma of Zealous Nationalism.* Grand Rapids: William B Eerdmans.

Jordan, Don and Michael Walsh (2008) *White Cargo: The Forgotten History of Britain's White Slaves in America.* New York: New York University Press.

Judt, Tony (2006) *Postwar: A History of Europe Since 1945.* Harmondsworth: Penguin.

Kabbani, Rana (1994) *Imperial Fictions: Europe's Myths of Orient.* London: Pandora Press.

Kahn, Paul W (1999) *The Cultural Study of Law: Reconstructing Legal Scholarship.* Chicago: University of Chicago Press.

Kampfner, John (2003) 'The British Neoconservatives' *New Statesman*, 12 May.

Kaplan, Amy (2002) *The Anarchy of Empire in the Making of US Culture.* Cambridge: Harvard University Press.

Kaye, Harvey J (2005) *Thomas Paine and the Promise of America.* New York: Hill and Wang.

Keane, John (2003) *Tom Paine: A Political Life.* New York: Grove Press.

Keddie, Nikki R (2007) *Women in the Middle East: Past and Present.* Princeton: Princeton University Press.

Keen, Sam (1986) *Faces of the Enemy: Reflections of the Hostile Imagination.* New York: Harper & Row.

Kelley, Donald R (2000) *The Human Measure: Social Thought in the Western Legal Tradition.* Cambridge: Harvard University Press.

Kelman, Mark (1990) *A Guide to Critical Legal Studies.* Cambridge: Harvard University Press.

Kelsey, Sean (2001) 'Staging the Trial of Charles I' in Jason Peacey (ed), *The Regicides and the Execution of Charles I.* Basingstoke: Palgrave, pp 71–93.

Kennedy, DM (1980) *Over Here: The First World War and American Society.* New York: Oxford University Press.

King, Richard H (2004) *Race, Culture, and the Intellectuals 1940–1970.* Washington, DC: Woodrow Wilson Center Press; and Baltimore: Johns Hopkins University Press.

Kirsch, Adam (2008) *Benjamin Disraeli.* New York: Nextbook/Schocken.

Kirsch, Jonathan (2009) *The Grand Inquisitor's Manuel: A History of Terror in the Name of God.* New York: HarperOne.

Klein, Christina (2003) *Cold War Orientalism: Asia in the Middlebrow Imagination, 1945–1961.* Berkeley: University of California Press.

Kluger, Richard (2004) *Simple Justice: The History of Brown v Board of Education and Black America's Struggle for Equality.* New York: Vintage.

Konefsky, Alfred S (2008) 'The Legal Profession: From the Revolution to the Civil War' in Michael Grossberg and Christopher Tomlins (eds), *The Cambridge History of Law in America, Vol II.* Cambridge: Cambridge University Press, pp 68–105.

Kostal, Rande W (2005) *A Jurisprudence of Power: Victorian Empire and the Rule of Law.* New York: Oxford University Press.

Kramnick, Isaac (ed) (1995) *The Portable Enlightenment Reader.* New York: Penguin.

Kramnick, Isaac and R Lawrence Moore (2005) *The Godless Constitution: A Moral Defense of the Secular State.* New York: WW Norton.

Kühl, Stefan (1994) *The Nazi Connection: Eugenics, American Racism, and German National Socialism.* New York: Oxford University Press.

Kynaston, David (2007) *Austerity Britain 1945–51*. London: Bloomsbury.

L'Engle, Susan (2001) 'Layout and Decoration' in Susan L'Engle and Robert Gibbs, *Illuminating the Law: Legal Manuscripts in Cambridge Collections*. London: Harvey Miller, pp 54–74.

Lake, Peter with Michael Questier (2002) *The Anti-Christ's Lewd Hat: Protestants, Papists and Players in Post-Reformation England*. New Haven: Yale University Press.

Lambert, Frank (2006) *The Founding Fathers and the Place of Religion in America*. Princeton: Princeton University Press.

Lambert, Frank (2008) *Religion in American Politics: A Short History*. Princeton: Princeton University Press.

Larson, Edward J (1997) *Summer for the Gods: The Scopes Trial and America's Continuing Debate Over Science and Religion*. New York: Basic Books.

Lauren, Paul Gordon (1983) 'First Principles of Racial Equality: History and the Politics and Diplomacy of Human Rights Provisions in the United Nations Charter' 5(1) *Human Rights Quarterly* 1.

Lauren, Paul Gordon (2003) *The Evolution of International Human Rights*. 2nd edn, Philadelphia: University of Pennsylvania Press.

Lawrence, Bonita (2004) *'Real' Indians and Others: Mixed Blood Urban Native Peoples and Indigenous Nationhood*. Lincoln: University of Nebraska Press.

Lerner, Michael (2006) *The Left Hand of God: Taking Back Our Country from the Religious Right*. New York: HarperOne.

Lestringant, Frank (1997) *Cannibals: The Discovery and Representations and of the Cannibal from Columbus to Jules Verne*. Translated by Rosemary Morris. Berkeley: University of California Press.

Levack, Brian P (1987) *The Formation of the British State: England, Scotland, and the Union 1603–1707*. Oxford: Clarendon.

Levit, Nancy and Robert RM Verchick (2006) *Feminist Legal Theory: A Primer*. New York: New York University Press.

Lewis, David Levering (2000) *WEB Du Bois: The Fight for Equality and the American Century, 1919–1963*. New York: H Holt.

Lewis, David Levering (2009) *God's Crucible: Islam and the Making of Modern Europe, 570–1215*. New York: WW Norton.

Lewis, Joseph (1947) *Thomas Paine, author of the Declaration of Independence*. New York: Freethought Press.

Lichtenstein, Nelson (ed) (2006) *Wal-Mart: The Face of Twenty-First Century Capitalism*. New York: New Press.

Lichtenstein, Nelson (2009) *The Retail Revolution: How Wal-Mart Created a Brave New World of Business*. New York: Metropolitan Books.

Likhovski, Assaf (1999) 'Protestantism and the Rationalization of English Law: A Variation on a Theme by Weber' 33(2) *Law and Society Review* 365.

Lilla, Mark (2007) *The Stillborn God: Religion, Politics, and the Modern West*. New York: Alfred A Knopf.

Limerick, Patricia Nelson (1987) *The Legacy of Conquest: The Unbroken Past of the American West*. New York: WW Norton.

Lincoln, Bruce (2006) *Holy Terrors: Thinking about Religion After September 11*. 2nd edn, Chicago: University of Chicago Press.

Lindgren, Erika Lauren (2009) *Sensual Encounters: Monastic Women and Spirituality in Medieval Germany*. New York: Columbia University Press.

Lindley, Keith (1997) *Popular Politics and Religion in Civil War London.* Aldershot: Scolar Press.

Linker, Damon (2006) *The Theocons: Secular America Under Siege.* New York: Doubleday.

Lipman, Joanne (2009) 'The Mismeasure of Woman' *New York Times,* 24 October, p 19.

Liss, Julia E (1998) 'Diasporic Identities: The Science and Politics of Race in the Work of Franz Boas and WEB Du Bois, 1894–1919' 13(2) *Cultural Anthropology* 127.

Little, Douglas (2001) *American Orientalism: The United States and the Middle East since 1945.* Chapel Hill: University of North Carolina Press.

Little, Patrick (ed) (2009) *Oliver Cromwell: New Perspectives.* Basingstoke: Palgrave Macmillan.

Locke, John (1690) *An Essay Concerning Human Understanding.* Oxford: Clarendon (1924).

Lombardo, Paul A (2002) '"The American Breed": Nazi Eugenics and the Origins of the Pioneer Fund' 65 *Albany Law Review* 743.

Lombardo, Paul A (2008) *Three Generations, No Imbeciles: Eugenics, the Supreme Court, and Buck v Bell.* Baltimore: Johns Hopkins University Press.

Loomba, Ania and Jonathan Burton (eds) (2007) *Race in Early Modern England: A Documentary Companion.* Basingstoke: Palgrave Macmillan.

Lopez, Ian F Haney (1996) *White By Law: The Legal Construction of Race.* New York: New York University Press.

Lorimer, Douglas A (1978) *Colour, Class, and the Victorians: English Attitudes to the Negro in the Mid-Nineteenth Century.* Leicester: Leicester University Press.

Lyons, Jonathan (2001) 'Bush enters Mideast's rhetorical minefield' Reuters, 21 September. hv.greenspun.com/bboard/q-and-a-fetch-msg.tcl?msg_id=006SM3.

Maalouf, Amin (1989) *Crusades Through Arab Eyes.* New York: Schocken.

MacCulloch, Diarmaid (2003) *The Reformation: Europe's House Divided 1490–1700.* New York: Penguin.

MacDougall, Hugh A (1982) *Racial Myths in English History: Trojans, Teutons, and Anglo-Saxons.* Hanover: University of New England Press.

McGrath, Alister (2004) *The Twilight of Atheism: The Rise and Fall of Disbelief in the Modern World.* New York: Doubleday.

Macinnes, Allan I (2009) 'The "Scottish Moment", 1638–45' in John Adamson (ed), *The English Civil War* (Problems in Focus). New York: Palgrave Macmillan, pp 125–52.

McLeod, Hugh (1984) *Religion and the Working Class in Nineteenth-century Britain.* Basingstoke: Macmillan.

McLeod, Hugh (2000) *Secularization in Western Europe, 1848–1914.* Basingstoke: Palgrave Macmillan.

MacMillan, Ken (2006) *Sovereignty and Possession in the English New World: The Legal Foundations of Empire 1576–1640.* Cambridge: Cambridge University Press.

MacMillan, Margaret (2009) *Dangerous Games: The Uses and Abuses of History.* New York: Modern Library.

Macpherson, CB (1962) *The Political Theory of Possessive Individualism.* Oxford: Oxford University Press.

McVeigh, Robbie and Bill Rolston (2009) 'Civilizing the Irish' 51(1) *Race & Class* 2.

Maga, Tim (2001) *Judgment at Tokyo: The Japanese War Crimes Trial.* Lexington: University of Kentucky Press.

Mahmood, Saba (2005) *Politics of Piety: The Islamic Revival and the Feminist Subject.* Princeton: Princeton University Press.

Maland, David (1982) *Europe in the Sixteenth Century*. 2nd edn, London: Macmillan.

Mancall, Peter C (1995) *Envisioning America: English Plans for the Colonization of North America, 1580–1640*. Boston: Bedford Books.

Mark, Joan T (1988) *A Stranger in her Native Land: Alice Fletcher and the American Indians*. Lincoln: Nebraska University Press.

Marrus, Michael Robert (1997) *The Nuremberg War Crimes Trial, 1945–46: A Documentary History* (Bedford Series in History and Culture). Boston: Bedford Books.

Martin, David (2005) *On Secularization: Toward a Revised General Theory*. Aldershot: Ashgate.

Matheson, Peter (2000) *The Imaginative World of the Reformation*. Edinburgh: T & T Clark.

Mathews, Donald G (1980) 'Religion and Slavery: The Case of the American South' in Christine Bolt and Seymour Drescher (eds), *Anti-Slavery, Religion and Reform: Essays in Memory of Roger Anstey*. Folkestone: Dawson, Archon, pp 207–32.

Mawani, Renisa (2009) *Colonial Proximities: Crossracial Encounters and Juridical Truths in British Columbia, 1871–1921*. Vancouver: University of British Columbia Press.

Mayhall, Laura E Nym (2003) *The Militant Suffrage Movement: Citizenship and Resistance in Britain, 1860–1930*. Oxford: Oxford University Press.

Mensch, Elizabeth (1990) 'The History of Mainstream Legal Thought' in David Kairys (ed), *The Politics of Law: A Progressive Critique*. New York: Pantheon, pp 13–37.

Mensch, Elizabeth (2001) 'Christianity and the Roots of Liberalism' in Michael W McConnell, Robert F Cochran, Jr and Angela C Carmella (eds), *Christian Perspectives on Legal Thought*. New Haven: Yale University Press, pp 54–72.

Meriam Report (1926), www.alaskool.org/native_ed/research_reports/IndianAdmin/Indian_Admin_Problms.html.

Mernissi, Fatima (1987) *Beyond the Veil: Male-Female Dynamics in the Modern Muslim Society*. Bloomington: Indiana University Press.

Merry, Sally Engle (2004) 'Colonial and Postcolonial Law' in Austin Sarat (ed), *The Blackwell Companion to Law and Society*. Oxford: Blackwell, pp 569–88.

Merry, Sally Engle (2006) *Human Rights & Gender Violence: Translating International Law into Local Justice*. Chicago: University of Chicago Press.

Michalski, Sergiusz (1993) *The Reformation and the Visual Arts: The Protestant Image Question in Western and Eastern Europe*. London: Routledge.

Micklethwait, John and Adrian Woolridge (2009) *God is Back: How the Global Revival of Faith is Changing the World*. New York: Penguin.

Midgley, Clare (1995) *Women Against Slavery: The British Campaigns, 1780–1870*. New York: Routledge.

Mihesuah, Devon A (1996) *American Indians: Stereotypes and Realities*. Atlanta: Clarity Press.

Mill, John Stuart (1850) 'The Negro Question' reprinted in the United States in *Littell's Living Age*, Vol XXIV, pp 465–69, edited by ED Littell.

Miller, Steven P (2009) *Billy Graham and the Rise of the Republican South*. Pennsylvania: University of Pennsylvania Press.

Mintz, Sidney W (1986) *Sweetness and Power: The Place of Sugar in Modern History*. New York: Penguin.

Moffatt, Allison (2006) 'Murder, Mystery and Mistreatment in Mexican Maquiladoras' 66 *Women & Environments International Magazines* 19.

Bibliography

Moghadam, Valentine M (ed) (2007) *From Patriarchy to Empowerment: Women's Participation, Movements, and Rights in the Middle East, North Africa, and South Asia.* Syracuse: Syracuse University Press.

Mohr, Richard (1999) 'In Between Power and Procedure: Where the Court Meets the Public Sphere' 1 *Journal of Social Change & Critical Inquiry* (e-journal).

Moreton, Bethany (2009) *To Serve God and Wal-Mart.* Cambridge: Harvard University Press.

Morgan, Edmund S (1975) *American Slavery, American Freedom: The Ordeal of Colonial Virginia.* New York: WW Norton.

Morgan, Thomas J (1890) 'Report of Commissioner of Indian Affairs Thomas Jefferson Morgan, 5 September' in Wilcomb E Washburn (ed) (1973) *The American Indian and the United States: A Documentary History,* vol II. New York: Random House, p 438.

Morton, Patricia A (2006) '"Document of Civilization and Document of Barbarism": The World Trade Center Near and Far' in Daniel J Sherman and Terry Nardin (eds), *Terror, Culture, Politics: Rethinking 9/11.* Bloomington: Indiana University Press, pp 15–32.

Mulcahy, Linda (2007) 'Architects of Justice: The Politics of Courtroom Design' 16(3) *Social & Legal Studies* 383–404.

Muller, Eric L (2007) *American Inquisition: The Hunt for Japanese American Disloyalty in World War II.* Chapel Hill: University of North Carolina Press.

Musson, Anthony (2001) *Medieval Law in Context: The Growth of Legal Consciousness from Magna Carta to the Peasants' Revolt.* Manchester: Manchester University Press.

National Labor Committee (2001) *Made in the USA? Clothing for Wal-Mart, JC Penny, Target and Sears made by Women held under conditions of indentured servitude: nightmare at the Daewoosa factory in American Samoa.* New York.

Nelson, Bruce C (1988) *Beyond the Martyrs: A Social History of Chicago's Anarchists, 1870–1900.* New Brunswick: Rutgers University Press.

Nelson, Craig (2006) *Thomas Paine: Enlightenment, Revolution, and the Birth of Modern Nations.* New York: Penguin.

Nesbitt, Nick (2008) *Universal Emancipation: The Haitian Revolution and the Radical Enlightenment* (New World Studies). University of Virginia Press.

Neusner, Jacob (1991) *Jews and Christians: The Myth of a Common Tradition.* New York: Trinity Press International and SCM Press.

Nicholson, Helen (2004) *The Crusades.* Westport: Greenwood Press.

Norris, Pippa and Ronald Inglehart (2004) Sacred and Secular: Religion and Politics Worldwide. Cambridge: Cambridge University Press.

Nourse, Victoria F (2008) *In Reckless Hands: Skinner v Oklahoma and the Near-Triumph of American Eugenics.* New York: WW Norton.

Novak, Michael and Jana Novak (2007) *Washington's God: Religion, Liberty, and the Father of Our Country.* New York: Basic Books.

Novak, Pierre (2000) 'Law: Religious or Secular?' 86(3) *Virginia Law Review* 569.

O'Brien, Sharon (1989) *American Indian Tribal Governments.* Norman: University of Oklahoma Press.

Oberman, Heiko A (2003) *The Two Reformations: The Journey from the Last Days to the New World.* New Haven: Yale University Press.

Odone, Christina (2001) 'Leave God Out of It: Bin Laden Invokes Allah, Bush talks of a Christian Crusade, Bad Religion Hides Dirty Politics' *The Observer* (London), 23 September.

Olund, Eric N (2002) 'Public Domesticity During the Indian Reform Era; or, Mrs Jackson is Induced to go to Washington' 9 *Gender, Place, and Culture* 153.

Omni, Michael and Howard Winant (1986) *Racial Formation in the United States: From the 1960s to the 1990s.* New York: Routledge & Kegan Paul.

Open Society Justice Initiative (2009) *Ethnic Profiling in the European Union: Pervasive, Ineffective, and Discriminatory.* New York.

Ordover, Nancy (2003) *American Eugenics: Race, Queer Anatomy, and the Science of Nationalism.* Minneapolis: University of Minnesota Press.

Orr, D Alan (2001) 'The Juristic Foundations of Regicide' in Jason Peacey (ed), *The Regicides and the Execution of Charles I.* Basingstoke: Palgrave, pp 117–37.

Pagden, Anthony (1993) *European Encounters with the New World.* New Haven: Yale University Press.

Paine, Thomas (2007) *The Thomas Paine Reader.* Radford: Wilder Publications.

Parsons, Lucy (1969) *Famous Speeches of the Eight Chicago Anarchists.* New York: Arno Press & New York Times.

Patterson, James T (2002) *Brown v Board of Education: A Civil Rights Milestone and its Troubled Legacy* (Pivotal Moments in American History). Oxford: Oxford University Press.

Persico, Joseph E (1995) *Nuremberg, Infamy on Trial.* New York: Penguin.

Phillips, Kate (2003) *Helen Hunt Jackson: A Literary Life.* Berkeley: University of California Press.

Pierce, Peter (1999) *The Country of Lost Children: An Australian Anxiety.* Cambridge: Cambridge University Press.

Pitts, Jennifer (2005) *A Turn to Empire: The Rise of Imperial Liberalism in Britain and France.* Princeton: Princeton University Press.

Polack, WG (1931) *The Story of Luther.* St Louis: Concordia Publishing House.

Ponting, Clive (2000) *World History: A New Perspective.* London: Chatto & Windus.

Porter, JM (1974) *Luther: Selected Political Writings.* Philadelphia: Fortress Press.

Porter, Roy (2000) *The Creation of the Modern World: The Untold Story of the British Enlightenment.* New York: WW Norton.

Preis, A (1996) 'Human Rights as Cultural Practice: An Anthropological Critique' 18 *Human Rights Quarterly* 286.

Prucha, Francis Paul (1979) *The Churches and the Indian Schools 1888–1912.* Lincoln: University of Nebraska Press.

Questier, MC (2006) *Catholicism and Community in Early Modern England: Politics, Aristocratic Patronage, and Religion, c 1550–1640.* Cambridge: Cambridge University Press.

Qureshi, Emran and Michael A Sells (eds) (2003) *The New Crusades: Constructing the Muslim Enemy.* New York: Columbia University Press.

Rahbek, Birgitte (ed) (2005) *Democratisation in the Middle East.* Aarhus: Aarhus University Press.

Razack, Sherene H (2008) *Casting Out: The Eviction of Muslims from Western Law and Politics.* Toronto: University of Toronto Press.

Redfield, Marc (2009) *The Rhetoric of Terror: Reflections on 9/11 and the War on Terror.* New York: Fordham University Press.

Reeve, LJ (1989) *Charles I and the Road to Personal Rule.* Cambridge: Cambridge University Press.

Reynolds, Henry (1989) *Dispossession: Black Australians and White Invaders*. St Leonards: Allen & Unwin.

Rhodes, Edward (2005) 'Onward, Liberal Soldiers? The Crusading Logic of Bush's Grant Strategy and what is Wrong with it' in Lloyd C Gardner and Marilyn B Young (eds), *The New American Empire*. New York: The New Press, pp 227–52.

Richardson, Brian (2005) *Longitude and Empire: How Captain Cook's Voyages Changed the World*. Vancouver: University of British Columbia Press.

Ritzer, George (2000) *The McDonaldization of Society*. Thousand Oaks: Pine Forge.

Rizzo, Helen Mary (2005) *Islam, Democracy, and the Status of Women: The Case of Kuwait*. New York: Routledge.

Roberts, Jan (2008) *Massacres to Mining: The Colonisation of Aboriginal Australia*. Impact Investigative Media Productions.

Robertson, Geoffrey (2005) *The Tyrannicide Brief: The Story of the Man who sent Charles I to the Scaffold*. London: Chatto & Windus.

Robertson, Lindsay G (2007) *Conquest by Law: How the Discovery of America Dispossessed Indigenous Peoples of their Lands*. Oxford: Oxford University Press.

Robinson, Robert (1788) *Slavery Inconsistent with the Spirit of Christianity*. Sermon preached at Cambridge on Sunday 10 February 1788, cited in B Stanley (2007) 'Baptists, Anti-Slavery and the Legacy of Imperialism' *Baptist Quarterly*, October, 284 at 285.

Rodriguez-Garavito, Cesar A and Luis Carlos Arenas (2005) 'Indigenous Rights, Transnational Activism, and Legal Mobilization: The Struggle of the U'wa People in Colombia' in Boaventura de Sousa Santos and Cesar A Rodriguez-Garavito (eds), *Law and Globalization from Below: Toward a Cosmopolitan Legality*. Cambridge: Cambridge University Press, pp 241–66.

Roeber, AG (2006) 'The Law, Religion, and State-Making in the Early Modern World: Protestant Revolutions in the Works of Berman, Gorski, and Witte' 31(1) *Law & Social Inquiry* 199.

Roediger, Dave (2009) 'Haymarket Incident' (retrieved 3 February 2009). Lucy Parsons Project, www.lucyparsonsproject.org/haymarket/roediger_haymarket.html.

Roediger, Dave and Franklin Rosemont (eds) (1986) *Haymarket Scrapbook*. Chicago: Charles H Kerr.

Roediger, David R (2005) *Working Toward Whiteness: How America's Immigrants Became White*. New York: Basic Books.

Roediger, David R (2007) *The Wages of Whiteness: Race and the Making of the American Working Class*. Revised edn, New York: Verso.

Romain, Jonathan (2009) 'The JSF Ruling is a Victory for Jews' *The Guardian* (London), 16 December.

Rosen, Lawrence (2006) *Law as Culture*. Princeton: Princeton University Press.

Rosenberg, Gerald (2008) *The Hollow Hope: Can Courts Bring About Social Change?* 2nd edn, Chicago: University of Chicago Press.

Roth, Kenneth (2000) 'The Charade of US Ratification of International Human Rights Treaties' 1(2) *Chicago Journal of International Law* 347.

Rourse, Victoria (2008) *In Reckless Hands: Skinner v Oklahoma and the Near-Triumph of American Eugenics*. New York: WW Norton.

Rublack, Ulinka (2005) *Reformation Europe*. Cambridge: Cambridge University Press.

Runciman, Steven (1987) *The History of the Crusades*, vols 1, 2 and 3. Cambridge: Cambridge University Press.

Russell, Conrad (2006) '1603: The End of English National Sovereignty' in Glenn Burgess, Jason Lawrence and Rowland Wymer (eds), *The Accession of James I: Historical and Cultural Consequences*. New York: Palgrave Macmillan, pp 1–14.

Said, Edward (1979) *Orientalism*. New York: Vintage.

Said, Edward (1997) *Covering Islam: How the Media and the Experts Determine How we See the Rest of the World*. Revised edition, New York: Vintage.

Sands, Philippe (2005) *Lawless World: America and the Making and Breaking of Global Rules from FDR's Atlantic Charter to George W Bush's Illegal War*. New York: Penguin.

Sarat, Austin (2007) 'Editorial' 3 *Law, Culture and the Humanities* 187.

Sarat, Austin, Lawrence Douglas and Martha Merrill Umphrey (eds) (2007) *Law and the Sacred*. Palo Alto: Stanford University Press.

Savage, Mike and Andrew Miles (1994) *The Remaking of the British Working Class*. London: Routledge.

Scalia, Antonin (2002) 'God's Justice and Ours' *First Things*, May, 17.

Schlag, Pierre (1997) 'Law as the Continuation of God by Other Means' 85(2) *California Law Review* 427.

Schmitt, Carl (1934) *Political Theology*. Cambridge: MIT Press (1985).

Schrecker, Ellen (1998) *Many Are the Crimes: McCarthyism in America*. Boston: Little, Brown.

Schwartz, Bernard (1996) *Decision: How the Supreme Court Decides Cases*. Oxford: Oxford University Press.

Scolding, Fiona (2009) 'The JFS Case has Far-reaching Consequences' *The Independent* (London), 16 December.

Scott, Joan Wallach (2007) *The Politics of the Veil*. Princeton: Princeton University Press.

Scribner, RW (1981) *For the Sake of Simple Folk: Popular Propaganda for the German Reformation*. Cambridge: Cambridge University Press.

Semmel, Bernard (1969) *Democracy Versus Empire: The Jamaica Riots of 1865 and the Governor Eyre Controversy*. Garden City: Anchor Books Doubleday.

Seymour, Hersh (2004) *Chain of Command: The Road from 9/11 to Abu Ghraib*. New York: HarperCollins.

Sharlet, Jeff (2008) *The Family: The Secret Fundamentalism at the Heart of American Power*. New York: HarperCollins.

Sharpe, James (2005) *Remember, Remember: A Cultural History of Guy Fawkes Day*. Cambridge: Harvard University Press.

Sheehan, Jonathan (2003) 'Enlightenment, Religion, and the Enigma of Secularization: A Review Essay' 108 *American Historical Review* 1061.

Shelley, Fred M, Adrienne M Proffer and Lisa DeChano (2006) 'Wal-Mart and Partisan Politics: From Agricultural Volatility to Red-State Culture' in Stanley D Brunn (ed), *Wal-Mart World: The World's Biggest Corporation in the Global Economy*. New York: Routledge, pp 203–11.

Sheridan, Richard (2000) *Sugar and Slavery: An Economic History of the British West Indies, 1623–1775*. Kingston: University of the West Indies Press.

Sherman, Daniel J and Terry Nardin (eds) (2006) *Terror, Culture, Politics: Rethinking 9/11*. Bloomington: Indiana University Press.

Shields, Mark (2005) 'The Real Scandal of Tom DeLay' CNN, 9 May, www.cnn.com/2005/POLITICS/05/09/real.delay (accessed 8 December 2009).

Shipman, Pat (1994) *The Evolution of Racism: Human Differences and the Use and Abuse of Science*. New York: Simon & Schuster.

Silbey, Susan S (1997) '"Let Them Eat Cake": Globalization, Postmodern Colonialism, and the Possibilities of Justice' 31(2) *Law & Society Review* 207.

Skidelsky, Robert (2009) *Keynes: The Return of the Master*. New York: PublicAffairs.

Sloan, Kim (2007) *A New World: England's First View of America*. Chapel Hill: University of North Carolina Press.

Smedley, Audrey (1999) *Race in North America: Origin and Evolution of a Worldview*. Boulder: Westview.

Smith, Adam (1776) *The Wealth of Nations, Books 1–3. Complete and Unabridged*. Scotts Valley: CreateSpace (2009).

Smith, Andrea (2005) *Conquest: Sexual Violence and the American Indian Genocide*. Cambridge: South End Press.

Smith, Rogers (1997) *Civic Ideals: Conflicting Visions of Citizenship in US History*. New Haven: Yale University Press.

Smith, Tom W (2009) *Religious Change around the World*. NOR/University of Chicago. Report prepared for the Templeton Foundation, news.uchicago.edu/files/religionsurvey_20091023.pdf.

Solow, Barbara L and Stanley L Engerman (eds) (2004) *British Capitalism and Caribbean Slavery: The Legacy of Eric Williams*. Cambridge: Cambridge University Press.

Sommerville, C John (1992) *The Secularization of Early Modern England*. New York: Oxford University Press.

Sonnenfeldt, Richard W (2006) *Witness to Nuremberg*. New York: Arcade Publishing.

Spater, George (1987) 'The Legacy of Thomas Paine' in Ian Dyck (ed) *Citizen of the World: Essays on Thomas Paine*. London: Christopher Helm, pp 129–48.

Spivak, Gayatri Chakravorty (1988) 'Can the Subaltern Speak?' in Cary Nelson and Lawrence Grossberg (eds), *Marxism and the Interpretation of Culture*. Urbana: University of Illinois Press, pp 271–313.

Spring, Joel (2007) *Deculturalization and the Struggle for Equality: A Brief History of the Education of Dominated Cultures in the United States*. 5th edn, New York: McGraw-Hill.

Spurr, John (1998) *English Puritanism, 1603–1689*. New York: St Martin's Press.

Spurr, John (2006) *The Post-Reformation 1603–1714*. Harlow: Pearson Education.

Stacey, Helen M (2009) *Human Rights for the 21st Century: Sovereignty, Civil Society, Culture*. Palo Alto: Stanford University Press.

Steigmann-Gall, Richard (2003) *The Holy Reich: Nazi Conceptions of Christianity, 1919–1945*. Cambridge: Cambridge University Press.

Steinberg, SH (1996) *Five Hundred Years of Printing*. London: The British Library & Oak Knoll Press.

Steinweis, Alan E (2001) 'The Nazi Purge of Artistic and Cultural Life' in Robert Gellately and Nathan Stoltzfus (eds), *Social Outsiders in Nazi Germany*. Princeton: Princeton University Press, pp 99–116.

Stephanson, Anders (1995) *Manifest Destiny: American Expansionism and the Empire of Right*. New York: Hill and Wang.

Steuter, Erin and Deborah Wills (2008) *At War with Metaphor: Media, Propaganda, and Racism in the War on Terror*. New York: Lexington Books.

Stoler, Ann Laura (1995) *Race and the Education of Desire: Foucault's History of Sexuality and the Colonial Order of Things*. Durham: Duke University Press.

Stolleis, Michael (2008) *The Eye of the Law: Two Essays on Legal History*. London: Birkbeck Law Press.

Stolzenberg, Nomi (2007) 'The Profanity of Law' in Austin Sarat, Lawrence Douglas and Martha Merrill Umphrey (eds), *Law and the Sacred*. Palo Alto: Stanford University Press, pp 29–90.

Strauss, Gerald (ed and trans) (1971) *Manifestations of Discontent in Germany on the Eve of the Reformation*. Bloomington: Indiana University Press.

Stremlau, Rose (2005) '"To Domesticate and Civilize Wild Indians": Allotment and the Campaign to Reform Indian Families, 1875–1887' 30 *Journal of Family History* 265.

Stumpf, Christoph A (2006) *The Grotian Theology of International Law: Hugo Grotius and the Moral Fundament of International Relations*. Berlin: Walter de Gruyter.

Sturm, Circe (2002) *Blood Politics: Race, Culture, and Identity in the Cherokee Nation of Oklahoma*. Berkeley: University of California Press.

Sugarman, David (1995) *A Brief History of the Law Society*. London: Law Society Publications.

Syse, Henrik (2007) *Natural Law, Religion, and Rights*. South Bend, Indiana: St Augustine's Press.

Tamanaha, Brian Z (2004) *On the Rule of Law: History, Politics, Theory*. Cambridge: Cambridge University Press.

Tamanaha, Brian Z (2006) *Law as a Means to an End. Threat to the Rule of Law*. Cambridge: Cambridge University Press.

Taylor, Carol M (1981) 'WEB Du Bois's Challenge to Scientific Racism' 11(4) *Journal of Black Studies* 449.

Taylor, Charles (2007) *A Secular Age*. Cambridge: The Belknap Press of Harvard University Press.

Taylor, Phillip M (2001) *British Propaganda in the Twentieth Century*. Edinburgh: Edinburgh University Press.

Taylor, Telford (1992) *The Anatomy of the Nuremberg Trials: A Personal Memoir*. New York: Knopf.

Therborn, Göran (1995) *European Modernity and Beyond: The Trajectory of European Societies, 1945–2000*. London: Sage.

Thompson, EP (1963) *The Making of the English Working Class*. London: Victor Gollancz.

Thomson, Ann (2008) *Bodies of Thought: Science, Religion, and the Soul in the Enlightenment*. Oxford: Oxford University Press.

Tigar, Michael E (with Madeline R Levy) (2000) *Law and the Rise of Capitalism*. New York: Monthly Review Press.

Tomlins, Christopher L (1985) *The State and the Unions: Labor Relations, Law and the Organized Labor Movement in America, 1880–1960* (Studies in Economic History and Policy: USA in the Twentieth Century). Cambridge: Cambridge University Press.

Tomlins, Christopher L (2001) *In a Wilderness of Tigers: The Culture of Violence, The Discourse of English Colonizing, and the Refusals of American History*. American Bar Foundation Working Paper #2105.

Toope, Stephen J (2006) 'Human Rights in the Use of Force after September 11th, 2001' in Daniel J Sherman and Terry Nardin (eds), *Terror, Culture, Politics: Rethinking 9/11*. Bloomington: Indiana University Press, pp 236–58.

Totani, Yuma (2008) *The Tokyo War Crimes Trial: The Pursuit of Justice in the Wake of World War II*. Cambridge: Harvard University Asia Center.

Trubek, David M (1972) 'Max Weber on Law and the Rise of Capitalism' *Wisconsin Law Review*.

Tusa, Ann and John Tusa (1983) *The Nuremberg Trial*. London: Macmillan.

Tushnet, Mark and Katya Lezin (1991) 'What Really Happened in *Brown v Board of Education*' 91 *Columbia Law Review* 1867.

Tutino, Stefania (2007) *Law and Conscience: Catholicism in Early Modern England, 1570–1625*. Aldershot: Ashgate.

Tyerman, Christopher (2006) *God's War: A New History of the Crusades*. Cambridge: The Belknap Press of Harvard University Press.

Uglow, Jenny (2009) *A Gambling Man: Charles II's Restoration Game*. New York: Farrar, Straus & Giroux.

Uglow, Jenny (2003) *The Lunar Men: Five Friends whose Curiosity Changed the World*. New York: Farrar, Straus and Giroux.

Umphrey, Martha Merrill, Austin Sarat and Lawrence Douglas (2007) 'The Sacred in the Law: An Introduction' in Austin Sarat, Lawrence Douglas and Martha Merrill Umphrey (eds), *Law and the Sacred*. Palo Alto: Stanford University Press, pp 1–28.

Unger, Roberto Mangabeira (1986) *The Critical Legal Studies Movement*. Cambridge: Harvard University Press.

US Department of Labor (2003) Bureau of Labor Statistics, Table No 37, Median Weekly Earnings of Full Time Wage and Salary Workers by Selected Characteristics.

Vale, Malcolm (1988) 'The Civilization of Courts and Cities in the North 1200–1500' in George Holmes (ed), *The Oxford Illustrated History of Medieval Europe*. Oxford: Oxford University Press, pp 297–351.

Van Caenegem, RC (1991) *Legal History: A European Perspective*. London: Hambledon.

Van Groesen, Michiel (2008) *The Representations of the Overseas World in the De Bry Collection of Voyages (1590–1634)*. Leiden: Brill.

Vance, Sandra S and Roy V Scott (1994) *Wal-Mart: A History of Sam Walton's Retail Phenomenon*. New York: Twayne.

Vandiver, Elizabeth, Ralph Keen and Thomas D Frazel (trans and annotated) (2002) *Luther's Lives: Two Contemporary Accounts of Martin Luther*. Manchester: Manchester University Press.

Vitkus, Daniel J (1999) 'Early Modern Orientalism: Representations of Islam in Sixteenth-and-Seventeenth-Century Europe' in David R Blanks and Michael Frassetto (eds), *Western Views of Islam in Medieval and Early Modern Europe*. New York: St Martin's Press, pp 207–30.

Voltaire (1755) *Toleration and Other Essays*. Translated, with an Introduction, by Joseph McCabe. New York: GP Putnam (1912).

Wakeham, Pauline (2008) *Taxidermic Signs: Reproducing Aboriginality*. Minneapolis: University of Minnesota Press.

Waldman, Steven (2009) *Founding Faith: How our Founding Fathers Forged a Radical New Approach to Religious Liberty*. New York: Random House.

Walters, Kerry S (1992) *The American Deists: Voices of Reason and Dissent in the Early Republic*. Lawrence: University of Kansas Press.

Walton, Sam with John Huey (1992) *Made in America: My Story*. New York: Doubleday.

Walvin, James (1980) 'The Rise of British Popular Sentiment for Abolition 1787–1832' in Christine Bolt and Seymour Drescher (eds), *Anti-Slavery, Religion and Reform: Essays in Memory of Roger Anstey*. Folkestone: Dawson, Archon, pp 149–62.

Warf, Barney and Thomas Chapman (2006) 'Cathedrals of Consumption: A Political Phenomenology of Wal-Mart' in Stanley D Brunn (ed), *Wal-Mart World: The World's Biggest Corporation in the Global Economy*. New York: Routledge, pp 163–78.

Washburn, Wilcomb E (1971) *Red Man's Land/White Man's Law: A Study of the Past and Present States of the American Indian.* New York: Charles Scribner's Sons.

Washington, Luther (1999) 'War Crimes After Nuremberg', www.law.umkc.edu/faculty/projects/ftrials/nuremberg/NurembergEpilogue.html (accessed 30 March 2009).

Wawrzyczek, Irmina (2001) 'Plantation Economy and Legal Safeguards of Sexual Discipline in Early Tobacco Colonies' in Helle Porsdam (ed), *Folkways and Law Ways: Law in American Studies.* Denmark: Odense University Press, pp 33–52.

Weber, Max (1904) *The Protestant Ethic and the Spirit of Capitalism.* London and New York: Routledge (1995).

Weber, Max (1922) *Economy and Society.* Berkeley: University of California Press (1978).

Wedgewood, CV (1967) *The Trial of Charles I.* London: Fontana.

Wiener, Martin J (2009) *An Empire on Trial: Race, Murder, and Justice under British Rule 1870–1935.* Cambridge: Cambridge University Press.

Wiessman, Robert (2003) 'Grotesque Inequality: Corporate Globalization and the Global Gap Between Rich and Poor', www.thirdworldtraveler.com/Third_World/Grotesque_Inequality.html (accessed 15 December 2009).

Wilke, Christiane (2009) 'Reconsecrating the Temple of Justice: Invocations of Civilization and Humanity in the Nuremberg Justice Case' 24(2) *Canadian Journal of Law and Society* 181.

Wilkins, David E (2008) 'Federal Policy, Western Movement, and Consequences for Indigenous People, 1790–1920' in Michael Grossberg and Christopher Tomlins (eds), *The Cambridge History of Law in America. Volume II. The Long Nineteenth Century (1789–1920).* Cambridge: Cambridge University Press, pp 204–44.

Wilkins, David E (2009) *Documents of Native American Political Development: 1500s to 1933.* Oxford: Oxford University Press.

Wilkinson, Charles F (1987) *American Indians, Time, and the Law: Native Societies in a Modern Constitutional Democracy.* New Haven: Yale University Press.

William, Tucker (2002) *The Funding of Scientific Racism: Wickliffe Draper and the Pioneer Fund.* Urbana: University of Illinois Press.

Williams, Eric (1944) *Capitalism and Slavery.* Chapel Hill: University of North Carolina Press.

Williams, Patricia J, *Alchemy of Race and Rights: Diary of a Law Professor.* Cambridge: Harvard University Press.

Williams Jr, Robert A (1990) *The American Indian in Western Legal Thought: The Discourse of Conquest.* New York: Oxford University Press.

Willis, James F (1982) *Prologue to Nuremberg: The Politics and Diplomacy of Punishing War Criminals of the First World War.* Westport: Greenwood Press.

Wills, Garry (2008) 'Two Speeches on Race' 55(7) *New York Review of Books.*

Wilson, Richard (1924) *Essays and Other Writings of Francis Bacon.* London: JM Dent & Sons.

Winant, Howard (2004) *New Politics of Race: Globalism, Difference, Justice.* Minneapolis: University of Minnesota Press.

Wise, Steven M (2005) *Though the Heavens May Fall: The Landmark Trial that Led to the End of Human Slavery.* Cambridge: Da Capo Press.

Witte, John Jr (2002) *Law and Protestantism: The Legal Teachings of the Lutheran Reformation.* Cambridge: Cambridge University Press.

Witte, John Jr (2005) *Religion and the American Constitutional Experiment.* 2nd edn, Boulder: Westview.

Witte, John Jr (2006) *God's Joust, God's Justice: Law and Religion in the Western Tradition.* Grand Rapids: William B Eerdmans.

Witte, John Jr (2007) *The Reformation of Rights: Law, Religion, and Human Rights in Early Modern Calvinism.* Cambridge: Cambridge University Press.

Witte, John Jr and Frank S Alexander (eds) (2008) *Christianity and Law: An Introduction.* Cambridge: Cambridge University Press.

Woolley, Benjamin (2008) *Savage Kingdom: The True Story of Jamestown, 1607, and the Settlement of America.* New York: Harper Perennial.

Wootton, David (1986) *Divine Right and Democracy: An Anthology of Political Writings in Stuart England.* Harmondsworth: Penguin.

Wormald, Jenny (1983) 'James VI and I: Two Kings or One?' *History* 68.

Wormald, Jenny (1985) 'Gunpowder, Treason and Scots' 24 *Journal of British Studies* 142.

Wormald, Jenny (1991) 'James VI and I, Basilikon Doron and The Trew Law of Free Monarchies: the Scottish context and the English translation' in Linda Levy Peck (ed), *The Mental World of the Jacobean Court.* Cambridge: Cambridge University Press.

Wormald, Jenny (1992) 'The Creation of Britain: Multiple Kingdoms or Core and Colonies'. *Transactions of the Royal Historical Society*, 6th ser, 2.

Yasuaki, Onuma (1986) 'The Tokyo Trial: Between Law and Politics' in C Hosoya et al (eds), *The Tokyo War Crimes Trial: An International Symposium.* Tokyo: Kodansha International, pp 45–52.

Zamir, Shamoon (2008) *The Cambridge Companion to WEB Du Bois.* Cambridge: Cambridge University Press.

Zec, Donald (2004) *Don't Lose it Again! The Life and Wartime Cartoons of Philip Zec.* London: Cromwell Press.

Zeman, ZAB (1984) *Heckling Hitler.* London: Orbis.

Zogby International poll 2004, www.zogby.com/index.cfm (accessed 24 November 2009).

Zweiniger-Bargielowska, Ina (2000) *Austerity in Britain: Rationing, Controls, and Consumption, 1939–1955.* Oxford: Oxford University Press.

Index

Numbers in *italics* refer to illustrations and captions.

Index